A History of
Homosexuality
in Europe

A History of Homosexuality in Europe

Berlin, London, Paris
1919-1939

Florence Tamagne

Algora Publishing
New York

Originally published as *Histoire de l'homosexualité en Europe*, © Éditions Seuil,
2000

Library of Congress Cataloging-in-Publication Data

Tamagne, Florence, 1970-
  [Histoire de l'homosexualite en Europe. English]
  A history of homosexuality : Europe between the wars / by Florence Tamagne.
      p. cm.
  Translation of: Histoire de l'homosexualite en Europe.
  Includes bibliographical references and index.
  ISBN 0-87586-252-7 (trade paper) — ISBN 0-87586-253-5 (hard) — ISBN 0-
87586-199-7 (e-book)
  1. Homosexuality—Europe—History—20th century. I. Title.

  HQ76.3.E8T3513 2003
  306.76'6'0940904—dc22
                              2003027409

This work is published with the support of the
French Ministry of Culture/National Book Center of France

Front Cover: On the Road to the Temple of Ceres: A Spring Festival
by Sir Lawrence Alma-Tadema (Dutch, 1836-1912)

Printed in the United States

Acknowledgments

I wish to thank my thesis director, Jean-Pierre Azéma, for his help and encouragement, as well as Anthony Rowley, Claude Courouve, Didier Éribon for their input, and the staff of the British Library in London, the Bibliothèque nationale in Paris and the Staatsbibliotek in Berlin for their help and their kindness. I am grateful to the British and German curators for their cooperation and help in my research.

My family has been a constant support, translating German documents, providing computer support, and designing the graphics. Christiane Dole helped with the images and kept me going throughout the writing of the thesis.

Finally, I thank Michel Winock and Richard Figuier, at Éditions du Seuil, who trusted me and gave this project the chance to succeed.

TABLE OF CONTENTS

FOREWORD

This work is the English-language translation of a doctoral thesis presented to the Institute of Political Studies of Paris, under the direction of Jean-Pierre Azéma, entitled, "Research on Homosexuality in France, England and Germany from the beginning of the 1920s to the end of the 1930s, based on information from partisan, police, legal, medical and literary sources January 1998."

The question of language is at the heart of this study and problems of vocabulary frequently occurred. It was common, in the inter-war period, to employ terms such as "invert" or "pederasts" to indicate homosexuals. The author elected to use those terms whenever they occurred in a historical perspective and signified a nuance of identity, often used by homosexuals themselves, without inducing negative connotations. It would be anachronistic to use the term "gays" to refer to homosexuals in the context of the 1920s and 1930s; and to make the reading easier, the full phrase "homosexuals and lesbians" is not always repeated when both groups are indicated — sometimes "homosexual" is used in a generic sense. Lastly, it is quite clear that although we may attach the term "homosexual" or "lesbian" to specific people's names, that does not necessarily mean that they regarded themselves as such.

Quotations were used extensively, as the best means of recreating the climate of the era and bringing the first-person accounts to life. This inevitably presents challenges, as most had to be translated into French, by the author; or into English, for this edition; or both. Where possible, idioms in the source language have been preserved in order to avoid distorting the meaning; in some cases, English sources have been rendered as indirect quotes — set off by dashes — since it would be impractical to repeat the entire research project from scratch.

INTRODUCTION

THE HISTORY OF HOMOSEXUALITY: A NEW AND CONTROVERSIAL HISTORY

Sexuality holds a place at the heart of human societies. However, the history of sexuality is quite a new field of study.[1] It stands at the crossroads of several disciplines — history, sociology, ethnology, anthropology, medicine — and so this history is still finding its way, oscillating between embarrassed silence and tempestuous logorrhea. Discussions of sexuality have usually been sheepish or provocative, seldom neutral and objective. In fact, sexuality is not fixed and certain, independent of any context; quite to the contrary, its position within a society reveals the relations of forces, the founding myths, the underlying tensions, and the insurmountable taboos. To Michel Foucault, the very concept of sexuality is an ideological construction. Every form of society would, in fact, have its own corresponding attitude toward sexuality.

The concept of sexuality is not only determined by culture, but also by class and gender. Thus, the traditional (so-called "middle-class") schema of sexuality is the monogamist heterosexual family. It may be associated with economic considerations (the woman does not work), ideological considerations (the woman does not have independent sexuality, she must embody the image of the "eternal" female and conform to her "womanly role"), and political considerations (the family is a factor of stability within society). This conformist model

---

1. See Denis Peschanski, Michaël Pollak and Henry Rousso, *Histoire politique et sciences sociales*, Bruxelles, Complexe, 1991, 285 pages; Jacques Le Goff (dir.), *La Nouvelle Histoire*, Bruxelles, Complexe, 1988, 334 pages.

was spread from the middle class to the working class starting around the end of the 19th century, as a result of the bourgeoisie's efforts to impose morality upon the masses. Under this highly restrictive definition of the sexual standard, any form of sexuality not conforming to that pattern was categorized as abnormal. Thus, under the combined pressures of religion, medicine, the law and morality, specific types were born: the child who masturbates, the hysterical woman, the congenital prostitute, the homosexual.

The history of sexuality cuts across many fields of human activity and history: it touches on the history of morals, changing attitudes, and in particular how our imagination has shifted over time: the history of representation, as well as the history of medicine, the law, the police, religion and, of course, political history. Literary history, art history, and the history of language also add to the picture. Attitudes toward sexuality can only be understood in a broad context. The history of sexuality, and thus the history of homosexuality, cannot be described in social terms alone. It sheds light on fields that seem to be quite unrelated, and gives us a better understanding of specific periods. This richness is, at the same time, its principal difficulty; the sources are many, and varied, and it is not immediately apparent that they are related to each other. Working to synthesize all these inputs, the historian sometimes realizes that he has ventured onto grounds which are foreign to him, like medicine and anthropology. As is true for any history of social attitudes, the historian must make an effort not to apply ulterior values to the population under study. He must also be fully conscious of his own prejudices and acquired views related to his education, his gender, his lifestyle, his social and cultural origin and his personal experience. Then we must consider whether the sources are neutral. In the field of social attitudes, representations and public opinion, we are constantly dealing with subjective documents and with personal testimonies, from which it is sometimes difficult to draw conclusions. Extensive use of historical literature as evidence can likewise entail involuntary distortions. With a question like homosexuality, especially, one may encounter silence, a lack of evidence, or false evidence. Thus with all humility it must be admitted that an ideal neutrality cannot be attained in the history of sexuality, nor even perhaps the approximate truth — much less in the history of homosexuality. We must be aware of that; but that does not mean we have to throw in the towel. There is a minimal truth that is worth seeking, exposing and analyzing. And that is what I will attempt to do in this work.

Homosexuality can be defined simply as a form of sexuality in which sexual attraction is directed toward a person of the same sex. That is a minimal definition which, nonetheless, raises various problems.[2] Indeed, we must specify what such a definition covers: will we consider as homosexuals and lesbians those people who are attracted only by individuals of their own sex, or will we also include bisexuals, who may be equally attracted by both sexes or who may have relations with both sexes? This is a real problem for, due to social constraints, many homosexuals have led a parallel lives, giving the appearance of being heterosexual. By the same token, for us to acknowledge that a person is homosexual, is it absolutely necessary that he should have had sexual relations with a person of his own gender or is it enough that he should have felt a purely platonic attraction? That presents another sizable problem: the term "homosexual" is a recent invention and does not really apply very well to the passionate friendships, female as well as male, of the 18th and 19th centuries. Still, should we exclude certain people from the study just because they did not see themselves as homosexual?

These questions are at the center of research on homosexuality, and the various answers that may be given often indicate an ideological standpoint. The very restrictive definition of homosexuality and lesbianism that is sometimes adopted in militant homosexual writings demonstrates a strong political desire to tie homosexual communities to a clear and exclusive identity, in complete opposition to the dominant heterosexual society. That is a phenomenon of withdrawal and rejection appropriate for a minority that wants to persist against a hostile and not very understanding majority. Thus Susan Cavin states that the feminine account of feminine events is ideally represented by feminist lesbians and separatist lesbians.[3] Certainly, she has a point. Until recent years the history of homosexuality remained *terra incognita*, and the terms "homosexual" or "lesbian" rarely came up at all, except to spice up a joke or to ruin someone's rep-

---

2. This is not the place to make a detailed analysis of the various theories on homosexuality. For a general view, refer to Michel Foucault, History of the sexuality, t.I, La Volonté de savoir, Paris, Gallimard, 1976, 211 pages; for English and American theories, see Kenneth Plummer, *The Making of the Modern Homosexual*, London, Hutchinsons, 1981, 380 pages, and David F. Greenberg, *The Construction of Homosexuality*, Chicago, the University of Chicago Press, 1988, 635 pages. Guy Hocquenghem is also interesting: *Le Désir homosexuel*, Paris, Éditions universitaires, 1972, 125 pages. For anthropological research on the origins of homosexuality, see Evelyn Blackwood, *The Many Faces of Homosexuality*, New York, Harrington Park Press, 1986, 217 pages.

3. Susan Cavin, *Lesbian Origins*, San Francisco, Ism Press, 1989, 288 pages, p.17.

utation. It took the remarkable works of homosexual historians like Jeffrey Weeks, Lilian Faderman, and Claudia Schoppmann to discover whole facets of social history that had been completely obscure. Furthermore, many studies on homosexuals leave out lesbians altogether, so that their history is even more overlooked.

Still, we must avoid going to the opposite extreme. The quite understandable desire of the gay community to take over homosexual history sometimes leads to a "revanchist" history, over-emphasizing the ghetto and awarding good and bad points depending on the degree of subservience to an exclusive concept of homosexuality. That leads to tiresome debates on whether so-and-so was actually homosexual, especially if we are talking about inter-war period. Virginia Woolf, for example, might be hailed by some as a complete, almost militant lesbian, an example for the lesbians of her era, whereas others refuse to regard her as such because she was married and she never defined herself as lesbian. Both positions seek to deny the complexity of human behavior and to reduce it to a preconceived model, one that lends support to one camp or another. This presents two clear dangers: the dilution of the concept of homosexuality in the infinite variation of individual experiences, and the ghettoization of homosexuality, since the term could no longer be applied to any but a very restricted group of individuals who satisfy all the political criteria of homosexuality: exclusive attraction, complete sexual relations, affirmed identity, overt militancy.

The history of homosexuality has to consider the distinction between homosexual conduct, which is universal, and homosexual identity, which is specific and temporal. Homosexuals do not necessarily define themselves as such, even if they find people of their own sex attractive or have sexual relations with them.[4] By the same token, society will not necessarily distinguish an individual in terms of his sexual practices.

---

4. Some were quite unaware of the very concept of homosexuality; that was very much the case before the end of the 19th century. Some considered that trait in their personality as generally meaningless, unimportant, and uninteresting; that attitude, too, was prevalent before the 20th century. Others flatly rejected the term "homosexual" because they felt it reflected characteristics that they did not share — that includes prostitute, and prisoners who practiced homosexuality for reasons of circumstance, but otherwise considered themselves heterosexual. Then, the problem of vocabulary is such that some men might admit they love other men, but reject the label of "homosexual" because they see it as having effeminate connotations.

The term "homosexual" itself can be perfectly pegged to a specific space and time. It appeared in the 19th century, in Europe, and gradually took hold more broadly. It seems to have been invented by the Hungarian Karoly Maria Kertbeny, in 1869 and it became more widespread after it was taken up by the medical community. Until that point in time, society did not distinguish the people, but the acts. Sodomy was condemned in many countries. Until 1939, the term "homosexual" was scarcely ever used and it only slowly gained currency. It competed with other terms, in particular "invert" and "uranist." These changes of vocabulary are not trivial: on the contrary, they testify to a shift in how the phenomenon was perceived, by society as well as by homosexuals themselves. Until the end of the 19th century only pejorative terms, insults, were used to indicate such people; homosexuality as a practice was not distinguished from sodomy. By employing the term "homosexual," doctors wanted to affirm their objective view of the phenomenon, their scientific approach, and their lack of prejudice. By adopting this vocabulary, homosexuals achieved a fundamental identity, but that was a step fraught with consequences: they also fell into a scientific and medical category and they seemed to amalgamate the word with the concept as it was defined by heterosexual society. The adoption of the term "gay" marked an important turning point in the second half of the 20th century. This choice illustrated the desire to get away from the pejorative and degrading connotations of the term "homosexual," and to reaffirm the homosexual identity only as a community, using non-value-laden language.

The history of homosexuality is not the history of sexual conduct, which is practically unvarying;[5] rather, it consists in studying the relations between homosexuals and society and observing the answers homosexuals have developed in order to affirm their identity. At the same time, one begins to wonder about homosexual identity and the validity of categorizing individuals according to their sexual practices. This is why I chose to adopt a "broad" definition of homosexuality. I regarded as being relevant to my topic any person having had homosexual liaisons, even temporary, even platonic ones. Similarly, in the context of representation and interpretation, I explored very broadly the topic of homoeroticism, i.e. a diffuse, even unconscious, attraction between people of the same sex.

---

5. Of course, this is relative. There are sexual fashions that come and go. In England, for example, homosexual relations evolved; during the Victorian era, child molestation enjoyed a considerable vogue. The practices of reciprocal masturbation, fellatio, and *coitus contra ventrem* were often preferred over sodomy.

RESEARCH IN HOMOSEXUALITY: METHODOLOGICAL PROBLEMS

Choosing to study homosexuality from a comparative viewpoint may seem to add an unnecessary complication. Why, indeed, not focus on just one country and study it thoroughly? Experience guided my choice. In an earlier work,[6] I concentrated my research on homosexuality in England (1919-1933).[7] It seemed obvious, then, that the fate of English homosexuals had been largely influenced by the example of Germany. Thus it became appropriate to study the two countries in parallel. On the other hand, in my readings, France appeared only anecdotally. That struck me as odd, and not very logical: in the political and intellectual fields, France of the 1920s and 1930s was a guiding light in Europe, if only because of the influence of Proust and Gide. It thus seemed to me that it would be instructive to include France in the study. Then, using the three countries as representative examples, one might draw a map of homosexuality in the inter-war period, define models, understand the interactions and perhaps distinguish some common ground and find the commonalities in the thinking and the lifestyles common to homosexuality in all three countries.

In the 1920s and 1930s, all three countries occupied a choice place on the European and international political scene. All three had taken part in the First World War. All three came out of it shaken æ although, obviously, Germany's situation was special. Shortly after the war, the three countries considered themselves liberal democracies equipped with parliamentary systems. Lastly, they were in constant interaction economically, commercially, politically, militarily, socially and culturally; so that it was no arbitrary decision to look at them all together.

Homosexuality, when it is studied, is often considered over the long term. Many works set out to embrace the history of homosexuality from Antiquity to the current day, pretending thus to imply that the subject is easily reducible and that changes occur only over the centuries, or even the millennia. Studying homosexuality over the long term means ignoring sudden changes and any characteristics specific to the period. For my part, I set out to prove that homosexu-

---

6. Florence Tamagne, *L'Homosexualité en Angleterre, 1919-1933*, DEA d'histoire du xxe siècle, under the direction of Anthony Rowley, IEP de Paris, 1991-1992, 188 pages.

7. The topic was in fact limited to England and Wales, because Scotland and Ulster didn't have the same legislation concerning homosexuality. Besides, Scotland and Ulster were special cases. The two regions would have required a far more in-depth survey, which seems at present very difficult, given the extreme scarcity of sources.

ality is a historical phenomenon that unfolds within a given political, economic and social context, and that it can be understood only in the light of events that are both internal and external to the homosexual community. The choice of the period proved to be a determining factor. From the English example, I had become convinced that the inter-war years constituted a crucial era, for homosexuals as well as for the concept of homosexuality. The end of the First World War opened a period of hitherto unknown homosexual liberation, the echo of which has survived until today in a fragmentary and largely mythologized way in the homosexual culture. Then again, the 1920s do not seem to have recorded major advances for the homosexual community. Furthermore, during the 1930s a particularly intense program of anti-homosexual repression was inaugurated under the Nazi regime in Germany. After the Second World War, the very notion of a homosexual golden age had disappeared and the fate of homosexuals in the concentration camps had become taboo. Twenty years of homosexual life had been wiped away. In fact, until very recently, the history of homosexuality during the inter-war period was almost completely blacked out, and the focus was placed instead on the late 19th and early 20th centuries, as well as the post-war period.

We are starting to question that convention, and the specific conditions of the inter-war period increasingly appear to be crucial for the history of homosexuality. This reversal of perspective comes from German historiography. The fact that homosexuals were sent to the concentration camps, and certain medical experiments that were conducted upon them, threw a sinister shadow over the history of homosexuality in Germany and inspired some major research projects. In France and England, a similar interest in the period has not yet evolved; thus, it was essential to study the 1920s and 1930s.[8]

The history of homosexuality has, until lately, been investigated primarily by the Americans, thanks to the gay liberation movement of the 1970s, particularly in the context of Gay and Lesbian Studies. This history has primarily focused on how the movement was formed, and on the homosexual identity, then on the upheavals linked to AIDS. However, some authors (both gay and lesbian), did look for traces of the homosexual way of life in centuries past, con-

---

8. Homosexuality during World War II seems to me to be a large enough subject to be addressed separately. The conflict changed the game considerably, both in terms of homosexual conduct and in the specific measures taken against it.

centrating in particular on the end of the 19th century, when homosexuality emerged as a "concept." Less research is being done in Europe.

England built on the American trend and developed its own analyses. But, there again, the authors were especially interested in the most recent period. Theoretical works on the homosexual identity and the construction of homosexuality proliferated. Works covering earlier eras are still rare. Outstanding among them is Jeffrey Weeks's book, *Coming Out — Homosexual Politics in Britain from the 19th Century to the Present* (1979), which offers a useful assessment of homosexuality in Great Britain. In Germany, as we have said, the younger generations tried to build a complete history of German homosexuality, so as to clarify the Weimar apogee and the Nazi repression. In France during the 1970s, under the leadership of Guy Hocquenghem, Jean-Louis Bory and Michel Foucault, theoretical and militant works proliferated æ albeit without an identical trend in historical research.[9] Currently, the post-war period is starting to be analyzed, but the earlier years are still largely ignored.

For any historian of homosexuality, finding sources remains the principal problem. Medical, literary, autobiographical, and propagandistic sources are fairly abundant and easy to find, even though a certain number of German works dealing with homosexuality and published between the two wars have disappeared æ either they were burned when Hitler came to power, or they were destroyed during the bombing. And still greater problems arise: personal testimonies from those days are rare, for obvious reasons. Populations were not polled on the subject, and the press remained very discreet. Legal and police sources are often vague and lacunar. Certain subjects are well covered by the available sources: the homosexual scene, homosexual movements, and homosexuality in the English public schools, in particular. Similarly, there are plenty of medical references, novels, and confessions from intellectuals and public figures of the time. The other side of the coin is obvious: very little is known about homosexuals in the lower middle class and the working class; popular reactions are not very reliable (for they are often reported by third parties); and the press generally abided by the code of silence, thus distorting any research that might

---

9. One might mention some works of varying size and interest, such as those by Guy Hocquenghem, *Race d'Ep. Un siècle d'images de l'homosexualité* (1979), Jacques Girard, *Le Mouvement homosexuel en France* (1981), Marie-Jo Bonnet, *Un choix sans équivoque. Recherches historiques sur les relations amoureuses entre les femmes, xvie-xxe siècle* (1981), Gilles Barbedette et Michel Carassou, *Paris gay 1925* (1981), Maurice Lever, *Les Bûchers de Sodome* (1985), Frédéric Martel, *Le Rose et le Noir* (1996).

rely on journalistic reports. Lesbians, moreover, suffer from an awkward disparity in the sources; in every field (especially the legal) the evidence and documents concerning homosexuals are more abundant than those dealing with lesbians. I tried, to the extent possible, to restore balance æ without always succeeding: as we will see, female homosexuality posed fewer social problems and thus it was less discussed. Moreover, many lesbians managed to lead a discreet life and did not seek to publicize their experiences. However, research on the history of lesbians is currently on the upswing and more books are appearing.

Finally, a comparison between three countries over a period of twenty years does not allow for much discussion of regional nuances. With regard to the homosexual scene, everything was concentrated in the capital cities, where the most homosexual activity took place. That does not mean, obviously, that there was no homosexuality in the provinces or countryside; far from it. But we have very little evidence about it. I tried, whenever possible, to shed some light on one or another provincial town. Regional study of the history of homosexuality, which is already well underway in Germany, will be of considerable interest for the history of social attitudes.

There remains the question of police and legal sources. Here, the study is quite out of balance in favor of England and, especially, Germany. There are not many English sources, but they suffice to enable us to draw a coherent picture of the repression of homosexuals. The sources primarily are composed of legal statistics, reports of homosexual lawsuits, official reports and notes from the police. Here again, regional studies would enable us to look more deeply into these data and to establish geographical nuances. The German files are superabundant, if dispersed far and wide. I was forced to restrict my research to certain nationwide studies. Several German researchers have begun very specific research projects studying one city in particular.

I am obliged to acknowledge that my research on France, in this respect, met with partial failure. It is a special case: homosexuality was not punished by French law in the 1920s and 1930s, so it is normal to find very few documents. Nevertheless, the discovery of a file on homosexual prostitution in the maritime regions tends to prove that there was some semi-official surveillance of homosexuals. Unfortunately, it is impossible to go further for the moment: all requests and inquiries made to the French National Archives and the Police Archives proved fruitless.

I tended to stay away from certain types of sources. It seemed counter-productive to spend vast amounts of time and energy collecting the testimony of homosexuals who lived during the inter-war period. There are not that many people concerned and, moreover, any such recollections related to a remote past, on a particularly subjective topic, would have to be taken with a large grain of salt. Distortions, even involuntary ones, may easily weaken the credibility of memoirs. I therefore preferred to rely on existing written testimonies and oral records, and I always read them with a critical eye. Press clippings were also used sparingly. Given the global character of this study, it was impossible to conclude a systematic examination of the press for each country. I examined the homosexual periodicals thoroughly, at least the remaining specimens æ for some of them, only two or three editions are available. Then, for each country, I focused on one national daily newspaper, which is used as reference, and I sometimes used other newspapers on specific points. By analyzing the press, it was possible to make a political reading of homosexuality. This research was done in Germany, where the leftist press was examined closely; I also made a thorough review of contemporary periodicals like *Gay News*. Cinematographic sources were very little used, except for three or four films that were emblematic of the period.

Many of the references required a critical reading, particularly the memoirs and the collections of memoirs written by homosexuals. They are invaluable, an irreplaceable source on the homosexual way of life. However, care must be taken, especially when the works were written many years after the events. As with oral testimony, distortions can creep in with the passage of time. It is less of a problem when sources are overtly partisan, one way or another — that in itself becomes a matter for analysis. I also made extensive use of the literature of the period, although I did not base my research mainly on literary sources. (That is a reproach often addressed to historians of homosexuality since, for lack of objective materials, they are obliged to emphasize the history of homosexuality as it can be discerned in literature. Nevertheless, literary works are an extremely useful source of information.) The writer is the witness of his time; the homosexual novelist brings his own perception of the situation, the heterosexual novelist always reflects some trend in public opinion. Thus, literature should not be excluded on the pretext of objectivity. There again, partisan sources can be as revealing as the most neutral analyses. The literary merit of the works was not considered; the œuvres of Proust, Virginia Woolf and Thomas Mann are examined along with the worst trash novels, each one giving its own view of homosexuality for a different public.

I do not claim that this work is exhaustive, but I think it has pulled together an extremely vast range of material. I hope that this work clarifies a subject that has been ignored over a period of history that is crucial, and that it will reveal, in addition to the different ways that homosexuality has been treated in the three countries, that the homosexual question, far from being a minor aspect of the history of sexuality, finds its place in the history of social attitudes and representations, serving through its faculty of attraction and repulsion to reveal the myths and fears of a society. Certainly, I do not claim to explain the inter-war period, Nazism and the beginnings of the Second World War exclusively on the basis of sexuality. It is quite obvious that the economic, political and social factors remain decisive. Neither do I propose to expound a theory of psychohistory, even if psychoanalytical theories are sometimes enlightening. Nevertheless, the study of homosexuality should allow us to gain a new understanding of certain fears on the part of the general public and the government, and perhaps to reassess the influence of sexual fantasies in the formation of the popular imagination.

PART ONE

A Brief Apogee: The 1920s, A First Homosexual Liberation
The homosexual — between dandy and militant

Sex, sex, sex, nothing but sex and jazz.

— T.C. Worsley, quoting his father, in *Flannelled Fool*

CHAPTER ONE
A MYTH IS BORN: THOSE FLAMBOYANT DAYS

The "Roaring Twenties." In homosexual mythology, the period just after the War conjures up a new freedom, the birth of homosexual movements, the extraordinary variety of the Berlin subculture. A new world, strangely modern and close to ours, seems to have had a brief and brilliant apogee. Is this wishful thinking or historical truth? Did "Eldorado" really exist?

In fact, the liberal tendencies that had begun to flicker through society before and during the First World War took concrete shape in the 1920s. Homosexuals, like many others, would benefit from the lax atmosphere in Europe in the wake of the war. In the countries on the winning side, it was a time for optimism and making hay while the sun shined; after the suffering and privations, people wanted to laugh and have a good time, and were readier to tolerate the expression of sexual peccadilloes.

The homosexual emancipation of the 1920s was fed by many streams: historically, it comes under the rubric of the movements at the end of the 19th century which tried, on the basis of new medical theories, to influence public opinion. It also bore traces of the scandals of the Victorian era and the shock of the First World War, fundamental events that resonated profoundly in the homosexual mind. And then, it was based on a culture of subversion, which created its own codes and defined its own boundaries. The language and clothing, the clubs, drag — all constituted bases of a homosexual identity in gestation and the bases of a "homosexual" liberation which, while it may now be seen in a context that is more or less mythical, was nonetheless real.

LOOKING BACK: 1869-1919

Among the legendary dates in homosexual history, some stand out. One is the night of June 27, 1969, the date of the Stonewall incidents. Others are more arbitrary, but are evidence of a conscious will to reconstruct the history of homosexuality and "homosexuals" from an identifying point of view. In 1869, the Hungarian writer-journalist Karoly Maria Kertbeny apparently used the term "homosexual" for the first time in an anonymous report calling for the abolition of criminal laws on "unnatural acts," addressed to Dr. Leonhardt, Prussian Minister of Justice. Even if it took several decades before the term stuck, this date, for many historians, marks a turning point, clearly distinguishing the sodomite (who offended God) and the homosexual (who offended society). In fact, the years 1869-1919 can be regarded as a major watershed in the history of homosexuality and as the foundation upon which the homosexual "liberation" of the 1920s was built.

One Scandal after Another

The scandals at the end of the 19th century hold a place apart, in this history. They certainly broke out in a paradoxical context. While urbanization, the guarantee of anonymity, and developments in medicine were leading to a greater sense of tolerance and while the beginnings of a homosexual "scene," even a "community," were seen, anti-homosexual legislation was strengthened and was used as a pretext for moral repression. This ambivalence is seen most clearly in England and Germany, with France experiencing a kind of counter-reaction.

The period is characterized by the development of openly homosexual movements and clubs, albeit in relatively restricted and elitist milieux — the aristocracy, the high bourgeoisie, the avant-garde. In England, the precursors of the sexual liberation of the 1920s were the Neo-Pagans. This group of intellectuals, linked to the Bloomsbury group, had its hour of glory just before the First World War. Centered around Rupert Brooke, leading light of Georgian literature, it included Justin Brooke, Jacques and Gwen Raverat, Frances Cornford, Katherine (Ka) Cox and the four Oliver sisters: Margery, Brynhild, Daphne and Noel. Coming together in Grandchester, in the country surrounding Cambridge, they sought to escape modernism by recreating a rural myth and developed an original lifestyle founded on worship of the body, freedom of movement, nudism, and co-ed bathing. The Neo-Pagans worked out a new paradigm for relations between men and women based on frankness and a free discussion of sexual questions. However, this rejection of social conventions still retained the strict observance of chastity before marriage for women, which led to frustration and repression. In this context, homosexuality represented a loophole; Rupert Brooke, who had already had homosexual adventures in his public school and then at Cambridge,[10] saw it as an easy and early means of obtaining sexual satisfaction.

His relationship with Denham Russell-Smith is remarkable in this sense. He reveals every little detail in a letter to James Strachey.[11] The detachment which he displays and his freedom in describing the sex act testify to a new approach to sexuality and homosexuality. Pleasure becomes possible, beyond the moral interdicts. Brooke began by playing with Denham the love games commonly played by the boys at public school, hugging, kissing and fondling each other. They went on that way for years, he says, until one calm evening when he masturbated him in the dark, without saying a word.[12] Denham then came to spend part of the holidays with Rupert, who decided to go all the way. One night, — I decided that the next day I would do it, not knowing at all how my partner would take it. simply wanted to have fun, and still more to see how it would be to remove the shame (as I saw it) of being a virgin.[13] Brooke does not express any remorse, only the fear that his partner would refuse him: —Very banal thoughts crossed my mind, like the Elizabethan joke about 'the dance of the bedclothes,' I hoped that he was enjoying it, etc. I thought of him only in the third person.[14] Here, homosexuality is no longer regarded as deviant, a monstrous vice, but as one form of sexuality among others.

The Neo-Pagans, due to their elitist nature, did not exert significant influence on British society but they did infuse a new spirit in the high bourgeoisie and the intellectual milieux. Their ideal of a body released of the Puritan constraints was taken up again shortly after the war. The death of Rupert Brooke, on the front in 1915, shook Victorian society. He became the symbol of all

---

10. Rupert Brooke had homosexual relations in his public school with Lucas St. John and Charles Lascelles, then at Cambridge with A.L. Hobhouse and Georges Mallory.

11. Cited by Paul Delany, *The Neo-Pagans: Friendship and Love in the Rupert Brooke Circle*, London, Macmillan, 1987, 170 pages, p.78-80.

12. *Ibid.*, p.78.

13. *Ibid.*

14. *Ibid.*, p.79.

the young soldiers sacrificed for their fatherland and he represented the idealized image of a radiant, fair and innocent youth that the world of the post-war period would struggle in vain to recapture. Sherrill Schell's photographs immortalizing the flower of English youth embodied a visual image that summarized all the longings of the nation in a time of crisis.[15] What is novel in this admiration, in the context of a society that was still deeply Puritan, it is that it is essentially homoerotic.

In France, Paris enjoyed a flattering reputation (especially among foreigners) as a capital of pleasures and haven of tolerance. Chic lesbians, mostly Americans, made Lesbos-on-Seine their paradise. One of the homosexual centers in Paris was the salon of Winaretta Singer, princesse de Polignac.[16] Married at the age of 22 to Prince Louis de Say-Montbéliard, she divorced very quickly. She knew she was a lesbian and wanted to be independent. In his book *Monsieur de Phocas*, Jean Lorrain draws a satirical portrait of her: "a multimillionaire Yankee whose greatest lack of discretion lay in her appearances at the theater in the company of a friend whose beauty was a little too conspicuous."[17] Her friends, the count de Montesquiou and the countess Greffulhe, advised her to marry Edmond de Polignac, who was also homosexual, in order to preserve her social position. She was soon receiving the best society and attracted many writers, in particular Proust. An American by birth, she was well acquainted with the Anglo-Saxon world. A friend of Henry James, she brought Oscar Wilde and Lord Douglas to the attention of the Parisian elite. They created a sensation. Paradoxically, only Montesquiou and Proust avoided them, finding them "decadent"!) Their flamboyant homosexuality made quite an impression and created the appearance of a new tolerance.

Sapphic love affairs were the fashion of the day, especially in high society. The countess d'Orsay, Princess Violette Murat, the Duchesse de Clermond-Thunder, princess Catherine Poniatowska, Countess Van Zuylen and, of course, Princess de Polignac herself were leading examples. The great courtesans also entertained female liaisons: Liana de Pougy, Émilienne d'Alençon, Liana de Lancy. Literary circles were especially rich in lesbians: Natalie Barney, Renée Vivien, Anna de Noailles, Gertrude Stein, Alice B. Toklas, and Vernon Lee were

---

15. Christopher Hassall, cited by Paul Fussell, *The Great War and Modern Memory*, Oxford, Oxford University Press, 1975, 363 pages, p.276.

16. Michael de Cossart, Une Américaine à Paris. La princesse de Polignac et son salon, 1865-1943, Paris, Plon, 1979, 245 pages.

17. Cited by Michael de Cossart, *ibid.*, p.98.

living in Paris. The city attracted many expatriate lesbians, who found an exceptional freedom and a fully-formed lesbian society in the capital. Natalie Barney's salon, at 22 rue Jacob, was a center of Parisian Sapphism.[18] Literary celebrities gathered there: Paul Valéry, Ford Madox Ford, Ezra Pound, Gide and Proust, and the finest flower of Parisian lesbians: Romaine Brooks (who would have an affair with the Princesse de Polignac), Dolly Wilde (Oscar's niece), Colette, Élisabeth de Gramont, Lucie Delarue-Mardrus, Rachilde, Gertrude Stein, Marie Laurencin, Marguerite Yourcenar, Mercedes d'Acosta, Sylvia Beach, Adrienne Monnier, Dorothy Bussy (Lytton Strachey's sister), Mata Hari, Edna St. Vincent Millais and Edith Sitwell. The atmosphere was relaxed, cosmopolitan, literary — or with literary pretensions — and well born. Inherently chauvinistic, they were for the most part quite oblivious to the other social classes.

France already symbolized a brilliant, theatrical, sometimes blatant homosexuality that was quite disengaged from political and social concerns. In the absence of repressive laws, homosexuals seemed to be well integrated into the society. However, this idyllic vision is misleading: for the majority of homosexuals who were not a part of high society and who lived in the obscurity of the provinces, homosexuality remained a stain that had to be kept carefully hidden.

Germany was different. There, by the end of the 19th century, a strong homosexual community existed and organizations like the Wissenschaftlich-humanitäres Komitee (WhK), under Magnus Hirschfeld, and the Gemeinschaft der Eigenen led by Adolf Brand, were forming to advocate the abolition of §175 of the Penal Code, under which "indecent acts" between men were punished with a five-year prison term. Their respective newspapers, *Jahrbuch für sexual Zwischenstufen* and *Der Eigene* were launched in 1899 and 1903. This detail explains why Germany, before 1914, had already built a solid reputation for sexual freedom. Travel in Germany, a normal part of an Englishman's university experience, was generally the pretext for such discoveries. Rupert Brooke went to Munich, the apex of the artistic avant-garde, in 1911. However, it was in Berlin that a homosexual scene worthy of the name was first coming together, with bars, clubs, and meeting places for women as well as for men.

In 1905, homosexuality was already such a fashionable topic that it was treated humorously in the German satirical newspapers. The Munich weekly

---

18. Gertrude Stein hosted a competing salon at 27 rue de Fleurus. For details on the life and adventures of Natalie Barney, see George Wickes, *The Amazon of Letters. The Life and Loves of Natalie Barney*, London, W.H. Allen, 1977, 286 pages.

magazine *Jugend* published a cartoon captioned, "The modern census," showing a middle-class German family being interviewed by the census official. The parents are asked: "How many children do you have?" And the mother answers: "Two girls, a boy, one uranian and three homosexuals."

In the three countries covered by this study, the Puritan backlash, based on a series of major scandals, badly shook the incipient homosexual communities. In England, the trial and condemnation of Oscar Wilde took on considerable symbolic importance.[19] The facts are well-known: after having received at his club an insulting note from the Marquis de Queensberry, calling him a "somdomite" [sic], Oscar Wilde filed suit for slander. The trial opened on April 3, 1895, but quickly turned to his disadvantage, several young male prostitutes having been called to testify. The case was eventually dropped, but it set off two further lawsuits, which began on April 26 and on May 22, in which Wilde was accused of offending morals and of sodomy. On May 25, he was sentenced to two years in prison, to the great joy of the public and the press.[20]

Oscar Wilde's trial, while it was unique in terms of the prominence of the individual in question and the scandal it caused, is just one of many examples of the outbursts of moral panic which haunted Victorian England. Wilde's sentence was the consummation of the victory of the Puritan party and it crystallized in the public view the image of the homosexual as a "corrupter of youth," a source of danger and depravity. A conspiracy of silence around homosexuality, intended to protect family morals, ensued. *The Lancet* newspaper, for example, said: — It is particularly important that such subjects are not discussed by the man in the street, much less by the young boy or the young girl.[21] To prevent such scandals from proliferating, Halsbury, with the support of the conservative Prime Minister Salisbury, drafted the Publication of Indecent Evidence Bill in 1896, prohibiting the publication of reports on trials relating to homosexuality. According to Salisbury, indeed, it was proven that the publication of details in lawsuits of this kind "entails the imitation of the crime."[22]

---

19. This topic still fascinates the popular imagination. In the period between the two wars, one notable publication in 1933 (a key year for homosexuals), was the book by Hilary Pacq, *Le Procès d'Oscar Wilde*, Paris, Gallimard, 263 pages.

20. See Richard Ellmann, *Oscar Wilde*, London, Hamish Hamilton, 1987, 632 pages.

21. *Lancet*, 9-26 November 1898, cited by Richard Davenport-Hines, *Sex, Death and Punishment*, London, Fontana Press, 1990, 439 pages, p.139.

22. Lord Salisbury, 20 March 1896.

Paradoxically, the Oscar Wilde trial was a catalyst for a new sense of identity among homosexuals. The case had revealed the existence of a homosexual lifestyle that was already solidly in place: Wilde was linked to a network of young male prostitutes who lived in an apartment at 13 Little College Street. It was not the first time that such events occurred: in 1889 and 1890, the scandal of Cleveland Street[23] exposed a similar group of young telegraphists.

In Germany, the homosexual question came to the fore as early as 1907, when the imperial regime of William II was suddenly shaken by a series of scandals. The journalist Maximilian Harden, in his newspaper *Die Zukunft*, accused two close friends of the Kaiser, Prince Philipp von Eulenburg and Count Kuno von Moltke, of being homosexuals. The motive was to discredit William II by casting suspicion on his entourage and upsetting Germany's international relations. Eulenburg and Moltke in fact were suspected of having given information to the First Secretary of the French legation in Berlin, Raymond Lecomte, who was himself homosexual. He was in a position to reveal to the Quay d'Orsay that Germany was bluffing during the Moroccan crisis of January-April 1906.[24] The episode was indisputably political in origin: an advisor to William II, and incidentally his best friend, Eulenburg was an anti-imperialist diplomat and favored a rapprochement with France. He quickly drew upon himself the resentment of the military and of Bismarck's disciples. Maximilian Harden organized a campaign against him, and focused on his homosexuality as an easy means of destroying his career and depriving him of influence, thus weakening the emperor at the same time without incriminating him directly. It seems that Harden did, indeed, have many compromising documents concerning William II's sexuality, but he preferred not to make use of them. It is quite clear that the charge of homosexuality was only a pretext in a more subtle political maneuver. During the period between the wars, as well, attacks on homosexuals were often only a means to a political end.

Harden started by making Eulenburg talk; he had forced him to resign from public affairs in 1902 by threatening to expose his private life. However, in

---

23. For details on the ring at Little College Street, see Richard Ellmann, *Oscar Wilde, op. cit.*, p.414-417; on the Cleveland Street scandal, see Jeffrey Weeks, *Sex, Politics and Society*, London, Longman, 1989, 325 pages, p.113-114.

24. For more details, see James D. Steakley, "Iconography of a Scandal: Political Cartoons and the Eulenburg Affair in Wilhelmin Germany," in Martin Duberman, Martha Vicinus and George Chauncey Jr. (dir.), *Hidden from History*, London, Penguin Books, 1991, 579 pages, p.233-263.

1906, Eulenburg renewed his political contacts, and that led to the campaign launched against him regarding his relations with General Kuno von Moltke, military commander of Berlin. It is possible that this campaign was launched under strong pressure from the military brass, which had just been just hit by a series of homosexual scandals as well. Given the charges, the Kaiser asked Moltke to resign and Eulenburg had to leave the diplomatic corps and turn in his medals.

As in England, with Oscar Wilde, one lawsuit followed another. Moltke filed charges against Harden. Adolf Brand, the leader of Gemeinschaft der Eigenen (the "Community of Special People"), a homosexual movement, accused the Chancellor of the Reich, Prince Bernhard von Bülow, of having an affair with his Secretary. Bülow sued him for calumny. Moltke's suit against Harden opened on October 23, 1907 and quickly turned sensational. Moltke's wife made devastating revelations about her husband's sexuality and Hirschfeld had to testify as an expert. He affirmed that Moltke's "unconscious orientation" could be described as homosexual. The purpose of this testimony was to denounce the hypocrisy of the government, which overlooked homosexuality in highly-placed figures but condemned it in others. This tactic did not pay off: on October 29, Harden was discharged and a new suit was opened, with Chancellor Bülow pursuing Brand for calumny. Brand was sentenced to eighteen months in prison. A little later, medical experts asserted that Moltke's wife was hysterical and Hirschfeld challenged her testimony. Harden was then sentenced to four months in prison. Once he was released, he continued his campaign against Eulenburg. The Eulenburg trial was never carried to its conclusion, for the prince fell seriously ill. He died in 1921, without being rehabilitated (unlike Moltke).

The Eulenburg case did serious harm to the homosexual cause. Eulenburg was disgraced and ruined, and the press and the general public now looked on homosexuals as traitors to the nation. The involvement of Hirschfeld, a Jew and a homosexual, in the lawsuit, added the idea of a conspiracy between the two groups with the aim of bringing down the Empire. Homophobic demonstrations became commonplace, often combined with anti-Semitic, antifeminist and anti-modernist actions. The number of arrests and indictments for homosexuality increased. The German homosexual liberation movement underwent a severe crisis. Financial support for the WhK fell by two thirds between 1907 and 1909. It is clear that Hirschfeld's intervention was a serious strategic error: the well-to-do homosexuals who had supported it, hitherto, now feared that they too could be penalized.[25]

24

It is clear that homosexuals in the three countries under study were in touch with each other from the very beginning of the century. The homosexual world already had a certain unity, superficial but real. In France, the princesse de Polignac's salon felt the backlash of a wave of Puritanism. The multiplying scandals reverberated deeply among these people of various stations and nationalities. Wilde's trial in 1895 shook this world of aesthetes and eccentrics; some turncoats became vehement moralists: Octave Mirbeau let loose a tirade against the aesthetes, Paul Le Bourget disavowed his homosexuality and fell in with Barres and the French nationalists. In 1903, Alfred Krupp committed suicide; the same year, the Baron d'Adelsward-Fersen was arrested in Paris after a scandal having to do with schoolboys; in 1907 came the Eulenburg affair. According to Michael de Cossart, "the shockwave was felt by the secret society of homosexuals throughout all of Europe."[26] This affair had extreme repercussions. Books were still being written about it after the First World War.[27] Proust mentions it in *Sodom and Gomorrah*: "There exists between certain men, Sir, a freemasonry about which I cannot speak, but which counts among its ranks, at this moment, the sovereigns of Europe — but the entourage of one of them, who is the emperor of Germany, wants to cure him of his illusions. That is a very grave thing and may lead us to war."[28] The French press started calling homosexuality the "German vice." Berlin was renamed "Sodom-on-Spree" and the Germans were called "Eulenbuggers." In the men's toilets, homosexual come-ons took a new form: "Do you speak German?"[29]

The scandals of the pre-war period left a lasting mark on the homosexual mind. The uproar showed how fragile were the attempts at homosexual emancipation, always at the mercy of the whims of ever-shifting public opinion — which was concerned with respectability and ready to name sacrificial victims, in a crisis, in order to redeem the "sins" of the nation.

---

25. See James D. Steakley, *The Homosexual Emancipation Movement in Germany*, New York, Arno Press, 1975, 121 pages.

26. Michael de Cossart, *Une Américaine à Paris, op. cit.*, p.95.

27.Maurice Baumont, L'Affaire Eulenburg et les Origines de la Première Guerre mondiale, Payot, 1933, 281 pages.

28. Marcel Proust, *A la recherche du temps perdu*, Paris, Gallimard, coll. "Bibl. de la Pléiade," 1988, t.III, 1952 pages, p.586-587.

29. See John Grand-Carteret, *Derrière "lui": l'homosexualité en Allemagne* [1907], Lille, Cahiers Gai-Kitsch-Camp, 1992, 231 pages.

They also revealed to those homosexuals who had been isolated that homosexual networks existed and that a homosexual culture was being formed. The First World War confirmed these trends.

The Shock of the First World War

The First World War represented a major founding myth in the homosexual imagination of the 1920s. The contradictory trends of the inter-war period originated in the War: liberalism and authoritarianism, pacifism and militarism, virility and femininity. Ambiguity was born from a certain confusion around the concept of homoeroticism, itself a consequence of the war. It could be associated with camaraderie, heroism, male beauty — and therefore with virility; just as it could be condemned as the incarnation of a lax rearguard, traitorous, impotent and thus female. Also, while the homosexual community of the 1920s may have recalled the First World War as a time of male friendships and while they may have developed a nostalgia for the sacrificed beauties, the War also led to a misogynist, militarist tendency expressed in antidemocratic movements and an apology for virile violence. In public opinion, too, liberal tendencies (and the pent-up desire for pleasure in the post-war period) clashed with repressive tendencies (including the confusion of homosexuality with decadence).

The homosexual, a traitor to the fatherland

War reveals a country's weaknesses. After 1914, each nation pulled together its forces to confront the threat. In Germany, England and France, the notion of holy unity was invoked to catalyze the coming together around national values. The war left little room for minorities and rendered suspect any and all forms of deviation. Homosexuals became a target of choice for the heralds of nationalism. In Germany, the homosexual movements retreated into prudent silence. Individuals remained vulnerable to rumors.

In D.H. Lawrence's *Kangaroo*, the hero, Richard Somers, is characterized by his constitutional weakness which makes him unfit to bear arms, his attraction to socialism and his sexual ambiguity. He becomes the scapegoat of the small village of Cornouailles, and each inhabitant begins to spy on him. He is finally obliged to flee to London, but he has difficulties all throughout the war.[30]

---

30. The novel is based on D.H. Lawrence's personal experiences during the war.

In England, the war was seized upon as an excellent occasion to purge the country of all its blemishes, in particular the sexual ones. Oscar Wilde's trial was still very much present in the public memory in 1914. It was a symbol of the decadence of the olden days, which would have to be eliminated if one wanted to make England a masculine and victorious nation. One of the broad topics in propaganda was the fight against pacifists, and grafted onto that theme one can find exhortations against sexual deviance, in particular homosexuality, considered a German weakness. This was a direct consequence of the Eulenburg episode, but it was also a handy way to designate homosexuality as a crime almost equivalent to treason.

The same phenomenon could be seen in France: in *Temps retrouvé*, Proust gives a perfect analysis of how the war changed the perception of Charlus' homosexuality. "Since the war, the tone had changed. The baron's inversion was not only denounced, but also his alleged Germanic nationality: 'Frau Bosch,' 'Frau van den Bosch' were his usual nicknames."[31]

The English army, for its part, enacted severe sanctions against sexual relations between men: two years of prison for any act, committed in public or in private; ten years in the case of sodomy. Officers were cashiered before being sentenced. In spite of that, homosexual activity still went on in the ranks: during the war, 22 officers and 270 soldiers were tried for homosexuality.[32] Homosexuality was not only a crime against the army, it was a crime against England at war. Civilians, too, became objects of attack and a veritable witch hunt started. The parliamentary deputy Noël Pemberton Billing launched a crusade against homosexuals.[33] In 1918, he published an article entitled, "The First 47,000," referring to the number of British homosexuals (according to him) known to the German secret service. They supposedly had a list that enabled them to blackmail people in high places and to extort state secrets. Billing reiterated his assertions before the House of Commons. He also went after the dancer Maud Allan, who was playing the role of Salome in the Oscar Wilde play. Allan charged him with slander. Billing protested that the way the play, and the way it was being performed, was targeted directly at sexual perverts, sodomites and lesbians, and said that at a time when Britain's very existence as a nation was in

---

31. Marcel Proust, *A la recherche du temps perdu*, op. cit., 1989, t.IV, 1728 pages, p.347.

32. According to Samuel Hynes, *A War Imagined. The First World War and English Culture*, New York, Atheneum, 1991, 427 pages, p.225.

33. The very witty Billing led a feisty campaign against the Jews, German music, pacifists, the Fabians, foreigners, financiers and internationalism.

danger, the producer J. T. Grein had chosen to put on the most depraved of all the depraved works by a man who already had been given the stiffest penalty available to the law for vice, for crimes against nature.[34] The trial was an enormous scandal and Billing was never seen as the defendant. He used the hearings as a soapbox to rail against homosexuality and posed as an honest patriot defending his country against those who were being led astray by Germany. He was acquitted.[35]

The hysteria over homosexuality shows the extent to which it could be regarded as pernicious and hazardous for the nation. The specter of having a homosexual traitor in power cropped up time and again during the inter-war period, and then, with greater and greater resonance during the Second World War and up to the paroxysms of the Fifties, during the Cold War, with the Cambridge spy scandal.

The front as a school in homosexuality

By bringing men closer together in situations of extreme danger, the war was a fertile ground for the development of homosexual friendships; and thus it served to relieve homosexuality of some of the tension and drama surrounding it. Warrior aesthetics is based largely on homoeroticism; by focusing on the male body, by accentuating virile characteristics, it strives to create an ideal male society. Saint-Loup, in *Temps retrouvé*, takes advantage of the war to live out a fantasy homosexual romance. The war represented a kind of ideal situation, his dreams fulfilled "in a purely masculine chivalric order, far from women, where he could risk his life to save his order, and in dying inspire a fanatical love in his men."[36]

Antoine Prost and Stéphane Audoin-Rouzeau both evoked "the fraternity of the trenches," a stereotype of the Great War:[37] in the trenches, soldiers and officers supposedly met each other as equals, helping each other, comforting each other, and feeling moments of intense sympathy. Similarly, in Germany, the universally worn Stahlhelm (steel helmet) became a unifying symbol that fostered the cult of "Frontkameradschaft." This enduring myth, promulgated by the

---

34. In Samuel Hynes, *A War Imagined, op. cit.*, p.227.

35. *Ibid.*

36. Marcel Proust, *A la recherche du temps perdu, op. cit.*, t.IV, p.324-325.

37. See Antoine Prost, *Les Anciens Combattants et la Société française, 1914-1939*, Paris, Presses de la FNSP, 1977, 3 volumes; Stéphane Audoin-Rouzeau, *14-18, les combattants des tranchées*, Paris, Armand Colin, 1986, p.50.

UNC's motto "United as [we were] at the Front," is based on a genuine, but fleeting, reality. After the war, only memories were left to testify to the magic of this solidarity. Still, we should not underestimate the impact of the experience. The testimony quoted by Stéphane Audoin-Rouzeau in *Les Combattants des tranchées* has strong homoerotic connotations, which has not been emphasized until now. The newspaper *Le Périscope* also said, in 1916: "[Because of all the misfortunes they have shared] they have conceived deep friendships for each other. Their shared memories and pains have left an indestructible bond which keeps them together. Thus they go around as couples, in the squads: two by two, as if the friendship could not extend to several people without being weakened and would lose its intensity if it were shared.... They are never seen without each other.... They are called comrades." *Poil et Plume*, in October 1916, said: "In the first-aid stations, a casualty who is failing will grab the first stretcher-bearer who comes along and whom he has never seen, and exclaim: 'Kiss me. I want to die with you'."

In fact, if the war allowed a blooming of hitherto discreet and timorous homosexuality, it also served as an eye-opener for men who, in normal times, would have looked on such relationships with contempt. Most people still thought of the homosexual as an effeminate and affected man. The friendships created in the trenches were built on a different logic, that of male societies welded together by a code of honor and shared experiences. Most of the homosexual friendships on the front were established between young officers and their men. J.B. Priestley[38] notes that it was largely members of the upper classes or of the well-to-do middle class, who had been prepared for such passions in their public schools, who welcomed the completely masculine way of life, freed of the complications associated with females. These passionate friendships, idealized and devoid of physical contact, were inspired by the youth, the beauty, the innocence of a young man, often an aide-de-camp or a soldier assigned to serve an officer. It was under such circumstances that Somerset Maugham met the young ambulance driver, Gerald Haxton, who was to become his companion. J.R. Ackerley[39] noted that his couriers and servants were selected on the basis of their looks; in fact, this desire to have the best-looking soldiers in one's service was common with many officers. He did not know, he said, whether any of the

---

38. Cited by Paul Fussell, The Great War and Modern Memory, *op. cit.*, p.273.
39. *Ibid.*

other officers took greater advantage than he did of this relationship of "almost paternal intimacy."

Many officers tried to sublimate what they regarded as guilty desires in an increased devotion to their men. Psychologist W.H.R. Rivers encountered several cases of officers who were torn by their sexual desires and a strict notion of duty and military discipline which obliged them to sublimate their feelings in a more impersonal interest for the fate of their men. Many cases of neurosis seem to have been the consequence of this conflict. Siegfried Sassoon, in his poems, expresses the pain (more mental than physical), and the guilt, he felt over his close companions who died.

But now my heart is heavy-laden. I sit
Burning my dreams away beside the fire:
For death has made me wise and bitter and strong;
And I am rich in all that I have lost.
O starshine on the fields of long-ago,
Bring me the darkness and the nightingale;
Dim wealds of vanished summer, peace of home,
And silence; and the faces of my friends. [40]

After the war, Sassoon fully acknowledged his homosexuality and went on to have relationships with Philip de Hesse, Gabriel Atkin, Glen Byam Shaw and especially Stephen Tennant. This conjunction between the former soldier, virile and tormented, and the decadent young dandy summarizes the shift that took place in homosexual circles after the war. Two opposite worlds attracted each other, with their own excesses, in their successive rebellions against the estab-lished order to create a new model of a "normal homosexuality," without con-straints.

The poet Wilfred Owen[41] seems to have had less difficulties accepting his homosexuality, probably because he was fully conscious of it before going to the front. His war poems[42] contain many homoerotic passages; Owen does not stop

---

40. "Memory" in *Collected Poems, 1908-1956*, London, Faber & Faber, 1984, 317 pages, p.105.

41. On Wilfred Owen, see Kenneth Simcox, *Wilfred Owen, Anthem for Doomed Youth*, London, Woburn Press, 1987, 166 pages.

42. *The Poems of Wilfred Owen*, edited by Jon Stallworthy, London, The Hogarth Press, 1985, 200 pages.

at evoking the beauty of his comrades, he shares their sufferings, he evokes the special bonds that tie them. While he denounces the horror of battle, with his aesthetic vision and his passion for the virile body he offers an original vision of life on the front:

Red lips are not so red
As the stained stones kissed by the English dead.
Kindness of wooed and wooer
Seems shame to their love pure.
O Love, your eyes lose lure
When I behold eyes blinded in my stead!...
Heart, you were never hot
Nor large, nor full like hearts made great with shot;
And though your hand be pale,
Paler are all which trail
Your cross through flame and hail:
Weep, you may weep, for you may touch them not.[43]

This is a very male perspective which bars from the outset any intervention by women. In this, Owen is a harbinger of homosexual relations in the post-war period, when men linked by a common experience preferred to stay to themselves, apart from women — whom they did not really know and whom they did not really trust.

Such fancies were not limited to the Officers' Club; romantic idylls also developed among the troops. Private Anthony French conceived a great passion for his fellow soldier Albert William Bradley, who died in his arms in September 1916. When he first set eyes on him, he was struck by his beauty, his youth, his face — pale and finely sculpted. He had a high, broad forehead, and his lips traced an odd curve that left a little dimple in his cheek.[44] Some of the soldiers, certainly, also came to worship their officers, as can be seen in the play by Robert Graves, *But It Still Goes On* (1931).

One of the favorite topics in the homosexual imagery of the era was that of bathing. Descriptions of naked soldiers bathing under the affectionate gaze of their officers crop up in many of the memoirs of ex-serviceman, expressing the

---

43. "Greater Love" (1917), *ibid.*, p.143.
44. Paul Fussell, The Great War and Modern Memory, *op. cit.*, p.274.

striking contrast between the vulnerability of the flesh (with strong erotic con-notations) and the aggressiveness of the external world.

> — A little further, a naked soldier was standing under a jet of water....
> And the beauty of this fragile, little blond thing, so white under the sun...
> was something so immense in itself that it pierced me with pain like a
> lance.[45]

Lastly, the war gave lesbians an unexpected opportunity. Many women participated in military operations, especially as military ambulance attendants. In *The Well of Loneliness*, Radclyffe Hall evokes this desire to serve and the oppor-tunity offered to women who were single and had no children to find a place in society. Stephen, one of her heroines, says she is afraid that they'd refuse people like her; her interlocutor puts a hand on hers and advises her, rather, that this war could give women of [her] kind their chance. "I believe you may discover that they need you, Stephen."[46]

Heroines indeed joined the London ambulance corps; and they found not only a place in society but a solidarity that was to be maintained after the war. One writer observed that

> — "feminine women," the nurses, had answered the call of their country
> superbly, and that should not be forgotten by England; but the others —
> who also offered the best that they had — they too ought not to be forgot-
> ten. They might have seemed a little strange (in fact, some of them were),
> and yet in the streets they were rarely noticed, although they walked with
> big steps, perhaps out of timidity, or perhaps out of a self-conscious desire
> to be useful, which often goes hand-in-hand with timidity. They had been
> active participants in the universal upheaval and had been accepted as
> such, for their merits. And although their Sam Browne belts held no guns
> and their hats and their caps lacked regimental badges, a battalion had
> been formed during those terrible years which never would be completely
> dissolved.[47]

---

45. Reginald Farrer, cited by Paul Fussell, *ibid.*, p.301. Bathing appears as a theme in both poetry and painting. Henry Scott Tuke, Frederick Walker and William Scott of Oldham specialized in portraying young men by the waterside. E.M. Forster had already suggested the erotic connotations of bathing, in *A Room with a View*. That freed George Emerson, Freddy Honeychurch and the pastor Beebe of their inhibitions in a pagan communion.

46. Radclyffe Hall, *The Well of Loneliness* [1928], London, Virago Press, 1982, 447 pages, p.271.

Thus the First World War brought to light the latent homosexual feelings in certain sectors of the male and female population, thus contradicting the stereotype of the depraved homosexual. In their work *History of Sexual Life during the World War*, Fischer and Dubois describe the living conditions in the prison camps. The soldiers gave in, they say, one after the other, to the temptation of relationships that went against nature. Even those who by temperament were most hostile to it were gradually drawn in by the supplications of their homosexual comrades, even those who might not have had the least idea, in civil life, of homosexuality.[48] The echo of these temptations is perceptible in contemporary satirical newspapers, which published caricatures depicting the "diva" of the regiment waited on by a horde of his admirers and where transvestite soldiers express sudden whims. After the war, the troubled consciences could no longer ignore the psychological shifts generated by combat. Still, over the "sexual liberation" of the "Roaring Twenties" a pall was cast, a feeling of incompletion: the young male prostitutes of the bars in Berlin, the homosexuals in the big, licentious cities were all haunted by the specter of death which always ran more swiftly than they, which pursued their least pleasures. On the other hand, the great homosexual myth of the inter-war period, in particular among English intellectuals, was to find "a friend," "a friend for life." This desperate search for a special partner seems reminiscent of the uncomplicated friendships of war-time, when fraternity between men could be exercised without constraints, without any thought of the world outside, the world of women, of mothers and sisters.

The war casts open the blinds

> *Tell England. You must write a book and talk to them,*
> *Rupert, about the schoolboys of our generation, who died.*[49]

The war left deep wounds. In England, 744,000 were killed and more than a half-million civilian deaths are ascribed to the conflict. The influenza epidemic of the winter 1918-1919 caused another 100,000-plus deaths. In Germany, 2 million men died in combat or from their wounds. Civilian deaths were 740,000 more than normal, never mind the deficit in the birth rate, estimated at 3 million.

---

47. *Ibid.*, p.275.

48. Cited by Richard Davenport-Hines, *Sex, Death and Punishment, op. cit.*, p.148.

49. Ernest Raymond, *Tell England: A Study in a Generation*, London, Cassell & Cie, 1922, 320 pages, p.314.

But the toll was highest in France: 1,300,000 died at the front, plus 150,000 other deaths related to the war, not counting deaths from disease. Thus, out of 8 million mobilized, there were 6.45 million survivors.[50] However, according to Antoine Prost, a large proportion of those mobilized never made it to the front, and so the number of ex-serviceman would actually be only about a million. However, about a sixth of the population was directly affected, if one includes war widows (600,000) and orphans (760,000), that is to say 7,500,000people.[51]

Many veterans' associations supported the legend of communion in the trenches and particularly emphasized that the survivors "had rights over us" (Clemenceau). The veterans' associations called for pacifism, driven by their memory of suffering and the horror of the war, which deeply marked people's minds psychologically and aesthetically as well. The heavy death toll was identified with the promising younger generation who went off to war with all their illusions, and were sacrificed. This feeling of youth in flower, mown down by guns, was ideally symbolized by the myth that developed in England around Rupert Brooke. Thus the post-war period, while idolizing the adolescent heroes for their beauty and their youth, opened the way to a latent homoeroticism in certain circles of society.

Worship of the body followed naturally in the wake of the great carnage of the war of 1914, and it is indissociable from the slogan, "Never again." Naturism, the rise of movements along the lines of the Wandervogel, and vestimentary liberation were partly the consequence of the great aesthetic shake-up of the war and a terrible fear of any attack on the body, especially the young body. The dominant moral values were replaced by the morality of survival, which gives priority to pleasure over the spirit of sacrifice.

The war transformed the family unit, and the number of orphans was one of the most immediate effects. The poet W.H. Auden, for example, ascribes his homosexuality to the absence of his father throughout the entire war period, and Christopher Isherwood, to his father's death in combat. Although such an explanation is partial and psychoanalytical, there could be some truth to it. The war was also followed by a steep rise in divorces, a consequence of the long separations during the war and the different courses lives will take; but there was also

---

50. Then there were the civilian casualties : some 570,000 died as a rsult of the evacuation, occupation, bombings, the higher infant mortality rate and the epidemic of Spanish flu.

51. Nevertheless, not all the war veterans and victims participated in the movement. At its apogee, in 1930-1932, it had about 3 million members.

a rise in the marriage rate. Widows were seen in two possible ways: ideally, they should hide away in their sorrow, faithful beyond death to "the dear departed," and devoted to the children. The merry widow, remarried and free, became a lightning rod for animosity and led to an obsession with woman-vampires, treacherously louche and sensualist, revived by the novel by Radiguet, *Le Diable au corps* (1923).

Added to that was the new disparity in numbers between men and women. In England, in 1911 there were 1068 women for 1000 men; by 1921, there were 1096; in 1931, 1088; and in 1939, there were still 1080 per 1000.[52] In France, according to Jacques Dupâquier, there were more than one million more women than men in 1931. The shortage of men would (falsely) be seen as a reason for the alleged proliferation of lesbians in the 1920s.[53]

Then, in contrast to the pacifism of the ex-serviceman, certain homo-sexuals in the 1930s, who were children in 1914, developed a mythical sense of the war — many young people had the impression that they had missed the major event of their lives. They had missed the solidarity forged in combat, and they could not prove that they were men. At Oxford, after the war, the younger students felt like second-class citizens while their seniors returned haloed in glory, and plaques lined the walls of the university enumerating the names of the war dead. At the same time, other movements derived from the war (like "Freikorps" in Germany) developed a homoerotic mystique around the worship of virility and the glorification of the soldier. Ernst von Solomon's works exem-plify this trend. Similarly, Max-René Hesse's novel *Partenau*, published in 1929, evokes the drama of "the return to normal" and certain soldiers' inability to accept the values of civil society. Lieutenant Ernst Partenau, 30 years old and the glory of the regiment, secretly falls in love with the brilliant Stefan Kiebold, 22 years old. Their relationship soon disturbs their superiors. Stefan tries to con-vince Partenau that this love is misplaced, and he ascribes it to the influence of the war years: "You refuse to see things as they are, now, or you can't see them, because for four years you lived in the extreme conditions of the No Man's Land, like a cave man, facing death every day, in an atmosphere of tension and hard

---

52. François-Charles Mougel, *Histoire du Royaume-Uni au XXᵉ siècle*, Paris, PUF, 1996, 600 pages.

53. An absurd idea: André Armengaud shows clearly that in France, for example, the feminine "excess" was resabsorbed in part by the decrease in male celibacy, and the high rate of marriage between Frenchwomen and foreign or younger men. See *La Population française au XXᵉ siècle* [1965], Paris, PUF, 1992, 127 pages.

masculinity. But we've gone back to women, long since."[54] Partenau commits suicide immediately thereafter.

Violence too becomes a dominant theme in a certain strain of homosexual literature. James Hanley's novel, *The German Prisoner* (1930),[55] exploits the topic of the war around a sadomasochistic homosexual phantasmagoria. The war here is seen as a catalyst of violence subjacent to a certain type of homosexual relations; the enemy is at the same time an object of hatred and of desire, the possible lover in times of peace and the symbol of a hostile nation. Unable to overcome the duality of their nature, the heroes give in to fatal impulses. The climax is reached when two English soldiers violate, then kill, the German prisoner, young, fair and beardless, matching the stereotype then in vogue; they are soon blown to bits, themselves. The cruelty and violence of the text reaches an unbearable pitch, revealing the frustrations of combat. Unable to accept their own homosexuality that surfaces at the front, the soldiers project it onto their enemy, denying it and destroying it at the same time. The text seems to synthesize all the fears related to homosexuality in times of war. The sexual tension reaches a paroxysm, the body becomes obsessive, but this discovery of sexual attraction for a man and worse yet, an enemy, is too brutal to be accepted. All the protagonists are blown away as if no trace must remain of such wayward actions, as if such a situation must at least be confined to war times.[56]

The loss of innocence is another major theme of the period, illustrated by the novel *Tell England* (1922), by Ernest Raymond. Here, the homosexuality of the pre-war period, displayed in the form of the passionate friendship between two pupils in a public school (a common topic in British literature), and the post-war world stripped of its illusions. The war highlights this shift — it is when his friend dies at Gallipoli that the hero, Ray, realizes that he loved him. Reminiscing about the idyllic scenes of their adolescence, he cries, "I loved you. I loved you. I loved you."[57] He is left alone with the awareness of his lost love and the vague sense that that love could not have existed unless it remained unrecognized — the ambiguity of the homosexual feeling which has no right to be declared in any definite way, and that is condemned as soon as it comes into clear existence. The entire novel is charged with homoeroticism and calls upon a latent homosexual culture that is there, waiting to be reactivated among English

---

54. Max-René Hesse, *Partenau*, Paris, Albin Michel, 1930, 323 pages, p.312-315.
55. James Hanley, *The German Prisoner*, London, ed. part., 1930, 36 pages, p.32-33.
56. *Ibid.*, p.36.
57. Ernest Raymond, *Tell England*, *op. cit.*, p.298.

readers from the middle class or higher. The attraction of the book rests in its worship of youth; homosexuality becomes a diffuse feeling of love and compassion for other boys, a way of still denying its sexual character while accentuating how widespread it is in the society.[58]

Thus the war marks a watershed in terms of sexuality, the revelations of the front having certain consequences once peace was restored. By awakening certain men to the profound truth of their own nature, it destroyed the entire edifice of lies and dissimulation which had enabled Victorian society to preserve its appearance of morality. From this point on, homosexuality was hard to cover up entirely, since it was clear by now that it involved more than a narrow segment of the population who were considered sick or depraved. It suddenly became a possibility for everyone.

Even if this acknowledgement was fleeting — or unconscious — it upset the foundation of sexual morals. Still, homosexuality was not freed from its underlying but ever so constraining myths: youth offered in sacrifice, pleasure dissolving in death, guilt before society's expectations, the impossibility of finding lasting satisfaction. All these themes persisted in the inter-war period, so that the liberation of morals remained hypothetical even among homosexuals, themselves. Those who called it decadence would persist, nonetheless, in associating the new visibility of homosexuality with the war, comparing it to a plague.

THE HOMOSEXUAL SCENE: SUBVERSIVE LANGUAGE

The homosexual scene is theater. It is not timeless; quite to the contrary. It follows the fads and fashions and interprets the latest trends. Homosexual fashions in speech, clothing, and gestures follow specific codes that help keep homosexuals in a world to themselves. In ways that are often imperceptible to the uninitiated, these evolving fashions delineate variations and sexual conventions. Knowing how to interpret the details enables one to penetrate to the very heart of homosexual life, to discern the secrets and to sort out what is part of homosexual reality and what is more a part of the mythology. The flamboyance of the homosexual scene of the 1920s, for example, takes its place among the founding myths of a culture, and gains importance mainly in subversion.

---

58. *Ibid.*, p.92.

Homosexual Talk: from "Slang" to "Camp"

The role language has played in shaping the homosexual identity was high-lighted by Michel Foucault in the first volume of his *History of Sexuality*. He drew attention particularly to their prolific talk about sex during times when middle-class families preserved a Puritanical silence on the topic. "Putting it in words" is an essential element of repression, but is also a means of getting around it, of subverting it. Sex, and homosexual sex in particular, was filtered and re-tran-scribed through a coded vocabulary, fixed expressions which made it possible to channel the discourse and at the same time to cut short the discussion, to render a final judgment from the heterosexual point of view.

But this same language, these same expressions can also be appropriated by homosexual speakers who void them of their usual meanings, deform them and transform them to the point of using them as the basis for defining their own identity. Talk about homosexuality then becomes something else altogether, a separate genre with its own rules and obligatory passages. Therefore, we will start by simply trying to delineate homosexual speech as such, the everyday speech, the designations, the labels.

It may seem anachronistic to talk about homosexual speech. Indeed, the term "homosexual" was not much used in those days in homosexual circles, except in medical books (often translated from German). Many homosexuals were unaware of the meaning of the term, or did not really see themselves as such. Worsley's characters stumble on this in his autobiographical *Flannelled Fool*, in a scene that may be paraphrased as follows.

—"You are a homosexual," she observed, pleasantly. "Really?" I asked, truly surprised. "Aren't you?" she insisted. "I don't know!" I answered, in all good faith...But was I? How could I say? Homo, I certainly was. Sexual, cer-tainly not. In any case, that word was not in everyday usage, as it is it now. In those days it was still a technical term, the implications of which largely escaped me; and in any case it implied being effeminate. Effeminatized, I certainly was not. Wasn't I, on the contrary, hard, at least a virile athlete?[59]

In fact, such designations are a function of the culture and the social milieu. Thus Alias, in Maurice Sachs's novel of that title, summarizes the situ-ation:

---

59. T.C. Worsley, *Flannelled Fool. A Slice of Life in the Thirties*, London, Alan Ross, 1967, 213 pages, p.25-26.

"He is a fag," he said to me (and every age, every class has its own way, like that, of indicating the same thing or ascribing the same characteristic, using different words: the schoolboy says "a fag" when the doctor says "homosexual" and a woman says "abnormal"; a journalist might say "invert," a strong man "a dirty aunt," a bartender in Montmartre: "queen," etc.)[60]

The bourgeoisie traditionally kept mum on this touchy subject. Discussing sexuality in public was out of the question, much less homosexuality. Girls especially were quite unaware of the existence of homosexuals or lesbians. When it became necessary to mention the question, a suitable vocabulary was terribly lacking. T.C. Worsley noted: — We had, in any event, in our godforsaken hole of a province, no word for those who nowadays one would summarily describe as queer.[61] In his public school, where homosexuality was frequent, "it remained unmentioned in everyday conversation." Many homosexual memoirs concerning this period corroborate these statements.[62] Very often, outside the mainstream there was greater freedom: lower-class workers had crude slang terms for homosexuals, whereas certain avant-garde circles, like Bloomsbury, could be very liberal.

It would be an error, however, to think that homosexuality was generally overlooked. If one studies the homosexual vocabulary in French, German and English communities, the multitude of designations is striking. Three categories of terms indicating homosexuals and their activities can be distinguished: scientific or medical terms; familiar or slang terms that heterosexuals used when talking about homosexuals — which sometimes were picked up by homosexuals themselves; and terms used within the homosexual community, often having a coded meaning.

Equivalent medical terms are found in all three languages: homosexual, lesbian, invert, uranian, uranist, unisexual, antiphysic, "indifférent," "occa-

---

60. Maurice Sachs, *Alias* [1935], Paris, Éditions d'Aujourd'hui, 1976, 220 pages, p.38.
61. T.C. Worsley, *Flannelled Fool, op. cit.*, p.74.
62. Anonymous homosexual testimonies, from people of all backgrounds, have been used to recreate the lifestyle homosexual during this period. The English comments include oral records preserved at the National Sound Archives, some of which have been published in *Between the Acts. Lives of Homosexual Men, 1885-1967* (ed. K. Porter and J. Weeks, London, Routledge, 1990, 176 pages), *Walking after Midnight. Gay Men's Life Stories* (Hall-Carpenter Archives, London, Routledge, 1989, 238 pages) and *Inventing Ourselves. Lesbian Life Stories* (Hall-Carpenter Archives, London, Routledge, 1989, 228 pages).

sionnel" (only due to special circumstances), intermediary. "One of those" could be used to indicate homosexuals. There are a vast variety of colloquial and slang terms; according to Brassaï, Parisian slang had more than 40 expressions for a homosexual but only six ways of designating a lesbian. Among most frequent French terms used in the 1920s and 1930s were *tante, tapette, pédé, pédale, jésus, mignon, lapin* (roughly, aunt, queer, fag, pedal, darling, sweetie, rabbit). For the women, *amazones, gouines, goulues, gousses, tribades* (amazons, dykes, — and literally, gluttons, pods, tribads). "My mother said 'pods,' and as I did not understand her she said to me: 'But don't you see, they are women with women.'... My buddies at the studio spoke among themselves of 'dykes.' None of that made much sense to me; I did not see myself as either a pod or a dyke — I never liked those words....[But] one never used the word 'lesbian.'"[63]

It was roughly the same in England: "We were a group of girls who were really lesbians; although we did not use that term, we knew what the word meant and we had used it.[64]

In German, *Schwule* was the term most often used. There were certain more pejorative terms like *Tunte* (queer). Other names were more specific, like *Puppen-junge* or *Strichjunge*, which designated the homosexual male prostitute. Young women were called *Lesbierin* or, more commonly, *Lesbe*, or sometimes *Tribadie*. *Bube* and *Bübin* are affectionate terms for a young male or female lover. More medical terms were also employed, like *Urnische* or *Urning* for "uranians." In the German and Austrian lesbian milieu, a color code was used: lesbians are *Lila, Violett, Mauve, Fliederfarben* (lilac color), *Veilchenblau* (purplish); the main Berlin lesbian club was called *Damenklubs Violetta*, the lesbian song is *Lila Lied*.[65] In England, among the most current terms were "to be so" (to be "like that") and TBH (To Be Had: "available").[66] "Queer" was already in use. This term seems to have been imported from Ireland, then spread throughout the theatrical circles. It only

63. Testimony of B., a dressmaker's apprentice born in Paris in 1910, recorded by Claudie Lesselier, in *Aspects de l'expérience lesbienne en France, 1930-1968*, mémoire de DEA de sociologie, Paris-VIII, under the direction of R. Castel, November 1987, 148 pages, p.93.

64. Testimony of Eleonor, farm wife, recorded by Suzanne Neild and Rosalind Parson, *Women like us*, London, The Women's Press, 1992, 171 pages, p.33.

65. See annexes (in volume 2 of this work). For more on this topic, see *Das Lila Wien um 1900, zur Ästhetik der Homosexualitäten*, Vienne, Promedia, 1986, 127 pages. Bear in mind also that Renée Vivien was nicknamed "la Muse aux violettes."

66. Cited in particular by Frank Oliver, a navy mechanic, in *Walking after Midnight* (*op. cit.*), John, a dancer and gigolo, in *Between the Acts* (*op. cit.*, p.137), and Gifford Skinner, a shopkeeper, ("Cocktails in the Bath," *Gay News*, n° 135, p.21-24).

took on its pejorative sense later. There were other alternatives in circulation as well, such as "to be musical," for example. Homosexuals called themselves by terms with pejorative overtones that also spread throughout the general public, like pansies, poofs (*tantes*) or Nancy boys (*tapettes*, queer). Lesbians also used "queer"; the public often identified them as "horsey," or "girls in collar and tie," an allusion to their masculine dress.[67] The terms "butch" and "fem" came later.

Homosexual slang (*parlare*) extended to many situations. Of course, it was used to indicate sexual practices of a range and variety that would be impossible to list completely. Making love with a boy could be called "shagging" someone, or "having a go" with someone.[68] Plain-sewing meant mutual masturbation; it was a contemporary term in homosexual slang borrowed from the navy, just like "Princeton-first-year," which indicated *coitus contra ventrem.*[69]

But the slang was not limited to sex; it left its mark on every aspect of homosexual life and thus came to embody what we know as high camp. High camp, a kind of exaggeration of homosexual postures and clichés, was a parody of the "normal life" of the rich and titled people who lived in Mayfair. The guys took the names of well-bred ladies, divided the year into "seasons," designated certain bars and restaurants as fashionable and used a secret terminology based on posing (camp), dressing up (drag) and satire (send up).

The best definition of high camp was given by Christopher Isherwood in *The World in the Evening*, where he explains,

> — You think that what is camp is an elegant young man with bleached hair, wearing a Gainsborough hat and a feather boa and who thinks he's Marlene Dietrich?... What I am talking about is high camp... true high camp is basically serious. One does not make fun of it, one uses it to make fun of himself. One expresses what is really serious through mockery, artifice and elegance.[70]

Camp helps homosexuals to formulate their own culture. According to Quentin Crisp (one of the best representatives of camp), camp came into being in the 1920s as a reaction to the crisis in sexual values, the upheaval of feminine and masculine roles that marked the period.

---

67. See Myrtle Salomon and Olive Ager at the National Sound Archives (Hall-Carpenter Archives), and Gifford Skinner, "Cocktails in the Bath," *loc. cit.*
68. Fred, a hobo, in *Between the Acts, op. cit.,* p.15.
69. W.H. Auden was the first to say that in print.
70. Christopher Isherwood, cited by *Gay News*, n° 60, p.19.

— All that game of stylizations which is now known by the name of camp (a word which I heard then for the first time) was self-explanatory in 1926. Women moved and gesticulated that way. Homosexuals wished to copy them, for obvious reasons. What is strange about camp is that it became fossilized. The mannerisms never changed. Now, if I saw a woman sitting with her knees together, one hand on the hip and the other lightly touching the hair on the nape of her neck, I would think: "Either she is reliving her last social triumph, in 1926, or she is a transvestite."[71]

The use of a specific language is the first act of homosexual differentiation. The slang functions as a secret code and brings homosexuals closer to trouble-makers and delinquents, who also have a need for anonymity and dissimulation. The linguistic expansion testifies to the cultural richness and the desire of homo-sexuals for affirmation. The middle-class world of silence, of non-designation, of refusal to name and thus to recognize, is opposed by the noisy world of homo-sexuality, the logorrhea of camp, the tendency to say it all, to say too much.

Dandies and Flappers: Homosexuals Have Style

> — *Blinded by mascara and rendered mute by lipstick, I paraded in the dark streets of Pimlico.... I wore a veil so thick that it completely obscured the road in front of me. That didn't matter. There were others to watch where I was going.*[72]

Among the myths associated with the 1920s, the flamboyance of style is the most persistent. In fact, membership in a group justifies the use of a vesti-mentary code that identifies its members. Certainly, what most homosexuals wanted was to be able to blend in with the mass of "normal" people and so they conformed to the canons of virility that were in vogue at the time, adding only the slightest variations to their appearance. According to Michel de Coglay, those who were willing to give themselves away through sartorial hints were in the minority and the "serious, intelligent and embarrassed homosexual" did not distinguish himself in any way.[73] The hair was worn very short at the nape of the neck and on the sides, brilliantined and combed in order to form a wave or plas-

---

71. Quentin Crisp, *The Naked Civil Servant* [1968], London, Fontana, 1986, 217 pages, p.26-27.

72. *Ibid.,* p.22.

73. Michel du Coglay, *Chez les mauvais garçons. Choses vues,* Paris, R. Saillard, 1938, 221 pages, p.137.

tered smooth like patent leather.[74] The suit was dark, of thick fabric, broad in cut, with the bottom of the trousers flared. This baggy fashion had some erotic advantages, as Gifford Skinner relates:

> — The average man wore his trousers very full cut and they went up almost to the chest. The underclothes, if one wore any, were quite as loose and left the genitals free. Any friction caused by walking could produce the most stark effect. In the street, homosexuals would stud their conversation with remarks like, "Did you see that piece?" or "Look what's coming — he's sticking straight out!" This was often an illusion caused by a fold in the clothing, but it was a pleasant pastime and didn't cost anything.[75]

Others, however, sought a departure from the ubiquitous classicism. Suits in electric blue, almond green or old rose were much admired, but few dared to wear them for fear of being kicked out of public places.[76] Certain accessories became homosexual signs of recognition, in particular suede shoes and camel's hair coats. Some dared to wear their hair long.

Any eccentricity was readily perceived as proof of inversion, leading to a little adventure for Quentin Crisp, a flagrant homosexual if ever there was one, when he presented himself at the draft board: While his eyes were being tested, they said to him, "You've dyed your hair. That's a sign of sexual perversion. Do you know what these words mean?" He just said yes, and that he was a homosexual.[77]

That does not mean that the man in the street could clearly identify a homosexual, that he knew enough to decipher the signs. However, any sartorial oddity was suspicious and could easily be seen as a sign of homosexuality. There was one way out: to be perceived as an artist, i.e. necessarily an "original." Crisp notes that the sexual significance of certain forms of comportment was understood only vaguely, but the sartorial symbolism was recognized by everyone. Wearing suede shoes inevitably made you suspect. Anyone whose hair was a little raggedy at the nape of the neck was regarded as an artist, a foreigner, or worse yet. One of his friends told him that, when someone introduced him to an older gentleman as an artist, the man said: "Oh, I know this young man is an artist. The other day I saw him on the street in a brown jacket."[78]

---

74. See Gifford Skinner, "Cocktails in the Bath," *loc. cit.*
75. *Ibid.*
76. *Ibid.*
77. Quentin Crisp, *The Naked Civil Servant, op. cit.*, p.115.

In the same way, the use of make-up was spreading, so that mere possession of a powder puff was enough to prove one's homosexuality for the police. Evelyn Waugh remembers sleazy young men in shirtsleeves standing in a bar, repairing the devastations caused by grenadine and crème de cacao with powder and lipstick.[79] This practice was still tainted with infamy and it generally was indulged in secrecy, sheerly for the titillation:

> — Sometimes I arranged to meet my friend George at the station. We would board in first class, for there was no conductor at that hour of the night and the compartments were private with a mirror on the wall. George was mad about make-up and initiated me. It was just brown powder bought from a theater shop on Leicester Square. Once applied, we would ask each other if it were visible. "Yes" meant that a layer had better be quickly removed. "No" meant the addition of a little more powder; and so on to Liverpool Street. Once in the subway and until the end of the line, we would sit in the corner very withdrawn, terrified at the thought of being seen and perhaps sent to prison.[80]

The very chic Stephen Tennant, taking tea with his aunt, was admonished: "Stephen, darling, go and wash your face." Thus we know that the practice was by no means limited to male prostitutes, but involved various social classes. However, it was far from being well accepted, even in the most exalted circles. At a ball hosted by the Earl of Pembroke, Cecil Beaton was thrown in the water by some of the more virile young men; one of them shouted: "Do you think the fag drowned?" According to Tennant, who was there at the time, the attack was caused by the abuse of make-up; he was convinced that it was Beaton's made-up face that so disturbed the thugs.[81]

In the 1920s, Stephen Tennant embodied homosexual aesthetics carried to its apogee. He was a great beauty, and he enjoyed using all the artifices of seduction and *l'art de la pose*, theatricality. In that, he exaggerated the prevailing fashion for dressing up. *Vogue*, in its spring 1920 edition, wrote that there was nothing more amusing than to dress up and paint one's face outrageously for, "as Tallulah Bankhead says, 'there is no such thing as too much lipstick.'"[82] Photo-

---

78. *Ibid.*, p.28.
79. Cited by Lain Finlayson, "Gay Dress," in *Gay News*, n° 60, p.19.
80. Gifford Skinner, "Cocktails in the Bath," *loc. cit.*
81. Cited by Philip Hoare, *Serious Pleasures: The Life of Stephen Tennant*, London, Penguin, 1992, 463 pages, p.85-86.
82. *Ibid.*, p.75.

graphed by Cecil Beaton, especially, Tennant looked like a prince charming. Even in his everyday wear, he stood apart from the crowd; his biographer Philip Hoare made much of his style, and his innate sense of theater which made him a symbol of the Bright Young People of the 1920s in London. Late in the decade, Tennant represented the most extreme of fashion — for a man, at least. His feminine manners and appearance were not diminished by the striped double-breasted suits he wore, in good taste and well cut, "which ought to have made him resemble any young fellow downtown." But Stephen's physical presence was enough to belie such an impression. He was large and imperious, but he moved with a pronounced step, affected, which was described as "prancing" or as "seeming to be attached at the knees." Each of his movements, from the facial muscles to his long limbs, seemed calculated for effect. He gilded his fair hair with a sprinkling of gold dust, and used certain preparations to hold the dark roots in check. "Stephen could very well have been taken for a Vogue illustration — perhaps by Lepappe — brought to life."[83]

The most famous Bright Young People had made their studies in Oxford, like Harold Acton and Brian Howard.[84] Acton was the first to wear very broad trousers (Oxford bags) in lavender. Together with Cecil Beaton, Stephen Tennant and other young society men they organized all kinds of themed evenings. Stephen Tennant's effeminate appearance caused ambivalent reactions. Some were simply struck: "I do not know if that is a man or a woman, but it is the most beautiful creature I have ever seen,"[85] the admiral Sir Lewis Clinton-Baker would say. Others were less indulgent. When Tennant arrived one evening dressed particularly outrageously, the criticism reached a boiling point. Rex Whistler, one of his friends, considered it regrettable that he had gone too far: "He posed as much as a girl." Rex's brother added, "Men should not draw attention to themselves. That was the only true charge against Stephen, and it was irrefutable." Parents also complained that their children spent time with Stephen. Edith Olivier noted that Helena Folkestone was complaining about how badly people spoke of Stephen, that he was hated by people who did not understand him. Olivier noted that they were out of touch with the times, since "nowadays so many boys resemble girls without being effeminate. That is the kind of boys that have grown up since the war."[86]

---

83. *Ibid.*, p.81.
84. See chapter three .
85. Cited by Philip Hoare, *Serious Pleasures, op. cit.*, p.81.
86. *Ibid.*

The main trends which we have just reviewed for men are also found among women. The woman of the 1920s is mythically associated with the flapper, summarized in a few visual stereotypes: hair cut short, short skirt, cigarette. This is a modern woman, independent, who takes care of her appearance, and goes to dance halls and especially the cinema. The flapper is a sign of the beginnings of the Americanization of European societies.

Her image was first broadcast by Hollywood films through actresses like Louise Brooks and Clara Bow, then by the great dressmakers like Poiret, Madeleine Vionnet, and Coco Chanel, as well as photographers like Edward Steichen, Horst and Beaton. The proliferation of women's periodicals spread the new fashion throughout all of society, thus contributing to the creation of a mass phenomenon.[87] The short hair, the short, fluids dresses that did not impede walking, were very symbols of independence. However, while this new fashion was indeed shocking, it was not always seen in negatively, especially among young people. The flapper, who hung around with young men of her age, was easily accepted as a comrade who could share common interests in sport or dancing, who was not physically timid, whom one did not have to treat with special care. Without exaggeration, one can see that the flapper perfectly embodied the other side of the homosexual tendency that suffused the post-war period. The companion from the trenches is substituted by an androgynous wife who, with her flat chest and her helmet of short hair, may even recall the ideal friend met during the war. Thus, Leslie Runciman, of Eton and Cambridge, with a homosexual past, ends up marrying the novelist Rosamund Lehmann, herself sexually troubled, for her ambiguous personality: "I know that it may seem extraordinary that I should wish to spend my life with a woman, but Rosamund resembles a boy much more than a woman. She has the spirit of a man."[88]

Beyond the traditional image of the flapper, the figure of the lesbian can be distinguished. While the flapper is accused of casting doubt on the value of femininity, her androgynous allure is mitigated by the feminine accessories: silk hose, fans, sunshades, boas. She ostentatiously flirts with her cigarette-holder. Her heavy make-up is accentuated by the plucked eyebrows and the feathers, fringes, and pearls which adorn her hair. While the criticism may have become

---

87. In France, *Le Petit Écho de la mode* (1880), *Modes et travaux* (1919), *Le Jardin des modes* (1923), *Marie-Claire* (1937). The anglo-saxon examples dominated, with *Harper's Bazaar* and *Vogue*, the French version of which came out in 1920.

88. Cited by Gillian Tindall, *Rosamund Lehmann: An Appreciation*, London, Chatto & Windus, 1985, 201 pages, p.47.

outspoken, it was first and foremost directed against unmarried women, those who worked, followed the fashions, and were easy targets of suspicion of deviant practices. In France, women had been prohibited from wearing men's clothes since about 1805. Those who still wanted to wear trousers were to address themselves to the police prefecture and to request a special permit. Several petitions had been submitted to Parliament early in the 19th century in the hope of abolishing this law, without success. However, right up until the 1920s, this taste for cross-dressing was not systematically related to lesbianism. On the contrary, the lesbians asserted their femininity. Liane de Pougy, for example, said, "We liked long hair, beautiful bosoms, pouts and glances, charm, grace; not woman-boys. 'Why would we wish to resemble to our enemies?' as Natalie-Flossie used to murmur."[89]

However, the lesbians of the avant-garde followed the example of Radclyffe Hall and Una Troubridge by exaggerating the flapper fashion.[90] Short hair was the fashion after the war, but Radclyffe Hall chose to affect the Eton crop, a cut much shorter and more masculine than was usual. When the fashion returned to longer and more feminine cuts at the end of the 1920s, she chose a crew-cut. She affected men's suits, ties and lace-up shoes. To accentuate her male appearance, she smoked cigars and adopted virile poses, feet apart and hands in her pockets.

It should be noted that the strict separation of roles adopted by the lesbian couple at the time led to a dichotomy in the costumes of the two partners. Radclyffe Hall, as a "true" lesbian (butch), found it appropriate to wear men's clothes, whereas Una Troubridge (fem) retained feminine elements in her attire. Her hair was never as short as Radclyffe Hall's, and she wore dresses and high heels. In France, Violette Leduc also distinguished herself by wearing a suit; her lover of the time, "Hermine," reproached her, saying that she was "imitating *them*." At the publishing house where she worked, they would tease: "I saw Violette Leduc at a concert; yes, in the same getup." This attitude was adopted intentionally: "I hardened my baroque face with razor-cut hair cut above the temples; I wanted to be a focus of curiosity for the public in the cafés, for the public promenading in the theater — because I was ashamed of my face, and at the same time I imposed it on others."[91]

---

89. Cited by Jean Chalon, *Liane de Pougy*, Paris, Flammarion, 1994, 389 pages, p.277.

90. See Katrina Rolley, "Cutting a Dash: The Dress of Radclyffe Hall and Una Troubridge," in *Feminist Review*, n° 35, summer 1990.

Cross-dressing was also very much in style among the lesbians in the inter-war period. Vita Sackville-West, for an escapade in Paris with Violet Trefusis on October 5, 1920, disguised herself as a young man, which enabled her to display her passion for her partner without risk:

> — I dressed myself as a boy. It was easy, I put a khaki band around my head, which was the style at the time and did not attract attention. I browned my face and my hands... My large size was useful. I looked like a rather neglected young man, a kind of student of about nineteen years old.[92]

But while these vestimentary extravagances might be seen in the eyes of the uninformed public as some vestige of aristocratic eccentricity, it was more difficult for anonymous lesbians to affirm their identity. Above all, they ran into maternal hostility: "My mother wanted me to wear the requisite feminine clothing. I wanted to wear shorts. At seven or eight years, I cut off my curls with a pair of manicure scissors. If I had been a boy, I would have had short hair. My mother struck me. They bobbed my hair and by the age of twelve years I had an Eton crop. There was a terrible argument, but I gave aristocratic examples to support my position."[93]

In the 1930s, the fashion turned once again toward a more feminine look and lesbians became even more conspicuous. The dresses were more colorful; they were longer, and the contours of the body were accentuated again. Hair remained short, but might be curly, waved or fringed. The only concessions to masculinity were sailor pants, then the beach pyjamas that came out in the 1930s; one might wear them at home, on the beach, in a boat; but they were still strongly associated with homosexuality. It became increasingly difficult for lesbians to go unnoticed. Peter Quennell, who met Vita Sackville-West in 1936, was struck by her unusual appearance. He noted that she was larger and more imposing than her husband who, standing by her side with his pink face, his

---

91. Violette Leduc, *La Bâtarde*, Paris, Gallimard, 1964, 462 pages, p.166. Violet Leduc is a very ambiguous personality and her testimony must be seen in context: she goes out with "Ermine," but also with "Gabriel," and it is he whom she seeks to please by dressing this way. At the same time, it is partly a provocation: she likes to be seen as a lesbian. Besides, the conspicuous clothing permits her to distract people from her "ugliness" — they are so struck by what "kind" she is that they no longer notice what she looks like.

92. Nigel Nicolson, *Portrait d'un mariage* [1973], Paris, Stock, 1992, 319 pages, p.151.

93. Olive Ager, National Sound Archives (Hall-Carpenter Archives).

briar pipe and his tweed jacket, looked like nothing so much as a graduate student, while she evoked a vigorous mixture of both sexes: Lady Chatterley and her lover in one and the same incarnation. Curls of thick black hair straggled out from under a wide-brimmed Spanish hat. — "She had very thick eyebrows, and very dark eyes; her cheeks were highly coloured and she made no effort to dissimulate the very visible moustache that Virginia had affectionately mentioned. She was wearing heavy earrings and a thin string of pearls that plunged down inside a lace blouse, and over it all great velvet jacket, while her legs, which Mrs. Woolf said called to mind the trunks of vigorous trees, were stuffed into gamekeepers' breeches and high boots laced to the knees."[94]

Thus, a pure homosexual vestimentary culture developed in the 1920s and 1930s. While it allowed homosexuals to identify one another more clearly, it also put them at the mercy of a society increasingly skillful at reading through the codes. —"Miss Runcible wore men's trousers, and Miles touched up his lashes in the dining room of the hotel where they stopped to lunch. They were asked to leave."[95]

MAGICAL CITIES, MYTHICAL CITIES: THE GEOGRAPHY OF WHERE TO MEET

Among the founding myths of the "homosexual liberation" of the 1920s, certain cities — Berlin, London, Paris — hold a special place. The richness of the homosexual scene in those towns, the profusion of homosexual hang-outs, the exuberance of the nocturnal festivities made them symbols of pleasure and permissiveness, the memory of which lingered on for decades. However, behind this glowing façade, the homosexual scene consisted more of tawdry bars, dismal provinces, and shame.

It may seem foolhardy to try to map out the homosexual and lesbian places in France, England and Germany in the inter-war period: after all, in all three countries, many meeting places were skillfully dissimulated in order to avoid drawing the attention of the police. An establishment could be shut down one week and reopen shortly in another location, under another name. In a small provincial town, there might very well exist a bar, a dance hall or a club that could be used as a meeting place for homosexuals, without advertising that fact.

94. Cited by Victoria Glendinning, *Vita, la vie de Vita Sackville-West*, Paris, Albin Michel, 1987, 437 pages, p.316-317.
95. Evelyn Waugh, *Ces corps vils*, Paris, UGE, coll. "10/18," 1991, 245 pages, p.167.

Unlike the analogous establishments in the capital, these haunts might be mixed and open to heterosexuals as well; but the proprietors were accommodating people, probably homosexual themselves.[96] In spite of the limitations, on the basis of existing sources we can draw an impressive and picturesque view of the homosexual scene in the inter-war period — a panorama of the "Roaring Twenties."

Berlin, A Homosexual Capital

In the 1920s, Berlin became an obligatory stopping place for European homosexuals. Visitors' accounts glow with enthusiasm: "Marcel, how you would like this big blond bitch of a city. I hopped over here from Venice. Joy keeps me from sleeping. There are great-looking young men..."[97] Many French works, whose writers were struggling to come up with a compelling subject, take on a tone of amused sympathy or virtuous indignation and simply enumerate the names and addresses of most of the homosexual bars and associations, some-times constituting a virtual guide to homosexual life in Berlin. Louis-Charles Royer, in *L'Amour en Allemagne* (1936), described how he "discovered" Berlin in June 1930:

> I walked into a bar to get some change and the barman asked me: "Are you French?" — "Yes." — "Pederast?" Well, I am not used to such direct assaults; my eyes blinked. The barman must have taken that for assent; he squeezed my hand in his own soft, be-ringed fingers: "Pleased to meet you." Then, taking a look at the clock, he added, "You were well informed. But you've arrived a little early. Come back tonight, around ten o'clock."[98]

Each of Royer's incursions into Berlin life plunged him into confusion. Wishing to step into a hotel with a lady, he was taken aside by the proprietor, who asked him whether his partner was a transvestite. Royer denied it vehe-

---

96. Research in the local and departmental archives would help us to understand the homosexual subculture in the provinces; but the current work forcuses on comparisons at the national level, and so such research has not been conducted. Nevertheless, in the present chapter and in Chapter Seven, I provide information on homosexual life in harbor towns like Toulon, Dover and Hamburg, which had a broad range of homosexual (but probably not lesbian) establishments.

97. Letter from René Crevel to Marcel Jouhandeau, late 1928, in *Masques*, n° 17, spring 1983, p.49.

98. Louis-Charles Royer, *L'Amour en Allemagne*, Paris, Éditions de France, 1936, 225 pages, p.2.

mently, to which the proprietor responded: "Well then, what are you doing here?"

As described by foreign visitors, the whole capital seemed to be in the hands of homosexuals.[99] While that is clearly an exaggeration, there admittedly was a great number of meeting places. Some clubs only operated for a few months; others became institutions. In the words of Charlotte Wolff, a young lesbian in the 1920s, and then a sexologist exiled under the Nazi regime:

> Homo bars and nightclubs had sprung up not only in the trendy dis-
> tricts of west Berlin, but also in the poor neighborhoods. One might see a
> line of Mercedes in front of the homo bars as well as in front of the upper
> crust lesbian nightclubs. Men and women, who may have been hetero,
> would greedily watch the comings and goings of the "underground soci-
> ety," which now goes by the horrible term "subculture." Some of those who
> came as onlookers would join in the fun and danced with partners of the
> same sex.[100]

Scandal is good publicity, and the more visible establishments, like Eldorado, started to attract more heterosexual tourists in search of exotic frissons. The community was very fragmented: not only according to the variety of sexual demand, but also according to social and cultural origins.

The male scene

The trendiest and best-known nightclub was Eldorado, on Lutherstrasse; it was famed throughout Europe for its transvestite shows. But this club only very partially reflects the homosexual life of Berlin, of which it gave a brilliant sketch. It was enlarged and reopened in 1927 on Motzstrasse, at the corner of Kahlkreuthstrasse. It was a meeting point for artists, writers, actors and society men; heteros and homos, Berliners and foreigners met there. At any rate, one had to be seen there. The Mikado, Bülow-Kasino and Kleist-Kasino also put on transvestite revues. The Mikado, which enjoyed an exceptional longevity, was opened in 1907 and closed in 1932-1933. The Silhouette, at 24 Geisbergstrasse, was also a meeting place for celebrities. There, one might find the homosexual actor Hubert von Meyerinck, Conradt Veidt, and Marlene Dietrich. The

---

99. They were already very numerous, before the war, for Magnus Hirschfeld speaks of more than 50000 homosexuals in the capital, in *Les Homosexuels de Berlin* (1908 (reedited., Paris, Cahiers Gai-Kitsch-Camp, 1993, 103 pages).

100. Charlotte Wolff, *Hindsight*, London, Quartet Books, 1980, 312 pages, p.73.

smartest clubs were in the west of Berlin, around Bülowstrasse, Nollendorfplatz up to Kurfürstendamm.

Then there was a host of homosexual clubs and bars, each one with its own distinct character, clientele and ambiance. Some put on shows, others were simply places to flirt and hang out, where one could find a partner for a dance or a night. These bars were the foundation of ordinary Berlin homosexual life; some bore evocative names (like the café Amicitia), others were perfectly anonymous — only the informed customer would know what to expect inside. Many were tastefully decorated, with boudoir-like soft lighting and upholstered banquettes to facilitate dialogue and enable clients to become acquainted, with the utmost discretion. These clubs were preferred by homosexuals of the middle class, and above all they sought to preserve their reputation and avoid embarrassing scenes, touts, gigolos and too-conspicuous personalities. Along Siegesallee were a multitude of bars, like Zum kleinen Löwen, at 7 Skalizer Strasse, Windsbona-Kasino, Marien-Kasino, the café Amicitia, Palast-Europa, and Palast-Papagei. This was "Homosexual Row," which led to the Brandenburg Gate. Conti-Kasino held theme evenings, a musical soirée on Tuesdays, an evening for the elite on Thursday, private parties on Saturdays. Kleist-Kasino, 14 Kleiststrasse, was frequented by the trade and banking clerks, lower-middle-class men who savored the furnishings, the cocktails and canapés.

The last category of establishments, the pubs and beer halls, were found primarily in central Berlin or to the north. Here, the workers and less fortunate could huddle; an unemployed man might be had for a beer and a tip. This is the type of bar that Auden and Isherwood visited during their stay in Berlin. "Cozy Corner" was, in fact, "Noster's Restaurant zur Hütte," 7 Zossener Strasse, near Hallesches Tor, a working-class neighborhood. It survived primarily due to its regular clientele; tourists avoided it, considering the neighborhood none too safe. In fact, there was nothing decadent about the establishment: it was decorated with photographs of boxers and bicycle racers, and the crowd consisted largely of young laborers who were out of work; they would sit, playing cards and waiting for customers, their shirts open to the navel and sleeves rolled up. The Adonis-Diele, Alexanderstrasse, Café Fritz, 1a Neue Grünstrasse, Marburger-Diele, Nürnberger-Diele, Klubhaus Alexander-Palast, and Hohenzollern-Diele were all similar.

The Karlsbad pastry shop and café, on Potsdamer Strasse, hosted the drug crowd, and gigolos:

The whole room was full of noisy men and young fellows, holding forth on one topic or another, making eloquently caressing gestures. A teenager, with great big eyes dilated by morphine, was lounging in the middle of the room; under his jacket, one could see his naked chest, and his feet were also naked, in sandals. He dipped and twisted to the muted yet feral sounds of a piano and violin, extending his arms, bending his wrists, wiggling, lying down, and standing up again abruptly...[101]

There were also numerous cabarets catering to soldiers. Along the promenades, soldiers would "be on the make, singly or in groups."[102] In his journal, Klaus Mann often evoked the homosexual subculture. Here, one can discover the names of small, unknown pubs and beer halls for the popular classes, such as *Lunte* ("fox tail" — which had a phallic connotation in slang).

Klaus Mann proves that it was entirely possible to live an open and even vibrant sexual life as a homosexual in the 1920s —

October 30, 1931: Went to the *Parisian*. Brought to my table a little sailor with a pretty nape, and who was an appalling liar. Stopped for a soup at the Jockey, made out with Freddy.

December 4: *With a nice enough young peasant (and with an enormous thing), in a place near Kaufingerstrasse.*

December 30: Went to the baths (and took a bath) and had a massage; I really like the place, but nothing happened — all the men were too fat; the masseur didn't dare to try anything, either.

January 2, 1932: With Babs, went to Lenbachplatz. *Found a boy called Narcissus. Went with him to B's place. All three. Funny enough, and vulgar, but exciting.*

January 17: ...to the Private Club, a convivial homo joint with a faux-fashionable atmosphere and a lot of transvestites. — Willy spent the night with me. *Love.*[103]

The female scene

Berlin also had a well-developed and rather well-known lesbian subculture, especially after *The Lesbians of Berlin* came out in 1928, written by Ruth Margarite Röllig with a preface by Magnus Hirschfeld.[104] The German capital

101. Willy, quoting Ambroise Got, in *Le Troisième Sexe*, Paris, Paris-Édition, 1927, 268 pages, p.52.

102. Magnus Hirschfeld, *Les Homosexuels de Berlin, op. cit.*, p.72.

103. Klaus Mann, *Journal. Les années brunes, 1931-1936*, Paris, Grasset, 1996, 452 pages, p.32, 37, 42 and 47-48. Italics in the original.

had a vast choice of lesbian establishments, around fifty of them, each striving to satisfy the demands of the clientele: "Here each one can find her own form of happiness, for they make a point of satisfying every taste."[105]

The very chic "Chez ma belle-soeur" ("My sister-in-law's") was a women's club located at 13 Marburger Strasse, but men were admitted, too. A 13-year-old bellboy greeted visitors. Frescoes on the walls endeavored to evoke Mytilene, and booths were shielded by curtains to mask the frolicking of the young women. It seems that this club was mostly a show place for the titillation of foreigners passing through town. Indeed, one young woman told Louis-Charles Royer that, "The 'real ones,' you know, don't come here."[106] Mostly, the distinguished lesbian would go to her private club; or she might put in an appearance at Topp and Eldorado, two large clubs where it was good to be seen. Dorian Gray, 57 Bülowstrasse, was one of oldest and better-known homosexual establishments. It was a mixed club, with certain days reserved for women and others for men. Friday, for example, was "elite day for ladies," with dancing alternating with stage shows. Theme nights included a Bavarian alpine festival, and a festival of the Rhenish grape harvest. The cuisine was refined Viennese, the atmosphere was traditional and of good quality. Salon Meyer, or Meyer Stube, was outside the center, in the west of Berlin, on Xantener Strasse. It was a miniature bar owned by two ladies; there was no live music but a gramophone lent some ambiance. The clientele were particularly refined: regular visitors included countesses, artists, and famous personalities. The Café Domino, 13 Marburger Strasse, received only the top-drawer lesbians. Frozen sherry, cocktails, and sparkling wine were sipped as jazz played in the background. The Monbijou was a very private club indeed, located in west Berlin at Wormser and Luther Strasse; it had some six hundred members. One could only get in if introduced by one of the members. The interior was very elegant, separated into many small and intimate rooms; under soft lights, surrounded by explicit illustrations, movie stars, singers and the lesbian intellectual elite sat comfortably ensconced in

---

104. Ruth Margarete Röllig (1887-1969) was a popular writer who published novels and serials in newspapers; she also worked as a journalist for several lesbian magazines such as *Die Freundin* and *Garçonne*. She hosted stage performers, homosexuals, lesbians and transvestites at home for evenings of singing, or spiritualism sessions.

105. Ruth Margarite Röllig, *Les Lesbiennes de Berlin* [1928], Paris, Cahiers Gai-Kitsch-Camp, n° 16, 1992, 140 pages, p.53.

106. Louis-Charles Royer, *L'Amour en Allemagne, op. cit.*, p.14.

leather easy chairs. Twice a year a great private ball was given at La Skala of Berlin.

In general, Berlin's lesbian establishments were characterized by a refined atmosphere, soft and indirect lighting, and sentimental music. Establishments opened and closed, as much due to the vagaries of fashion in the lesbian community as to police action. Hohenzollern, located at 101 Bülowstrasse, was one of the first cafés to tolerate and protect lesbians; in 1928, it suffered from competition from newer establishments and lost its reputation. Maly und Jugel was a very private club located 16 Lutherstrasse. Window panes covered with thick curtains blocked out the street; inside, the décor was a subdued play of garnet red and pearl gray, with light-colored paintings, deep armchairs and a piano. The atmosphere was chaste; people came by the couple and there were none of those theatrical scenes of the "clubs for foreigners."

The lesbian newspaper *Die Freundin* provides some information on these female meeting places. They tended to pop up in the same neighborhoods, even in the same streets; some establishments hosted different clubs on different days of the week. Very often, the same lesbians were frequent visitors to several of these establishments, and the same formulas were found in two or three clubs. Damenklub Harmonie met every Wednesday with the Exchange-Festsäle, 32 Jakobstrasse; the Association des Amies Thursday in Köhler's Festsäle, 24 Meerstrasse, the Club Heiderose every Sunday at the Kollosseum, 62 Kommandantenstrasse. Verona-Diele was at 36 Kleiststrasse. In 1928, the Damenklub Tatjana opened; it met Wednesday in Alexander-Palast; in 1929, the Erâto club opened at 72 Kommandantenstrasse. At the same address, the Damenklub Sappho occupied the second floor; it met on Tuesdays, Thursdays and Saturdays from 7:00 PM, and Sundays from 5:00. The Kölnerhof Hotel hosted lesbians on Monday and Thursday from 5:00 until 8:00 PM. New names and addresses appeared each year until 1932, when new lesbian clubs appeared for the last time: Manuela, 26 Joachimstaler Strasse; Monokel-Diele, 14 Budapester Strasse; Geisha, 72 Augsburger Strasse.

Not all the lesbians preferred the fashionable clubs; some simply went to the local cafés or even to shady joints in bad neighborhoods. Auluka, at 72 Augsburger Strasse, was off-color to the point of extravagance. The Café Olala, Zielenstrasse, was rather coarse; as many men went there as women. The Topp Cellar, or Toppkeller, 13 Schweinstrasse, was a hideaway for women where men are tolerated as consumers and onlookers; they held contests like "the most beautiful lady's calf." Sometimes, late in the evening, famous singers, actresses, and dancers would come in, but the general atmosphere was rather sordid. Charlotte Wolff describes one scene:

> — A strange creature, a large woman who wore a black sombrero and looked like a man, directed the dancers with an eagle eye. She invited us to join them, and we spread out in a circle around her. She stood at the center of the circle and gave commands in a hypnotic voice. We stepped forward and back, holding a glass with one hand and our neighbor with the other. This went on until we received the order to drink and to throw our empty glasses over our shoulders.[107]

The Tavern, Georgestrasse, was a private jazz club that was used as the model for the Skorpion in A. E. Weirauch's lesbian novel. One room was reserved for the ladies; there was smoking, dancing, and drinking. Beer festivals, masked balls, and sorties on the beach were periodically organized. The atmosphere was crude, and fairly sexual; arguments were frequent. Here the most haggard women in Berlin would turn up, prematurely haggard and faded.

The Club des amies was for women of the popular classes; it held balls two or three times a week in Alexander-Palast in Landsberger Strasse; Saturdays and Sundays were packed. Violetta, 37 Bülowstrasse, was very popular; it was a center for homosexual young women in business, saleswomen, manual laborers, and lower level employees. Dances were held, and conferences and cultural events, and a sporting group offered excursions. Violetta took as its mission to make love and harmony reign, to fight against contempt for homosexuals, and to fight against the extension of §175 of the Penal code to women. Many women came there dressed as men; evenings were organized in order to help people meet each other; and Das Lila Lied was sung ("the mauve song," the lesbian anthem of Berlin). During certain festive evenings, each woman was entitled to pick up a large number at the cloakroom, which she should wear very visibly. Toward midnight, "mail" would be delivered, and each woman could write the number of anyone whom she found interesting. Every means was employed to help them find partners: when the "Tyrolian" was played, no woman should remain seated; everyone was to step forward, dance, and change partners.

In 1929, Violetta and the Monbijou club were combined; to celebrate this event, a great festival was organized on September 15 in Amerikanischen Tanzpalast, 72 Kommandantenstrasse. The two clubs then met at this address every

---

107. Charlotte Wolff, *Hindsight, op. cit.,* p.76-77.

Wednesday, Saturday and Sunday. For the Christmas festivities in 1929, a great masked ball was held.

At the Café Princess, 4 Gleditschstrasse, each Thursday "the merry shrews" would meet; the evening went on until everyone was drunk. Other lesbian clubs also met here. "The Magic Flute" was a dance hall located Kommandanturstrasse where the readership of the lesbian newspaper *Frauenliebe* would meet. The masculine lesbians (Bubis) were clearly distinguishable from the female lesbians (Mädis).

Each week, masked balls and dances were announced in *Die Freundin*. On April 23, 1927, a great ball was planned at the Exchange-Festsäle; September 2, a great costume ball was held in Alexander-Palast. On February 4, 1928, a great masked ball marked Mardi Gras. Florida, at 72 Kommandantenstrasse, organized a costume ball on October 3, 1929. In fact, there was quite a lot of dancing in Berlin. Big costume balls were frequently held to bring together the homosexuals of the city, and homosexuals who were visiting made a point of attending. Vita Sackville-West wrote, — We went to ball of Sodomites. A great number of them were dressed as women, but I suppose that I was, in this respect, the only authenticate article."[108]

Christopher Isherwood went to a Christmas ball in 1929 at In den Zelten. He met the great actor Conradt Veidt there. Foreign journalists tended to write rather frightened descriptions of these evenings. Oscar Méténier attended a masked ball at Dresdner Strasse, the Dresdner-Casino. Inside there were 400–500 people, all in costume and all of them men. Half were dressed as women. Méténier was especially struck by the calm and the reserve of this assembly. Only the waltz, the scottish, mazurkas and polkas were danced; no one looked astonished and no one laughed; the most eccentric groups did not draw attention. Everyone was having a good time without worrying about the neighbors.

He noticed moreover that the police tolerated these gatherings. They delivered special permits; but they did use the occasion to create a register of homosexuals. This policy enabled them to monitor the groups discreetly while tolerating activities that did not disturb the law and order.

---

108. Letter from Vita Sackville-West to Virginia Woolf, January 1929, in Louise de Salvo and Mitchell A.Leaska (ed.), *The Letters of Vita Sackville-West to Virginia Woolf*, London, Hutchinson, 1984, 473 pages, p.366.

Triumph of the amateurs

Not all the homosexual spots had to do with sex. They were at the same time meeting places, hangouts, private clubs, and conference halls; various establishments depending on a homosexual clientele enabled their members to be among their own kind, to discuss their problems, or simply to get acquainted. The Berliner League of Friendship met Tuesdays in a room at 89 Alt-Jakobstrasse. The Association of Friends and (Female) Friends held its meetings at No. 32 on the same street. It organized costume balls, conferences on literature, art, the sciences, and group excursions. However, dating was the main point of most of these establishments, which gave homosexuals a place where they could do as they pleased without danger and where they meet new people discreetly.

However, even with all these bars and clubs, there was still sex in the parks and public urinals. There were always men in the bushes in the Tiergarten; they would flee when the police made their rounds: "Near a pool, ten agents surrounded four young little urchin lads aged about fifteen to twenty. They, too, seemed to be wearing a type of uniform: silk shirts with Danton collars, full cut trousers in a light fabric, and patent leather shoes."[109]

Berlin became the temple of male prostitution in the inter-war period. In *Homosexuals of Berlin* (1908), Hirschfeld already noted the existence of many safe houses, which mostly catered to homosexuals of the higher social classes and officers who feared blackmail. But street prostitution in particular increased in the 1920s, following the economic crisis of 1920-1923, then that of 1929.[110] There were something like 650 professional male prostitutes (*Strichjunge, Puppenjunge*) in Berlin in the 1920s but, if one counts the casual or occasional ones, the number would be closer to 22,000, an enormous figure.[111] Before the war, there were

---

109. Louis-Charles Royer, *L'Amour en Allemagne, op. cit.*, p.68.

110. From 1920 to 1923, Germany suffered from galloping inflation as a consequence of the war, the global economic crisis, the imposed payment of damages, and then of the occupation of the Ruhr. The gold mark, which was worth 46 paper marks in January 1922, was worth 84,000 in July 1923, 24 million in September, 6 billion in October, and 1 trillion in December. Workers were hit hard by unemployment and the erosion of their spending power, because the wages did not keep pace with the inflation rate. In 1923, there were 210,000 unemployted in Berlin.

111. Richard Linsert, militant communist and a member of the WhK, surveyed 100 young prostitutes in Berlin, which allows us a good look at their sociological profile. His conclusions were published in 1929, in *§ 297, Unzucht zwischen Männern* (Berlin, Neuer Deutscher Verlag, 130 pages). See chapter tw.

approximately 12,000 male prostitutes, including 400 professionals. That means there was an increase of more than 60%! [112]

Male prostitutes tended to congregate more in the north and east of Berlin, most of them on Friedrichstrasse; there might have been about sixty there, on average. There must have been a hundred pubs that allowed male prostitutes. Boys frequented the public places that attracted many people: fairs, expositions, festivals, pedestrian ways, train stations, parks. They came from all sorts of backgrounds; hotel employees, horse grooms, hunters, telegraphists, drivers, salesmen and, of course, soldiers. The number of soldiers who became prostitutes dropped after the First World War, following the measures taken by the Ministry of Defense. In particular, soldiers in civilian clothes were stationed at high-risk locations and were ready to intervene if they saw a soldier soliciting.

The majority of young people whom Richard Linsert studied had no professional qualification. Forty-nine had turned to prostitution after losing their jobs. However, 19 were only prostituting themselves to cover some extra expenses and to make a little pocket money. The others gave various reasons: for fun, to pay for something specific, to pay the rent, out of laziness. From the sexual point of view, 31 said they were heterosexual, 34 homosexual, 22 bisexual. Eleven acknowledged masochistic tendencies; 5, sadistic; 5 were cross-dressers. Thirty-six admitted to being alcoholics, 6 cocaine addicts. 73 lived alone, 19 stayed with their parents, 6 were homeless. While the part-time male prostitutes were hooking in their everyday clothing, the most elegant (*Klassejungen*) invested in fetishistic accessories (shoes with high heels, boots) and make-up. Those who wore a uniform were preferred: sailors, drivers, soldiers. Some, even at the age of twenty or more, dressed as schoolboys while soliciting: that was a sure success. Hirschfeld met the male prostitute known as B, who was very fashionable; he had about 20 to 25 customers a month and approximately 300 a year. Ten percent of them were from Berlin, 50–60% from the provinces, 30–40% were foreign (mostly French and American).

The rates varied according to the popularity of the boy; a top male prostitute could make on average 20–30 RM (Reichsmark); Klassejunge got approximately 10 RM. The prices could go down as low as 50 pfennigs. Most of the boys made less than 5 RM a day. The weekly profits varied between 10–12 RM and 60–80 RM. Professionals and de luxe prostitutes were more expensive. Some boys simply asked for a place to spend the night, a meal, maybe some gifts. Those

---

112. I 1920, Greater Berlin had 3.8 million inhabitants; in 1939, there were 4.3 million.

who practiced prostitution at a hotel were expected to give part of what they earned to the night porter. Unlike the women, the boys were paid after consummation. Fairly often, clients would take off; and blackmail was not uncommon. Most of the boys hoped to find some rich man who would pick them up and take them along on a trip. Such couples did travel, in the guise of uncle and nephew, or master and servant.

A boy's career was generally rather short; amateur male prostitutes worked the sidewalk a year and a half, on average. They began at around the age of 17 years (although some started as early as 14), and most were through by age 22 (although some were still at it, at age 30). Of the hundred boys met, three worked for the police: in the local jargon they were known as *Achtgroschenjungen*. If they stayed out of jail and did not catch any disease, the boys could hope to start a business and find a normal life.

Berlin was not the only city marked by an increase in male prostitution. A survey carried out by Dr. Hans Muser in 1933, *Homosexualität und Jugendfürsorge*, focused mostly on the town of Hamburg, which had a strong homosexual subculture based on the harbor traffic. The district of Sankt Pauli was famous for its shady bars where men could dance together and pick up a sailor for a few marks. It is there that Stephen Spender spent several months between 1930 and 1933.

Among the homosexual establishments was the Hamburg Society for Scientific Exploration, which offered medical consultations and excursions for men and women. Then there were the Adonis-Bar and the Three-Stars, which had made names for themselves. Women met Thursday evenings at Phaline. There were approximately 3,000 male prostitutes in Hamburg. As in Berlin, some solicited downtown, others in the bars.

Until 1924, most of the boys plied their trade in the central station, especially in the fourth class waiting room. In 1924, the police made a sweep and cleaned up the station; the prostitutes then spread throughout the whole city. Further police operations in 1928 and 1929 led the male prostitutes to regroup in homosexual joints. The number of prostitutes varied with the season; in the summer, they flowed out of Berlin looking for the tourist clientele. Statistics from the Office of Youth Affairs showed a net increase in amateur prostitution, in connection with the economic crisis. In 1929, 13% of male prostitutes only occasionally dabbled in it, and 87% were professionals. In 1930, no more than 40% were professionals; in 1931, 46%. By the same token, the proportion of minors involved was on the rise. In 1925, 11% of the male prostitutes were minors; 35% in 1926; 49% in 1928; 52.8% in 1930. Competition was fierce; the customers wanted young boys, the supply was abundant and the older ones could not find any takers. Often, in order to keep their customers, they refused to let the new ones in on where homosexuals could meet.

The number of unemployed who resorted to prostitution kept going up, too. In 1925, 48% of the registered male prostitutes were unemployed; in 1931, it was 83%! The Office of Youth Affairs in Hamburg undertook to rehabilitate the young men by finding them steady jobs and keeping an eye on them. Some of the young men were sent back to their home regions.

The German homosexual scene thus seems to have been particularly vibrant. It offered a wide range of services to satisfy any desire, from simple entertainment to ultra chic dance halls, from timid pick-ups to the unrestrained hunt for sex. While Berlin was clearly the center, the provinces had something to offer, too.[113] Anyone who read the good homosexual newspapers (which were available to anyone by subscription and under discreet wrappers), could not miss finding out about such and such establishment in their area, or that "friends" met regularly at a small and nondescript café. For many who would not have dared to solicit in the street nor to approach obvious male prostitutes, the clubs were the entrée to the homosexual community.

London, or the Glamour of Uniforms

The homosexual scene in London in the 1920s, lively as it was, was but a shadow of that in Berlin. There were far fewer establishments, and they were certainly less picturesque. The large costume balls that gave the German capital such a reputation were lacking altogether and homosexual dances were rare. The homosexual associations had no money, so there were practically no meeting places at all. The London scene was also more spread out and harder to identify

---

113. For a study on the homosexual scene in a provincial German town, see Cornelia Limpricht, Jürgen Müller and Nina Oxenius, *"Verführte" Männer, das Leben der Kölner Homosexuellen im dritten Reich* (Cologne, Volksblatt Verlag, 1991, 146 pages). To a far greater extent than in France or in England, German towns of a certain size tended to have specialized establishments and, especially, a local headquarters for various homosexual associations. Thus, the *Deutsche Freundschaftsbund* was flourishing all over Germany. In Brunswick, its offices were at 3 Schlossstrasse. In Karlsruhe, meetings were held at Prinz Wilhelm, 20 Hirschstrasse. There were affiliates in Eisenach, Weimar, Frankfurt, Krefeld, Leipzig, Saarbruck, and Dortmund. In Breslau, Sagitta welcomes homosexuals; in Chemnitz, there was the club Nous; Kassel had the club Fortuna. In Düsseldorf, the Club of Noble Sociability met at the restaurant Neue Welt. In Dortmund, one would go to "Heinrich Burstedde" for dancing, and in Frankfurt, to the café Reichsland.

than the scene in Berlin. On the other hand, London led the field in terms of military prostitution and the parks were the favorite place for homosexual assignations.

Not much of scene at all

Given the frequent police raids, homosexual life in London was primarily restricted to the night: and one had to be initiated to know the main meeting spots. These places generally did not set out to attract a homosexual clientele; they were places that were taken over by homosexuals, without the owners always knowing whom they were dealing with.

The Maida Vale neighborhood was known for its very "gay" atmosphere; many homosexual artists and writers settled there and so the place was soon colonized. Lionel Charlton, Tom Wichelo, Stephen Spender and his friend Tony Hyndman, William Plomer and J.R. Ackerley lived there. In London, homosexual evenings started in the galleries of the theaters and the variety halls, in particular the Prince of Wales, Holborn and the Palladium, which were used as meeting places and hunting grounds. A few became favorites, including those of G.S. Melvin, Bartlett and Ross, which put on transvestite spectacles. Various plays were very popular with homosexuals. In *The Green Bay Tree*, by Frank Vosper, a homosexual aristocrat picks up a working-class boy and remodels him in his own image. Similarly, *Children in Uniform* (the English version of *Jeunes Filles en uniformes* by Christa Winsloe) was a great success. After the theater, homosexuals headed off to certain cafés.

"The Cri" was located in the basement of the Criterion hotel. Most of the homosexual clients took the service entrance on Jermyn Street, but some triumphantly entered by the grand staircase on Piccadilly and were greeted by applause. Famous transvestites were regulars there, like "Lady Lavender," a big blond twenty-year-old (who was in fact more like forty), or "Rosie, Baroness Bothways," a Welshman of indeterminate age who dressed sumptuously and was covered with gold chains and bracelets. In spite of his reputation as a millionaire, Rosie was in fact cook for a very rich old homosexual who lent him his clothes and jewels for his nightly excursions in the West End.

Coventry Street Corner House became a cult spot. Homosexuals would spend the evening there, but they might also turn up during the afternoon, in a room on the first floor that they called the Lily Pond. The café was run by two old ladies who never noticed a thing, no matter how flagrant their guests might be. Sundays, one could go to a tea salon called "The Tea Kettle," located one minute from Piccadilly Circus. There were no exclusively homosexual clubs; but certain clubs that catered to people in show business were mainly homosexual, like Caravan Club, Rumbaba Club, Apollo Club and Florida. Neither were there many homosexual pubs. There was the Cavour Bar and JB's, in Leicester Square; Dickens on Edgware Road, "The French Hour" and York Minster in Soho; the ground floor of "Queens," in Coventry Street, was a homosexual haunt as was Pakenham, next to the Wellington barracks where the soldiers of the Guard gathered; The Running Horse, near Shepherd Market, was very much in fashion at one time; and, finally, the Long Bar of the Restaurant Trocadero, in Shaftesbury Avenue, which was reserved for men.

The police from time to time descended on the pubs, took names and arrested potential homosexuals. That meant the end of the pub as a homosexual meeting place. Sometimes all it took was for a group of homosexuals to meet at a café and find the owner obliging, and it would end up becoming a homosexual favorite. Quentin Crisp and his friends met in a café on Old Compton Street called the Black Cat; he said it resembled a dozen other cafés in the area, with a horseshoe-shaped bar area that was rarely cleaned, a linoleum floor in black and white squares and mirrors everywhere. There he and his counterparts would sit, while "one dull day succeeded another, loveless night followed loveless night"; and they sipped tea, combed their hair and tried each other's lipsticks.[114]

For the women, the places for socializing were far fewer, and there was no comparison with Berlin and Paris. The Orange Tree Club, which opened in 1921, became very famous and women could dance together there. In the 1930s, Gateway's Club, or Gates, became the lesbian center of the city. Radclyffe Hall gives a rather sordid description of the female bars in *The Well of Loneliness*. For her, the Narcissus and Alec's Bar were the symbols of all that homosexuals lacked, even if they did offer some place to meet: "Where could one go if not to the bars? There was no other place where two women could dance together without causing comments or ridicule, without being looked at like monsters."[115]

One of the great homosexual events of the London season was the charity ball organized by Lady Malcolm at the Albert Hall. Initially, it was intended for domestics and tickets had to be obtained. But as it was a costume ball, it served

114. Quentin Crisp, *The Naked Civil Servant, op. cit.*, p.28.
115. Radclyffe Hall, *The Well of Loneliness, op. cit.*, p.403.

as a pretext for all kinds of fun. Famous women were represented. The final procession was a great moment. The ball evolved with the passing of the years until it became a drag ball.

Pick-ups and prostitutes

In London, solicitation principally took the form of "cottaging"; it consisted in making the rounds of the various urinals of the city looking for quick and anonymous meetings. The most likely places were the urinals at the Victoria and South Kensington stations and the public toilets at Marble Arch and Hyde Park Corner. The urinals were frequently subjected to police raids; and there were often agents provocateurs, which made it all the more dangerous. Then other places were used as pick-up sites, like the arcades of the County Fire Office in Piccadilly Circus, the Turkish baths at Jermyn Street, the isolated streets of Bridge Places, Dove Mews, Dudmaston Mews or Falconberg; in Clareville Street, Leicester Public garden or Grosvenor Hill, one could find somebody for the night.[116]

Most of the male prostitutes operated around Piccadilly Circus and Leicester Square. Quentin Crisp remembers his astonishment at discovering this shady world. There he was, wandering along Piccadilly or Shaftesbury Avenue, when he ran into some young fellows standing at the crossroads. One of them said to him, "Isn't it terrible this evening, darling? Not a man on the horizon. Dilly isn't what it used to be." Crisp adds that the "Indian boy" at school had stunned the students by telling them that there were male prostitutes in Birmingham, but they'd never believed that they would really see one themselves. Now, "there they were — and recognizable to everyone — or almost everyone, posing like fashion models, with hand on hip and hip thrust forward."[117] One could take his conquest to a cheap hotel on the West End; J.R. Ackerley found some in Mayfair's Shepherd Market, a zone known for prostitution. You could rent a room there, no questions asked. The location was not very promising, however: "11 Half Moon Street. It is in this kind of room that one commits suicide."[118]

---

116. See Richard Davenport-Hines, *Sex, Death and punishment, op. cit.*, p.146.
117. Quentin Crisp, *The Naked Civil Servant, op. cit.*, p.26.
118. J.R. Ackerley, note dated 1921, cited by Peter Parker, *A Life of J.R. Ackerley*, London, Constable, 1989, 465 pages, p.40.

In addition to the professionals, there were docile characters whom one would first take along to dine, and there were boys who were kept.[119] As in Germany, but to a lesser degree, male prostitution expanded due to unemployment. At the Cat and Flute in Charing Cross, young workmen would be found. The contemporary practice was that two would sit together and share a beer. A client would approach and offer to pay for the second one. After a moment one of the boys would step away, leaving the two others together. These boys were not necessarily homosexual, but got into prostitution due to the economic situation. Some of them said they were "saving up to get married."[120] The rates were set, with 10 shillings added if there were sodomy.

Soldiers (mainly from the Guards brigade) and sailors made up another category of prostitutes. Unlike the workmen, they were not in prostitution as a result of need but rather by tradition. The best places to meet them were the London parks, especially Hyde Park, Kensington Gardens and Saint James Park, Tattersall Tavern in Knightsbridge, and the Drum, by the Tower of London, for sailors.[121] The guards' red uniform and the sailors' costumes exerted a fascination and an erotic attraction that was constantly evoked by contemporaries: "everyone prefers something in uniform." Any national costume or traditional equipment can be sexually stimulating and there are as many eccentric sexual tastes as there are kinds of costumes.[122]

The sailors' uniform was particularly appreciated for the tight fit and especially for the horizontal fly. Moreover, while soldiers generally had very little time to share, sailors had many weekends. For a walk in the park, a soldier received about 2 shillings; a sailor might get up to 3 pounds. Stephen Tennant wrote about this fascination, noting one sailor's tight little derrière.[123] Anecdotes from those days include the story of an evening organized by Edward Gathorne-Hardy where a contingent of soldiers of the Guard were invited as special guests; in another, a soldier was offered as a gift to the master of the house.[124] To the soldiers, prostitution was a tradition; it seems that the young

---

119. For details on the life of men who were kept as lovers, see John and Bernard in *Between the Acts, op. cit.,* 137-143 and 117-124; as for professional gigolos, see Tony, *ibid.,* p.114-150.

120. Cited by George Mallory, "Gay in the Twenties," *Gay News,* n° 30, p.9.

121. See Chapter Seven, as well.

122. Quentin Crisp, *The Naked Civil Servant, op. cit.,* p.96.

123. Cited by Philip Hoare, *Serious Pleasures, op. cit.,* p.158.

124. Cited by Peter Parker, *A Life of J.R. Ackerley, op. cit.,* p.114.

recruits were initiated by their elders as they were being integrated into the regiment. The customers were designated twanks, steamers or fitter's mates. A good patron was preferred; thus Ackerley received a letter one day announcing the death of one of his lovers — and another soldier from his regiment offering himself as a replacement. This part-time prostitution allowed soldiers to get some pocket money, which they then spent on drinks or with prostitutes of their own. These activities were not entirely safe, for many a soldier or sailor could turn out to be quite brutal. Charles Damon, a former turn-of-the-century decadent, a relic of Oscar Wilde's circle, is supposed to have murmured to Noël Coward: "My dear, my ambition is to die crushed between the thighs of a soldier of the guard!"[125]

While London obviously had a far vaster choice of homosexual entertainment, there were also some good places in the provinces. In the big cities, especially university towns, homosexuals could get together at certain pubs (the Still and Sugarloaf at Cambridge, for example). The big annual rowing race between Oxford and Cambridge was a good occasion to meet. That is where J.R. Ackerley met E.M. Forster, Colleer Abbott, Lionel Charlton, Tom Wichelo, Harry Daley, their various lovers, and quite a number of police officers, soldiers, sailors and other young delinquents who were linked by a common secret.

In the 1920s, J.R. Ackerley, Raymond Mortimer and Eddy Sackville-West, *inter alia*, went to Portsmouth. In the 1930s, due to increased repression in the capital, more of them turned up in harbor cities, in particular Brighton, which was easily accessible for the evening by the 6:00 PM. rapid train for 4 shillings round trip, or for the weekend for only 10 shillings. One of the discreet locations that accepted homosexuals was the hotel The Old Ship, which had a wing reserved for men only. The room doors did not close, which allowed for easy coming and going. Several pubs were accepted homosexuals, in particular Pigott's, on St. James Street; the Eastern, in Montpellier Street; and the Star of Brunswick. A section of the beach was reserved for men and, in fact, homosexuals took it over.[126] The city of Dover was also favored by homosexuals, where four regiments were stationed along with a considerable number of

---

125. Cited by Philip Hoare, *Noel Coward: A Biography*, London, Sinclair-Stevenson, 1995, 605 pages, p.81.

126. All descriptions of the homosexual "scene" in London and the provinces has been reconstructed from the testimonies of Roy, Sam, Bernard, Barry and John, in *Between the Acts*; the testimony of Gifford Skinner, "Cocktails in the Bath," *loc. cit.*; of Galileo, "The Gay Thirties," *Gay News*, n° 54, p.11-12; and of George Mallory, "Gay in the Twenties," *loc. cit.*

sailors. J.R. Ackerley went to many pubs, the British Queen, Granville, Prince Regent, and Clarendon; he had an apartment where he invited many friends. The city was host to homosexual celebrities like T.C. Worsley, Graham Bell, Christopher Isherwood, W.H. Auden, Stephen Spender, E.M. Forster, Jack Sprott, and John Hampson; Lionel Charlton and Tom Wichelo settled there for good; William Plomer lived there for a year. Forster jokingly said that, if a bomb fell on the city, it would have freed the country of almost all its undesirables.[127]

The rates were low: 10 shillings on average, but nothing was guaranteed; many male prostitutes were dishonest and dangerous; the city was organized around sex; the sailors and the soldiers who prostituted themselves then spent their money on girls. The myth of Dover was boosted by W.H. Auden's poem, "Dover," which evokes with many an ambiguity and double entendre the night life and homosexual meetings, and describes the atmosphere of a city whose rhythm followed the venal relations by which its populace passed the time:

> Soldiers crowd into the pubs in their pretty clothes,
> As pink and silly as girls from a high-class academy;
> The Lion, The Rose, The Crown, will not ask them to die,
> Not here, not now: all they are killing is time,
> A pauper civilian future.
>
> ...
>
> The cries of the gulls at dawn are sad like work:
> The soldier guards the traveller who pays for the soldier,
> Each prays in a similar way for himself, but neither
> Controls the years or the weather. Some may be heroes:
> Not all of us are unhappy. [128]

London's homosexual scene seems to have been more traditional than the German scene: it was on the defensive, which is a sign of greater police repression and less tolerance for overt display. The English homosexual scene

---

127. Cited by Peter Parker, *A Life of J.R. Ackerley, op. cit.*, p.212.

128. W.H. Auden, *Collected Shorter Poems, 1927-1957*, London, Faber & Faber, 1966, 351 pages, p.98. The Lion, The Rose and The Crown are names of pubs that were frequented by soldiers and homosexuals. W.H. Auden slips in references that would be understood only by those in the know.

had merely infiltrated the city, rather than springing up within it. And, due to the higher level of repression, the clubs and the pick-up scene were more directly sexual: there was little time and opportunity for small talk and idle chat, much less a real exchange of information. In the bars, simply asking for a cigarette was enough to pick up a partner, without attracting the attention of anyone else. In essence, the English homosexual culture was an underground culture, closed to the uninitiated, inaccessible to timid, and concentrated very closely in obscure districts of London and the ports.

Paris, Montmartre, and Getting Caught

Paris held a special position in the 1920s. In a climate of relative tolerance, many specialized homosexual and lesbian establishments were opened, and the capital gained a reputation for the variety of its night-time pleasures.[129] When the Nazis cracked down in Berlin in the mid-1930s, Paris essentially became the new center of homosexual life.

Dance time

The homosexual venues were mostly found in one of three locations: Montmartre, Pigalle and Montparnasse. Since the end of the 19th century, Montmartre had been the main gathering place for Parisian lesbians, where they could be seen sitting together at the sidewalk cafés or dancing at the Moulin-Rouge. Lulu de Montparnasse opened The Monocle, on Edgar-Quinet boulevard — one of the first lesbian nightclubs. All the women there dressed as men, in Tuxedos, and wore their hair in a bob. Paris had many homosexual bars: Tonton, on rue Norvins, in Montmartre; la Petite Chaumière; Palmyre, on place Blanche; Liberty's; Rubis; Tanagra; Récamier; The Maurice Bar; Chez Ma Cousine on rue Lepic; Graff, place Blanche (where Crevel was a regular); the Clair de lune, on

---

129. Gilles Barbedette and Michel Carassou present serious research on Parisian homosexual meeting places between the wars, in *Paris gay 1925* (Paris, Presses de la Renaissance, 1981, 312 pages), and Brassaï in *Le Paris secret des années trente* (Paris, Gallimard, 1976, 190 pages). I will thus repeat some of their conclusions. To round out the list, I also consulted the testimony of Willy (*Le Troisième Sexe, op. cit.*), Charles-Étienne (*Notre-Dame-de-Lesbos*, Paris, Librairie des Lettres, 1919, 309 pages, and *Le Bal des folles*, Paris, Curio, 1930, 255 pages) and Michel du Coglay (*Chez les mauvais garçons, op. cit.*) Most of these establishments did not survive more than a year, as a result of police raids, the frequent scandals that ruined the reputation of the clubs, and the clientele's insatiable desire for something new.

place Pigalle, was open from three in the afternoon until five o'clock in the morning and was popular with marines and soldiers; and Mon Club, at the end of a dead-end off the avenue de Clichy, where salesmen and office workers met in the basement. There were also Chez Leon, near Les Halles; la Bolée, on the Rive Gauche, in the passage des Hirondelles; and Chez Julie, rue Saint-Martin. La Folie, on rue Victor-Massé, became the Taverne Liégeoise on rue Pigalle. Les Troglodytes was a private club.

The Petite Chaumière ("the little thatched cottage") was a picturesque establishment that drew sensation-seeking foreigners. The scene is described in *Le Troisième Sexe*, by Willy:

> The pianist gives a prelude to a shimmy, and as if on cue the professionals who are paid to give the viewers a spectacle immediately latch onto one another. They undulate more than dance, and thrust their pelvises obscenely, shimmying their bosoms and delicately grasping the leg of their trousers, which they raise above their shiny boots with each step forward, all the while winking at the customers. They wear very fine clothing, and some appear to have built up their chests with cotton wadding. Others wear low-cut kimonos, and one of them wears an Oriental costume all in silver lamé.[130]

Many of these establishments are reputed to have engaged in drug trafficking, too. "Almost all the bars for pederasts in Montmartre, or near the porte Saint-Denis and the porte Saint-Martin, are cocaine dens, where selling and using are common."[131]

However, it was at the homosexual balls that they could get together on a large scale. Such events were very popular in those times. The Sainte-Geneviève Mountain dance, with accordion music, was held behind the Pantheon, and evolved into a drag ball on the day of Mardi Gras. Male and female couples were seen, and women danced together. Magic-City, on rue Cognacq-Jay, was the most famous. A drag ball for men of all ages and every social background, it was banned after February 6, 1934. Following this prohibition, homosexuals tried unsuccessfully to revert to "normal" balls and ended up slipping off to the outskirts of town. For instance, to celebrate Christmas in 1935, a hundred homosexuals traveled fifty kilometers outside of Paris, by coach, for their midnight supper.

---

130. Willy, *Le Troisième Sexe, op. cit.,* p.173-174.
131. *Ibid.,* p.177-178.

Magic-City, due to its sinful reputation, attracted spectators as well as homosexuals, so that inverts were often greeted by a crowd of gawkers:

> For it was a very Parisian thing for some [of the "normal people"] to come and visit the "aunties" at Magic every year. Their presence was always a nightmare for me; not because I was afraid of being spotted by them, since I might well be just a dilettante, but because I knew what homosexuals had to fear when these "Peeping Toms" showed up at these balls... For them, the aunties at Magic represented Sodom, whereas in fact they were nothing more than a disturbing caricature.[132]

This was the central topic of Charles-Étienne's novel, *Le Bal des folles* (1930). Despite the fictionalized aspect, one can assume that the author paints a fairly true-to-life picture, especially with regard to the ambiance and the reactions of the onlookers. He places himself in the position of the viewer who is completely foreign to the homosexual milieu, who discovers, with a mixture of amazement, distaste and amusement, the largest gathering of Parisian "queens," and he describes how the crowd gathered to watch the transvestites shouts insults and threats.[133] Others comment, "How can they be allowed to insult the world this way! Today, we are entitled to respect as much as to fun."[134]

People came there to be seen, and certainly to see others:

> After the bruising attack outside, here the reception was more restrained, but quite as bitter, inside. All along the balustrade, clusters of people perched, climbed, and packed together to the point of smothering, raised a mocking jeer: two hundred heads with eyes flaming and mouths hurling insults... a Greek chorus of poisonous epithets, ridicule, and slurs....[135]

This was certainly the greatest homosexual attraction in Paris, not to be missed for anything in the world. Through their costumes, the transvestites expressed all the exuberance and vitality of a community kept closely under wraps all the rest of the year and wildly satirized the "normal" world through exaggerated, almost archetypal feminine and virile characters: countesses

---

132. Alain Rox, *Tu seras seul*, Paris, Flammarion, 1936, 403 pages, p.258.
133. Charles-Étienne, *Le Bal des folles, op. cit.*, p.153.
134.*Ibid.*, p.154.
135. *Ibid.*, p.155.

dressed in crinoline, mad virgins, Oriental dancers cavorting with sailors, hoodlums, and soldiers.

Pretty much the same ambiance prevailed at the Wagram Ball, which was also held during Lent. Charles-Étienne's description of it, in *Notre-Dame-de-Lesbos*, sounds like Magic-City. His portraits of the transvestites give us a good idea of the general color. "Didine" was one example: "Stuffed into a yellow brocade dress, wearing a red wig topped by a trembling tiara of paste, the dress low-cut and in the back naked to the waist, revealing the physique of a prize fighter, a man climbed the staircase, twisting adroitly and with meticulous gestures lifting the long train of her skirt."[136]

The list of the nicknames is particularly revealing: Fontanges, Sévigné, Montespan, the Duchess of Bubble, the Infante Eudoxie, the Mauve Mouse, the Dark One, Sweetie Pie, Fréda, the Englishwoman, Mad Maria, the Muse, the Teapot, the She-wolf, Sappho, Wet Cat, Little Piano, Princess of the Marshes, Marguerite of Burgundy, etc. This was a triumph of camp, a tinsel aristocracy that mocked the traditional hierarchies and values. Like Magic-City, the Wagram Ball attracted a crowd of spectators, but of lower-class origins. "From the Avenue des Terns to the parc Monceau, from la Muette to l'Étoile, all the laborers from the surrounding area would flock to 'Wagram.' It was something of a ball for the household help, but others came, too, from Point-du-Jour and La Villette, looking for a treat...."[137]

These were the homosexual centers in Paris; some second-tier locations existed as well: the Champs-Élysées was the "in" place for a lofty clientele including members of parliament and men of letters; the English gathered at a tea house opposite the Tuileries; others congregated at the porte Saint-Martin while the Champs-de-Mars was monopolized by the Italians. The Gaumont cinema was a notorious place for pick-ups, as was the Berlitz bazaar, on the broad boulevards. And finally, there were several dance halls in the Bastille neighborhood, especially in rue Lappe, where tipsy sailors and colonial troops could be seen. This was not strictly speaking a homosexual scene, but men could dance together and one could easily find a partner for the night.

Daniel Guérin describes the atmosphere of this workingman's neighborhood:

---

136. Charles-Étienne, *Notre-Dame-de-Lesbos*, *op. cit.*, p.62.
137. *Ibid.*, p.67.

I was a regular at one of the popular dance halls on rue Lappe, near the Bastille, where workmen, prostitutes, society women, johns, and aunts all danced. In those relaxed and natural days, before the cops took over France, a chevalier could go out in public with a mate of the same sex, without being considered crazy. From its little loggia the orchestra, dominated by the accordion, carried us away on its tantalizing rhythms. Once in a while some tough would try to start a fight, but not very seriously; the whores fussed with their chignons. When there was a raid, it was rare and paternalistic, the so-called morality brigade was lenient and discreet. We sat in peace and sipped our traditional *diabolo*.[138]

However, not all the witnesses shared Guérin's enthusiasm. "What you see there are little delinquents, not too carefully washed but heavily made up, with caps on their heads and sporting brightly colored foulards; these are guys who, when they fail to make a buck here, will certainly be found hauling coal or other cargo."[139]

Night life

As a city of homosexual delights, Paris distinguished itself from Berlin by the large number of pick-up joints and prostitution. Although there were practically no places for meeting and socializing, the baths and even homosexual flophouses were innumerable.

In certain public urinals, also known as tea-houses or tea cups, solicitation was unrestrained. The urinals were round, with three stalls; one could discreetly observe the activity next door and join in, if one wished. If you were caught, you risked three months to two years in prison for offending public decency and a fine of 500 to 4,500 francs. Homosexuals mostly circulated around the urinals on the grand boulevards, in the railway stations, at the Invalides, the Champs-de-Mars, the Trocadéro, and the Champs-Élysées, in Montmartre, Montparnasse, the boulevard de Courcelles, Edgar-Quinet boulevard, Haussmann boulevard, Malesherbes boulevard, at the Batignolles, Père-Lachaise, la Villette, les Halles, the Latin Quarter and at the Observatory.

Those were places for hunting solo; in the public parks, especially the Bois de Boulogne and the Bois de Vincennes, the well-born mingled with male prostitutes and hustlers of all sorts; then, too, there was the more romantic Park Monceau, where homosexual couples strolled in summertime, and finally the

138. Daniel Guérin, *Autobiographie de jeunesse*, Paris, Belfond, 1972, 248 pages, p.169.
139. Willy, Le Troisième Sexe, *op. cit.*, p.162-163.

Tuileries, where queens known by their *noms de guerre* would meet: Mme. de Lamballe, Mme. de Pompadour, etc.[140] According to Daniel Guérin, the barge Noïé, moored at the canal Saint-Martin near the Bastille, was a homosexual joint. Lastly, the swimming pools were still good places to try one's luck. Guérin especially cites the UCJG pool (Union of Young Christians), on rue Trévise, where visitors would swim naked after exercising or taking a walk, and the one on rue Pontoise, where people would slip, two by two, into the cabins to make love.[141]

Male prostitution in Paris was well organized; in contrast to Berlin and London, most of the male prostitutes were professionals and operated within specialized establishments. Even Proust, as early as in *A la recherche du temps perdu (In Search of Lost Time)* mentioned these male brothels where the most demanding clients could be satisfied. The middle-class customer was reassured by the "family" atmosphere; he had quite a wide choice, the décor was acceptable, and there was relative anonymity. The fear of robbery, aggression and blackmail were also reduced.

Certain houses were equipped to satisfy the more extreme requests. Maurice Sachs noted,

> I had not hitherto even suspected that there was any homosexual activity going on there. Someone suggested that I try an establishment on XXX Street which, operating under the cover of a public bath, dissimulated an active business in male prostitution, where soft lads too lazy to seek regular jobs earned money to bring home to their wives by sleeping with men, for it is striking that this deviant youth neither derived pleasure nor became habituated to the practice of these infamous vices.[142]

Willy also mentions these establishments; one on rue Tiquetonne, in another part of Les Ternes, and another near Saint-Augustin:

> Having identified a young man whose style is particularly pleasing, one slips some small change into the young bath attendant's damp hand, and he promptly notifies the attractive young man that a Monsieur wishes a massage session. And then one is shut up in a private cubicle with a curtain at the door, and, hey, presto! Your soul mate appears, and sets to work in his capacity as a masseur to restore movement to the unresponsive member.[143]

---

140. Michel du Coglay, Chez les mauvais garçons, *op. cit.*
141. Cité in Gilles Barbedette and Michel Carassou, *Paris gay 1925*, *op. cit.*
142. Maurice Sachs, *Le Sabbat* [written in 1939, publié en 1946], Paris, Gallimard, 1960, 298 pages, p.194.

Another place, on rue de la Folie-Méricourt, was arranged to facilitate sexual exchanges: "...all along both sides of the bath, benches were arrayed around tables in small, separated niches, where patrons sat together in bath-robes, with piano music emanating from a semicircular stage at the back of the room."[144]

Many male prostitutes worked independently, in a fairly cohesive world having its own codes, slang, and signs of recognition.[145] Most of the gigolos used *noms de guerre*, often inspired by show business: Mistinguett, Baker, Greta, Marlene, Gaby, Crawford, or Mae West. Sometimes they were disguised, and always heavily made up: "All the painted youth of the boulevard de Clichy were there, including Messaline, with her dyed hair."[146]

Cross-dressers operated mainly at Pigalle, in Clichy, and Rochechouart, but there were also some in Montmartre. The rates and the means of payment varied. On the first go, a gigolo could earn 200 to 300 francs a night, but there-after the tariff might drop to 50 francs; and he still had to pay the hotel a fee, on top of the price of the room. On the other hand, if the customer were rich, the hotel paid a commission to the male prostitute. There were subscription systems for timid customers, family men who did not want to be noticed; they could see the prostitute once a week, or twice per month, for example.

The gigolos lived together and formed a subculture within the Parisian underworld. They installed themselves in the promenades of Parisian theaters, where they targeted their next customers and flaunted their charms: "The 'ladies' (as they were called) chatted. Then, as the hour advanced, Olga set off for a date at the steam bath, Titine seduced a strapping man and Birdie readily accepted the first serious invitation presented."[147]

---

143. Willy, Le Troisième Sexe, *op. cit.*, p.181.
144. Alain Rox, *Tu seras seul*, *op. cit.*, p.282.
145. For a good description of the milieu, see François Carlier, *La Prostitution antiphy-sique* (1887; reedited., Paris, Le Sycomore, 1981, 247 pages): The head of the morality brigade at the Paris prefecture between 1850 and 1870 used various terms to distinguish between prostitutes ("honteuses," "persilleuses," "travailleuses") and clients ("tantes," "tapettes," "corvettes," "rivettes"). See also Francis Carco, *Jésus-la-Caille* (1914; Paris, Mercure de France, 250 pages), Charles-Étienne, *Les Désexués* (1924; Paris, Curio, 267 pages), Michel du Coglay, *Chez les mauvais garçons* (1938; *op. cit.*).
146. Francis Carco, *Jésus-la-Caille*, *op. cit.*, p.76.
147. Francis Carco, *Jésus-la-Caille*, *op. cit.*, p.151

Not every male prostitute operated the same way. Along with the beautiful young men strolling the boulevards, there were tougher characters whose main concern was to make the customer cough up some money, by any means necessary. These boys often operated in pairs: while one was working the urinals, the other lurked, club in hand, ready to jump on the recalcitrant customer. Some carried fake unemployment cards, which protected them from arrest for vagrancy. Unlike the gigolos, they were not so much homosexuals as little thugs looking for an easy buck. They would justify their actions by bragging and by denying the sexual aspect of their profession: "I took that job because I said to myself that it was cleanest — or the least dirty, and the least risky. What's the big deal? In any case, robbing these old bastards, I do their kids and their wives a service."[148] The robbed and cheated customer was in a bind: if he filed a complaint, the police would mock him, insult him, and even abuse him, so he was hardly likely to call attention to what had happened.

In many instances, a "guy" controlled one or more male prostitutes. "He was not up to the level of Charlot-des-Halles, who had eight or ten minors under his control, and who disdained him entirely."[149] Commonly, young boys who had not yet been initiated into their profession would work under the wing of an older male prostitute. "A stout brunette, La Marseillaise, ran two pale little apprentices and pocketed their receipts. Both minors, Pompom-Girl and Lolotte would trot along nicely in front of her, and she would announce, 'I have two good-looking boys, here, Mister.'"[150]

Cross-dressers worked the same territory as women prostitutes, who often complained of unfair competition. The two types of prostitution were not, however, entirely at odds with each other. Sometimes, a pimp might have both girls and boys, and a prostitute might sometimes get together with a gigolo: "How often does a girl fall in love with a Jesus? The ladies didn't have any compunction over taking the most ambiguous artists from the Moulin Rouge as lovers. They were all free agents."[151] This sort of goings on was viewed very unfavorably in the homosexual world, as the butches did not like to see anyone horning in on their prerogatives and having the "drips" ridicule them. "You don't know Birdie. She cannot stand the mignards. She sees red. When she heard that

---

148. P'tit Louis, cited by Michel du Coglay, *Chez les mauvais garçons, op. cit.,* p.39.

149. *Ibid.,* p.239.

150. *Ibid.,* p.134.

151. Francis Carco, *Jésus-la-Caille, op. cit.,* p.104.

a woman had deceived her man with an aunt, it was he who felt like a cuckold and who wanted to be avenged."[152]

Social exclusion added to the problems of financial dependence. Gigolos were not accepted; they were scorned by just about everyone, including many women. Therefore, they were particularly vulnerable to the settling of accounts in the underworld. This was a chauvinist milieu where it was important to affirm one's virility, even one's brutality; gigolos were suspected of being rats and were not trusted. Paradoxically, for this reason they were often denounced to the police by thugs looking to put themselves in a good light: "He knew Corsica's instinctive hatred for ambiguous couples and, like Corsica, he hated Bamboo, Birdie and others who were of the same species but did not show it. Indeed, in Montmartre he satisfied his urge to violence by encouraging the police to take action, meanwhile declaring, in the bars: 'Death to the she-asses and death to the aunts!'"[153] Also, very often, the gigolo was the designated fall guy, sacrificed without remorse, rejected by the very circle from which he came. His life expectancy was relatively short and he often ended his days in indigence: the trade was profitable only during a youth that quickly faded,[154] and the hopes of moving over into other criminal sectors remained slim, since the reputation of such people made them complete outcasts from the start. Moreover, gigolos were often addicted to opium and coke, which accelerated their decline.

In the 1920s and 1930s, professional male prostitutes faced competition on their own terrain by unregulated soliciting on the part of young workmen. André Gide, in his journal, mentioned his astonishment at this trend. "According to Roger [Martin], nine out of ten young men who resort to prostitution are by no means homosexual. They do it without any sense of repugnance, but solely for the money, which by the way enables them to maintain a mistress, with whom they like to go about during the day."[155]

---

152. *Ibid.*, p.65.

153. *Ibid.*, p.9-10.

154. An article appeared in *La Vie parisienne*, 1934, p.1307, showed that some of them managed to get away with it for quite a long time: a young fellow dressed in a navy uniform and beret was the main attraction at a certain homo nightclub in Montmartre. He spoke like a child, and had big eyes. The police put an end to his reign. They asked him for his papers, and he took out his military record, saying: "I am a war veteran, here is the list of campagns I was in from 1914 to 1916." "The old gentlemen must have fallen out of their seats; the evidence was incontrovertible: the 'boy' was 40 years old!"

155. André Gide, *Journal, 1889-1939*, Paris, Gallimard, coll. "Bibl. de la Pléiade," 1951, 1374 pages, 24 October 1932, p.1144-1145.

The economic crisis may have encouraged temporary prostitution, but it seems that this phenomenon was less widespread in France than elsewhere, perhaps because the crisis hit there later.[156] Amateur prostitution in Paris is explained not so much by any urgent financial need as by the allure of the good life, expensive gifts, sometimes an introduction into a higher social milieu, and a general atmosphere of sexual license. "It is so easy to allow oneself to be caressed by any hand, when one closes one's eyes. And then, without expecting it in the least, one ends up finding that one has developed a taste for it."[157]

These amateur male prostitutes were likely to come to grief. Having been introduced to another world, the lad soon felt ill at ease at his work place and hoped to escape from it by becoming attached to a patron. This kind of adventure generally ended in misery, for it was the working-class origin of the boy and his amateurism that so fascinated the customer. Joining the crowd of professional male prostitutes, painted and jaded and spewing slang, the working boy lost his principal attraction:

> A child of the poor neighborhoods,... who can no longer stand to look at Nini, now that he has learned to appreciate the torso of the young man to whom he has sold himself as a joke, just to "try it,"... One day, he throws away his workman's tools... A pot of cream softens the face. Now, in the evening, he goes to the dance halls. Foreigners like places such as Notre-Dame...he quickly learns how to choose the prettiest ties. He has a whole collection of them. He dances well, he sings. He makes an art of it.[158]

These boys were a mainstay of cosmopolitan Parisian night life. Professional prostitutes recruited middle-class men from Paris or the provinces, habitués with well-defined tastes and not very much interested in trying something new — and even less interested in having their reputations compromised by showing up at trendy places. But amateurs, workmen, gangsters and sailors on leave were very much in demand. It is they whom the rich foreign tourists, especially the Americans, wanted to meet in order to have a good story to tell when they went home. Proud and trembling with false outrage, they could say

---

156. Germany's industrial output fell, starting in 1929. By spring 1930, the crisis hit Great Britain. France was not affected until fall of 1931.

157. René Crevel, *Mon corps et moi*, Paris, Éditions du Sagittaire, 1926, 204 pages, p.54-55.

158. *Ibid.*, p.57-58.

that they had had an adventure with a real operator. René Crevel gives us a little vignette:

> The little scoundrel was shaved so smooth, his neck looked so white — draped as it was in a beautiful red scarf, waiting at a table with a glass of wine; a friend to help you forget the rain and loneliness of the night,... The teasing and flirting might include a little English learned from American soldiers during the war. The foreigner would invite the boy to dance. A girl, in love with the lad, insulted him when he left with the foreigner. He caressed her hair and gave no reply to her abuse.[159]

These were the very lads that the top celebrities of Paris liked to show off and offered to their friends as prized gifts. Cocteau's and Crevel's crowds would spend the evening in trendy nightclubs, forging and demolishing the reputations of young men filled with illusions. A remarkable beauty, an appealing physique, a reputation for toughness brought them fleeting glory on Montmartre, the envy of their peers, and a gold watch. But callous society men were soon bored and rejected those whom they once had adored.

The homosexual life in the countryside is more difficult to research. Toulon was characterized as "a charming Sodom,"[160] and Cocteau raved about it in *Le Livre blanc* (1928): "From every corner of the world, men enamored of male beauty come to admire the sailors who stroll by, singly or in groups, responding to winks with a smile and never refusing the offer of love."[161] Marseilles attracted many homosexuals in search of exoticism and sailors on leave. Stephen Tennant stayed there several times, drawing ideas from harbor life for his drawings and his novel, *Lascar*. Daniel Guérin, embarking for Beirut, made a pass at a young fellow and from that point onward was propositioned continuously, throughout the whole voyage, by all the most virile deckhands.

Similarly, André Gide draws an enthusiastic portrait of the town of Calvi:

> In Calvi, every male, grown up or not, is involved in prostitution. Even that word is inadequate, for pleasure seems to drive them more than a desire for profit... At the many public dances, men only dance with each other, and in a very lascivious way. Little boys, from eight years and up, go along with their big brothers when they go off to frolic in love with foreigners, who take them along on the beach, to the rocks, or under the pines;

---

159. *Ibid.*, p.161-162.
160. See Chapter Seven.
161. Jean Cocteau, *Le Livre blanc* [1928], Paris, Éditions de Messine, 1983, 123 pages, p.56.

they keep watch in the neighborhoods and sound the alarm in case anybody seems to be approaching; they make propositions on their own behalf, or enjoy themselves as "Peeping Toms." Any hour of the day or the night, always ready.[162]

This makes it very difficult to determine how many homosexual locales there were outside of Paris. Willy solves the problem in one sentence: "It would take Bottin to enumerate all the various commercial centers in the provinces that have a thriving trade in pederasty."[163] This enthusiasm seems suspicious; indeed, while some bars and some hotels in the large provincial towns no doubt accepted homosexuals, cruising was restricted primarily to nighttime and, unlike Germany, there was no organized structure to handle the desires of the homosexual clientele.

Thus, the main distinction in the 1920s homosexual scene was the creation, in addition to the traditional networks of cruising and prostitution, of quasi-legitimate establishments doing regular business and openly accepting homosexual customers. For the first time, it became possible to show up as homosexuals, to go to specialized bars, to come on to one another without danger, at least in the capitals. This sense of security was tremendously important to expanding the phenomenon: it encouraged contact, allowed dialogue, facilitated meetings: in the bars, in the dance halls, a community was created. "During work hours, homosexuals formed an integral part of society, for the most part indistinguishable from anyone else performing a job. But, during their free time, they became very distinct, a class apart."[164] At the same time, this sense of security fostered the illusion that society was undergoing a radical moral shift: living without constraint, in a protective cocoon, one sometimes forgot that the external world had changed little. In England and Germany, homosexuality remained a crime. For some, the return to "law and order" in the 1930s was a painful surprise.

* * *

The 1920s were a flamboyant time. The homosexual imagination is stoked, like everyone else's, by visual stereotypes, evocative names, magical places which

---

162. André Gide, *Journal, op. cit.*, 3 September 1930.
163. Willy, *Le Troisième Sexe, op. cit.*, p.185.
164. Galileo, "The Gay Thirties," *loc. cit.*

by their very names are part of the background mythology and become compo-
nents of homosexual identity. In this construction of the imagination, which is
essential, what matters is not so much the historical truth — with all the insults,
ridicule, scorn and exclusion it entails — but the power of the symbols, and the
power that we still ascribe to them. The success of these founding myths is
undeniable. They served as the basis for the homosexual liberation of the 1920s,
which resulted in the creation of the German homosexual movement and the
emergence of a virtual cult of homosexuality among the English elite; in addition,
they served as a reference for the homosexual liberation movements of the Sev-
enties.

CHAPTER TWO
LIBERATION ON THE MOVE: THE GOLDEN AGE OF HOMOSEXUAL MOVEMENTS

The homosexual apogee of the 1920s is more than just the mythical context. It is no exaggeration to speak of a homosexual liberation in the 1920s, but that is precisely because the emancipation took concrete forms, from activist groups to networks of mutual aid. Indeed, while we today usually associate homosexual movements with the 1970s, they actually came into being far earlier. The first groups, founded in Germany at the end of the 19th century, had already become fairly significant. They were mainly geared to repealing anti-homosexual laws, but they also showed ambitions to establish a clear identity and a community, and they took on a mission to inform and educate the public. As we will see, the lack of unity thwarted them in achieving these objectives. The movements had various priorities and were sometimes at odds with each other, and the lesbians mostly kept to the sidelines.

Besides, homosexual militancy did not really take hold in England and France before the Second World War. Liberation took different forms in those two countries. In England, attempts were made to form homosexual organizations, but they were only a sidebar to the "cult of homosexuality" which characterized the period.[165] And finally, compared to the democratic and militant German models, France presented an individualistic model, less assertive and centered on exceptional figures.

---

165. See Chapter Three.

THE GERMAN MODEL: COMMUNITARIANISM AND MILITANCY

Germany holds a special place in the genesis of homosexual movements, serving as the cradle of homosexual militancy and a model of organization for other European movements. Since about 1890, German homosexuals tried to enroll public opinion on their side; they particularly concentrated their efforts on the abolition of §175 of the Penal Code, which condemned homosexual acts between men.

Magnus Hirschfeld, Prefiguring the Militant Identity

Magnus Hirschfeld[166] was born on May 14, 1868 into a Jewish family in Kolberg, on the Baltic coast. After studying medicine in Munich and Berlin and after travelling to the United States and North Africa, he settled in Magdeburg and then in Berlin, in the district of Charlottenbourg. One of his homosexual patients committed suicide the day before his marriage, and that apparently led him to take an interest in the homosexual question. The subject was in vogue at the time, and Hirschfeld was one of those liberal doctors who advocated a scientific rather than a criminal approach to homosexuality.

He developed a highly complex theory on the origins of homosexuality, which he regarded as innate: a theory which can be summarized by the famous formula, "The heart of a woman trapped in the body of a man." According to his theory, there are "intersexual" levels, a subtle classification of human beings according to various degrees of hermaphrodism and intermediate sexuality. Hirschfeld published his first book on the subject in 1896, under the pseudonym Th. Ramien, Sapho und Sokrates. Thirty more followed. Hirschfeld's theories on homosexuality were covered most broadly in his principal work, *The Homosexuality of Men and Women* (1914) (in English from Prometheus Books, September 2000, Michael A. Lombardi-Nash, trans.; Vern L. Bullough, introduction), a monument at over a thousand pages which elaborated on all the forms of homosexuality. It is densely documented: the articles and interviews are supplemented by questionnaires the doctor distributed to his patients, especially those in the working classes. *Homosexuals in Berlin* (1908) and *Von einst bis jetzt* (Then and Now) (1923), are early histories of the German homosexual movement, whereas *A Sex-*

---

166. For a biography of Magnus Hirschfeld, see Manfred Herzer, *Magnus Hirschfeld, Leben und Werk eines jüdischen, schwulen und sozialistischen Sexologen*, Francfort-sur-le-Main/ New York, Campus, 1992, 189 pages.

ologist's World Tour (1933) enabled him to compare sexual practices and the perception of sexuality in various countries. But Hirschfeld was not merely a theorist of homosexuality: he created the first German homosexual movement, the WhK (Wissenschaftlich-humanitäres Komitee, or the Scientific-Humanitarian Committee).

The Beginnings of the WhK (1897-1914)

The WhK was founded in Berlin on May 14, 1897 by Hirschfeld, a doctor, psychiatrist and sexologist; Max Spohr, editor; Eduard Oberg, administrative civil servant and lawyer; and the former officer Franz Josef von Bülow. This was a major event in the history of homosexual movements, as it marked the first time that an organization was created with the acknowledged goal of defending homosexual rights. It was declared to be politically independent. The Committee had several goals:[167] first of all, to secure the abolition of §175, then to inform the public about homosexuality, and finally to involve homosexuals in defending their own rights. WhK was a rational and effective organization; it took full advantage of the modern media to promote its cause and to lobby for reforms.

In 1897, Hirschfeld launched a petition in favor of abolishing §175. The petition called for the suppression of anti-homosexual laws, except for the use of force, public disturbance, or acts concerning minors below the age of sixteen. Six hundred signatures were quickly collected, including the names of now prestigious artists like Hermann Hesse, Thomas Mann, Rainer Maria Rilke, Stefan Zweig, Lou Andreas Salome, Karl Jaspers, Georg Grosz, Gerhart Hauptmann, and Engelbert Humperdinck (German composer, 1854-1921); politicians such as Rudolf Hilferding, Karl Kautsky, and Eduard Bernstein; sociologists like Max Scheller and Franz Oppenheimer; sexologists like Richard von Krafft-Ebing; theologists including Martin Buber and scientists such as Albert Einstein. Foreign figures including Emile Zola and Leo Tolstoy signed the petition. Certain highly-placed homosexuals like Alfred Krupp, however, refused.

In 1914, the petition linked the names of 3000 doctors, 750 university professors and 1000 others. It did not go unnoticed. Hirschfeld managed to interest

---

167. Within the WhK, a board of some 70 people discussed and decided the major issues; seven of them were elected to an executive committee, of which Magnus Hirschfeld was president until 1929. There were also one or two secretaries, who were the only two members to be paid for their work.

some leftist politicians in the cause. August Bebel (a founder of German Social Democracy) made a speech on January 13, 1898, at the Reichstag, calling on the other members of Parliament to sign and support the petition. Hirschfeld regarded it as a great success to be received by Rudolf Arnold Niebarding, head of the Justice Ministry for the Reich. He is supposed to have told Hirschfeld, at the time: "The hands of the government are tied until the public understands that your requests are a question of ethics and not some sexual or scientific whim. You must educate the public so that they understand what would be the result if the government gets rid of Paragraph 175."[168]

The Committee stepped up its campaign; it sent letters to Catholic priests, to members of the Reichstag, officers in the administration, mayors and judges. In 1905, the question of §175 was raised before the Reichstag; Bebel and Adolf Thiele called for its abolition, alleging that, according to Hirschfeld's works, 6% of the population was homosexual or bisexual and that thousands of Germans were likely to be threatened with blackmail. Liberals and conservatives opposed it in the name of moral order and the vitality of the German people; the law remained unchanged. By this date, the WhK appears to have had 408 members.

Hirschfeld was busy on other fronts, as well. He put together international conferences to disseminate information on homosexuality, published reviews and bulletins on homosexuality and sent them to the commissions charged with reforming the Penal Code in Germany; he also sent them to the public libraries at home and abroad. He promoted all kinds of information on homosexuality: medical, of course, as well as legal, historical, anthropological, literary; debates and scientific studies. In 1901, he published a pamphlet entitled *Was soll das Volk vom dritten Geschlecht wissen?* ("What should people know about the third sex?"). It went through nineteen editions and more than 50,000 copies were printed. It included a list of famous homosexuals, accompanied by assurances as to homosexuals' morality, their desire to be integrated in society, their compliance with the prevailing laws. The tone was consciously soothing; this was a first attempt to legitimize homosexuality and Hirschfeld had no intention of coming across as a provocateur. WhK publications were always careful not to defy contemporary morals: "Nothing could be farther from our aims than to violate the province of the Church," he wrote in *Jahrbuch für sexual Zwischenstufen*.[169]

---

168. Cited by James D. Steakley, *The Homosexual Emancipation Movement in Germany*, New York, Arno Press, 1975, 121 pages, p.31.
169. Jahrbuch für sexuelle Zwischenstufen, n° VI, 1904.

Hirschfeld produced original and innovative works. Anxious to collect all possible information on homosexuality, he launched a major research project in 1903 covering the students in Charlottenburg and metal-workers in Berlin. More than 8000 questionnaires were sent out,[170] listing precise questions about sexual practices. Of the students who responded, 1.5% said they were attracted to members of their own sex, and 4.5% said they were bisexual. Among the workers, 1.15% declared themselves to be homosexual, and 3.19% bisexual. Hirschfeld concludes from these surveys that 2.2% of the population was homosexual and 3.2%, bisexual.

While this study is open to criticism (the selected sample is not very representative of the population as a whole), it marked a new and sociological approach to homosexuality. A protestant pastor, Wilhelm Philips, in Plötzensee, filed charges against him for the "distributing indecent writings"[171] and slander on behalf of six student co-plaintiffs. Hirschfeld reported many cases of homosexual suicides, including one in particular at the Charlottenburg technology school, and insisted on the need for information and for compassion. In the end, he was only fined 200 marks, the court system having thrown out the charges of indecency.

The Eulenburg Affair (1902-1907, in which many of the men closest to Kaiser Wilhelm II were accused of homosexuality and possibly treason) was a serious blow to the WhK, and caused it to lose most of its financial support. In 1910, the new draft of a reformed penal code proposed extending the prosecution of homosexual acts to lesbianism, evidencing the less tolerant attitude toward the homosexual question. Feminists reacted by organizing meetings and by voting in support of a resolution condemning the law. Helene Stöcker's Bund für Mutterschutz und Sexualreform ("Union for the protection of mothers and sexual reform") met with Magnus Hirschfeld in February 1911. Until this point, lesbians had kept their distance from the Committee, but the link between activism and legal pressure became too important. In the 1912 elections, the

---

170. 3000 questionnaires were sent to students in Charlottenburg, and 5721 to metal workers; 1696 students and 1912 metallurgists responded. In 1901, a Dutch medical student, Lucien von Römer, conducted a comparable survey with 595 students at the University of Amsterdam;he arrived at very similar results: 1.9 % homosexuals, 3.9 % bisexuals, according to Manfred Herzer, *Magnus Hirschfeld, op. cit.*, p.63. Certain authors, like Richard Plant, mention 6611 questionnaires, with the same results.

171. Cited by John Lauritsen and David Thorstad, *The Early Homosexual Rights Movement (1864-1935)*, New York, Times Change Press, 1974, 91 pages, p.22.

WhK sided with those parties who supported the homosexual cause. It published inserts in newspapers, hailing the possibility of seeing members of the "third sex" elected to the Reichstag. The WhK kept at it during the next several elections, working to develop a political awareness among its members.[172]

The apogee and decline of the WhK (1919-1933)

Soon after this defeat, the Committee had another prime opportunity to fight for homosexual rights, on the occasion of the change of regime. For Hirschfeld, 1919 was a banner year; he founded the Institute für Sexualwissenschaft ("Institute for sexual science") in Berlin, and bought a building from Prince von Hertzfeldt at 10 In den Zelten. Visitors were greeted at the entryway by the inscription, "Dolori et Amori Sacrum" ("dedicated to pain and to love"); the WhK slogan was Per Scientam ad Justiciam ("justice through science"). The Institute had two main functions: as a scientific research center, it intended to collect all the existing documentation on homosexuality; and it also comprised a library and a museum. At the same time, it was expected to serve as a center for homosexuals seeking medical help, or psychological support, or who simply wished to meet friends.[173] A hand-picked group of doctors, scientists and politicians attended the inauguration on July 1, 1919. Magnus Hirschfeld gave a speech and presented the Institute as "the first and the only one of its kind in Germany and in the world," and he underscored its political leanings: "Our institute can be described as a child of the revolution."[174]

The Institute quickly became famous abroad and attracted doctors, sex researchers, intellectuals and journalists. André Gide, Édouard Bourdet, René Crevel, and Christopher Isherwood all came to visit. The literature of those days is full of references to the Institute, which seems to have become an obligatory stop for any visitor who knew anything about Berlin. The diplomat Ambroise

---

172. Unfortunately, it is impossible to know what influence the WhK had on the homosexual vote. While one faction of the homosexuals already felt a strong sense of identity and probably voted accordingly, it is likely that most of them, who were less engged in militancy, voted as a function of other concerns.

173. Scientific research concerning sexuality extended to four domains: biology, pathology, sociology and ethnology. The reception center was also divided into four sections: "Marriage and professional counsel," "Psychopathological states and nervous illnesses," "Psychological sexual problems" and "physical sexual problems." The medical team was under the direction of Magnus Hirschfeld, neurologist Arthur Kronfeld, dermatologist Friedrich Wertheim and radiologist August Bessunger.

174. Jahrbuch für sexuelle Zwischenstufen, January-June 1919, p.51.

Got, in *L'Allemagne à nu (Naked Germany)* (1923), and the journalist Louis-Charles Royer in *L'Amour en Allemagne (Love in Germany)* (1936) give their French readers lengthy descriptions of the Institute. Royer was received by Dr. Abraham, an associate of Hirschfeld, who asked him to fill out a 48-page so-called "psychobiological questionnaire." The staircase doubled as a photo gallery. The museum featured portraits and photographs of famous inverts and transvestites. Vitrines displayed material relating to specific cases: fetishists, sadists, Siamese twins, hermaphrodites. In Hirschfeld's own office hung a portrait of the Chevalier d'Éon. Royer sat in on some interviews; he met two pedophiles who requested to be castrated.

One of the most important WhK publications, the *Jahrbuch für sexual Zwischenstufen (Annals for the sexually in-between)*, was published regularly between 1899 and 1923. It was the first newspaper in the world focusing on the scientific study of homosexual conduct, and included articles on medical and sociological studies, reports on WhK activities and press reviews on homosexuality, biographies of famous homosexuals and literary essays on inversion. *Jahrbuch* published an annual report on the activities of the Institute für Sexualwissenschaft: in the year 1919-1920, 18,000 consultations were held, for a total of 3500 people (two-thirds of them men), including 30% homosexuals. After 1923, because of inflation and the economic crisis, *Jahrbuch für sexual Zwischenstufen* was no longer issued; in 1926, it was replaced by *Mitteilungen des WhK (WhK Information)*, which was published until 1933.

During the 1920s, Hirschfeld travelled extensively, to conferences in Germany and abroad, tirelessly spreading his vision of the third sex and agitating for homosexual rights. He made a lecture tour in 1922 in the Netherlands, Vienna and Prague. In 1930, he went to the United States and China; in 1932, he toured Europe and spoke at several events in Switzerland and France. He also continued to fight unremittingly for the abolition of §175, making much of the risks of blackmail. Hirschfeld quoted incredible sums: one victims supposedly paid 242,000 marks over the course of several years, and someone from Munich paid 545,000 marks.[175] Some victims committed suicide to avoid shaming their families.[176]

To influence public opinion on the subject, the WhK used the cinema. Hirschfeld was involved in the first militant homosexual movie, *Anders als die Andern (Different from the Others)*. The film was commissioned by the producer and director Richard Oswald, who specialized in social cinema with an educational purpose. A press screening was held on May 24, 1919, in Berlin's Apollo-Theater, before it was shown to the public. The lead role, that of Paul Körner, was played by Conradt Veidt, the future hero of *Das Kabinett des Doktor Caligari (Dr. Caligari's Office)*.[177] The melodramatic plot means to be edifying: a famous violinist, a homosexual, is not free to express his love. Persecuted by a blackmailer, he is finally denounced to the police. His reputation demolished, he commits suicide. The moral of the film is underscored by Magnus Hirschfeld, who plays the part of the understanding doctor who campaigns for the recall of §175 and advocates more social tolerance for homosexuals — who are not responsible for their condition.

Predictably, the film sparked a public debate. It received many very eulogistic reviews in the press, which underlined its serious approach. But there were also attacks from those supporting the moral order and from anti-Semitic circles. A special screening took place on July 17, 1919, at the Prinzess-Theater in Berlin, for researchers, writers and various famous personalities. Hirschfeld also received very many letters from both celebrities and anonymous sources, expressing variously their support or indignation. In fact, the film was quite a hit, but incidents took place on several occasions while it was being shown, and as a consequence the police banned it in certain cities, like Munich and Stuttgart. After October of that year, it could not be shown anymore except to doctors or scholarly organizations. In spite of this limitation, the film remains a milestone in the fight for homosexual freedom. Due to its broad distribution in Germany, it was an important means for disseminating homosexual propaganda and it helped to inform the public about a cruel injustice.

WhK also fought to modify §297, which related to male prostitution and which envisaged, in the new draft laws, sentences of up to seven years of forced labor. Richard Linsert, a communist, published in pamphlet form a compendium

---

175. In n° 19 of *Mitteilungen des WhK* (January 1929), Hirschfeld mentions the case of a man from Leipzig who had to pay first 600, then 200 marks. When they demanded another 264 marks, the victim filed a complaint for blackmail and the thieves were sentenced, one to 3 years in jail and 3 years of loss of civic rights, another to 9 months in jail, the third to 6 months in jail. Such cases were rare, because the victim usually was unwilling to press charges for fear of being condemned in turn on morality charges, and for fear of the inevitable social disgrace.

176. A 1914 questionnaire covering 10000 homosexuals showed that one quarter of them had attempted suicide. 51 % did it out of fear of being arrested, 14 % following a case of blackmail, 8 % because of family conflicts, 2 % because of sexual trouble with their wives. 18 % of these suicides were homosexual couples. 3 % succeeded.

177. Tall the information about the film is drawn from *Jahrbuch für sexuelle Zwischenstufen*, January-June 1919, p.1-51, which includes a very comprehensive press review.

of interviews with key people on this question, $297, *Unzucht zwischen Männern* (1929). This adds up to a solid report on the state of male prostitution in Germany,[178] and it contains various appeals for modifications to the penal code, from Heinrich and Klaus Mann and Alfred Döblin, *inter alia*. WhK also continued its parliamentary lobbying.

When a new Minister for Justice was appointed (Otto Landsberg, a socialist), Hirschfeld took the occasion to send him a congratulatory letter *cum* petition,[179] asking for a new commission to address the question of penal reforms to be made up of doctors, sexologists and criminologists as well as lawyers. Landsberg ensured Hirschfeld of his goodwill but the new draft law of 1919 still condemned homosexuality. Thereafter, each new Minister for Justice received a letter from the WhK and various information packets.[180] The Reichstag deputies were also sent reports calling for the removal of that paragraph and giving scientific explanations of the origins of homosexuality. For the 1924 elections, the WhK sent the deputies a report comprising a history of German laws on homosexuality and listing the many public figures who had signed the petition. Magnus Hirschfeld stressed that some 1–1.5 million Germans were homosexual, that is to say about 100,000 voters, and that they would be voting according to the deputies' position on $175. WhK therefore asked the various parties to publicly state their positions on the issue.

These pressure tactics did not have the desired effect and the WhK tried on several occasions to increase its impact by taking joint actions with other German homosexual movements. In 1922, the writer and lawyer Kurt Hiller, a close collaborator of Hirschfeld's, published "$175: die Schmach of Jahrhunderts!" ($175: The shame of the century!), a violent lampoon criticizing members of Parliament. According to him, no political party had yet taken a clear stand in defense of homosexuals. Hiller asked for SPD to present Magnus Hirschfeld as a candidate in the next elections. This request went without response. In fact, the WhK briefly considered founding a homosexual party at the national level, which would participate in the elections with the aim of defending the rights of

---

178. See chapter one.

179. BAB, R 22/FB 21764.

180. *Ibid.* 21 July 1921, Minister Gustav Radbruch; 29 April 1923, Chancellor Wilhelm Cuno; 25 September 1925, Hergt. 16 October 1929, the day that $ 175 disappeared from the new draft of the legal code, Magnus Hirschfeld sent to the Minister of Justice a new appeal, regarding issues related to $ 175 that were still open.

"the third sex." This attempt ended in failure, and Hirschfeld bitterly commented, in 1927:

> Without going into a discussion of the merits of these efforts and how important the final success would be, we must stress that all the efforts to create a "mass organization" for homosexuals have, in the final analysis, failed. It is not true that homosexuals form a kind of "secret society" with all kinds of secret signals and arrangements for their mutual defense. With the exception of a few minor groups, homosexuals have almost no feelings of solidarity; in fact, it would be difficult to find another class of humanity that was so unable to organize itself to ensure its elementary rights.[181]

Starting in 1919, the WhK also tried to unite the various German homosexual movements in order to step up the pressure. On the initiative of Kurt Hiller, an action committee (Aktionausschuss) was founded on August 30, 1920, bringing together the WhK, Gemeinschaft der Eigenen, and Deutscher Freundschaftsverband, in order to organize the fight against §175. Interested individuals were invited to send donations to the lawyer, Walter Niemann, and a separate account was opened at Deutsche Bank. In January 1921, Hiller called for all German homosexuals to join in the fight to assert their rights: "The liberation of the homosexual can be only be accomplished by homosexuals themselves." The Action Committee reformulated the old WhK petition and wrote new pamphlets, which it sent in great quantity to the Reichstag deputies.

At the same time, the new Minister for Justice Gustav Radbruch, USPD, proposed a new draft law, in which homosexual activity between consenting adults was not condemned. Radbruch was himself a signatory of the WhK petition, and two months after taking office, in December 1921, he received a WhK delegation. Nonetheless, because of political instability, Radbruch's draft law never went into effect.

The Action Committee also had to contend with internal tensions. Deutscher Freundschaftsverband, now called Bund für Menschenrecht, had a new director, the editor Friedrich Radszuweit; he took a very aggressive stance that led to the successive withdrawal of Gemeinschaft der Eigenen, and then of the WhK.

In the wake of this failure, Hiller then reached out to heterosexual groups that were seeking legal reforms on sexual matters. In 1925, the Kartell für die

---

181. Cited by James D. Steakley, *The Homosexual Emancipation Movement in Germany*, op. cit., p.82.

Reform of Sexualstrafrechts (Association for the reform of the penal code in regard to sexual issues) was founded, bringing together the WhK and five other organizations.[182] In 1927, in response to a new draft law that still maintained the repression of homosexuality, Kurt Hiller drafted an alternative (Gegenentwurf)[183] that better protected individual rights; this set off an intense polemic in the press and had the merit of bringing to the public's attention the question of abolishing $175.[184] The Association also proclaimed the equality of women, and called for liberalizing laws relating to marriage and for contraceptives and abortion services to be made available. Once again, the pleas of homosexuals were drowned out in the broader cacophony and the Association failed to make its mark.

In 1929, the decriminalization of homosexuality was accompanied by additional riders that irritated the WhK.[185] By now, the WhK was slowly crumbling and little by little lost its influence. Hirschfeld had to step down, in the face of increasing criticism from his own adherents, especially his former friend Richard Linsert. He set off on a new series of travels, which became the basis for his book *A Sexologist's World Tour*, published in Switzerland in 1933. During the three last years of its existence, the WhK was a shadow of itself. The economic crisis that hit Germany in 1930 and the increasing political tensions did nothing to improve the chances of creating a more tolerant environment;[186] and with the loss of its

---

182. At the time of the opening meeting, 19 January 1925, participants in the Cartel included the Deutscher Bund für Mutterschutz, Gesellschaft für Sexualreform, Gesellschaft für Geschlechtskunde, Verband für Eherechtsreform, WhK and the Department for Sexual Reform of the Institut für Sexualwissenschaft. Deutsche Liga für Menschenrecht joined soon thereafter. WhK was the only homosexual organization to participate in the Cartel.

183. The editorial commission was composed of Magnus Hirschfeld, Kurt Hiller, Felix Halle, Arthur Kronfeld, Richard Linsert, Heinz Stabel, Helene Stöcker, Felix A. Teilhaber, Siegfried Weinberg and Johannes Werthauer.

184. The WhK published 55 newspaper and magazine articles relating to the counterproposal, in n. 10, 11 and 13 of its *Mitteilungen des WhK*.

185. See Chapter Seven and the annexes.

186. In 1929, unemployment was at 8.5 %; it reached 14 % in 1930, 21.9 % in 1931 and 29.9 % in 1932 — that is, 5.6 million registered as being out of work and probably another million undeclared. Politically., March 1930 was the end of the big coalition. When he came to power, Heinrich Brüning imposed presidential, antiparliamentary government. At the Reichstag elections on 14 September 1930, the NSDAP had more than 18 % of the votes. The last years of Weimar were marked by a paralysis of the system. See Detlev J.K. Peukert, *La République de Weimar*, Paris, Aubier, 1995, 288 pages.

leader, the WhK was left with no clear direction. There were no new initiatives undertaken during this period.

Assessing Magnus Hirschfeld's record

Given his notoriety and his role as a precursor, Magnus Hirschfeld was a lightning rod for all sorts of abuse and insults. The very symbol of homosexuality in Germany, his name became a household word. He was the prototypical homosexual militant, and at the same time he represented medicine's new supremacy in the field of sexuality. He was active on all fronts, and made many enemies.

WhK was at its most successful early in the century. After the War, it never quite managed to re-establish its influential position. WhK celebrated its twenty-fifth anniversary on May 15, 1922, an event commemorated by a booklet published by *Jahrbuch für sexual Zwischenstufen*. Hirschfeld assessed the organization's progress to date. He noted that the task of the WhK had been "to research and to educate." The movement had not failed in this mission and would continue its work undaunted: "All these things are seeds, which must bear fruit; but the harvest is not yet ripe and the time for the harvest and for rest has not yet come."[187]

Five years later, at its thirtieth anniversary in 1927, the press (mostly on the left) echoed this commemoration and emphasized what had been achieved.[188] An article in the May 14, 1927 edition of *Vorwärts* was eulogistic, but it underlined the principal failure of the WhK: its inability, despite all the pressure exerted, to decriminalize homosexuality. In fact, the Committee's failure was mainly political. Wishing to avoid being tied to any one party, Hirschfeld guaranteed the independence of his organization but deprived it of any real support in Parliament.

Still, the WhK's nonpartisan stance was only relative. Hirschfeld, who greeted the revolution of 1918 with enthusiasm, was a member of the SPD (Germany's Social Democratic Party) and his closest collaborator, Kurt Hiller (1885-1972), who joined the WhK in 1908, belonged to a group of pacifist revolutionaries and was editor of the newspaper *Das Ziel (The Goal)* 1916-1924). Both were anti-Bolsheviks. Another WhK leader, Richard Linsert, was a member of

---

187. Jahrbuch für sexuelle Zwischenstufen, January-June 1922, p.5-15.
188. Strongly positive articles were published in Le Vorwärts, Welt am Montag, Welt am Abend, and Sächsiches Volksblatt, Volksstimme Chemnitz, Berliner Volkszeitung, Berliner Börsen-Courier, Neue Berliner 12 Uhr-Zeitung, and Neue Zeit.

the KPD. In addition, because he hoped to spare the public's sensibilities, Hirschfeld made himself the unwitting accomplice of the most conservative movements. He was convinced until the very end that he would be able to win over his interlocutors to common sense and tolerance. He never despaired of convincing the conservatives, and made repeated, even humiliating appeals to them. As an example, we have a letter which he sent to the deputies of the Bavarian Popular Party (BVP), on January 29, 1925: "We request, resolutely, Right Honorable Deputies, that you take all that into consideration and we hope that your psychological discernment and your love of mankind will lead you to rally to our cause...."[189] He was even more diffident in his approach to the Nazi party.

He became the target of virulent attacks from the far right, who set to work undermining his public events. In several German towns, including Stettin and Nuremberg, he was prevented from giving his talks. In Hamburg, in March 1920, he was attacked by demonstrators armed with stink bombs and fireworks. In Munich, events took a dramatic turn. He had decided not to avoid the city despite having received threatening letters; as he stepped forward to give a conference on October 4, 1920, he was attacked, shoved, and jeered at, the crowd spat at him from above, and he was pelted with rocks; he was seriously wounded. Some nationalist newspapers even announced that he had died.

The *Bayerischer Kurier* of October 24 took the occasion to denounce his theories and to warn its readers against his pernicious influence. *Deutschnationale Jugendzeitung* (Nos 33-34) went still further: "The bad penny still turns up. The famous Dr. Magnus Hirschfeld was severely wounded during a conference in Munich. It has now been learned that he is expected to recover from his wounds. We are not afraid to say that it is regrettable that this infamous and very impudent corrupter of the people ("Volksvergifter") has not yet met the end that he so very much deserves!"[190] A few days after the incident, Hitler himself went to Munich and briefly commented on the event.

Another incident occurred in Munich in 1921; and in 1922, during a conference in Vienna, a young man shot at him. After 1929, Nazi persecution increased to the point that it was almost impossible for him to appear in public. Even after his death, he was excoriated as a typical representative of Weimar. In the lampoon *Die Juden in Deutschland* (1936), published by the Institute for the

---

189. Cited by Joachim S. Hohmann, *Sexualforschung und -aufklärung in der Weimarer Republik*, Berlin, Foerster Verlag, 1985, 300 pages, p.36.

190. Cited by *Jahrbuch für Sexuelle Zwischenstufen*, July-October 1920, p.105-142.

Study of the Jewish Question, Hirschfeld is featured in the chapter on "Jews and Immorality."

Even so, Hirschfeld long believed that the Nazi party might come out in support of the abolition of $175. Prior to each election, he sent letters to sound out the NSDAP's position on homosexuality. Early in 1932, Mitteilungen des WhK published an anonymous letter from a homosexual member of the SA (Sturmabteilung, "Attack Section)" under the title "National-Socialism and Inversion," which explained that there were many homosexuals in his party and they were tolerated without any problem. Kurt Hiller responded by citing many examples of Nazi homophobia; he concluded that the NSDAP was on this ground either fundamentally reactionary or profoundly hypocritical. Nonetheless, the letter was used again and again by homosexual movements to convince themselves that Nazi hostility was only temporary and was intended merely as a sop to public opinion.

The ultimate failure of the WhK must be viewed in context. The Committee not only had to fight the conservative parties, but also many of the German homosexual militants — especially the second largest German homosexual movement, Gemeinschaft der Eigenen — who considered his activities counterproductive and antithetical to the homosexual cause. Moreover, Hirschfeld had to face the scathing irony and the skepticism of foreign commentators, above all the French, who looked on his work as nothing but fantasy and charlatanism. Willy, who devoted a whole work to the "third sex," had this to say:

> His idealism is perfectly combined with a certain cupidity betrayed by all the noisy advertisement of his periodical, his film, and even of his institute and the consultations given there.... He has an admirable knack for exploiting the perverse curiosity of his contemporaries.[191]

Some French homosexuals judged his activity harshly; René Crevel's *Êtes-vous fous?* (Are You Nuts?) (1929), is a severe indictment against him. Crevel depicts him under the guise of Dr. Optimus Stag-Mayer, an abominable charlatan who specializes in conducting absurd operations.[192]

In sum, Hirschfeld's record as a homosexual militant remains mixed. The Committee never comprised more than five hundred members, and Hirschfeld was constrained to note that the majority of homosexuals were not ready to fight

---

191. Willy, *Le Troisième Sexe*, Paris, Paris-Édition, 1927, 268 pages, p.47.
192. René Crevel, *Êtes-vous fous?*, Paris, Gallimard, 1929, 179 pages, p.141-142.

for their rights. Some activists felt that his endless propaganda only served to exasperate the public and made homosexuals a more obvious target for extremists. However, in spite of all his errors of judgment and his appetite for power and honor, it is hard to deny Magnus Hirschfeld a unique place in the history of homosexual movements. Thanks to him, it became possible to discuss homosexuality in Germany, on a scientific and humanistic basis. The insults and abuse to which he was subjected clearly show that his adversaries did not under-estimate his power of persuasion and the originality of his combat.

Adolf Brand and "Der Eigene," An Elite and Aesthetic Homosexuality

Adolf Brand (1874-1945) followed a very different course from that of Magnus Hirschfeld.[193] He had to give up his post as a professor because of his anarchistic opinions and his association with free-thinkers. An assiduous reader of Max Stirner, he named his newspaper in direct reference to that philosopher's principal work.[194] To him, anarchism and homosexuality went hand in hand: as an affirmation of one's right to his own body and as a stand against the inter-vention of the State, the Church, the medical profession and middle-class morals. He cited Nietzsche as an example.[195]

Brand founded the newspaper *Der Eigene*, in 1896, but it lasted only for nine issues, then ran out of money. In 1898, Brand tried to start over, advertising the newspaper as "the first homosexual periodical in the world." After seven issues, he was fined 200 marks by the County Court of Berlin on March 23, 1900. His partners, Hanns Heinz Ewers and Paul Lehmann, were fined 50 and 150 marks. A third attempt, in January 1903, led to a new conviction November 1903 and he spent two months in prison for immorality. Editor Max Spohr had to pay a fine of 150 marks. Publication recommenced, nonetheless, and *Der Eigene* became a landmark in homosexual history. Brand also published a supplement to the newspaper, *Eros*, and he published many shorter works on homosexuality, poems, news, essays and lampoons; and he published photographs of beautiful young men in mannered, homoerotic reviews, like *Blätter für Nacktkultur, Rasse und Schönheit*, and *Deutsche Rasse*.

---

193. See Harry Oosterhuis and Hubert Kennedy (dir.), *Homosexuality and Male Bonding in Pre-Nazi Germany*, New York, The Haworth Press, 1991, 271 pages.

194. Der Einzige und sein Eigentum. See also Chapter Six.

195. Hansfried Hossendorf, "Nietzsche und der Jugend," *Der Eigene*, n° XI/2, 1926, p. 34-35.

Like other homosexual reviews of the time, *Der Eigene* had the ambition of serving as a forum on homosexuality, and encompassed scientific, literary, artistic, and historical articles, poems, news bulletins and photographs of stunning, naked young men. However, the general tone strove to be lofty and edifying, and the production quality was high. The leading contributors included Elisar von Kupffer (1872-1942), a homosexual aristocrat and a follower of aestheticism, and Edwin Bab (1882-1912), a doctor.

Der Eigene adjusted its political content according to the times. In 1932, only literary pieces and homoerotic photographs were published, as had been the case in the publication's early days, for the political climate was becoming less tolerant. By way of contrast, the years 1919-1931 are remarkable for the wealth of topics covered, the many philosophical discussions and political views expressed. Like most homosexual newspapers, it ran a large section of classified advertisements; they helped make it a success, for they enabled homosexuals to make contact anonymously; some were simply seeking friends, others were looking for jobs: "Student from good family, 22 years, fair, admires physical and intellectual celerity, seeks a real man, understanding friendship (reciprocal), encouraging, similar age or an older student. Letter with photograph to be sent to the editor if possible"; "Saar region: male, 29, seeks exchange of ideas with distinguished men, very pure, 25-20 years, student if possible, living in the Saar, Rhineland or France. No anonymous replies," (Eros, N °7). The newspaper was condemned regularly for immorality, and on January 3, 1922, the County Court of Berlin fined it 5000 marks.

In 1903, Brand and Benedict Friedländer (1866-1908), a philosopher and biologist, had also founded Gemeinschaft der Eigenen (the "Community of special people"), a homosexual association. Among the founding members were Friedländer, Wilhelm Jansen — the founder of the Jung-Wandervogel, the painter Fidus, the writers Caesareon, Peter Hille, Walter Heinrich, Hans Fuchs and Reiffegg (a pseudonym of Otto Kiefer), the composer Richard Meienreis, writer and professor Paul Brandt, Dr. Lucien von Römer, and the legal counselor Martha Marquardt.

After the war, Brand tried to expand his movement beyond Berlin and abroad, without much success. We do not have membership statistics for Gemeinschaft, nor subscription information for Der Eigene, but the movement does seem to have grown during the post-war period. Like the WhK, the Community of special people actively lobbied the Ministry of Justice.[196] The Ministry was given a massive report on May 29, 1929, with all kinds of documents favorable to the homosexual cause — including several issues of *Der Eigene* and *Eros*, and various propaganda articles.

However, even though several members of Gemeinschaft were also members of the WhK and were contributors to the same periodicals, political and strategic differences, exacerbated by the competition between Brand and Hirschfeld, led Gemeinschaft to attack the WhK. From a theoretical and ideological point of view, the two associations were very different. Whereas Magnus Hirschfeld was driven by rationalist and humane ideals, Brand held a romantic and antiquated vision of the German culture. The avant-garde nature of some of his positions on sexuality was contradicted by his reactionary bases: Friedländer preached nudity, and was himself a member of a nudist organization since 1893 — but his reasons were mainly related to hygiene;[197] by the same token, when he praised pedophilia, he was focusing only on the spiritual and educational aspect of this relationship and denied its sexual implications.

Fascinated by the Greek model, the Community was strongly antifeminist and rejected industrialization and the principal assets of modernity, which it interpreted as signs of decadence. The ideal, they felt, was that of a male community linked by bonds of honor, something like knighthood, which would express its aesthetic sense through the veneration of beautiful, heroic young people.

These aspirations reprise many of the themes in German romanticism: admiration for the Christian Middle Ages, faith in the humanistic values of the Renaissance, love of nature and worship of friendship, as expressed by Goethe and Nietzsche. The movement was also close to the philosophy preached by the poet Stefan George, who entertained a circle of male admirers bound by a love of Greece and homoerotic relations, as well as the exaltation of nature. In fact, the Community of Special People shared some of the same aspirations as other German movements like Wandervogel.

Theorists like Hans Blüher and Gustav Wyneken had close ties to the Community, with which they shared a elitist and aesthetic vision of homosexuality. The program of Gemeinschaft der Eigenen fits directly in line with this:

---

196. BAB, R 22/FB 21764.
197. Adolf Brand, "Nacktkultur und Homosexualität," *Der Eigene*, n° VII/1, 1919.

[It] stands for the social and moral rebirth of love between friends, the recognition of its natural right to existence in public and private life, as was the case at the height of its reputation, when it encouraged the arts and shaped the evolution of freedom in Ancient Greece. [Gemeinschaft] will foster, through words and images, through art and sports, the worship of adolescent beauty, as was the case during the apogee of Antiquity... [It] naturally stands for the elimination of all laws contrary to the law of nature. It seeks in particular the abolition of §175, because it constitutes a permanent attack by the State on the right to personal freedom. By the same token, it opposes §184 [on obscene publications] and all the restrictions that derive therefrom.[198]

Gemeinschaft der Eigenen especially refuted the vision of homosexuality that was being disseminated by Hirschfeld. Benedict Friedländer was one of the first to denounce the theory of "the third sex," which he considered humiliating and untrue. Similarly, Adolf Brand saw Hirschfeld as being largely responsible for homosexuality's bad image in Germany. A pamphlet by St Ch. Waldecke, published by Der Eigene, took on the WhK: "Das WhK, warum STI zu bekämpfen und centre Wirken schädlich für das deutsche Volk? (WhK: why it should be fought and why its activities are harmful for the German people).[199] He denounced the attempt to label homosexuality a medical problem and stated that association with the left was dangerous — for, in fact, leftist newspapers had denounced Krupp, Eulenburg and Wyneken. Hirschfeld, he asserted, confused love and friendship, pederasty and homosexuality.

Brand and Friedländer repeated these charges and took particular exception to Hirschfeld's excluding pedophiles so as to make homosexuals respectable, and categorically rejected the idea of setting a sexual majority at the age of sixteen. This special relationship did not, in their eyes, preclude marriage: most of the leaders of the Community were married and were bisexual.

Lastly, the strategic options of the two movements were very different. Brand several times came out in favor of a mass "outing" of famous homosexuals. In 1905, he published a lampoon accusing Kaplan Dasbach, the leader of Zentrum (who was savagely opposed to the abolition of §175), of being homosexual.[200] At the time of the Eulenburg Affair, as was mentioned above, he called

---

198. Adolf Brand, *Die Bedeutung der Freundesliebe für Führer und Völker*, Berlin, Adolf Brand, 1923, 32 pages, p.5.

199. Berlin, Adolf Brand, *Der Eigene*, 1925, 18 pages. Most of it comprises a speech given in Berlin, 27 January 1925, at the Gemeinschaft der Eigenen.

200. Brand serait ainsi l'un des précurseurs de l'*outing*.

the Chancellor of the Reich, Bernhard von Bülow, a homosexual; a lawsuit ensued and he could not show any proof. The WhK did not support him in these moves. In this unsettled context, the Community of Special People did not hesitate to use anti-Semitic arguments against Hirschfeld; "as a Jew" he was an "unsuitable leader" for a movement against §175, since he represented "an oriental point of view" on sexuality and love.

In the early 1920s, Gemeinschaft and the WhK temporarily set aside their disagreements and cooperated within the Action Committee in order to prepare a new campaign for the abolition of §175. Like Hirschfeld, Brand felt the need to mobilize his troops, for the atmosphere of moral tolerance allowed homosexuals to let down their guard rather than continue their fight. "The younger generation which follows us often forgets that we are still in mid-combat . . ."[201]

This lull was of short duration: in 1925, Adolf Brand started in again on Hirschfeld. The increasing influence of two young authors within the Community, Ewald Tscheck and Karl Günther Heimsoth, seems to have played a part in this change of attitude.[202] Both were ardent opponents of the theory of "the third sex." Number 9 of *Der Eigene*, 1925, became an attack on Hirschfeld, who was once again subjected to violent attacks, anti-Semitic and otherwise.[203]

In fact, there were contradictory political leanings within the movement and, like the WhK, Gemeinschaft had difficulty finding a middle ground. In 1928, Brand asked all the parties to state their position on the abolition of §175. In 1925, he had been very disappointed by the immobility of the SPD — he had urged his readers to give them their votes, and yet, once they were in power, they had ignored the homosexual cause. Even so, in an article entitled "Rightist Parties and Love Between Friends," he recalled that the right had always been an enemy to homosexuals and he thus suggested voting for the Socialists, the Communists or Democrats.[204]

While some members of Gemeinschaft, like Heimsoth or Hanns Heinz Ewers, became Nazi sympathizers, Brand himself seems to have cherished few

---

201. *Der Eigene*, n° VII/1, 1919.

202. See Manfred Herzer, "Die Gemeinschaft der Eigenen," in *100 Jahre Schwulenbewegung*, Berlin, Schwules Museum, 1997, 384 pages.

203. In the preceding numbers, in 1924 and 1925, he was subjected to anti-Semitic attacks in "Bücher und Menschen" by Valentin Schudell (*Der Eigene*, n° VII/8, 1924) and in "Freundesliebe und Homosexualität" (*Der Eigene*, n° VIII/9, 1925), where it was suggested that a "Jewish committee" was endangering "German eros."

204. *Der Eigene*, n° XIII/8, 1928.

illusions as to the true nature of the NSDAP, even if he was troubled by the homoerotic resonance of the movement. The sexual revelations about Röhm reinforced his conviction that the Nazis were hypocrites who refused to admit what was going on in their own ranks: "With the Röhm trial, the German public will finally have its eyes opened to the fact that the most dangerous enemies of our cause are often homosexual themselves, who help, consciously, through political hypocrisy and lies, to destroy again and again any moral victories we may have obtained through all our efforts."[205]

In sum, Gemeinschaft der Eigenen offered German homosexuals another model. Elitist and anti-modernist, it associated the worship of male beauty with the denunciation of contemporary society and it exalted individualism over communitarianism. This criticism, anarchistic and romantic at first, took on increasingly nationalist and reactionary tones in the 1920s. At the same time, the movement offered a positive image of male homosexuality, repositioned historically, artistically and culturally, which could have been used as the basis for a strong sense of identity, independent of medical theories and somewhat immune to society's judgment.

However, Brand's hostility to the WhK contributed significantly to the failure of the German homosexual movements. By fostering division, by excluding "effeminate" homosexuals, by defining homosexuality very restrictively, he played into his opponents' hands and obstructed the creation of a strong and unified homosexual movement.

Homosexual Magazines and Popular Organizations

After the First World War, there was an explosive expansion of homosexual associations in Germany.[206] The two pioneering movements, the WhK and Gemeinschaft der Eigenen, were joined by a multitude of local or exclusive cliques, with names like Freundschaft (friendship), Klub der Freunde und Freundinnen ([male- and female-] "friends club"), and Freundschaftsbund ("friendship association"), which transformed the homosexual movement into a mass movement, as far removed from the elitism of Brand as from the scientific vocation of the WhK. Most of these clubs were the result of private and local initiatives and were not related to each other. Their intention was to provide a

---

205. Adolf Brand, "Politische Galgenvogel: ein Wort zum Fall Röhm," in *Eros*, n° 2, 1931, p.1-3.

206. On this subject, see *100 Jahre Schwulenbewegung, op. cit.*

social space for homosexuals where they could talk, have fun and exchange thoughts. Many of them had separate sections for men and women, and it was these associations that gave lesbians the opportunity to organize themselves for the first time.

Many of these associations were largely known by their periodicals; most managed to survive only a few years, since mass circulation magazines monopolized the market to such an extent. *Der Hellasbote* ("Greek messenger"), founded by Hans Kahnert in 1923, targeted both male and female readers. The price, in May 1923, was 300 marks; and it was mainly literary in scope: poems, homosexual news, and readers' views on subjects of their choice. In the June 9, 1923 edition, Ernst Bellenbaum, a reader, suggested that the best way to influence public opinion would be to have frequent coverage in the national press. He proposed regularly sending material on the homosexual movements to the socialist, communist and democrat newspapers. The magazine went out of print in 1925.

The number of homosexual periodicals grew tremendously during the 1920s, thanks to the liberalization of the press following the end of war-time censorship.[207] *Die Fanfare* was published from 1924 to 1926, by the writer Curt Neuburger (who had also founded an independent club, Internationaler Freund Bund, IFB). He was strongly opposed to the leading homosexual movement, Bund für Menschenrecht. In 1927, *Phoebus-Bilderschau* was founded by Kurt Eitelbuss; it published only illustrations. These reviews addressed very different publics: some were high-brow and were intended for a cultivated readership, others were more populist; some advocated a return to nature and, using sporting events as a pretext, published photographs of naked athletes in suggestive positions; others were reserved for women and defended the flapper. Addressing a mainstream homosexual public, who were eager to enjoy their sexuality in peace but avid for information on the homosexual community, meeting places and available entertainments, the reviews sought to tread a fine line, maintaining their neutrality politically and socially. However, the main period-

---

207. James D. Steakley tried to draw up a list of these periodicals: Agathon, Die Blätter für ideale Frauenfreundschaften, Blätter für Menschenrecht, Das dritte Geschlecht, Die Ehelosen, Der Eigene, Eros, Extrapost, Die Fanfare, Frauenliebe, Die freie Presse, Der Freund, Die Freundin, Die Freundschaft, Freundschaft und Freiheit, Das Freundschaftsblatt, Der Führer, Garçonne, Geissel und Rute, Der Hellasbote, Die Insel, Jahrbuch für sexuelle Zwischenstufen, Ledige Frauen, Der Merkur, Mitteilungen des WhK, Monatsberichte des WhK, Mundbrief, Phoebus-Bilderschau, Die Sonne, Der Strom, Die Tante, Uranos. Some magazines printed hundreds of thousands of copies, others were very small.

icals of the time, *Die Freundschaft, Das Freundschaftsblatt, Flapper* and *Die Freundin* were in fact official organs of the larger homosexual associations.

"Der Deutsche Freundschaftsverband"

On August 13, 1919, Karl Schultz founded the review *Die Freundschaft*, subtitled *Mitteilungsblatt des Klubs der Freunde und Freundinnen* (News bulletin of the Club of friends and [female] friends). It was sold openly at newsstands. Number 2 was banned and for a few weeks the publication came out under the title of *Der Freund. Die Freundschaft* found its market very quickly, and in 1922 it absorbed two of its former competitors, *Freundschaft und Freiheit*, published by Adolf Brand, and *Uranos*, by René Stelter. The editor of *Die Freundschaft* was Max H. Danielsen, but he was replaced in 1922 by the former Secretary of the WhK, Georg Plock. It was a monthly, published in Berlin at 1 Baruther Strasse.

The fact that this was an official publication based in homosexual clubs is attested by the fact that Berliner Freundschaftsbund (Association of Berlin friends) was inscribed in the register of associations by the local court on September 28, 1920.[208] In fact, *Die Freundschaft* was a serious newspaper that published fundamental articles on homosexuality, calls to decriminalize it, and stories about the status of homosexuals through the ages. It constantly recalled the homosexual legacy. The newspaper was copiously illustrated with suggestive photographs, but with an aesthetist bent. It was also famous for its classified advertisements, which allowed German homosexuals and sometimes those abroad to find one another. These ads, like those for homosexual establishments, brought in money.

The first articles were signed pseudonymously. A debate on that subject concluded that the use of pseudonyms detracted from the struggle to assert homosexual rights, and from then on, most of the writers used their real names. The review was known abroad, and it became the symbol of German homosexuality. Ambroise Got, who visited Berlin and was shocked by Germanic morals, noted that the review *Die Freundschaft*, despite its high price (50 pfennigs), was a big success: "It is difficult to get this newspaper, unless you look for it the very day it comes out. In downtown Frankfurt and Berlin, and many other cities, where there are many colony of 'transvestis' [sic], it is snapped up as soon as it goes on sale, and it is futile to look for it at the newsstands the following day; as for back issues, they are untraceable."[209] *Die Freundschaft* was a child of the

208. WhK fut was registered there on 2 June 1921.

November revolution. Politically, it came out clearly in support of the Weimar Republic. However, the review was primarily concerned to pull together the incipient homosexual community.

"Friendship Associations" (Freundschaftsvereine) were formed in several large towns in 1919 and later; they offered their members concerts, debates, conferences, social afternoons, and sporting events. They often had a conference room, a library, a medical section and a legal aide, and sometimes specific sections for younger people and women. On August 30, 1920, these various associations were unified under the name Deutscher Freundschaftsverband (DFV), which encompassed Berliner Freundschaftsbund and the Hamburg, Frankfurt-am-Main and Stuttgart sections. Gradually, other clubs became affiliated and the DFV organized congresses to help the various members to meet and discuss militant action. The first congress was held in Kassel on May 27 and 28, 1921, the second in Hamburg, April 15-17, 1922. The DFV sought to oversee all the homosexual organizations and hoped to lead the militant activity. As it turns out, it quickly fell into crisis, not having any sway over the earlier movements like the WhK and Gemeinschaft der Eigenen, which still had influence. In any case, it soon faced competition from a new movement that took off on the wings of its charismatic founder.

"Der Bund für Menschenrecht"

Friedrich Radszuweit (1876-1932) set up a ladies' clothing store and a retail business in Berlin in 1901. He became involved in the homosexual movement in 1919 and, due to his talent as an organizer, was named chair of Vereinigung der Freunde und Freundinnen, a Berlin-based homosexual club. He renamed it the Bund für Menschenrecht (Union for human rights), or BfM, in May 1922. The following year, he succeeded in incorporating the DFV and several other homosexual clubs into it. He split off from *Die Freundschaft*, which took a dim view of his authoritative methods; the newspaper went on without him until 1933.[210] In the meantime, Radszuweit founded many periodicals, and they became the most influential in the homosexual press. These were the *Blätter für Menschenrecht* (Pages for human rights), February 1923; *Die Freundin* (The [female] friend), September 1924; *Die Insel* (The island), November 1924; and, *Das Freundschaftsblatt* (The friendship sheet), June 1925. Radszuweit opened a

---

209. Ambroise Got, *L'Allemagne à nu*, Paris, La Pensée française, 1923, 248 pages, p.103. Also cited by Alain Rox, *Tu seras seul*, Paris, Flammarion, 1936, 403 pages, p.269.

bookshop on August 1, 1923, and then a publishing house, Friedrich Radszuweit Verlagsbuchhandlung, 9 Neue Jakobstrasse. In January 1924, he launched a collection of homosexual writings entitled "Volksbücherei für Menschenrecht."

The movement's official organ was *Blätter für Menschenrecht*, a monthly (sometimes weekly) review that covered literary and scientific information and defined the association's positions: fighting for the abolition of §175, fighting for the social integration of homosexuals, fighting against blackmail, and calls for free legal help. *Das Freundschaftsblatt*, a traditional homosexual review, appeared on Thursdays and cost 20 pfennigs. In addition to traditional medical, social, and literary articles, it carried considerable political content. Indeed, Radszuweit frequently used the newspaper as his personal platform, which enabled him to influence great numbers of homosexuals, many of whom were not militant. He hoped by this means to sensitize an increasing number of "inverts" and encourage them to become more politically engaged in the struggle for social recognition. For example, the lead headline on November 1932 was: "Should We Vote?" Radszuweit made much of the decisive role that homosexuals could play in determining their own fate. Like other homosexual organizations, before each election Bund für Menschenrecht sent out questionnaires to various political organizations asking them to state their position on §175 and it encouraged readers implicitly to vote for those parties who were favorable to the cause. Nevertheless, it also underlined the ambiguity of the leftist parties: on November 10, 1932, it denounced an article published in the communist newspapers *Berlin amndt Morgen* and *Welt amndt Abend*, which termed homosexuality a "middle-class vice," along with prostitution, sadomasochism and bestiality.

Bund für Menschenrecht became the largest German mass organization for homosexuals. Whereas the DFV had succeeded in signing up 2,500 members by 1922, BfM already had 12,000 in 1924 and, in August 1929, it reached its apogee at 48,000, including 1,500 women members. Almost every town in Germany had a group related to Bund für Menschenrecht; the addresses published in the group's publications were most often only post office boxes. Affiliates were formed in

---

210. The magazine only lasted one year because it was denounced, apparently by Radszuweit, and registered on the list of "pornographic and slimy" publications. A meeting organized by Danielsen on 4 May 1928 at the Alexander-Palast was attended by some two hundred people; it ended in great confusion after a talk by Brand Adolf, originally entitled "§ 175 and the elections" but in which he accused Radszuweit of having denounced the magazine to the authorities (BAB, R 22/FB 21764). The DFV was unable to stand up to the BfM and the power of Radszuweit.

Switzerland, Austria, Czechoslovakia, and even in New York, Argentina and Brazil. BfM printed more than 100,000 copies of its periodicals every month. *Die Insel*, priced at 30 pfennigs, hit a record press run of 150,000.

BfM was also active politically. It organized a demonstration in May 1925 against the Army Minister, Otto Gessler, for the dismissal of homosexual soldiers from the Reichswehr. In August 1926, it forwarded a complaint to President Hindenburg regarding the dismissal of homosexual civil servants. BfM also spoke out during the lawsuit over $175, seeking to get the case dismissed or to lessen the penalties. Its members were eligible for legal aid and many of them were defended by the famous lawyer Walter Bahn, who was active in the homosexual movement. Like the WhK and Gemeinschaft der Eigenen, BfM peppered the Ministry of Justice with letters, petitions, bulletins and reports. In 1925, it sent a letter to Justice Minister Frenken, questioning his position on homosexuality, and reminding him that there were 2 million homosexuals — not an insignificant portion of the populace.[211] It wrote to the Justice Minister of the Reich and all the Justice Ministers of the different Länder, or states, on April 20, 1925, recapitulating the fundamental causes of homosexuality and emphasizing the normality of homosexuals.[212] On August 27, 1926, it sent the ministry a whole series of booklets on the question and a copy of the review *Blätter für Menschenrecht* and, in 1927, all the deputies were sent the pamphlet, "$175 Muss abgeschafft werden! Denkschrift an den deutschen Reichstag zur Beseitigung einer Kulturschande" ($175 must be repealed! Calling on the German Reichstag to eliminate a cultural disgrace").

BfM shared the goals of the WhK and Gemeinschaft, but was fundamentally opposed to Magnus Hirschfeld's theories. Like Brand, Radszuweit rejected the notion of a "third sex" and refused to equate homosexuals with "effeminates." He did, however, publish a periodical specifically for transvestites, *Das dritte*

---

211. BAB, R 22/FB 21764. Nine questions were posed to the Minister : 1) What does the minister think of homosexuality, does he think it is innate or acquired? 2) Does he know that there are 2 million homosexuals in Germany? 3) Does he think that homosexuality endangers public morality? 4) Does he think that 2 million Germans should be marked with infamy, as they currently are? 5) Does he believe that homosexuality can be eliminated, thanks to $ 175? 6) Does he plan to keep the paragraph in the new draft? 7) Did he remember that in 1910 and 1911 many public figures had been in favor of suppressing that law? 8) What does he think about that? 9) What does he think of the thousands of signatures on the petition?

212. BAB, R 22/FB 21764.

Geschlecht, which included advice on how to dress effectively enough to pass undetected. This heavily illustrated magazine cost 1 mark.

Unlike the WhK, BfM took an intolerant attitude toward homosexual minorities. Looking to increase the sense of normalcy and to foster social integration, it rejected those who did not fit the mold, especially "queens," pedophiles and male prostitutes. Furthermore, BfM's opposition to §175 was more limited than that of Hirschfeld, which prevented them from working together effectively. Thus, on October 9, 1929, Radszuweit sent the Prussian Minister for Justice a list of resolutions that had been adopted by the Bund für Menschenrecht at its plenary session on September 20 and 23.[213] They claimed immunity only for homosexual acts between consenting adults, and recommended setting the age of sexual majority for boys at eighteen years and, *inter alia*, recommended prosecution of male prostitution. The draft law formulated by the Kahl Commission in 1928 was practically identical to this, but it had been vigorously attacked by the WhK, which preferred the total decriminalization of homosexual acts except where violence was involved.

This difference of views hampered the homosexual struggle, and the governments took advantage of these dissensions to grant only partial reforms. BfM did not get along any better with Gemeinschaft der Eigenen, which considered itself the refuge of the "enlightened." Furthermore, the homosexual movements never really managed to involve the lesbians into their fight, and this only accentuated the divisions.

Lesbians, at the fringes of the homosexual movement

The beginnings of lesbian militancy in Germany date to the 1920s. Until then, women were ascribed minor roles within the WhK, and Gemeinschaft der Eigenen was strictly a male organization. The proliferation of "friendship clubs" in Germany allowed the creation of lesbian sections. Most of the clubs accepted both men and women, but the two groups had their own conference rooms and held their own demonstrations. Often, the buildings were reserved on different days for the men or women. BfM was organized according to the same schema, and it offered women their own organizations and a wide range of activities; it also published *Die Freundin*, a well-received magazine that became the symbol of lesbianism in the 1920s.

---

213. GStA, I.HA, Rep.84a, 8101.

Die Freundin started out as a monthly, then became weekly; it had a large press run. A supplement for transvestites, "Der Transvestit," was eventually dropped. It was published from August 8, 1924 to from March 8, 1933. Its goal was spelled out in Number 3: "Die Freundin will defend the equal rights of women in social life. Die Freundin will foster ideal friendships by publishing articles by our readers, and we invite every woman who feels qualified to send articles and works that they feel are suitable."[214]

The magazine responded to the aspirations of the lesbian public, which sought to be affirmed independently and to be recognized within the homosexual movement as its own entity. Women had their own section within BfM where they could meet together and discuss their problems. However, these sections were often kept out of the movement's main activities: political actions, the fight for rights, and parliamentary representation; and BfM itself was run by men. *Die Freundin* was a specifically lesbian newspaper, but it was not written exclusively by women. Like most homosexual periodicals at that time, it offered a range of articles on varied subjects. Historical articles extolling the glory of lesbians of ages past (Rosa Bonheur, Christine of Sweden, Sappho, etc.) predominated; with basic articles on the problems facing lesbians in Germany (loneliness in the rural areas, work-related problems, confrontations with the police); and cultural articles (homosexual meetings, homosexual life in foreign countries, and reviews of books, plays and movies likely to interest the homosexual public); then there were scientific/medical articles speculating about the origins of homosexuality, political articles calling for solidarity, news, and homosexual poems, as well as photographs of attractive young women.

In addition to various ads for lesbian establishments and dances and all the homosexual events of the week, there were several pages of personal advertisements, which were the magazine's main selling point. These ads were not restricted to lesbians; advertisements for male couples and even heterosexuals also ran. They were an immediate success, as they met a real need in the lesbian community. Not every woman was comfortable going to lesbian establishments and preferred discretion over militancy. By the time No. 8 came out, the classified advertisements took up more than half a page: "Berlin, nurse seeks partner to chat at tea time."[215] "Transvestite selling a well-stocked ladies' wardrobe, very cheap, like new."[216] "Cologne: a woman in the professions, brimming with life,

---

214. *Die Freundin*, n° 3, 1924.
215. *Ibid.*, n° 8, 1924.

loves swimming, seeks partner."[217] "Modern couple, 38-42 years, with comfortable house, seeks a similar couple in Königsberg to get acquainted."[218]

The plight of lesbians outside the city was a frequent topic. Many wrote in to express their anguish and isolation. One such letter dated March 7, 1927, from Elisabeth S., says: "How I envy my comrades and my friends in Berlin! It must not be too difficult for them to meet a nice girl. There are so many meeting places, cafés, clubs... My only solace is that there are even more women who are abandoned, like me. With longing, I still await my best friend."[219] A married woman wrote to say that her husband, after having learned that she was homosexual, allowed her to visit her friend: "I wish that other married women, like me, might meet with such understanding from their husbands with respect to their homosexual inclinations and thus be able to live in friendship, tying their life to that of their friend for eternity."[220] For other women, *Die Freundin* seemed a life saver, which delivered them from despair: "As nobody could understand me or my nature, I have cut myself off from my homeland and my parents."[221]

Die Freundin was the definitive reference point for lesbians of the 1920s.

> We had only a few cents; we would buy a few clothes and — my most urgent desire, in those days — we could sometimes 'go out.'...I would buy *Die Freundin* as often as I could (i.e., seldom). There were classified advertisements there, letting us know what was going on. In this way we managed to attend a Christmas ball for a few hours at a lesbian association. There was a large hall with a stage. And choirs... We also went to a homosexual place on Bülowstrasse, once. For an hour or two. That's all.[222]

Lesbian readers of *Die Freundin* were modern women, who worked, who were up on all their rights and ready to demand they be respected. Thus, it seemed likely that they could be mobilized for specific causes and join an alliance pushing for the abolition of $175, even though it related to them only indirectly. Bund für Menschenrecht used the periodical for its own publicity and

---

216. *Ibid.*, n° 13, 1927.
217. *Ibid.*
218. *Ibid.*, n° 22, 1929.
219. *Ibid.*, n° 4, 1927.
220. *Ibid.*, n° 6, 1927, Letter dated 4 April 1927.
221. *Ibid.*, n° 7, 1927, Letter dated 18 April 1927.
222. Testimony of Gerda M. (1904-1984), who lived in Berlin with her lover since the 1930s, unemployed at the time. Cited by Kristine von Soden and Maruta Schmidt (dir.), *Neue Frauen, die zwanziger Jahre*, Berlin, Elefanten Presse, 1988, 176 pages, p.162.

tried to recruit new members by expounding its views before a favorably-disposed audience. In No. 10, 1928, an article entitled "Homosexual women and the elections" tried to guide lesbians to vote for parties on the left.

These calls seem to have resonated with very few lesbians. The political messages drew no reaction in the Letters to the Editor, whereas the social and medical articles launched polemics. Looking to mobilize the female public, Friedrich Radszuweit and Lotte Hahm, director of the lesbian club Violetta (one of the city's most famous establishments) launched a new association, Bund für ideale Freundschaft ("Union for ideal friendship"), whose statutes were published in *Die Freundin* No. 22, May 28, 1930. It is implicitly stated that, while there is a time for fun and games, they must also think about fighting for their rights. By this return to its roots, the magazine exhibited a growing unease in the face of a political climate that was not getting any friendlier, and a concern over the continuing passivity of lesbians.

In July 1930, for the first time, a police incident at a meeting of Bund für Menschenrecht is mentioned. The newspaper echoed the shock that went through the homosexual community and published a long protest against this aggression. In February 1931, a young woman wrote to testify to her professional troubles. She wore short hair and male clothing; her appearance earned her insulting remarks from her customers and the boss demanded that she change her behavior or be fired. She resigned herself to reverting to a feminine appearance. In 1932, the classified advertisements disappeared, signifying the end of the publication in the form that first won it its following.

Even so, the newspaper could not make up its mind to face certain questions and it refused to take sides, for fear of putting off some of its readers and attracting reprisals. In 1928, *Die Freundin* clearly encouraged readers to vote for the SPD, but it gradually backed away from the political aspect of homosexuality.

Hitler's shadow weighed on BfM, and Radszuweit was unsure as to what stance to adopt with the NSDAP. His lack of political acumen became cruelly apparent when he decided to publish "A Letter to Adolf Hitler," on August 11, 1931, asking Hitler to spell out his views on homosexuality. He recalls certain remarks the Nazi press made with reference to homosexuals ("When we are in power, they will all be hanged or expelled"), but presumes that Hitler is merely misinformed on the subject. He then pleads in an almost humiliating tone on behalf of homosexuals. In fact, he stoops so far as to state that homosexuality is not a "Jewish plague." Anticipating Hitler's possible accession to power, he offers to support him if he agrees to take homosexual interests into account. He goes on to stress how important homosexuals have been within the Nazi party — a strategy which he supposed, mistakenly, would be to their advantage: "I think, Mr. Hitler, that you also, in the interest of your party, can accept these requests, and [I wish] that in your party's platform you will give up any prosecution of homosexual conduct and that, during consultations for the drafting of the new penal code, the deputies of your party will decide to abolish §175. Several hundred thousands of homosexuals will be grateful to you, many of them being members of your own party."[223]

Radszuweit did not receive any reply to his letter. He continued, however, in the same vein right up until his death, on April 3, 1932. One of his last articles, dated March 30, 1932, is an attack against the left for using Röhm's homosexuality to discredit him. After Radszuweit's death, *Die Freundin* stuck to the same line.

The 1932 issues attest to a very clear degradation of the situation of German homosexuals. Suicides are announced one after another, along with stepped-up police activity and the closing of homosexual establishments. On March 8, 1933, a little more than a month after Hitler came to power, *Die Freundin* disappeared.

Die Freundin was not the only lesbian periodical. *Die Blätter für ideale Frauenfreundschaften* (BiF) had the unique quality of being the only lesbian periodical produced entirely by women. The other female publications were produced by male homosexual groups which accepted women but did not make the lesbian cause their priority. Many articles in fact were written by men — the height of irony, and proof that, unfortunately, the lesbian community was sorely lacking in cohesion and organization. And then Selma Engler, the editor of BiF, went to join the team at *Die Freundin*.

Deutsche Freunschaftsverband was reconstituted and in 1928 tried to publish a magazine to compete with *Die Freundin*; *Frauenliebe und Leben (Female Love and Life)* made a brief appearance but did not have much success. The first issue defined the its objectives: "[It aims] to serve as a link between homosexuals and heterosexuals; it will address various topics in the fields of science, art, sport, fashion and personal life, include exchanges of opinion."[224] In fact, unlike *Die Freundin, Frauenliebe und Leben* was aimed not at the emancipated, even militant,

---

223. *Die Freundin*, n° 32, 1931, Letter dated 11 August 1931.
224. Frauenliebe und Leben, n° 1, 1928.

lesbians of Berlin but the modern woman who was interested in female topics, looking for useful recommendations and anecdotes rather than a serious analysis of the lesbian situation in Germany. The newspaper regularly emphasized the things that heterosexuals and lesbians had in common, in order to work toward a future of mutual tolerance and comprehension. The layout was directly derived from that of traditional women's magazines, enlivened here and there with more specific details: photographs of famous lesbians, Sapphic poems, sections on beauty and astrology, exercises designed to help one maintain one's figure,[225] and articles on lesbian life.[226]

Frauenliebe was soon replaced by another magazine, *Flapper*, which was published from October 1930 to October 1932, with a printing of 10,000 copies. Continuing in the same vein as *Frauenliebe*, *Flapper* was addressed to the average woman, emancipated and sympathetic to the feminist movement but not necessarily lesbian.

German organizations like the BfM are evidence of homosexuals' desire to forge a community in the 1920s. While its founder, Friedrich Radszuweit, was adamantly militant, it is by no means clear that all his members and all his readers shared that feeling. Most homosexuals wished above all to discover the new homosexual scene, to find like-minded people, to be able to socialize with their own kind. They were engaged in this effort in varying degrees: the true militants were relatively few, and the list of names of those who took the lead in the main organizations and published articles in the periodicals shows that. Often, the same people were the motivating force behind two or three periodicals and were the leaders of various organizations and clubs. There were many association members, 48,000 for BfM alone, but far fewer than the readership of the magazines and newspapers. However, the German experience, in spite of its limitations, was exceptional and was evidence of an early awakening of a homosexual identity in Europe in the 1920s.

---

225. Dr Agnes Shelter, "Heimgymnastik für lesbische Frauen" ("Gymnastics at home, for lesbians"), *ibid.*, n° 2, 1928.
226. Dr Eugen Gürster, "Hosenrolle und Frauenemanzipation" ("Transvestism and women's emancipation"), *ibid.*

THE GERMAN MODEL AS AN INFLUENCE ON HOMOSEXUAL MOVEMENTS

The German model, although unique, did have some echoes in Europe and the wider world, mostly due to the influence of Magnus Hirschfeld. Indeed, one of his goals had been to create a worldwide organization with the aim of spreading new ideas on sex and psychiatry, of informing the public and securing rights for sexual minorities. The impact of the movement, although limited, allowed for a homosexual awakening in other countries besides Germany and inspired the formation of homosexual movements in some of them, such as England. However, these movements never managed to catch on in a big way and their actions remained largely symbolic.

The World League for Sexual Reform: A Homosexual Internationale?

In 1921, Magnus Hirschfeld launched a series of world congresses for sexual reform, which led to the constitution of a World League for Sexual Reform[227] made up of scientists, doctors, and intellectuals who were anxious to encourage the sharing of new ideas. The homosexual question fit in with the general liberalization of sex that marked the 1920s. Doctors were anxious to improve sexual hygiene, and feminists were calling for gender equality and the recognition of female sexuality, the right to divorce, access to contraception and the liberalization of abortion; and psychoanalysts, educators and theorists of all kinds all had a part to play. The medical influence was considerable, and testifies to the new emergence of doctors interested in sexuality.

The League chose Berlin as the site for its first congress in 1921, evidence of how important the German movement was in the sexual avant-garde in those days. The League published its newspaper and generally met at Hirschfeld's Institut für Sexualwissenschaft. The League was run by an executive central committee composed of the president and five other people. The international committee consisted of deputies (a maximum of three per country) of the various affiliated countries. Three honorary presidents had been appointed: Hirschfeld, Havelock Ellis and Auguste Forel, which in itself makes clear what was the philosophy of the movement. According to Wilhelm Reich, the League included "the foremost sexologists and sexual reformers in the world,"[228] and

---

227. The reports could be published in German, English and French. The League was known as *Weltliga für Sexualreform, World League for Sex Reform* and *Ligue mondiale pour la réforme sexuelle.*

included representatives of the Western capitalist countries and the USSR. Indeed, the list of the international committee for the congress of Copenhagen in 1928 shows that an impressive number of countries sent representatives,[229] many of them celebrities.[230] Membership in the League was open to anyone who "worked for sexual reform on a scientific basis" and to "associations pursuing similar goals." Each association was represented by a member. At its high point, the League had 130,000 members, divided into various affiliated associations. Resolutions were passed by a simple majority. Each individual had a vote; associations could vote for 500 members, but they could not vote for more than five choices. The annual fee was as high as 5 shillings, but members were encouraged to give more, if they could. The League's newspaper, *The Journal for Sexual Reform*, sold for 12 shillings (9 shillings for members).[231]

At the first congress in Berlin, the homosexual question was approached from various angles.[232] Dr. H.C. Rogge (Dutch) gave a talk on "the significance of Steinach's research into the question of pseudo-homosexuality." Dr. C. Müller (German) established the linkage between "Psychoanalysis and sexual reform" and he explained in detail why §175 was harmful: "The paragraph represents a confusion of social and moral law...homosexual activity is not in itself harmful to society; socially harmful excesses can be pursued in court without calling it an attack on morals."[233] Several other speakers addressed the abolition of §175, in particular Kurt Hiller in "The Law and Sexual Minorities." His speech concluded with the words: "§175 is the shame of this century."

The League held its second congress in Copenhagen in 1928. The committee included about thirty members, by then. At this congress, the goals of the

---

228. Cited by Jeffrey Weeks, *Sex, Politics and Society*, London, Longman, 1989, 325 pages, p.185.

229. England, the United States, Canada, Germany, France, Russia, Austria, Switzerland, Czechoslovakia, Italy, Holland, Belgium, Spain, Japan, Norway, Sweden, Denmark, Iceland, Lithuania, Egypt, Liberia, Argentina, Chile, the British Indies and Malaysia.

230. Norman Haire and Dora Russell for England, Margaret Sanger the United States, Max Hodann and Helene Stöcker for Germany, Victor Margueritte for France, Alexandra Kollontaï for Russia.

231. For information on the League, cf. "Constitution of the WLSR," in WLSR, *Sexual Reform Congress, Proceedings of the Second Congress*, Copenhague, 1-5 July 1928, Levin & Munksgaard, 1929, 307 pages.

232. All these presentations are covered in Dr A. Weil (dir.), *Sexualreform und Sexualwissenschaft*, Vorträge gehalten auf der erste internationale Tagung für Sexualreform auf sexualwissenschaftlicher Grundlage in Berlin, Berlin, Julius Püttmann, 1922, 286 pages.

233. *Ibid.*, p.144.

League were explicitly defined and its statutes were revised. The League's goals were expressed in a general resolution adopted at the end of the congress, July 3, 1928:

> The international congress for sexual reform on a scientific basis appeals to legislative bodies, the press and the people of all countries to help create a new social and legal attitude (based on knowledge based on scientific research in sexual biology, psychology and sociology) towards the sexual life of men and women. Currently, the happiness of an enormous number of men and women is sacrificed to false sexual standards, ignorance and intolerance. Therefore it is urgent that many sexual problems (women's place, marriage, divorce, contraception, eugenics, marriage, unmarried motherhood and illegitimate children, prostitution, sexual anomalies, sex murders, sex education)... be re-examined from a judicious and impartial viewpoint and dealt with scientifically.

The League especially called for "political, economic and sexual equality between men and women," "the liberation of marriage (and especially of divorce) from the tyranny of the Church and the State," "the control of conception, so that procreation may be undertaken only voluntarily, and therefore only with the necessary sense of responsibility," "the improvement of the human race through the application of the knowledge of eugenics," "the protection of unmarried mothers and illegitimate children," "a rational attitude toward sexually abnormal people and especially with regard to homosexuals, both men and women," "the prevention of prostitution and venereal diseases." It advocated that "disorders of the sexual instinct [be] considered as essentially pathological phenomena, and not, as in the past, as crimes, vices or sins"; that "only sex acts which compromise the sexual rights of another person [be] regarded as criminal"; that "sexual acts between responsible adults, undertaken by common assent, must be viewed as private matters"; and, finally, that "systematic sex education" be provided.

The League was tackling an ambitious, exhaustive and progressive program. It was connected to a legislative platform. It proposed that sexuality was a special field, subject to comment only from scientists and not the government, the Church or public opinion. Information and education were to be used to bring an end to outdated behaviors, transform people's attitudes and bring about changes in legislation.

The question of homosexuality is explicitly addressed in item 6 and indirectly in item 9. Homosexuality is seen as strictly a private matter; the law has nothing to say, since it does not impinge on the sexual rights of others. Nevertheless, it should be noted that homosexuals are defined as abnormal, which makes it difficult to improve their public image. This formulation is clearly the result of a compromise between the various factions represented in the League.

The World League for Sexual Reform did not stop at voicing pious wishes, expressing its views and publicizing the medical and sociological advances in the field of sexual research. It developed various activities intended to ensure the application of the points of its program, as enumerated in the League's statutes. It was to achieve its goals "by serving as a link between organizations and individuals of all countries which share its point of view," "by disseminating scientific knowledge on sexuality," "as a combatant all the forces and the prejudices that bar the road to a rational attitude with regard to these questions." The principal methods adopted were "to publish or encourage the publishing of technical and popular scientific works aimed at reforming sexuality on a scientific basis," "to produce an international journal on sexual reform," "to conduct an international congress," disseminate "propaganda via conferences," "collect all the laws and statistics relating to sexuality in every country," and to "draft laws and assist in the development of legislation as regards sexuality."

Obviously, the League saw its key activities as being mainly in the field of information and education. An intellectual and scholarly organization, it was geared more to reflection than to action. While the prominence of some of its members gave it some measure of influence at the government level, and while it could contribute to influencing public opinion through its publications and conferences, it remained invisible on the ground. There was no direct pressure paced on the government (petitions, demonstrations, press campaigns).

In this, the League was different from, for example, Wilhelm Reich's Sexpol. Specifically, it did not consider practical measure, for example in the field of contraception. However, it must be said that it was made up of many associations which were, themselves, active on the ground in confronting the daily problems of homosexuals. The League had an international vocation; it had neither the means nor the structures necessary for local action. It was rather a coordinating body that defined a political outlook shared by the various associations working for sexual reform.

The League's third congress was held in London in 1929. It was a great success in terms of audience; 350 deputies took part in it, compared to just 70 deputies who had participated at Copenhagen in 1928. Portugal was the only European country not to send a representative. Several participants testified to the importance of the homosexual question within the League, even if, according to Dora Russell, practically all the presentations were intended to inform or influence public opinion rather than to instigate political action.[234] R.B. Kerr addressed the fundamental topic of "the sexual rights of single people." H.F. Rubinstein gave a talk on "Sex, censure and public opinion in England," dealing with the lawsuit against Radclyffe Hall for *The Well of Loneliness* (1928). His remarks against the Minister for the Interior, Sir William Joynson-Hicks, were particularly severe; it was he who had initiated the condemnation of the book. Rubinstein said that, "Under his government, the administration seems to take as its goal to refuse any public discussion of the problem of homosexuality."[235]

George Ives, in "Taboo attitudes," also underscored the role of the press in the treatment of homosexuality: "There are certain forms of criminal activity that are not reported by the newspapers and of which most decent women are ignorant and prefer to remain ignorant," as the *Evening News* had asserted, for example. During the Radclyffe Hall trial, *Daily Express* had expressed its view by saying: "There are certain vices in the world, which, since they cannot be treated, must be endured, but in silence."[236] The question of "the taboo" seems to have been particularly topical, with Bertrand Russell analyzing "the taboos on sexual knowledge." He charged that "the condemnation of *The Well of Loneliness* brought out into the light of day another aspect of censorship, i.e. any discussion of homosexuality in the form of fiction is illegal in England."[237] Lastly, H.S. Sullivan talked about links between homosexuality and schizophrenia in "Antiquated sexual culture and schizophrenia."

By the time of the fourth congress, held in Vienna in 1930, the committee had 2,000 members. Homosexuality was addressed in several forums; Dr. Fritz Wittels, in "Sexual Distress," explained the increase in homosexuality in Germany as a consequence of the moral rigidity of German women.[238] Ernst Toller explored the relationship between "Detention and homosexuality," Elgar

---

234. Dora Russell, *The Tamarisk Tree, My Quest for Liberty and Love*, London, 1975, 304 pages, p.218.

235. WLSR, *Sexual Reform Congress*, London, 8-14 September 1929, Kegan Paul, 1930, 670 pages, p.308-309.

236. *The Evening News*, 12 November 1920, *Daily Express*, 5 September 1928, cited *ibid.*, p.342. George Ives also cites the *Daily News*, 25 August 1927, the *Pall Mall Gazette*, 16 July 1921, the *Star*, 7 August 1927, the *Daily Express*, 8 September 1927.

237. *Ibid.*, p.401.

238. WLSR, *Sexual Reform Congress*, Vienna, 16-23 September 1930, Vienna, Elbemühl, 1931, 693 pages, p.45.

Kern spoke about "the difficulty of living in women's prisons." Finally, Sidonie Fürst addressed the "Problem of the unmarried woman" and Dr. Hermann Frischhauf dealt with "Some psychoanalytical experiments on young sexual delinquents."

The last congress was supposed to take place in 1932 in Moscow; that was cancelled, and it was held finally in Brno. The 1933 congress was scheduled to be held in Chicago but it did not take place, for the accession of the Nazis in Germany dealt the organization a fatal blow. The goal of the League had been to convince governments of the rationality of sexual reform; with Europe facing economic depression and a gathering threat from fascism, these concerns paled by comparison.

The League was finally dissolved in 1935 by Norman Haire and Dr. Leunbach, after Hirschfeld's death. It had succeeded, however, in promoting a new outlook in many different countries, and it had served as a forum for the discussion of homosexuality as well as contraception and divorce. Reformist, but progressive, it contributed to changing public opinion. It also inspired national initiatives elsewhere, particularly in Great Britain.

A Lackluster Performance on the Part of English Activists

Toward the end of the 19th century, some marginal homosexual experiments had been tried in England. In the 1890s, George Ives founded the order of Chaeronea,[239] a homosexual secret society whose purpose was to organize a "homosexual resistance" and to promote reforms. Lawrence Housman was involved — a friend of Carpenter and Wilde; and Montague Summers, future Secretary of the homosexuality sub-committee of the British Society for the Study of Sex Psychology (BSSP); John Gambrill; Francis Nicolson — treasurer of the BSSP; and A.E. Housman, brother of Lawrence, an academic and poet. This initiative did not achieve much. English homosexual militancy was characterized in the 1920s by its great discretion. If one excludes the outstanding figure of Edward Carpenter, one finds few remarkable personalities. The only homosexual movement, the BSSP, would have liked to become the British equivalent of the WhK but it was too timid to have any real impact.

---

239. On Ives and the Order of Chaeronea, see Jeffrey Weeks, *Coming Out. Homosexual Politics in Britain from the 19th Century to the Present*, London, Quartet Books, 1979, 278 pages, p.118-127.

Edward Carpenter, socialist utopian and homosexual

The leading English homosexual activist from the end of the 19th century to the early 1930s was, without a doubt, Edward Carpenter (1844-1929).[240] Carpenter was born in Brighton into a well-to-do family. In his autobiography, *My Days and Dreams*, he breaks his life into four parts: from 1844 to 1864, he lived in Brighton in a world that tried to be fashionable and which detested.[241] He was at Cambridge from 1864 to 1874l then, from 1874 to 1881, he was lecturing in the north of England. Beginning in 1881, he devoted himself to the working class and his research on homosexuality. He noted that he could trace his passionate desire for a male relationship back to his earliest childhood, but that this desire could not be expressed, indeed, it did not have any chance of being expressed.[242]

Carpenter's sexual reformism falls under the broader rubric of a utopian socialism. The sexual question fits into his logic: civilization (defined by access to private property) "disintegrated and corrupted man" from the inside, "and destroyed the unity of his nature."[243] To build a better world, then, would require restoring man to his real nature by placing the body and sex back at the center of human concerns.

During the 1880s, Carpenter distinguished himself by his defense of feminism, more than anything else, and by his role within the socialist movement in Sheffield. By 1890, the sexual question came to the fore, as much for personal reasons (his relationship with George Merrill began in 1891) as political. His meeting with a wise Indian, "Gnani," revealed to him the Hindus' more tolerant attitude toward sexuality and he wanted to publicize it. In 1894, he published three essays entitled, *Sex Love, Woman,* and *Marriage,* at Manchester Labour Press. In 1896, *Love's Coming of Age* came out, including a chapter on the "intermediate sex." It had to be pulled off the market, given the repercussions of the Oscar Wilde trial. In 1902, he published *Iolaus: An Anthology of Friendship, A Collection of*

---

240. Long forgotten by history, Edward Carpenter's role in the history of gay and the socialist movements has been rediscovered. Homage was paid to him in 1944 on the centenary of his birth and articles were published in the *Time Literary Supplement, The Spectator, The Listener,* and *The New Statesman.* His book *Towards Democracy* was reissued. E.M. Forster gave a talk on BBC on 25 September 1944 But, these efforts toward rehabilitation remained without effect until the end of the sixties.

241. Cited by Jeffrey Weeks, *Coming Out, op. cit.,* p.68.

242. Edward Carpenter, *Selected Writings,* vol.1, *Sex,* reedited., London, Gay Men Press, 1984, 318 pages, p.83.

243. Cited by Jeffrey Weeks, *Coming Out, op. cit.,* p.71.

Essays on Homoeroticism; in 1908, *The Intermediate Sex*; and in 1912, *Intermediate Types among Primitive People*. Several essays on Walt Whitman and Shelley could be added to this list.

The writings of his friend Havelock Ellis, and of sexologists like Otto Weininger and Magnus Hirschfeld, influenced Carpenter in the development of his theory, with elements derived from Lamarckian philosophy, Hindu mysticism and the poetry of Walt Whitman incorporated as well. Much of this writing seems very dated, today, but it was highly innovative at the time. Carpenter was the first to call for a liberation of sexual morals and he influenced several generations of readers. What made him unique among his contemporaries was that he distinguished sex from procreation. At the same time, while not neglecting the sentimental aspect, he maintained that it was vital to rehabilitate the physical pleasure of sex in order to remove shame from the act of love. In *The Intermediate Sex*, he expounded his theory on homosexuality. He refers to Ulrichs's idea ("the heart of a woman in the body of a man)" and refutes the notion that homosexuality is a sign of degeneracy. Like others, he seeks to classify "uranians" in several categories. He distinguishes extreme cases ("queens," etc.), which he suggests are not very representative of "average" homosexuals who, he says, are not recognizable physically but who are characterized by a greater sensitivity and a greater emotional complexity (as far as males), and (as far as females) a penchant for order and a strong sense of organization. Homosexuality may come in any degree, but it is necessarily instinctive, congenital and ineradicable. For Carpenter, homosexuality can only be "acquired" if the person is carried away by curiosity, lubricity or a lack of women. However, in his view bisexuality would become standard in the new society. He also strives to demonstrate that uranians are positive forces within a nation and he emphasizes their contribution as inventors, professors and artists.

Carpenter shows his limitations when it comes to female sexuality. He declares that the division of labor between the sexes is the result of biological differences between men and women; that woman is more primitive, more sentimental, more intuitive and closer to nature than is man. Nonetheless, he advocates social and economic independence for women and calls for a reform of marriage and for birth control options to be made available.

Carpenter would not have had such a great and long-lasting effect if he had been only a theorist. He became a model, a "prophet" for many homosexuals because he practiced what he preached. In fact, his private life is closely connected with his writings. Constantly seeking a loving relationship that would satisfy him fully, he suffered long years of frustration. After various attempts with craftsmen or Socialists (George Hukin, George Adams, Bob Muirhead and James Brown), he met George Merrill, in 1890, in a railway compartment. They never parted. Merrill was twenty years old. He grew up in a working-class family in Sheffield. He was sexually confident and liberated, but his rather vulgar speech and manners shocked Carpenter's friends. Beyond a certain paternalism on behalf of Carpenter, their relationship rested on a sincere and mutual affection. After a few years, Merrill moved to Millthorpe, Carpenter's home. The notion of two homosexuals living together more or less openly did not sit well with their neighbors, or even their friends, but Millthorpe took on a kind of symbolic luster as a kind of homosexual paradise. The property became a place of pilgrimage for all kinds of working class and progressive homosexual movements who sought to win Carpenter over to their cause. The reception was always very cordial, be it for personalities like Goldsworthy Lowes Dickinson, political friends like Edith Lees and Olive Schreiner, or the isolated homosexual in search of a guide.

Scandal was never far from their door and Carpenter had to be mindful of his reputation. In 1909, he was attacked by the puritanical M.D. O'Brien, a member of the Liberty and Property Defence League, which published a lampoon entitled "Socialism and Infamy: The Homogenic or Comrade Love Exposed. An Open Letter in Plain Words for a Socialist Prophet." He alleged that there was an international Whitmanian plot afoot that intended to weaken the moral fabric of society.[244]

---

244. Cited by Jeffrey Weeks, *ibid.*, p.81. A police dossier revealed the existence of an inquest on Carpenter; many witnesses provided staggering testimony concerning sexual advances supposedly made by Merrill. A young man who spent several weeks with Carpenter revealed that he tried three times to have sexual relations with him and confessed to being a homosexual. Given these different statements, the Procurator drew the following conclusions: "Edward Carpenter is one of the leaders of a secret organization that is political in nature, whose members are linked by homosexual practices"; "the leaders of this secret and criminal organization have as their goal to destroy civilization"; they recognize themselves by a secret sign: "The hand is placed on the thigh, and pushed strongly." Beyond the anecdotal aspect of the famous homosexual plot, which here takes on a particularly ridiculous nature, it is hard to understand why, given the existence of such a file, the police remained inactive. It is possible that Carpenter's links to socialist movements raised questions about his real goals. Rather than indict him on morality charges, the procurator may have sought to pin him with a more serious crime — national treason, perhaps. Carpenter's book, *Homogenic Love*, was withdrawn from sale, but the sanctions didn't spread to the author (HO 144/1043/183473).

Carpenter's influence can be seen in the works of the Bloomsbury group, which placed individual relations at the center of its concerns, in the philosophy of homosexual novel *Maurice* by E.M. Forster, and even in D.H. Lawrence's writings. Robert Graves wrote to Carpenter from Charterhouse to tell him that *Iolaus* and *The Intermediate Sex* had enabled him to understand his true nature. Carpenter's influence was also considerable on the British Labour and Socialist movements, the feminists, and even abroad.[245] And last but not least, Carpenter served as president of the BSSP in 1914.

"British Society for the Study of Sex Psychology" (BSSP): A timid reformism

Carpenter was active in the only English homosexual movement of the 1920s, the British Society for the Study of Sex Psychology (BSSP), which was founded in July 1914 by former members of Chaeronea. Lawrence Housman was named president, and Edward Carpenter was appointed honorary president for life. The very neutrality of the name shows how hard the group tried to be discreet. Far from flaunting itself as a homosexual association, the BSSP sought to hide its affiliation and dissimulated even its ties with the WhK. In fact, Magnus Hirschfeld had played an essential role in launching the society. In 1912, he had created a British affiliate of the WhK and, the following year, had come to make a speech at the 14th International Medical Congress, held in London. He created a sensation there by exhibiting various diagrams and photographs of men and women who "proved" the existence of "an intermediate sex." This conference was a revelation for many of the doctors who were present, for sexuality and above all homosexuality were very little studied. The BSSP was founded partly to cure this ignorance.

The society defined its activities and goals in one of a publication entitled, "Policy and Principles," wherein it sets itself the task of "the study of problems and questions relating to sexual psychology, in their medical, legal and sociological aspects."[246] Additional aims were to educate the public on sexuality and thus to pave the way for the necessary reforms.

---

245. Cited by Jeffrey Weeks, *Coming Out*, op. cit., p.80-82. The publication de *Love's Coming of Age* led, for example, to the formation in Italy of a group dubbed the "Union of young men," which discussed and reflected on problems of sexuality.

246. *Policy and Principles*, BSSP, n° 1, 1915, 14 pages, p.3. On la BSSP, see aussi Jeffrey Weeks, *Coming Out*, op. cit., p.128-143.

Three working groups were formed. The first was focused on sex education, the second on sexual inversion and the third on heterosexual problems. A private library for members was established; and a sub-committee for libraries to tried to gain access to the British Library's catalogue of "private matters," which included a list of works kept out of circulation due to their sexual content. Monthly talks were held for the public at large, throughout the 1920s, and 17 conferences were published in the form of bulletins. Various subjects were addressed, but the study of homosexuality remained the central concern. The first bulletin stated the question of homosexuality clearly, criticizing the conservative approach adopted by the medical, government and society milieux, which basically refused to tackle the subject. The second one announced the BSSP's stand in favor of homosexuality, with the publication of "The Social Problem of Sexual Inversion," an abridgement of Hirschfeld's famous text, "Was soll das Volk vom dritten Geschlecht wissen?" The abridged version recommended the liberalization of social and legal attitudes with respect to homosexuality, noting that there were efforts underway in Germany to modify the law and the criminal code but offering the opinion that England would not be ready for such a move until homosexuality was better understood; "[t]herefore, our goal is to discuss and elucidate this question."[247] Several pamphlets were distributed on the subject of homosexuality.[248] A special sub-committee was created and speeches were given by various public figures; Ives, or example, explored "the Greco-Roman view of youth" and "the condition of the adolescent."

What influence did the BSSP have? In July 1920, it had 234 members, which seems to have been its average size. Up to forty or fifty people might show up at the meetings and BSSP publications were distributed widely. Still, it is quite unlikely that it succeeded in reaching the general public; its influence was mainly within the progressive intellectual milieux. G.B. Shaw, E.M. Forster, Maurice Eden and Cedar Paul (defenders of birth control, working within the Independent Labour Party, then the Communist Party), Vyvyan Holland (the son of Oscar Wilde), and the dramatic author Harley Granville-Barker were members. Radclyffe Hall, Una Troubridge, Bertrand and Dora Russell were very much involved.[249] The society also had contacts abroad, with Hirschfeld and his

---

247. The Social Problem of Sexual Inversion, BSSP, n° 2, 1915, 12 pages, p.3.

248. Lawrence Housman, *The Relation of Fellow-Feeling*, BSSP, n°4; Harold Picton, *The Morbid, the Abnormal and the Personal*, BSSP, n°12; Edward Carpenter, *Some Friends of Walt Whitman*, BSSP, n°13; F.A.E. Crews, *Sexuality and Intersexuality*, BSSP, n° 14; H.D. Jennings White, *Psychological Causes of Homoeroticism and Inversion*, BSSP, n°15.

colleagues, of course, but also with Margaret Sanger in the United States, the Chicago Society for Human Rights, and the French Society of Sexology. Alexandra Kollontaï, the Russian feminist, was a member of the BSSP's honorary committee in the 1920s. Thus, the BSSP has a mixed record; it managed to spark some discussions of homosexuality in a difficult environment and it followed a cautious course, looking to educate society in this area. However, it cannot claim to have made any practical difference. The BSSP stuck to a line that was reformist rather than radical, and it shied away from militant action. Nevertheless, one might agree with Jeffrey Weeks in noting that until the beginning of the 1930s, it was the principal British organization to deal with homosexuality, and that, in itself, is a kind of achievement.[250]

THE FRENCH WAY: INDIVIDUALISM COMES UP SHORT

Unlike Germany and England, France did not experience the formation of homosexual movements in this time period. Perhaps the tolerant legal context accounts for their reticence with regard to associations — there were no repressive laws on the books that required a concerted fight; but French individualism also played a role. The communal approach, more typical for the Anglo-Saxon or Germanic countries, was not part of the French make up. Asserting homosexual rights was thus left to a few key figures, who personally identified with the homosexual cause.

Marcel Proust, Witness of Days Long Past

This is not the place to embark on a complete analysis of Proustian sexuality, but we can take a look at the overall influence his work may have had on the perception of homosexuality. His *Sodom and Gomorrah* can be considered as the starting point in the debate on homosexuality in France.[251] Proust does not

---

249. Edith Sitwell refused to support it, declaring that she would never have thought that there was any need to encourage them [homosexuals], and [that] indeed we have more than enough of them now, without making any new ones," (cited by Philip Hoare, *Serious Pleasures: The Life of Stephen Tennant*, London, Penguin, 1992, 463 pages, p.151).

250. Jeffrey Weeks, *Coming Out, op. cit.*, p.137.

251. For everything concerning how *La Recherche* was received, I relied on the fundamental work by Eva Ahlstedt, *La Pudeur en crise. Un aspect de l'accueil « A la recherche du temps perdu » de Marcel Proust, 1913-1930*, Paris, Jean Touzot, 1985, 276 pages.

reveal the central topic of his work in any brutal way;[252] homosexual allusions are sprinkled throughout *Swann's Way, Within a Budding Grove*, and *Guermantes*, but they drew little attention. In *Swann*, for example, there is the Sapphic scene between Mlle Vinteuil and her friend. The only reviewer to comment on it was Willy, who alluded to it in *Le Sourire*, June 18, 1914, and then with delight:

> And mind that you keep this away from young ladies, if you know any who have retained their innocence — anything can happen — Proust shows us a sentimental sadist, almost a child, moving in with an older friend, a vicious alexandrine who enjoys (*inter alia*) a bad reputation, refuses to close the shutters when they play their games, and says: 'If anybody should see us, it will be even better.' She ends up picking up the portrait of her complaisant friend's papa off the piano and spitting in his face.[253]

Within a Budding Grove appeared in July 1919 and won the Goncourt prize on December 10. In *L'Action française* of December 12, Leon Daudet compares Proust to the great moralists. Most of the reviews are favorable. *The Guermantes Way, Part I*, was published in autumn 1920. Paul Souday, in the November 4, 1920 issue of *Le Temps*, refers to "a nervous aesthete, a little bit morbid, almost feminine." Still, there was nothing to indicate what the later reactions would be. The critics were mostly preoccupied with questions of form and style, and Proust's talent as a moralist, rather than any hint of immorality.

It was only upon the publication of *Sodom and Gomorrah* that the truth burst out into the open when the character of the baron de Charlus, partially based on the count Robert de Montesquiou, a Parisian dandy and notorious homosexual, was revealed in full light. Even then, the critics hesitated to tackle the subject head-on. *Sodom and Gomorrah I* followed *The Guermantes Way, Part II*, and Souday, for example, devoted nine-tenths of his May 12, 1921 review to the first volume. Others were more aggressive. Gustave Binet-Valmer,[254] in *Coemedia*, May 22, 1921, went on the attack:

---

252. He wrote to his publishers in 1912 to warn them that it would be an "indecent" book with characters who were "pederasts." However, he insisted that this aspect of the book be kept secret until the final revelation.

253. Cited by Eva Ahlstedt, *La Pudeur en crise, op. cit.*, p.30.

254. Binet-Valmer, a novelist and journalist, had himself published a homosexual novel, *Lucien*, which was quite a success. He was also an ardent patriot, decorated during the war, and vice-president, then president, of the Ligue des chefs de section, an association of war veterans.

In 1910, disgusted by the morals which I saw being promoted in certain salons, I imagined what a great man might suffer, whose son would bear the burden of too sumptuous a heredity. In the example here at hand, I have frequently stated my admiration for the meticulous genius of Mr. Marcel Proust... but if this monument is to be crowned by four volumes which study sexual inversion, I think that this is hardly the proper time... we do not want any more of the aberrations of a false aristocracy (and international, at that) to invade our literature. I detest snobs.

Many publications considered it prudent to warn the reader. *L'Action française* of August 6 noted: "Let us mention, finally, that in its last pages the Proust book introduces the first chapter of the continuation. Its title is such that we hesitate to print it in these pages, never mind the subject matter. What a rage to defy all conventions!"[255]

Even so, not all the critics were unfavorable. Paul de Bellen, in *La Libre Parole*, July 1, was very positive, but his position did not have anything to do with acceptance of homosexuality: "To repress vice, it is necessary to have the courage to denounce and show it as being odious." It was left to Roger Allard, in the September 1 *NRF*, to emphasize the innovative aspect of the subject. He saw this as "a date in literary history," which "breaks a spell, the aesthetic spell of sexual inversion."

With *Sodom and Gomorrah II*, published in May 1922, reviewers had to stake their positions. It became difficult to avoid the subject and, in fact, there was certainly no "conspiracy of silence" regarding this work. Still, some critics worked brilliantly in the sphere of euphemism and allusion, and often relied on their readers' imagination to appreciate what was going on.[256] Proust was even congratulated on the absence of obscene details. Souday, in *Le Temps* of May 12, 1922, noted that the book is more discreet than its title suggests:

> Mr. Proust avoids making us eye-witnesses to repugnant scenes. He does not directly describe the corrupt excesses of these perverts, but studies their psychology through their vice. This is very bold, and in essence not too interesting, but is useless rather than truly scandalous. Moreover, in

---

255. Signed "Orion," the collective pseudonym of Eugène Marsan and Lucien Dubech.
256. Only Binet-Valmer, in *Coemedia*, Roger Allard in *NRF* and André Germain in *Les Écrits nouveaux* used the term "inversion."

spite of the rather off-putting title, Proust has taken care not to devote all seven or eight hundred pages to this antiseptic and repellent study, which in sum remains episodic in this volume and all its precursors. And indeed, that is all that it deserves: it is even more than one would have wished.

In fact, Souday, like many others, admires Proust *in spite* of his chosen subject matter, which interests him not at all — it seems shocking and repugnant to him, and he concedes to refer to it only indirectly, allusively and morally, i.e. allowing the judgment of vice through the description of the hero's misfortunes. The work may have raised questions about Proust's objectivity, but no one made any allusion to his private life. At this time, only Proust's closest circle of friends was aware of his homosexuality and few suspected him of having direct involvement in the subject matter. Rumors about his sexual orientation may have been whispered here and there, but were made public only after his death.

Proust died on November 18, 1922 and the remainder of his writings were published posthumously. From this point onward, the attacks became more and more acute, against both his work and his person. Lucien Dubech authored a particularly violent article published on April 25, 1923, in the *Revue critique des idées et des livres*, asking: "Do You Read Marcel Proust?" He himself did not read him; he compared his writings to pornography, and suggested that they reflected a "foreign" influence.

The Captive was published in February 1924. Some reviews were positive, especially Souday's, but Franc-Nohain, in *L'Écho de Paris*, sees Proust as "a sick person" and "a pornographer." *Le Mercure de France* took an original stance; Raphaël Cor, in an article signed "Bergotte," calls for tolerance for homosexuals. It cannot be insignificant that this gesture comes in connection with a volume dealing with lesbians, a less shocking subject for the public than male homosexuality. *Albertine disparue* (1926) (English translations exist, entitled *The Fugitive*, or *The Sweet Cheat Gone*) was not so well-received: Proust was not forgiven for the sudden "inversion" of Saint-Loup.

The release of this title more or less coincided with the first rumblings about Albertine's "real" gender and Proust's morals. The year 1926 was a defining year for homosexuality in literature in any case: Gide brought out *Les Faux-Monnayeurs (The Counterfeits)* and drew thunderbolts from Souday. *Time Regained* was first published in serial in the NRF in 1926, but arrived in the bookshops only in November 1927. The book was greeted as a great literary event. By now, one could speak of homosexuality directly; the debate was focused on the moral question and how it related to the arts. Proust's talent was broadly recognized, but the question of inversion continued to pose a problem. In fact, he was condemned for having broached the subject, and he was held responsible for starting a "homosexual trend" in literature. Some remained resolutely hostile, such Louis Reynaud in *La Crise de notre littérature* (1929): "Proust, we repeat, is a sick and depraved intellectual. He brings us the feelings of a sick and abnormal being, a very particular psychology case from which others will find perhaps nothing worth retaining."

Thus, studying how Proust's writings were received in the French press makes it plain what a fundamental role *Remembrance* played in instigating a public debate on homosexuality in France. Before him, the subject was scarcely discussed. His example opened the door to homosexual writings and discussions. Even if he had relatively few readers, the polemic reached such scope that the subject matter became quite public. Simply mentioning his name or his works was enough to evoke certain images, among cultivated people. But, how original was Proust when it comes to homosexuality and what was his impact on the French homosexual population?

Indeed, if one studies the description of homosexuality as it is given throughout *Remembrance*, Proust seems to be firmly rooted in times gone by. His experience of inversion is typical of the end of the 19th century. Despite the "enlightened" medical theories, it was still charged with a very heavy sense of shame. According to George Painter,[257] Proust was probably not conscious of his inclinations until the age of twenty, when he experienced ardent friendships for platonic comrades alternating with crushes on girls.

His relationship with Reynaldo Hahn marked a decisive stage in the identifying process; he understood that his friendships were only the sublimation of a repressed desire and he also discovered shame: he had to lie to his mother, to hide a truth that could have killed her. Thus, in Proust, one does not find acceptance of homosexuality — much less homosexual pride. The slow maturation of his characters seems modeled on his own painful process, and seems to be an ultimate fight to deny the obvious and to try to stick to an ideal and fictitious normality, precisely that of the narrator. The evolution of Proust's sexuality shows a progressive loss of illusions in love and a turn toward carnal satisfactions; by the same token, his search for an ideal friend gradually dissolves into a

---

257. George D. Painter, *Marcel Proust* [1959], Paris, Mercure de France, reedited 1985, 2 vol., 464 and 515 pages.

search for a sexual partner. The young aristocrats whom he admired, like Antoine Bibesco, were replaced by young working class boys, like Alfred Agostinelli, and then gradually gave way in the final years to the professionals at Albert Le Cuziat's secluded house, the hôtel Marigny, rue de l'Arcade in Paris. This gradual decline looks like a metaphor of Proustian homosexuality: inversion is vice, and it can only turn out badly. Any attempt to color it with noble and generous feelings is only a fraud; it must don the face of brutal sex, unhealthy perversion, prostitution. The reader also suffers one disillusionment after another, as the characters with whom he sympathizes plunge deeper and deeper into the abysses of vice and corruption. The final revelations of Albertine's double life seem to mark the ultimate stage of a reality test: even the charming lesbians prove they are damned; their innocent games give way to perversions equal to those of Charlus and their degradation is illustrated perfectly by Vinteuil's profaning of the photograph. The homosexual commits his first crime by betraying his parents; this original sin cannot be erased. There is a kind of predestination in this: born into vice, the invert has no choice but to show his vice.

Thus, as innovative as Proust's work may be, from the point of view of homosexual theory it remains more representative of late-19th-century thought than that of the inter-war period. His decision to make the narrator heterosexual may be logical from the point of view of his work, but it sets up a certain confusion as to whether the author himself is homosexual. Proust transcribed, in a striking yet fictionalized way, the usual line used by sexologists on those rare occasions when they dared to touch upon the subject of homosexuality. The meeting between Charlus and Jupien, which serves as a revelation to the narrator, reads like a botany or zoology treatise. Homosexuality is compared to "an incurable disease" and inverts are constantly associated with Jews, whose dark destiny and bad reputation they share. Proust incorporates a number of other prejudices that were in vogue early in the century, like the readiness to charge people with treason and conspiracy. In his anxiety to provide a meticulous description of the homosexual world, he gives examples that end up looking more like a list of cautions. He reinforces the notion that homosexuals are very numerous but go undetected by the ordinary population — an impression that is confirmed as revelations mount, indicating that most of the characters in the novel, who had hitherto been above suspicion, exhibit dubious proclivities: "...these exceptional beings, for which we feel so sorry, are actually a whole crowd, as will be seen in the course of this work, and for a reason which will be revealed only at the end; and they themselves complain of being rather too numerous than too few."[258]

Proust heads off any accusations in advance; he neither encourages nor supports the formation of a homosexual movement, because he is persuaded that it must fail.

> [B]ut one would in any case like to avoid making the same disastrous mistake that happened when the Zionist movement was encouraged, by which I mean creating a sodomist movement and rebuilding Sodom. The sodomists, as soon as they got there, would leave the city again so as not to be considered part of it; they would take wives and entertain mistresses in other cities, where they would enjoy every sort of proper entertainment. They would only show up in Sodom when they were in dire need, the way hunger drives the wolf out of the woods — in other words, things would continue to go on as they do now in London, Berlin, Rome, Petrograd and Paris.[259]

Proust's severity misled some of his critics. The chapter on "Sodom" was considered "moral" and "scholarly." Jacques Rivière himself, who did not yet know Proust's true nature, was delighted by the tone of the work: "I have heard a distorted notion of love being promulgated too often not to feel a delightful sense of ease in hearing someone speak about it in such a healthy, balanced way as you."[260] André Gide harshly judged Proust's descriptions, which he felt painted too nice a picture of vice, uncontrolled passion and excessive images of perversion: "We have yet, this evening, to speak of hardly anything but uranism; he says he reproaches the 'indecision' which led him to round out the heterosexual part of his book by transposing 'to the girls' side' all that his homosexual memories contained that was gracious, tender and charming, so that he had nothing left for Sodom but the grotesque and the contemptible. But he takes great offense when I say that he seems to have wanted to stigmatize uranism; he protests; and I understand finally that what we find deplorable, a laughing matter or an abomination, does not appear repugnant to him."[261] Gide is also hostile to Proust's Platonic references, which equate homosexuals with the "original androgyne":

---

258. Marcel Proust, *Sodome et Gomorrhe* I, *A la recherche du temps perdu*, Paris, Gallimard, coll. "Bibl. de la Pléiade," 1988, t.III, p.32.

259. *Ibid.*, p.33.

260. Cited by George D. Painter, *Marcel Proust, op. cit.*, p.388.

261. André Gide, *Journal, 1887-1925*, Paris, Gallimard, coll. "Bibl. de la Pléiade," 1996, 1 840 pages, May 1921, p.1126.

"Even worse: this offending of the truth is likely to please everyone: the hetero-sexual, whose warnings it justifies and whose loathings it flatters; and the others, who will now have an alibi and who will benefit by their scant resem-blance to those whom he portrays. In short, given the general tendency to cow-ardice, I do not know any writing which is more likely than Proust's *Sodom* to encourage wrong-headed thinking."[262]

In fact, it was the "aunts'" tragic destiny that first fascinated Proust, their mystery, their flagrant perversion. A standardized homosexuality, uniform, undifferentiated, and militant like the Germans', managing to integrate into society more or less, would have interested him very little. His work has the merit of crudely exposing to the eyes of the public, for the first time, the vicissi-tudes of homosexual life, its codes and its pitfalls, its passions and its dramas, its flaws and its beauties.

Proust, a guilt-ridden homosexual, persuaded that he belonged to "an accursed race," could not propagate a positive image of homosexuality, much less pass a precursor of homosexual militancy. According to Gaston Gallimard, André Gide accused Proust of "setting the question back by fifty years." Proust is said to have answered: "For me, there is no question — only characters."[263] Still, Proust's extraordinary impact on French public opinion is undeniable: for the first time, inversion became a trendy topic, one that could be discussed, com-mented on, and analyzed — even if not necessarily in positive terms. And that was a fantastic revelation.

André Gide, A Militant Homosexual?

André Gide, constantly cited by French homosexuals, is a very ambiguous figure. Indeed, just like Proust, Gide built his view of homosexuality on his own personal experience. Gide was not a militant homosexual in a strict sense: he did not fight for homosexual rights, and he did not found any movement or create a magazine for them. However, by agreeing to go public on his sexuality, by pub-lishing *Corydon*, by publicly acknowledging his pederasty, he found himself in the position of a spokesman or a representative for French homosexuals. He neither wished for it nor saw it coming; but it fell to him because, at least at first, there really was no one else who might have filled such a role. As a consequence, French homosexuals identified with Gide's thoughts on a wide scale, despite the

---

262. *Ibid.*, 2 December 1921, p.1143.
263. Cited by Marcel Erman, *Marcel Proust*, Paris, Fayard, 1994, 286 pages, p.227.

fact that his ideas were quite specific and not readily applicable to most of them. Moreover, this completely eliminated lesbians from the field of reflection, as they were of no concern to Gide. Proust had briefly brought the Gomorrahns out of the closet; Gide sent them back.

Like Proust, Gide had a "before" and "after."[264] Before *Corydon*, Gide had a reputation as an austere moralist, which he owed to his Protestant origins and his interest in ethical problems. The book *Strait is the Gate (La Porte étroite)* (1909) was even considered rigid, cold, and depressing due to its merciless vision of Christian morals. *The Immoralist (L'Immoraliste)* (1902) was very well-received and Michel's attraction to young boys was prudently left unmentioned, except by Rachilde, who made witty allusions to Gide's sexuality in the July 1902 *Le Mercure de France*. *Saül*, presented at the Vieux-Colombier Theater in 1922, drew a sharper reaction. Several critics reproached Gide for choosing an improper subject, but their tone remained moderate — since the episode was drawn from the Bible. It was *Corydon* (1924) that definitively established Gide as a homosexual writer.

Since 1895, Gide had been keeping a file entitled "Pederasty," in which he collected information on the subject with the aim of writing a scholarly work on the question. It was apparently in 1908, during a trip to Bagnols and England with Ghéon, Copeau and Schlumberger that he wrote the first two dialogues. On May 22, 1911, a first version of *Corydon*, including the first two dialogues and part of the third, was published anonymously in Bruges under the name of C.R.D.N. Only twelve copies were printed. On March 5, 1920, 21 copies were published anonymously. It was only in May 1924 that *Corydon* appeared in its final form.

In his journal, Gide explains that he delayed publishing this text for so long in order to avoid disappointing those who were dear to him. Now, he feels more mature, more sure in his mind, and ready to reveal his thoughts. He also intends to respond to *Sodom and Gomorrah*, which irritated him deeply, and to Remy de Gourmont's book, *Natural Philosophy of Love (Physique de l'amour)*. An essay on the sexual instinct, published in 1903, included a chapter on "the question of aberrations." His principal influences were Hirschfeld, Moll, Krafft-Ebing, Raffalovitch, Havelock Ellis and Freud. He feels an urgent need to reveal to the world his true nature, even if it means ruining his reputation: — "I cannot wait any more... I have to obey an internal need, more imperative than anything! Under-

---

264. Here I refer to Eva Ahlstedt's book, *André Gide et le Débat sur l'homosexualité*, Paris, Jean Touzot, 1994, 291 pages.

stand me. I need, need, to finally dissipate this cloud of lies in which I have hidden since my youth, since my childhood... I am choking in it!"[265]

The work is composed of four dialogues, in which Dr. Corydon[266] encounters a heterosexual visitor, who plays innocent. The first two dialogues discuss homosexuality in nature, and the latter two speculate about its social consequences. In fact, this fundamental work sheds light on both André Gide's personality and the French model of homosexuality.

The Eulenburg trial serves as a pretext for the meeting between Corydon and his interlocutor. He has known Corydon for a long time, but he had kept his distance out of moral compunction. Now, he decides to question him in order to understand uranism better. His prejudices are clear from the very start of the visit: he is surprised not to find the apartment decorated in a more feminine style, but notes the presence of a photograph reminiscent of Michelangelo and a portrait of Walt Whitman. Gide uses this character as a "herald of normality." Instinctively recoiling from homosexuality, he grudgingly admits the cogency of certain arguments. He learns to understand Corydon better, in the course of the discussion, respects him and admires his courage, but he cannot overcome his innate hostility. He learns tolerance, but not approval.

In the first dialogue, Corydon expresses his desire to write a "Defense of pederasty"; he wishes there were a martyr for the cause, "somebody who would advance ahead of the attack; who, without fanfare, without bravado, would brave reprobation and insult; or better, someone of such prestige and probity that reprobation would be forestalled..."[267] Here, we recognize the ambition of Gide, himself.

Corydon then gives a dramatic recollection of his first awakening. He rejected overtures of love from his girlfriend's brother, who then commits suicide. This drama led him to look into the subject. Gide, like his contemporaries, intended to pique his readers' interest and, to get around any sense of distaste or contempt, drew on their compassion and pity. However, this introduction is misleading: Gide — and Corydon — are not positioned as victims. They are proud of their orientation and are rather persuaded of their superiority.

---

265. Cited by Roger Martin du Gard, *Notes sur André Gide (1913-1951)*, in *Œuvres complètes*, Paris, Gallimard, coll. "Bibl. de la Pléiade," 1983, t.II, 1 432 pages, p.1375.

266. Corydon was the name of one young shepherd who was in love with another, in Virgil.

267. André Gide, *Corydon* [1924], Paris, Gallimard, reedited 1991, 149 pages, p.20.

Corydon immediately drew lines. Now, there was only talk of "normal pederasts" and not, like the doctors, of "shameful uranists," plaintive and ill. Already, a large portion of homosexuals were judged and kicked out. Gide's dialogues relate only to his own passion: pederasty. On other matters, he shared the prejudices of heterosexuals. Clearly, such a limitation played a fundamental part in the definition of homosexuality in France. Unlike in Germany, which had militant movements for the great mass of homosexuals as well as for pederasts (Der Eigene), the former had no real defenders in France.

Gide was the proponent of an elitist, aristocratic, intellectual homosexuality. His model was Platonic, his references, Greek. To explain the origins of homosexuality, Corydon plunges into natural history first, as medical works do. Then he attacks the notion that homosexuality is a vice "against nature." Heterosexuality, he suggests, is a matter of "habit" and not of nature, for everything in our society and our education heads us in that direction. If homosexuals persist in their inclinations in spite of all the inducements otherwise, it is because their passion is dictated by nature. The third dialogue considers homosexuality in the cultural context. Gide contrasts the "natural" and superior beauty of man to the artificial and "false" allure of woman. He draws parallels between beauty and art, and associates the exaltation of male beauty with historical periods of glory and ostentation, and the celebration of "Venusian" qualities with the centuries of decline and decay. Lastly, the fourth dialogue looks at the pederast's place in society. The male having far more resources than can be directed to the reproductive function, he seeks alternative outlets for his desire. In a monogamist society, prostitution or adultery are the only other options. Corydon proposes a historical, healthy and noble solution, that of ancient Greece. Again, like most of homosexuality's defenders at that time, who sought to bolster their remarks with lists of heroes and men famous, Gide evokes the last brilliance of Sparta and the Sacred Band of Thebes in support of his thesis. Lacedaemon is not just a random example: the city embodied the warlike spirit, courage, and virile force, the characteristics most diametrically opposed to those popularly ascribed to homosexuals. Gide pleads, here, for his own way of life. His relationship with Marc Allégret was thus copied on the Greek tutelary and pedagogic model. The fourth dialogue ends with this demonstration. The visitor leaves without a word — by no means convinced, but with no arguments left.

What are we to conclude? Gide was not a zealot. His defense of pederasty was moderate; and in his other books, he always stressed control and measure, and not abandonment to instinct. However, given the author's social position, the works are courageous. One might even say there is some bravado, an almost puerile will to lay bare his heart, at last.

Gide set to work to rehabilitate homosexuality and fell into a long tradition that was well represented in Germany by Adolf Brand's group, Gemeinschaft der Eigenen, and teachers like Gustav Wyneken. The general tone of his essay exudes a clear sense of superiority. Pederasts are intellectuals, artists, aesthetes, who know how to distinguish true beauty and who care more for the heart than the body. Is Gide's work original, then? For France, it was, since no one else there was really defending homosexuality, and Proust's works remained under wraps. However, such work was already well underway in Germany and England, and Gide was hardly innovative if we compare him to Hirschfeld, Carpenter or Brand. His originality was in the use of the sophisticated and didactic form of the dialogue, which makes the explanation more pleasant to follow. One might well ask whether Gide's work was in step with its time. Gide started out early in the century, precisely when his foreign neighbors were publishing their essays. By 1924, *Corydon* seems rather obsolete. Pederasty was not at the heart of the issue during the inter-war period; on the contrary, what was needed was recognition of homosexuals in general, "inverts," "pederasts," "sodomites" or what-have-you, without distinguishing between the different types and tendencies. For all the anonymous homosexuals, *Corydon* may have offered some consolation, but hardly any hope. Few could see themselves in this portrait of a moral, even moralistic, pederast who justifies his "vice" on the basis of artistic taste and pedagogical concerns.

Gide was extremely distressed upon the book's release; he was apprehensive over the public reaction and expected to be pilloried: "When it comes to *Corydon*, I compare myself to that caricature by Abel Faivre, depicting a man lying across the train tracks, his head on the rail, waiting for the train that will slice him in pieces. He pulls out his watch and exclaims, "Sapristi! The Express is late!"[268]

This concern was matched by a certain impatience and a more or less conscious will to provoke things. In August 1924, he was particularly chagrined by the lack of publicity given his book: "Corydon is on sale, but almost nobody knows it, for it is not being promoted by reviews nor in the bookshops."[269]

---

268. A letter from André Gide to Dorothy Bussy, 26 December 1923, in *Correspondance André Gide/Dorothy Bussy, January 1925-November 1936*, Paris, Gallimard, Cahiers André Gide, 1981, t.II, 650 pages, p.448.
269. Id., 4 August 1924, *ibid.*, p.476.

Actually, Corydon was received fairly coolly. The courage of the author was appreciated, but no one dared pass judgment on his theories. Most critics did not feel qualified to discuss the question. Jean de Gourmont was the most virulent; in the *Mercure de France* of October 1, 1924, he said Corydon was "an apology for pederasty" and that Gide wrote the book "to make people talk about him." In the *Journal littéraire*, Léon Pierre-Quint noted that "the work seems quite dated,... André Gide, intending to give us a scholarly and philosophical work, has given us a work in the style of the poet in J[ean]-B[aptiste] Rousseau."[270] Willy was openly scornful: "The dialogues of Corydon, heavily scented with the laboratory and hospital, are hardly likely to excite the salacity of one's colleagues and then, even if they contain some clever remarks here and there, one senses the aggressive intolerance of the Great Writer who, as part of an insulted minority, has the impression that it, and only it, now represents Truth, the Beautiful, and the Healthy."[271]

Among the most violent reactions was that of François Nazier, who published *The Anti-Corydon, an essay on sexual inversion*, in 1924. A parody of *Corydon*, it starts with a dialogue between Sappho and Casanova. Diogenes, Alcibiade, Lucien de Samosate, Verlaine, and Rabelais are all invited to speak, in turn. Nazier's main quarrel was with Gide's lack of originality and especially his militant and pontificating tone: "Corydon is only a demonstration, a shocking one, 'tis true, of the strange fury of proselytism that, like a sacred delusion, overtakes the sectarians of 'reverse love.'"[272]

Corydon's influence could still be felt until the end of the 1920s. A famous article by Marcel Réja, entitled, "The revolt of the cockchafers," was published in the *Mercure de France* on March 1, 1928, making direct reference to the book. The article is an anti-homosexual lampoon, the cockchafer or maybug symbolizing the inverts who were multiplying so rapidly in literature. The person who was responsible for this situation is indicated clearly: "Corydon, or rather André Gide, having declared without the least nod to decency that homosexuality, far from being a monstrosity, a vice, is the most normal, the most advisable thing in the world, and having tried to prove it to us by conclusive reasoning, it is André Gide whom we fight — courteously, but relentlessly."

---

270. *Journal littéraire*, n°12, 12 July 1924, p.12.
271. Willy, *Le Troisième Sexe, op. cit.*, p.109.
272. François Nazier, *L'Anti-Corydon, essai sur l'inversion sexuelle*, Paris, Éditions du Siècle, 1924, 126 pages, p.11.

Even homosexuals themselves sometimes greeted *Corydon* with reserve. Klaus Mann noted in his journal: "Many judicious elements, not much new; on the whole, it's rather moving;" and especially: "It is dangerous to establish a clear distinction between 'normal pederasts' and 'inverts,' since the line is fluid and even the individual may find himself on one side and then the other (as Gide himself proves); the only difference is more a question of quality than of predilection."[273]

After *Corydon*, Gide ignored the advice of his friends, who recommended prudence, and placed himself right at the center of the debate on homosexuality. *The Counterfeiters* was published in February 1926. The book presents two homosexuals, Édouard, a pederast, and the count Robert de Passavant, an "invert" according to Gide's classification. The two men are competing over the friendship of a young boy, Olivier Molinier. Édouard embodies all qualities of the pederast according to Gide: attentive, discreet, anxious to educate and protect the elect of his heart, fearing to be rejected by a carefree youth keen for pleasures; in his quest, he is paradoxically encouraged by the child's mother, who wishes for a sure guide for her son; pederasty receives the ultimate imprimatur here: "I understand how precarious a boy's purity can be, even if he seems to be well protected. Moreover, I do not believe that the purest adolescents make the best husbands later; nor even, alas, the most faithful," she added with a sad smile. "Finally, the example of their father has made me wish for other virtues in my sons. But I am afraid they may fall into degrading vice, or get into bad company. Olivier is easily led. You will have the courage to restrain him. I believe that you will be able to do him good. He only listens to you."[274]

The only evocation of sexual intercourse between Édouard and Olivier is summarized in two lines, and even then a certain puritanical reserve is felt: " 'Next to you, I am too happy to sleep.' He wouldn't let me leave until morning."[275]

---

273. Klaus Mann, *Journal. Les années brunes, 1931-1936*, Paris, Grasset, 1996, 452 pages, 10 and 12 July 1932, p.76. *Corydon* was translated into German in 1932 and published by Deutsche Verlagsanstalt. By contrast, it was not publishedin England until after the war.

274. André Gide, *Les Faux-Monnayeurs*, Paris, Gallimard, 1926, 499 pages, p.398. The mother's attitude recalls that of Mme de Bricoule in *Les Garçons* by Henry de Montherlant, who preferred her son have relations with his schoolmates rather than hanging around with loose girls.

275. *Ibid.*, p.403.

The criticism was more abundant now and came from the popular press; opinions remained divided. The literary qualities of the book were acknowledged, but there were too many homosexual characters. Some started to suspect that Gide's obsession was becoming less controlled. Many found the book so tedious that they doubted it could have much of an impact, but others worried about the readers' reaction. Paul Souday summarized the general feeling in *Le Temps* (February 4, 1926):

> Oh! there is nothing crude here, as far as the words themselves. Everything is very discreet, cloaked, and a very innocent reader might conceivably get through it without understanding what is going on. However, it is only too clear. Really, it becomes unbearable, especially with this serious tone and this insipid sentimentality. From that perspective, it is ridiculous! Let's quit talking about the Ancients! Morals have changed!

This article inspired a survey on "homosexuality in literature," in the review *Les Marges*. The results were published on March 15, 1926. The review's editorial committee had put together a questionnaire which was sent to several writers. They were asked if "the preoccupation with homosexuality had developed after the 1914-1918 war" and whether the introduction of homosexual characters into literature could have a harmful effect on morals and the arts. Most of the authors agreed on the development of homosexual literature since the war, although some, like Michel Pay, recalled that during the *Belle Époque* Sapphic literature was very widespread. Some, like Gerard Bauer, said that "Marcel Proust was like the Messiah for these people and, with a kind of genius, released them from their bondage." Others blamed psychoanalysis; and still others said that literature only mirrors the evolution of society. Henri Barbusse saw the development of homosexual literature as proof of the degeneracy of society and attributed it to "a declining phalanx of intellectuals." He issued a call to young people to purify their minds. André Billy blamed "nervous exhaustion from the war, sports, the extreme cerebral quotient of all contemporary art." Charles Derenne only saw it as nothing but snobbery and "fun," even though he himself would condemn inverts "to be whipped and sent to hard labor." Clement Vautel thought it was just a means of shocking the public. In fact, most saw very little danger in it, and they merely sighed or made fun of it. Jean Cassou did not express any interest in the question; André Billy and Pierre Bonardi said people should be allowed to write whatever they wanted; and François Mauriac cautiously explained that there was nothing to condemn nor to tolerate. Ambroise

Vollard, as a good Catholic, did not read such works and Leon Werth, who found all that quite repugnant, also abstained.

However, there were some zealots who decided to clean up this scourge, be it through censorship or, if it came to that, why not an auto-da-fé? "I could not have noticed the expanding presence of homosexuality in literature, because I immediately destroy any book that might reflect such a thing," declared Charles Derenne. Robert Randau also asked that homosexuals be kept from spreading "the microbe of their special literature." Others, like Charles-Henry Hirsch, recommended that doctors ally with legislators to choke off "this disgusting aberration." Camille Mauclair exclaimed: "Imagine the sexual practices between two men and try not to vomit!" He concluded, in a gripping way, unconsciously revealing how public opinion linked homosexuality and foreigners, treason and national threat: "We got over Boches, we will get over the pederasts." George Maurevert called for a return to order, a national rejuvenation: "When France has become again what she ought to be — with the help of a strong man, if need be — these wicked morals will disappear on their own." He added: " 'Men make the laws, but women make the morals, as La Bruyère said. The day when a good, honest Frenchwoman ejects a flamboyant fag from a salon or stops an over-dressed dandy at the door, with a hand in his face, the morals will change over-night. And the men will make the laws." The satirical magazine *Fantasio* published a report on the survey on April 15, 1926, and underlined, rightly, the novelty of the debate. The sentence was clear, nevertheless: "We have had enough of literature full of pederasts."

Gide reached an apogee in the revelation of his homosexuality by publishing *If It Die — An Autobiography (Si le grain ne meurt)* in October 1926. Writing to the critic Edmund Gosse to justify his attitude, he said:

> Dear friend, I have a horror of lying. I cannot hide under that conventional camouflage that systematically disguises the works of X,... Y,... and so many others. I wrote the book to "create a precedent," to give an example of frankness, to enlighten some, to reassure others, to force public opinion to take account of things that are being ignored or that one tries to ignore, to the great detriment of psychology, morals, art... and society. I wrote this book because I would rather be hated than to be admired for being something that I am not.[276]

---

276. 16 January 1927. Cited by Eva Ahlstedt, *André Gide, op. cit.*

If It Die is a valuable testimony; in it, Gide confesses his homosexuality, and analyzes its progression and his homosexual awakening. At times, Gide seems to want to apologize for his vice; other times, he glorifies it and takes pleasure in shocking the reader with salacious anecdotes. He retraces the course of how his homosexuality unfolded, evoking his first concerns at school, the abrupt reve-lation that he was different: "I am not like the others! I am not like the others,"[277] he acknowledged to his mother. But it was in Tunisia that he first experienced pederasty with young Arab boys like Ali and Athman: "On the threshold of what we call sin, would I still hesitate? No, I would have been too disappointed if the adventure had ended in the triumph of my virtue — which by now was con-temptible to me, a horror."[278]

By yielding to the call of the flesh, Gide diverged from his Protestant edu-cation and gave in to pagan values. Anxious to show that homosexuality is not a burden, he presents his adventures in an idyllic way. His attempts at seduction always result in success and a complaisant partner, especially in North Africa. Gide moves in a world that is largely fantasy, where his homosexual desire is always divined, foreseen, fulfilled, with no obstacle barring his road, not even his own scruples. The press received *If It Die* with mixed reviews; several writers praised Gide's courage and sincerity but others, like Souday and Gourmont, reproached him for showing his dirty laundry. Henri de Régnier in *Le Figaro* was very unfavorable.

And after *François Porché, L'Amour qui n'ose pas dire son nom* (*François Porché, the Love which dares not say its name*) (1927) was published, the attacks against André Gide began in earnest. Pierre Lièvre's article in *Le Divan*, July-August 1927, was incendiary:

> So that we categorize the works of André Gide among those things which are so corrupted by their ending that they are debased and destroyed in their entirety and to the very core. This is a draught that we do not want to drink anymore, because the last mouthful leaves a horrible aftertaste. It is a romantic supper at the end of which the criminal warning makes us forget all the foregoing pleasures: "You have been poisoned, Ladies and Gentlemen"... It is this pleasure [of perverting] that, in combination with his love of children — which we will not deign to grace with the name that

---

277. André Gide, *Si le grain ne meurt* [1926], Paris, Gallimard, coll. "Folio," 1986, 372 pages, p.133.
278. *Ibid.*, p.299.

he has borrowed from the Greek — fills him with such indulgence for these vicious kids, petty thieves, poachers, assassins, tricksters, and cheats whose baser instincts he flatters, and a seductive and rotten troupe of which peoples his works like a choir of evil cherubim.

His novels may legitimate homosexuality, and *Corydon* remains the landmark book of the inter-war period as regards homosexuality, but it would be an overstatement to claim that Gide was a militant. His discourse remains that of an intellectual who defends his singularity from a certain height. His argumentation principally aims at showing that homosexuality is legitimate, that it must be tolerated, and also that the homosexual is a solitary being, one who chooses his own way and who is thus to some extent superior to the others.

Gide was indignant at his contemporaries' cowardice; they let him fight alone at the front line:

> X and T keep repeating that they have had enough of pretence, that they are resolved from now on to speak frankly, to face up to the public, to burn their ships, etc. But they do not burn anything. The courage they take pride in is a courage that does not cost them anything of that which they still hold onto. And, in the new book that they give us, they take great care that their "confessions" are of such a kind and are so speciously dissimulated that only the very astute can read between the lines; so that they do not have anything to retract if they convert later on or if they think they have a chance of getting into the Academy.[279]

But he never managed to hide his own feelings of guilt, which are plain in his confessions to Roger Martin du Gard; he confides that he is the product of generations of Puritanical Protestants and concludes: "I pay for them, I am their punishment."[280]

"Inversion," An Isolated Attempt at a Homosexual Review

There was no homosexual movement in France during the inter-war period. However, a homosexual review did exist, fleetingly, on the German model. (This was not the first French homosexual periodical; Marc-André Raffalovitch and Jacques d'Adelsward-Fersen had already founded *Akademos* in 1909.[281]) *Inversions* was created by Gustave Beyria and Gaston Lestrade in 1924.

---

279. André Gide, *Journal, 1889-1939*, Paris, Gallimard, coll. "Bibl. de la Pléiade," 1991, 1374 pages, 8 December 1929, p.960.
280. Roger Martin du Gard, *Notes sur André Gide, loc. cit.*, p.1373.

Beyria was born in 1896; he was an unmarried office worker. Lestrade was born in 1898; a postal worker, he lived with a 24-year-old Swiss tapestry maker, Adolphe Zahnd.

What is most striking about it is that it was such a marginal initiative; it had nothing to do with the Parisian homosexual cliques. The publication had no literary godfathers, and neither was it an emanation from the medical community. Of course, it echoed the theories then in vogue, but it was not the publishing organ of any specialist in homosexuality. In fact, the only French homosexual review was the work of perfect unknowns and it received no external aid. It was published anonymously, at 1 rue Bougainville. Its high price (1,50 F) made it a luxury, which few could afford. It was sold at newsstands, but one could also subscribe and even receive it in a discreet wrapper.

Only five issues were published before it was banned. The first issue came out on November 15, 1924. *Inversions* called itself "not a review on homosexuals but a review for homosexuals." "We want to cry out to inverts that they are normal and healthy beings, that they have a right to live their lives fully, that they owe nothing to a morality created by heterosexuals — they do not have to standardize their impressions and their feelings, to repress their desires, to conquer their passions."

Various authors in homosexual circles contributed to the review, such as the "theorist" of androgyny, Camille Spiess, and the writer Axieros; but no leading light participated. *Inversions* was directly inspired by the Greek model and, like Der Eigene in Germany, made frequent references to Antiquity. The review owed much to the German movements: it communicated the scientific discoveries of Hirschfeld and sexologists from across the Rhine. And, like the German periodicals, it offered a varied panorama of subjects relating to homosexuality. The first issue included an article on the Oscar Wilde trial, medical commentary, an article on inversion in pigeons, a book review and the traditional classified advertisements, very modest (they disappeared in No. 2). Starting with No. 3, the review was going to be called *Urania*, which would draw less attention. That change never took place, because an investigation was

---

281. In the previous centuries, France had known seen fledgling homosexual organizations come and go, in particular the Ordre de la Manchette, inthe 17th century, and the Secte des Ebugors (an anagram of "bougres") in the 18th. Under the Second Empire, an association called the Société d'Émiles use dto meet in a house in the Grenelle neighborhood. See Claude Courouve, *Les Homosexuels et les Autres*, Paris, Éditions de l'Athanor, 1977, 155 pages.

already underway for offending public morality. By No. 4, the German influence is strongly felt, especially in an article by Numa Praetorius on homosexuality in Germany. There was also a survey for readers: "Has *Inversions* outraged your good morals? In your opinion, does the investigation against this review constitute an infringement of your freedom of thought and the freedom of the press? What is your opinion on homosexuality and homosexuals?" Several public figures responded, expressing a tolerant opinion on homosexuality, for example Suzanne de Callias (Ménalkas), Claude Cahun, Henry Marx, Havelock Ellis, Camille Spiess and George Pioch, a close relative of Eugene Armand. The review was banned after that, but it managed to publish another issue under the name of *L'Amitié (Friendship)*. Most notably, it included an article by St Ch.Waldecke, one of Adolf Brand's and Der Eigene's collaborators.[282]

The periodical attracted sarcastic remarks from its competitors. With the exception of *L'En-dehors*, Eugene Armand's anarchistic publication, the other newspapers reacted very negatively; *Fantasio* in particular attacked *Inversions*. Under the headline, "Let's be French! Long Live Women, for Heaven's Sake!," it gave vent to a standard condemnation of "inverts," which it repeated from then on. It proclaimed its clear opposition to the "Anglo-Saxon gangrene" and asserted the French heterosexual "tradition."[283] As for *La Lanterne*, it suspected Germany of having a hand in it.[284]

The disappearance of *Inversions* did not make any waves. Willy, in *The Third Sex*, makes an ironical reference to this French misadventure: "I do not deplore the disappearance of *Inversions*, which was too dumb to be believed; but in the end, we should ask, all the same, what the public wants: that everyone be left in peace, or that all delinquents should be locked up, without distinction."[285]

Except for *Inversions*, there is no trace of any French homosexual militancy. This odd fact was noted at the time, especially by German observers. Numa Praetorius (a pseudonym of Eugen Wilhelm), in his article, "In connection with homosexuality in France," in *Jahrbuch für sexual Zwischenstufen* in 1922, devoted five pages to the subject. He supposed that there must be fewer homosexuals in France than in Germany, and he suggested that the absence of anti-homosexual

---

282. Gilles Barbedette and Michel Carassou mention the existence of the review *Inversions* in their work, *Paris gay 1925*, Paris, Presses de la Renaissance, 1981, 312 pages. See also AN, BB 18 6174/44 BL 303 and Chapter Seven.

283. *Fantasio*, n° 427, 15 November 1924.

284.*La Lanterne*, 19 November 1924.

285. Willy, *Le Troisième Sexe, op. cit.*, p.108.

laws and the feminine mythology (specific to France, according to him) must be factors. Similarly, in *The Third Sex* Willy observes: "This ornamental sword of Damocles [§175] allows fagots who are conscious and organized to make themselves out to be martyrs, to make claims, and even to attract significant numbers of heteros to support them."[286]

Also, while France did have an organized homosexual subculture, there was no militancy, and French homosexuals remained determinedly individualistic. That is certainly due to the more favorable social climate than in the neighboring countries, but it also had to do with a certain political immaturity. Discussions on homosexuality remained confined to the literary sphere, consideration to be a private sphere — unlike that of political writing or social lampoons.

It was only because there was so little discourse that Marcel Proust and André Gide came to be seen as the heralds of the homosexual cause. Talking openly about homosexuality was already a militant act. The French homosexual intellectuals did not present a united front; Proust and Gide defended opposing theories and Jean Cocteau, another outstanding figure on the French homosexual scene, squared off against Gide.[287] Far from helping French homosexuals advance, the visibility of homosexual personalities served as a handicap, reinforcing the idea of a vice reserved to an intellectual elite or stuffy sensation-seeking middle class, and paralyzing anonymous initiatives.

* * *

Were the 1920s the golden age of homosexual movements? To some extent, yes. Many homosexual associations were formed and it was the apogee of German militancy. However, this success was tempered by other failures and shortcomings. Throughout the profusion of periodicals, and lobbying efforts, what is striking is the discordance of the voices, the disagreement and the competition between the principal leaders, the lack of a common platform or even of a common definition of homosexuality. The exclusion of lesbians, whose impact within the movements was almost nil, is another proof of how fragmented the

---

286. *Ibid.*, p.58-59.

287. Homosexual rivalry, stirred by the quarrel around Marc Allégret, is reflected in books from those days, such as *Les Monstres sacrés* de Cocteau (1919) ou *Les Faux-Monnayeurs* de Gide (1926).

German homosexual community was. These divisions were surely one of the main reasons for the political failure of the movements.

Moreover, in an environment of increasing sexual liberation, in which the homosexual subculture flourished, securing rights seemed like just one more tedious and formal consideration. This shallow approach had no repercussions under Weimar, but it took on a tragic significance after 1933. Still, we should not undervalue the attempts at organization and the assertion of rights. As precursors, these movements were courageous, generous and vivifying. They testify to the precocity of the aspirations to form a community, which took their first concrete forms in Europe, and a diverse approach to the problem. Already in the inter-war period, there were many ways of affirming oneself as a homosexual or lesbian — as a militant protestor, as in Germany, through subversive integration, as in England, or via sensual individualism, as in France.

CHAPTER THREE
AN INVERSION OF VALUES: THE CULT OF HOMOSEXUALITY

The militant groups are certainly the most recognized aspect of the homosexual liberation movement of the 1920s. However, if we are looking to explain the homosexual apogee, its cultural impact, its resonance in public opinion, we must look at a phenomenon that is less well-known but is perhaps more representative of the novelty of the period: the propagation of a model of homosexuality in the British upper classes, and especially among the intellectuals.

Although closely tied to the development of the German homosexual scene, the "cult of homosexuality"[288] was specific to England, and particularly to the years 1919-1933. The traditional aversion to homosexuality gave way, in certain sectors of the society, to a tolerance that soon shifted into approval, and then to adulation. Homosexuality was spread in the public schools, the universities, and the intellectual circles. It became a fashion, a life style, a sign of recognition in certain classes and certain circles. The cult of homosexuality in England was the basis by which homosexuals gained entry into certain British institutions and began to permeate the literature, thereby imperceptibly molding the society.

Of course, this does not mean the triumph of the forces of progress, or tolerance for homosexuals as a group. Moreover, very few lesbians were part of this and there was very little parallel in France and Germany. However, in spite of its

---

288. Noel Annan uses this expression in his book, *Our Age: English Intellectuals between the Wars: A Group Portrait*, New York, Random House, 1991, 479 pages. In my view, it perfectly reflects the state of mind of the time, at least among the British upper class and intellectuals.

limits, the cult of homosexuality did constitute a unique subversive phenomenon in the traditional institutions and the affirmation of a positive difference. In fact, the counter-reaction, which dates from the mid-1930s, was never
complete because this pro-homosexual climate had caused an upheaval in the
education of at least two generations of young men.

SEDUCED IN THE PUBLIC SCHOOLS

The public school[289] was commonly held to be a den of vice where homosexuality was the rule (at least until the introduction of co-education in the
Sixties). This is not limited to England; other European boarding schools and
religious colleges also had a naughty reputation, usually associated with a confined group engaging in promiscuity. However, the English public school has
certain distinctions. First, it is basically the only form of schooling available for
the middle- and upper classes. (In France or Germany, there are more options
available.[290]) These children are principally raised in boarding schools and live
only among their schoolmates. They spend little time with their parents, except
during the holidays; and they have almost no contact with the external world,
particularly girls.[291] Then, as we will see, the hierarchical and self-managed

---

289. The *public schools* system is composed of two levels. The nine biggest ones provide
entrée to the *upper class* and the future élite of the nation. Seven are boarding schools:
Winchester (founded in 1382), Eton (1440), Westminster (1560), Charterhouse (1611),
Harrow (1571), Rugby (1567), Shrewsbury (1552). Two are day schools: St Paul's (1509)
and Merchant Taylors (1561). Most of the *public schools* were founded more recently; they
are for youngsters of the *middle class* and their graduates tend to become executives and
middle managers in business, administration and the liberal professions. The best known
are Cheltenham (1841), Marlborough (1842), Rossall (1844), Radley (1847), Lancing
(1848), Epsom (1853), Clifton (1862), Haileybury (1862), and Malvern (1865). To get a
sense of the influence of the *public schools*, we can take one example: in 1937, 19 ministers
out of the 21 in Chamberlain's cabinet came from a public school. The *public schools* are in
any case the private preserve of a tiny privileged minority, which Tawney estimated at 3%
of the families in 1939 (cited in François Bédarida, *La Société anglaise du milieu du XIXe siècle à
nos jours*, Paris, Éditions du Seuil, coll. "Points histoire," 1990, 540 pages).

290. Antoine Prost thus recalls that in France, at the end of the 19th century, the
boarding school model was largely — but not exclusively — used in private establishments, and was not common for public lycées. Besides, the boarding schools were more
for children from the countryside than the city. And finally, affluent families could always
pay for a tutor. See *Histoire de l'enseignement en France, 1800-1967*, Paris, Armand Colin, 1968,
524 pages.

operation of the school encourages special relations to form between the pupils. Lastly, the English public school often regards homosexuality as normal and the pupils, at various times, may consider it the latest fashion to boast of their homosexual relations. This topic is common in British literature, even though school headmasters and educational authorities often try to refute it.[292] Thus, the phenomenon of "best friends" often goes beyond mere friendship, and it would be foolish to pass it off as a minor thing. The public school largely determines the pupils' future life; it is both a model and a reference. By making homosexual experimentation a standard part of adolescence, it encouraged greater tolerance toward homosexuality in adulthood. By disseminating a cult of homosexuality among the elite, it set the stage for more open homosexuality.

The Public Schools, Fostering the Cult of Homosexuality

The public schools are for youths from about ten to eighteen years old. The boarding school system is used for almost all pupils, who spend six years living in an exclusively male milieu for most of the time. Such living conditions, at the age of full sexual awakening, are hardly helpful to one's development as far as sex and love. While heterosexual encounters might be possible during the holidays, the boys do not always take advantage of the opportunity. There is a very strict code of honor in force in the public schools, and the boys tend to scorn girls or, at least, to ignore them. Thus, it is no surprise that romantic or erotic friendships develop within the schools.

The public schools were always dens of sexual iniquity. In Eton, in particular, the dormitory where 52 pupils slept was well-known for the sexual frolicking and persecution that went on; parents were strongly advised not to send their children there, if their health was fragile.[293] Throughout the 18th and the 19th centuries, orgies and torture were commonplace in the schools. In the 1920s and 1930s, the situation began to change. However, a palpable erotic excitation

---

291. Here, I am going to study mainly homosexuality among boys, but I will also touch on this question in the girls' schools. The problem there was nearly identical, anyway. For this survey I rely on the book by John Gathorne-Hardy, *The Public-School Phenomenon, 597-1977*, London, Hodder & Stoughton, 1977, 478 pages.

292. See Rennie Macandrew, *Approaching Manhood, Healthy Sex for Boys*, London, The Wales Publishing Co, 1939, 95 pages, p.67.

293. Shelley was tortured there and all his life suffered physical and psychological consequences from it. See John Gathorne-Hardy, *The Public- School Phenomenon, 597-1977*, *op. cit.*

continued to haunt the corridors. When individual rooms began to be assigned, first by Dartington and Eton, this only further encouraged sexual activity. Robin Maugham describes his life at Eton in 1929, in his autobiography, *Escape from the Shadow*. [294]

Homosexuality was in fashion to a greater or lesser extent, depending on the school and the year. All it took was for enough of the boys in one class to have reached sexual maturity, and they would quickly promote such practices. Quentin Crisp notes that, in his public school, it was customary to have an orgy on the eve of the last day of every quarter. Goldsworthy Lowes Dickinson remembers the atmosphere in the corridors of Beomonds, and writes of a scene in the locker room where a crowd of admirers watched an older boy masturbating against a younger one.[295] Cecil Beaton entered Harrow in January 1918 and stayed there until 1922; he says the situation varied from dormitory to dormitory; in some, there was little sexual activity, and in others "bad behavior" went on openly.

Beaton himself acquired a bad reputation, because he was so good-looking that everyone assumed he was extremely sexually active. He says that he was calm, weak and rather effeminate, avoided sports, dressed with care, and tried to look beautiful in order to please himself; but that because of his good looks he was thought to be a little whore. Everything he did was seen as reinforcing that view, and he became ill as a result. While other people were sleeping around, his only partner was Gordon Fell-Clark.[296] A class like that might be followed by one that is more reserved, or even hostile to homosexuality.

What was different about the inter-war period, and especially the years 1919-1933, is that homosexuality seems to have been everywhere, then. One witness of the time says that he had fun at school; he "got along" well with his mates; at that time, it was seen as a good thing to be homosexual. "Almost all the boys had sexual experiences together."[297] At Oundle, in 1920, when Director Sanderston asked who had been passing notes to their classmates, half of the school stood up. To paraphrase an alumnus:

---

294. Robin Maugham, *Escape from the Shadow* [1940], London, Cardinal, 1991, 472 pages.
295. Dennis Proctor (ed.), *The Autobiography of G. Lowes Dickinson*, London, Duckworth, 1973, 287 pages, p.53.
296. Cited by Hugo Vickers, *Cecil Beaton*, London, Weidenfeld & Nicolson, 1985, 656 pages, p.23.
297. Dudley Cave, in *Walking after Midnight. Gay Men's Life Stories*, Hall-Carpenter Archives, London, Routledge, 1989, 238 pages.

— There was an enormous amount of sex, enormous. I had my share of it, but I would have liked even more. You passed somebody a slip of paper: "Would you like to go for a walk with me on the moor?" If he agreed, one could be pretty sure that he would be obliging. The boys adored carrying notes from A to B, if they lived in different houses. One did not have much time. We had to hurry. There was an ideal moment to make love, between dinner and study time. One could slip into the study hall with somebody who had caught one's eye.[298]

Homosexuality in the public schools could take many forms, including the most brutal. G. Lowes Dickinson speaks of cruel events at Charterhouse. In Wellington, in the 1930s, young boys were violated. In Bedford, during the same period, an alumnus admits that he and his comrades masturbated regularly another pupil, New. One day they noticed two live electric wires hanging from the ceiling, and practically burned the boy's penis off: "...there was a terrible flash and he howled. I swear to you that his penis changed color. I still hear his cries today."

Other practices were less dangerous. J.R. Ackerley describes how the older boys would make passes at the younger ones, sitting on their beds, evening after evening, whispering and masturbating. He says that one clever fellow had opened the seams of the pockets in his trousers, so that his hands — or those of one of his obliging peers, would have direct access to the treasure.[299]

It is impossible to know what proportion of boys had sexual intercourse; John Gathorne-Hardy suggests that 25% of them made love on a regular basis. Romantic friendships were formed, as well as erotic crushes. Indeed, the fear of being caught, added to timidity, and a strict separation by age group made sexual intercourse difficult. John Betjeman says: "The only thing that held me was love. I never would have dared to touch anybody. I thought that I would go to prison — or hell."[300] Often, and naturally, the boys were still too young, too shy, or too frightened to perform the act, even with a boy whom they loved. In a letter to a friend, the writer and critic Cyril Connolly recalls a failed experiment:

---

298. Cited by John Gathorne-Hardy, *The Public-School Phenomenon, op. cit.*, p.163-164; and in the following anecdote (p.164).

299. J.R. Ackerley, *My Father and Myself* [1968], London, Penguin, 1971, 192 pages, p.70-71.

300. Cited by John Gathorne-Hardy, *The Public-School phenomenon, op. cit.*, p.166.

"I have spoken to you, I believe, of my fatal repression our last night in the bathroom, and how timid and awkward I was when he tried to embrace me."[301]

These differences in conduct only represent different stages in sexual evolution. Precocity and promiscuity in the schools often went side by side with the purest chastity, sometimes maintained out of very lofty sentiments — the desire not to sully the purity of a budding love. In these cases, love relationships were copied on the heterosexual model. One of the boys should be younger, beautiful, and of another social class, if possible. He needed to be protected and to some extent played the part of the girl. Above all, the relationship between the young boy and his elder was to remain chaste. It was not the fulfillment of desire that mattered, but the innumerable difficulties that stood in the way of winning over the chosen one.

The relationships that sometimes cropped up between pupils and teachers may also be seen in this light. T.C. Worsley notes that while he was assistant headmaster at a famous public school (which he does not name), "there too, a majority of professors were definitely homoerotic to a greater or lesser degree."[302] Worsley, a homosexual himself, described the situation facing the faculty when it came to their loves or their desires:

> —It was a weakness in my position because I had less control over my expressions than [my most prudent colleagues]; but perhaps even more because I was conscious of it. It was not that I had any real reason to feel guilty, since I did not have any physical desire for any of the boys, even for those with whom I finally "fell in love." And it was the same for my other colleagues in the same situation. We eventually discovered that only one of them had acted scandalously.[303]

Indeed, it seems that, while a significant proportion of the teachers in the public schools were homosexual, most never satisfied their inclinations with their pupils. Worsley supposes that the overall homoerotic climate in the school tempered the urge: "The generalized homoeroticism that I discovered in the organized sports rituals satisfied my inclinations sufficiently so that I kept them 'pure'."[304]

---

301. Cited by Humphrey Carpenter, *The Brideshead Generation, Evelyn Waugh and his Friends*, London, Weidenfeld & Nicolson, 1989, 523 pages, p.23.

302. T.C. Worsley, *Flannelled Fool. A Slice of Life in the Thirties*, London, Alan Ross, 1967, 213 pages, p.74.

303. *Ibid.*, p.75.

In the girls' schools, the pattern was fairly similar, although somewhat attenuated. Also, since there were fewer such schools, we have fewer memoirs; scandals were extremely rare and it is difficult to draw any conclusions. Sexual intercourse seems to have been much rarer than among boys, even though each school had its share of lesbians. However, no scenes of debauchery have been described that would compare to those evoked above. The most widespread phenomenon seems to have been the crush, when a girl (between the ages of eleven and fourteen) fell in love with an older girl who did not reciprocate.

As among the boys, these romantic friendships were patterned on the heterosexual diagram. The older girl represented the boy; but she could also embody a heroine or the absent mother. The younger girl showed her affection by carrying her books and notepads, leaving candies under her pillow or making her bed. There would be endless discussions analyzing how the older girl dressed, how she talked, the gestures she made; but each girl kept secret her personal contribution to the worship of the loved one. The relationships were perfectly innocent: a smile, a simple hello was enough to make a younger girl happy for a week. It seems that sexual intercourse would have rather signified a failure in the process in love, which consisted in large part in identifying with the loved one. Differences in age and authority intensified the desire. By the age of fifteen, it was more common to have a crush on one of the mistresses, and the pupils vied for their favors:

"— Signorina is part of Miss Julie's clan."

"— Fancy," says another, "the German mistress is a widow!"

"— Yes," the first one answers. "But she is in Miss Caral's clan!"[305]

Teaching seems to have attracted a significant number of homosexuals, female as well as male. In England, as in France and Germany, teachers were supposed to be unmarried. Many of the women were in teaching because they had not managed to marry, and sometimes their attitude expressed a sense of revenge, fear and hostility toward men. But, for their pupils, they represented an example of social success, which increased their prestige. That partly explains the frequent sense of fear and dislike for men that girls raised in public schools expressed in those days. When they left school, they asked their favorite mis-

---

304. *Ibid.*, p.89.

305. See *Olivia*, by Olivia (pseudonym of Dorothy Bussy, sister of Lytton Strachey and close friend of Gide), Paris, Stock, 1949, 148 pages, p.26.

tresses to write to them. This they readily did, and often took the opportunity to go on giving advice aimed at enabling them to face the outside world without succumbing to its temptations.

Ambiguities in the System

The attitude toward sex in the public schools reflects deep-seated institutional hypocrisy. It seems that, in spite of all the Puritanical and repressive speeches, a certain laissez-faire attitude prevailed. Homosexuality among teens was seen as benign, almost an obligatory rite of passage in one's sexual life.[306] Even so, the post-Victorian moralizing frenzy reached its heights in these establishments. The director of Charterhouse, for example, "would make obscure and alarming references to the sexual vice [masturbation]."[307] The obsession with masturbation reached dizzying proportions: sermons were devoted to it, boys prayed to be delivered of it, and they were obliged to be confessed on this subject. Some schools set up highly complex systems to counter any temptations; at Rossall, the Masters were not permitted to be in a room alone with a pupil for more than ten minutes, and even then they had to leave the open door. The older boys had to keep away from the younger ones, and they were all under constant surveillance. Anything that related to sex was severely repressed. Works that were considered dangerous, such as D.H. Lawrence's writings, were censored. Queenswood, a women's college, banned *Gone With The Wind* in the 1930s and the pupils' mail was read. T.C. Worsley's headmaster at Marlborough once told him that he might see a kind of white matter running from his intimate parts; — Don't worry, he said, it's just a kind of disease, like measles.[308]

School authorities were often very severe in dealing with what they regarded as major crimes. At Lancing, Tom Driberg was denounced to the director by two little boys whom he had tried to seduce; he was deprived of his position as prefect[309] and was isolated for the rest of the quarter. In fact, forbidding romantic friendships only made them more appealing; it was a game that broke the routine of school life. And for that reason alone, there was little likelihood of breaking them up. Quentin Crisp relates the outcome of a homosexual scandal in his school: one night, one of the boys walked from one end of his

---

306. See Chapter Five.
307. Dennis Proctor (ed.), *The Autobiography of G. Lowes Dickinson, op. cit.*, p.54.
308. T.C. Worsley, *Flannelled Fool, op. cit.*, p.47.
309. An older schoolmate, responsible for discipline; see below.

"house" to the other, to get to his friend's bedroom. The two boys could have met without the least risk at any time of day in a secluded spot; but desire is stoked by the atmosphere of challenge, of danger. The boy was caught., and he was thrashed in front of the whole school. Instead of being chastened, he was lionized. A fan-club developed around him and he became all the more desirable. The administration had to expel him in order to put an end to it.

While he was a pupil at Lancing, Evelyn Waugh tried to start a discussion on the subject of homosexuality. As an editorial in the school newspaper, he published a fictitious conversation between a visitor and a schoolboy like him. He wanted to show that passionate friendships between pupils were not necessarily disruptive or corrupting, and that the authorities were wrong to intervene in an area that did not concern them.

A few years before, his brother Alec had launched a great offensive against the public schools through his acclaimed novel, *The Loom of Youth* (1917).[310] In a less well-known work, *Public-School Life. Boys, Parents, Masters* (1922) he gives a very detailed description of homosexuality in the public schools, defends romantic friendships and denounces the hypocrisy that surrounded the subject.[311] Noting that the system of the public schools is (in this respect) contrary to nature, he says that one must expect results contrary to nature. He calls the time spent in public school a phase of sexual transition; and says that most of the "active immorality in the schools" takes place between fifteen- and sixteen-year-old boys; not, as is frequently imagined, between the younger and older boys." He says that, like everything else at school, homosexuality has to conform to rules; there are rules for everything, and friendships, like personalities, must fit the mold. It is the endless talk about homosexuality that keeps interest alive and ensures that the phenomenon will be reproduced.

Waugh also highlights some neglected aspects of homosexual life in the public schools. First of all, having 18- or 19-year-old boys in some of the houses can only create a difficult climate, for at this age sexual impulses more definitely demand physical satisfaction. Then, romantic friendships can have harmful consequences for the younger boys. A young one who becomes the friend of an older boy finds himself suddenly propelled to the top of the school hierarchy; he gets to know other boys in the upper forms, and he receives various privileges; boys

---

310. *Loom* has many meanings : not only a weaving apparatus, or to "appear," but, in Old English, "penis."

311. Alec Waugh, *Public-School Life. Boys, Parents, Masters*, London, Collins Sons & Co, 1922, 271 pages.

in his own form become jealous or hate him, and he loses contact with reality. When his guardian leaves the school, he finds himself alone and unwanted. Moreover, constantly separating love from sex can cause trouble for the lads later in life. To change this situation, Waugh became an advocate of coeducation; he called for a freer discussion of these subjects, and for better public information:

> — There is so much ignorance to dissipate; the ignorance of the mothers, the ignorance of the fathers who have not themselves been in public school, the conspiracy of silence among the pupils, alumni and masters. We make too much of immorality, and at the same time we do not pay enough attention to it. The headmasters assure us that it only crops up occasionally, but their attitude is like that of a doctor who suspects his patient has a grave illness and simply goes on observing him, looking for signs.

These attempts to start a discussion of homosexuality were not the only ones and it wasn't only the pupils who were concerned. Worsley, as an assistant headmaster, with the assistance of some young teachers, prefects, and pupils, tried to fight the reactionary spirit of the older teachers, whom he called the Old Guard. One Hoffman, in particular, promulgated such an insidious, oppressively suspicious atmosphere that it was nauseating. "Hoffman looks at each boy as if he thought he was expecting a baby!"[312] The Old Guard would make examples of those pupils suspected of homosexuality. The atmosphere at the college was noxious, charged with rancor and suspicion and poisoned by denunciations and accusations of "sexual misconduct," "calls from parents in tears" and expulsions in the wake of "anti-vice campaigns."

Worsley was fully aware of the ambiguity of the situation and recognized that to defend the pupils was hardly any better than seeking to condemn them at all costs. In the end, he admitted to himself that the grounds for his moral indignation at Hoffman's attitude toward sex could reasonably be considered suspect.[313] Initially, his quarrel was with the relentless inquisition to which the faculty subjected the pupils, and the despotic control which they exerted. During a council debate over repealing the rule requiring school caps to be worn while inside the college, Worsley learned that the Old Guard was resolutely opposed to repealing it because the caps had different-colored ribbons indi-

---

312. T.C. Worsley, *Flannelled Fool*, *op. cit.*, p.101.
313. *Ibid.*, p.107.

154

cating which dormitory the pupils belonged in, which enabled them to catch boys who were talking with pupils from other dormitories. The director of the college was upset to find out that there was a "law" prohibiting pupils from different houses or dormitories speaking to one another. The cap-wearing rule was repealed at once and it was announced that all the pupils of the college could speak to each other freely. On another occasion, a sexologist was invited to speak in the college. "The feeling of outrage that that produced was extraordinary. But what made the question even more outrageous was that when the sexologist arrived, it turned out to be a woman!"[314]

In any case, the public schools were clearly one of the main forums for spreading, discussing and understanding homosexuality. This preoccupation with homosexuality was so overwhelming that school authorities sought to continue to influence their pupils even after they left school. When Cyril Connolly left Saint Cyprian, he was subjected to the usual "exhortation on the seed" from the chaplain and the director, the gist of which was: — We were departing for a world of temptations.... We were to name any boy who had tried to get into our beds, we were warned never to go with a boy from another school, never to become friends with a boy more than a year and a half older than us and, above all, not to play with ourselves.[315]

Given this apparent desire to maintain a high level of morality in the public schools, the rampant homosexuality must give us pause. In Eton, the director William Cory was certainly an adherent of the cult of beauty, especially when it came to the individual, the particularly fine young man. He allowed himself some very romantic friendships with certain pupils.

Some schools, and not only the public schools, were regular training grounds in homosexuality. Valentine Ackland, briefly attending the Domestic Training College of Eastbourne, a professional school, was plunged into an entirely lesbian universe. The director was butch and the other teachers encouraged crushes and affairs.[316]

In most cases, it seems that as long as there were no scandals, liaisons and sexual intercourse between pupils were tacitly allowed, even approved, by those in charge, who saw their job primarily as training gentlemen who would be respectful of British traditions and loyal citizens of their country. This respect

314. *Ibid.*, p.132.
315. Cited by Humphrey Carpenter, *The Brideshead Generation, op. cit.*, p.23.
316. See Valentine Ackland, *For Sylvia: An Honest Account*, London, Chatto & Windus, 1985, 135 pages, p.68.

was learned early on, at the public school, and was reflected in the attachment the alumni felt for their school and the formation of what in adulthood would be the "old boy network," a kind of guild, which allowed graduates of the big schools to identify each other, to stay in touch, and to help each other enhance their careers and social positions. This friendship-loyalty bond neatly prefigured the future attachment of the pupil to his fatherland, England. In that sense homosexual relations, whether based on deep love or physical passion, between boys who would later be called upon to run the country together, or at least to work toward the same goal according to the ideals which were inculcated during school, could well be an asset. They helped to weave a stable social fabric.

The most obvious symbol of the tacit social acceptance of homosexuality in the name of social cohesion is the institutionalization of the system of fag and prefect.[317] Originally intended to protect young people from pressure from the older boys, it soon became a form of slavery that included sexual aspects. This was reinforced by the fact that the public schools followed a self-management scheme whereby the prefects were responsible for handling interpersonal conflicts and discipline, with the masters and the directors not intervening directly. This inevitably led sometimes to excesses.

The boys were enormously dependent on each other; they learned management skills and developed a sense of responsibility, but were still bound by diffuse erotic feelings, as shown by the memoirs of the very frank Christopher Isherwood. He recounts his elation when, for the first time, he had an office and two fags to clean it. The "fags" were two new boys named Berry and Darling; he had great fun calling out, "Berry, Darling!" and admits that he was as little suited for authority as most of his comrades, in fact less so than many, and despite having begun with the friendliest intentions, soon became unstable, taking offense at imaginary signs of treason. His mood shifts upset his "fags," and generally, he says, he acted like any low level manager. Office holders at that school could beat their fags and were rather encouraged to exert that privilege.[318]

On the whole, the school directors' attitude toward homosexuality seems to have been particularly hypocritical. Sex becomes all the more desirable when

---

317. A *fag* is a young student who has to obey the orders of an older boy (the *prefect*); he performs household duties and various services. The system was widespread in the the the *public schools* from the beinning of the 19th century following the wave of reforms inaugurated by Dr Thomas Arnold at Rugby.

318. Christopher Isherwood, *Lions and Shadows*, London, Methuen, 1985, 191 pages, p.26-27.

it is laden with so many prohibitions. Public school boys were obsessed with sex, reflecting the fundamental contradiction which is at the heart of the post-Victorian system: "Nobody must masturbate and yet everyone does it; thus, everyone must become an idiot and yet nobody does so; homosexual attraction is a sin, however it is widespread, and cannot be stopped, even among eminent professors."[319]

Did the homosexuality that was practiced in the public schools between 1919 and 1939 induce homosexuality in the pupils? That is a difficult question. It was precisely those alumni who had experienced intense homosexual relations, and then married, who savagely denied being homosexuals. A Hailesbury alumnus recalls: "Oh yes, there were tons of sex. Does that make you a fag? — certainly not. The most active person that I knew at that time became a formidable womanizer."[320] In the same vein, Alec Waugh, in *Pleasure* (1921), depicts a romantic friendship that is nearing its end; passage into adulthood and entry into society entails marriage and heterosexuality; woe to anyone who failed to realize that school was only a brief interlude. Each one had to come to terms with what was coming. They would forget their friends, would fall in love with a girl, and all the rest would turn out to have been just a stupid prelude.[321]

However, the list is long of those who first discovered their future homosexuality or bisexuality through their experiences at school.[322] It seems reasonable to conclude that, if the public schools did not actually produce homosexuality, they at the very least sensitized boys to any latent homosexual inclinations; and so they enabled many boys to clearly determine their sexual identity. The main problem lay in the world outside that condemned homosexuality; once they became active members of society, alumni often had difficulty owning up to what they may have liked to consider youthful indiscretions. Noël Blakiston, in his letters to a former friend at Eton, Cyril Connolly, strives to prove to him that their relationship was always normal and that they were never homosexual. Yet when Connolly married, at the age of,[323] he admitted that, "of

---

319. John Gathorne-Hardy, The Public-School Phenomenon, *op. cit.*, p.92.

320. Cited by John Gathorne-Hardy, *ibid.*, p.164.

321. Alec Waugh, *Pleasure*, London, Grant Richards Ltd, 1921, 320 pages, p.44.

322. Among the famous examples from this period are W.H. Auden, Christopher Isherwood, Stephen Spender, E.M. Forster, Cyril Connolly, Cecil Beaton, J.M. Keynes, Goldsworthy Lowes Dickinson, Lytton Strachey and Bertrand Russell.

323. Cyril Connolly, A Romantic Friendship, The Letters of Cyril Connolly to Noel Blakiston, London, Constable, 1975, 365 pages.

course, the problem is that I am still homosexual, emotionally."36 This, certainly, contributed to the lack of comprehension that prevails between the two sexes, and partly explains the frequent failure of marriage and the sexual dissatisfaction among the bourgeoisie. The boys' regrets are sometimes echoed by the fears and regrets of the girls. According to Martha Vicinus, "many women seem to have found a more complete love during their adolescence than any they ever feel for a man."[324]

Institutional ambiguity with regard to adolescent homosexuality had twofold consequences: having accepted homosexual practices at a given age, it becomes more difficult to resist them later on; moreover, those pupils who had homosexual experiences tended to keep on having them in the future, or at least to consider them favorably. "The men of the British upper class are homosexual in everything except their sexual life."[325] It shows in their lifestyle: together in their clubs, hunting, in the City, they live in an exclusively male environment that recreates as far as possible the atmosphere of the public schools. If homosexuality became a fashion in the 1920s, if homosexuals had a chance to express themselves more freely, it is primarily because many members of the leading classes were secretly allied with them.

Paradise Lost: The English Model

The cult of homosexuality, as we have seen, started in the British education system, which, in point of fact, tolerated homosexual practices. It was bolstered, above all, by the exaltation of adolescent love affairs, and mythologized by the literature of public schools and the memories of the alumni. This is uniquely British.

Indeed, various first-hand accounts exist, telling of homosexual practices in the boarding schools in France and Germany, but adolescent loves were not cherished as dearly and homosexuality was considered, at best, as an obligatory rite of passage, and at worst as a disastrous consequence of an education system mired in vice. To understand better what was different about the English model, we can take a closer look at what was taking place in the neighboring countries.

---

324. Martha Vicinus, "Distance and Desire: English Boarding-School Friendships, 1870-1920," in Martin Duberman, Martha Vicinus and George Chauncey Jr. (dir.), *Hidden from History*, London, Penguin Books, 1991, 579 pages, p.219.

325. A testimony cited by John Gathorne-Hardy, *The Public-School Phenomenon, op. cit.*, p.178.

In France and Germany, as in England, education experts did warn that boarding schools were dangerous, and fostered homosexuality. In Germany, surveys were conducted in the schools to try to determine how widespread homosexuality was. In 1928, a synthesis was published by the National Ministry for Education, entitled, "Sittlichkeitsvergehen in höheren Schulen und ihre disziplinare Behandlung" (Attacks on morals in the secondary schools and their disciplinary treatment). The survey was conducted between 1921 and 1925, with a population of 552 pupils — 467 boys and 85 girls. A total of 36 boys acknowledged having had homosexual experiences; no girls. That is a very weak result, but of course one must take account of the undeclared cases. The authors of the research distinguished two different groups: that of older boys who took the active role, going out with younger boys who were passive. For the most part, they did not have sex but only mutual passion, kisses, and caresses. Then, there are the boys who were "victims of seduction by an adult," who were lured by gifts (theater tickets, alcohol, etc.). These conclusions were repeated in 1936 by Gerhard Reinhard Ritter in *Die geschlechtliche Frage in DER deutschen Volkserziehung* (The sexual question in German popular education). It called the rate of homosexual acts in colleges very high, but suggested that this represented only "acquired," not "real," homosexuality.

Indeed, it is difficult to determine how widespread homosexuality was in the French and German schools, for alumni accounts on this subject are quite rare. However, there are a few reports that seem to substantiate the claim. Golo Mann, in his memoirs entitled *A German Youth*, speaks quite naturally about his early loves: "One day, at school or in the yard, I saw Erika and Klaus with a boy whom I liked enormously, without knowing why. But from then on, I was in love, without knowing the cause and without even knowing the word.... It was my first love for the bigger kids in the playground, and it was not to be the last."[326] Even though the school was co-ed, the officials were terrified that any homosexual activity might take place. The headmaster, Kurt Hahn, was a closet homosexual himself; he carried out a virtual Inquisition against what he termed "promiscuity" and which was considered to start when a pupil put a hand on the shoulder of another. In the spring of 1925, a new pupil arrived at the boarding school and Golo fell vaguely in love. The headmaster was suspicious and forbid to them to go bicycling together for Pentecost.

---

326. Golo Mann, *Une jeunesse allemande*, Paris, Presses de la Renaissance, 1988, 412 pages, p.27-28.

For Golo Mann, the adolescent years did not cause any real problem or raise any question; it was a normal and transitory phase. But others were permanently scarred by their experiences in school. The novelist Ernst Erich Noth was at the center of a tragedy at the College of Steglitz. Günther Scheller shot and killed the apprentice cook, Hans Stefan, on June 27, 1927, and then committed suicide. Scheller was seeking revenge for being supplanted in the favors of a rich patron who was known to invite his protégés on trips to Paris. Noth himself had been known to take advantage of his charms: "I was considered a pretty boy; perhaps I was. The caresses of the old man were not always innocent, but his infirmities prevented him from lavishing more specific favors on me."[327] For Noth, homosexuality was acceptable and profitable: "And yet, in spite of the very 'prudish' public discourse, pederasty was already an indisputable reality in Germany at that time. Since the third grade, we already knew that some of our peers, all sons of good families, were making pocket money by regularly visiting some old Berlin degenerates."[328] Such accounts, although extreme, do tend to indicate that homosexual experiences were relatively widespread in German schools.

The French were not left behind. In *Le Livre blanc (The White Book)* (1928), Jean Cocteau depicts a scene at the Condorcet College, in Paris: "The senses were awakened and flourished unrestrained, and grew like crab grass. There were only perforated pockets and soiled handkerchiefs." He notes, however: "But Condorcet was a college of externalities. These practices did not go as far as falling in love. They hardly went beyond the scope of a clandestine game."[329] In *Les Enfants terribles (The Terrible Children)* (1925), he evokes a schoolboy's emotions: "This love was all the more devastating as it preceded knowledge of love. It was a vague, intense feeling, for which there was no remedy — a pure desire without sex and without any goal."[330]

In like fashion, in *The Sabbath* Maurice Sachs tells of his education in a school that was run "according to the English method." Sachs felt "a chaste love" for his captain, then he was "wised up" by one of his buddies. Another one

327. Ernst Erich Noth, *Mémoires d'un Allemand*, Paris, Julliard, 1970, 506 pages, p.57.
328. *Ibid.*, p.98.
329. Jean Cocteau, *Le Livre blanc* [1928], reedited, Paris, Éditions de Messine, 1983, 123 pages, p.22-23.
330. Jean Cocteau, *Les Enfants terribles* [1929], reedited, Paris, Grasset, 1990, 130 pages, p.19.

granted him favors in exchange for a tennis racquet. The general atmosphere recalled that of the boarding schools and the cadet academies:

> A great wave of sensuality swept through the school. A luxurious sur-feit washed over everybody, in every grade level, and it is no exaggeration to say that out of a hundred pupils, more than fifty were making love with each other. Only the very youngest were exempt, or some boys of solid vir-tue voluntarily kept away from these games. The older ones went after the younger ones. Sometimes we'd go, eight or ten at a time, to roll around and fondle each other in the hay in a barn.[331]

As elsewhere, the vice was ignored, even tolerated by the school author-ities for a while. Then, like a thunderbolt, they made a clean sweep.[332]

> It was surprising that the authorities seemed not to see a thing. One day, something came to their attention and they suddenly undertook a major clean-up campaign. I had, as it was considered at the time, the honor of appearing pretty high up on the list of pupils who were dismissed, and we were sent home with such remarkable courtesy that our parents, fortu-nately, were easily deceived... I think the reason for this indulgence lies in the fact that more than one of our teachers, and particularly the English ones, were guilty.[333]

So, homosexuality was hardly absent from French or German schools. However, it would be too much to say that there was a cult of homosexuality. Indeed, there is an essential difference between the educational institutions of the three countries: in France and Germany, there were boarding schools and there was no co-education;[334] but the boarding school was not the only form of schooling. Consequently, most pupils spent less time alone together; they had the restraining influence of their families; and they stayed in contact with society. Special friendships might have developed, but a "cult of homosexuality"

---

331. Maurice Sachs, *Le Sabbat* [written in 1939, publié en 1946], Paris, Gallimard, 1960, 298 pages, p.35. To the French, England is a prime example of depravity in the schools. In *La Liberté ou l'Amour!* (1924), Robert Desnos presents a scene of lesbian sadism in a British boarding school, "Humming-Bird Garden," where the mistress enjoys whipping the girls.

332. Violette Leduc was thrown out of school for having a sentimental and sexual relationship with one of her comrades, "Isabelle." See Violette Leduc, *La Bâtarde*, Paris, Gallimard, 1964, 462 pages.

333. Maurice Sachs, *Le Sabbat, op. cit.*, p.35.

334. Except for some experimental schools, like Wyneken's at Wickersdorf.

would not be likely to evolve, since that presupposes the existence of a micro-society, partly independent of adults and controlled by a system of codes that the pupils were held to, under penalty of being snubbed and excluded. One might hypothesize that day schools, by releasing pupils from the authoritative influence of the group, only allow for the formation of those homosexual friend-ships that were inevitable, i.e. between boys who would have been homosexual whatever the circumstances. Boys in a boarding school who try out homosexu-ality, in imitation, or out of social pressure, simple curiosity or to gain confi-dence, do not have the opportunity in a more open school system. Thus, homosexuality has less chance to develop on a large scale and to have a lasting impact on a whole generation. That would especially explain the contrast between French homosexual individualism — the result of personal homosexual experiences and free of any group influence — and the English cult of homosexu-ality, resulting from a shared homosexual culture and homosexual history.

An examination of the literature is particularly convincing in this respect. The public school novel is almost a genre of its own, in English literature; and, along with works aimed at teenagers directly, one finds accounts intended for the nostalgic adult. By emphasizing the group spirit, "fair play," the latent homo-eroticism of a unisex society, the author allows the reader to identify easily. The reader internalizes his homosexual experience as an obligatory rite of passage, a decisive test that proves his integration into the society. French literature, and incidentally German literature, are strikingly different. Neither considers the homosexual experience as anything but a rupture of solidarity, an assertion of the ego, a will to set oneself apart. The reader, even if he recognizes himself in the novel, relives an incidence of rejection, either radical or disguised (a penchant for secrecy, codes, messages, etc.). Homosexuality can never constitute a common reference in adult society. It is concealed and considered to have been a unique experience.

We can verify that hypothesis by reviewing a whole series of literary works. In Germany, the novel *The Cadets*, by Ernst von Solomon (1933) transposes the vocabulary, conventions, and rules identical to those of the most sexually emancipated English public schools onto a Prussian military academy:[335]

---

335. See also Robert Musil, *Les Désarrois de l'élève Törless* [1906], Paris, Éditions du Seuil, 1960, 260 pages.

There was a new boy in the barracks. Emil Tillich was the smallest boy in the company, but his limbs were nimble, his eyes full of life and he was well formed. "A nice rabbit," said Gloecken — and I hated him for it. It was the first time that such a remark had annoyed me. I spat back, "You, you always think of 'those things' right away." But he was only expressing the general opinion. Everybody liked Tillich.[336]

The arrival of the pretty new boy led to all sorts of changes in the behavior of his comrades: rivalries intensified, each one tried to outshine the others and to spend as much time with him as possible. Goslar went out of his way to have the boy in his swimming class.[337] The narrator, Schmidt, was in love with Tillich, but was afraid that Goslar had already monopolized him. He soon discovers otherwise:

> During a walk, outside the institution, he simply took my arm. At first, that frightened me. He held my arm so calmly that at first I thought maybe he had no ulterior motive. And then, this took place on the little paved path that went around the meadow and which, by a hallowed tradition, was reserved for pupils of the upper classes. If Tillich was walking there, it became obvious to everyone that I had him. He could not have been unaware of that."[338]
> [From then on, the two boys had a perfectly traditional romantic friendship. In the pupils' honor code, a system equivalent to that of the English fags and prefects was semi-official.] He bore the seal of my friendship. If somebody hurt him, he was attacking me. Of course, there were no secrets between us, except with regard to feelings which a delicate modesty kept us from revealing. It is true that he had to polish the buttons of my uniform, to keep my things in order and to give me his larger slice of bread during recreation. That was well-established tradition. But, in exchange, I was always there when he needed me."[339]
> [Schmidt, like many public school boys, wants to preserve his love from any sexual temptation, any risk of moral debasement. The character of Goslar allows him to create a revealing contrast between this penchant for chastity and the sexual tension that reigned inside the school.] "Obviously, there remained the possibility of kissing. But between desire and realization stood a wall... Goslar, for his part, did not seem to suffer from any such

---

336. Ernst von Salomon, *Les Cadets* [1933], Paris, Correa, 1953, 277 pages, p.167-168.
337. *Ibid.*, p.169.
338. *Ibid.*, p.171.
339. *Ibid.*, p.172.

inhibition. I found his behavior coarse, low, "proletarian," as we said in such cases. He maintained a noisy cheerfulness with respect to Tillich, grabbing his buttocks during exercises and, during work, never passed by his chair without giving him a friendly cuff on the ear.[340]

It all ends in disillusionment; Schmidt discovers that Tillich has been deceiving him from the very beginning with Goslar and avenges himself by humiliating him.

The system goes on, just the same. As Gloecken observes: "A true rabbit is afraid of any lasting ties."[341] In the homosexual micro-society of the school, a young boy, if he is pretty, if he has the good luck to be appealing, has a considerable advantage over his comrades. Far from being a victim of the system, he is the principal beneficiary and reserves the right, when he grows older, to have "rabbits" in his turn.[342] In the end, it is romantic boys like Schmidt who suffer most from the ambient cynicism.

Another German work, *The Child Manuela, or Girls in Uniform* (1934) by Christa Winsloe, is quite representative of the existence of homosexuality within the boarding schools.[343] This book was made into a play and then a movie. Christa Winsloe was clearly inspired by her personal experience. She was sent as an adolescent to an institution for noble girls in northern Germany. In the book, written in a simple and straightforward style, the young Manuela is sent to a military college for girls, when a scandal breaks out: she is believed to have fallen in love with a young man. In fact, she loves his mother. At the boarding school, the atmosphere is charged with secret passions. Pupils wear lockets engraved on the inside with the initials of a professor, in a heart pierced by an arrow. At the same time, pupils are falling in love with each other, offering gifts and exchanging notes. Manuela falls passionately in love with the most popular mistress who, in turn, is not insensitive to her affection — but hides her feelings. In the end, Manuela reveals her feelings — to the whole school — during a costume ball. The scandal is enormous. The director speaks of "abnormal feelings," and upbraids the teacher, saying: "And do you know what the world — our world — thinks of this kind of women?" Manuela is isolated from her com-

---

340. *Ibid.*, p.173.
341. *Ibid.*, p.174.
342. See also, in 1929, *Classe 22* by Ernst Gläser and *Alf* by Bruno Vogel.
343. This novel, first adapted for the theater by its author in 1931, was followed by a movie that was a big success the same year and was published only in 1934.

rades and her teacher; in desperation, she throws herself from the window. Miss von Bernburg holds her in her arms one last time as she lies on the paving stone.

In fact, compared to the English works, German works relating to homosexual loves at school depict a more morbid and sadistic atmosphere. The ties between the boys are clearly established in terms of power and competition, and those who struggle to keep their loves pure are bound for disillusionment. In the girls' schools, the strict rules relentlessly prevent any personal expression and deny the pupils any right to tenderness and freedom. This depressing and negative presentation of the situation in the schools explains why no cult of homosexuality developed; readers who could have found any childhood memories in these books were not encouraged to recall them in positive terms.

This situation is less striking in France, where the majority of homosexual writers evoked their adolescent years in a context other than the boarding school. They were more sheltered. Furthermore, the education system placed its emphasis on intellectual prowess and not on sports. Relationships between boys were not based on physical violence and brutal games. Lastly, French literature dealing with homosexuality in the schools was generally not written by homosexuals seeking to regain the happiness of their lost loves, but on the contrary by those who opposed homosexuality and who sought to discredit the type of education that fosters it.

The most famous work in France was *Claudine à l'école* (*Claudine at School*) (1900); that came before the era we are looking at, but it still has quite an impact. Unlike other French authors, Colette did not approach the subject from a moralistic and morbid angle. The adventures of Claudine and her friends are shown as normal, amusing, part of the accepted adolescent amorous adventures, a prelude to more lasting attachments — to men. Only the relationship between Aimée and Miss Sergent turns sinister, precisely because the director is no longer a girl and she places Aimée in a perverse, socially unacceptable situation. Unlike the English novels, the book aimed above all to titillate the reader and for that sole purpose makes many a Sapphic allusion.[344]

The account that comes closest to the English cult of homosexuality is that of Henry de Montherlant, in his very fictionalized book, *Les Garçons* (*The Boys*). Montherlant relates his adolescence at the college of Sainte-Croix, in Neuilly, from January 1911 (when he was admitted) to March 1912 (when he was thrown out). This short episode made a lasting impression on him and he recalled it time

---

344. On Claudine, see Chapter Five.

and time again. He brings it up once in *La Ville dont le prince est un enfant*, a play that was written in 1929 (but only published in 1951).[345] His memory of this period sounds quite like the English accounts: "Love made the college fabulous."[346]

Montherlant developed two themes in *The Boys*: adolescent love and the fascination which it exerts on adults. The heart of the work is the relationship between Alban de Bricoule and Serge Souplier, which fits into an extremely precise and codified protocol. The school of "Our-Lady-of-the-Park" is divided into groups of boys classified according to various aesthetic criteria and their stage of sexual awakening. "Those who were part of this coterie, which they called 'the Group,' all wore their ties outside of their jackets, as a rallying sign. But Louchard, who was not part of them, started to wear his tie on the outside, too. Then everyone in the clique put theirs back inside."[347] Lists of "protégés" were circulated, and were known even to the professors — who maintained this atmosphere of homoeroticism: "Binet said to Salins: 'Brulat as a protégé, what an idea! How could you choose him, with his big ears! When one takes a protégé, one chooses one with lovely, sweet little face.' I asked him: 'And you, Sir, did you have little protégés when you were our age?' He replied: 'Oh! Me, I had tons of them!'"[348]

The system was classic: "An older one is 'going' with a younger one? OK. But two of the older boys together?... Revolting, or rather, unthinkable."[349] Love often took the form of "torture": the older boys made martyrs of the younger ones to prove their interest in them. The whole school seemed to be centered around love affairs: "After studies (or before), the only occupation and the only concern, at Our-Lady-of-the-Park, were these friendships."[350] The atmosphere was permeated with sex, and everything that happened all day had erotic overtones: " 'And this 'Park' vocabulary!...One would think we were talking about the shows at the Moulin-Rouge. Couldn't you speak a little differently?' — 'Everyone talks like that here, the abbots and Profs as well as the kids, as you very well know.'"[351]

---

345. Montherlant reprised this work in 1947, encouraged by the publication of *Amitiés particulières* by Roger Peyrefitte (1943); similarly, *Les Garçons*, which he had been working on since 1919, did not come out until 1969.

346. Cited by Pierre Sipriot, *Montherlant sans masque*, t.I, *L'Enfant prodigue, 1895-1932*, Paris, Robert Laffont, 1980, 500 pages, p.39.

347. Henry de Montherlant, *Les Garçons*, Paris, Gallimard, 1973, 549 pages, p.187.

348. *Ibid.*, p.26.

349. *Ibid.*, p.35.

350. *Ibid.*, p.91.

Alban and Serge become friends; it all starts in a relatively traditional way: admiration, kisses, caresses; they are baptized "the ideal couple." In this closed adolescent world, complications inevitably originate from the few adults who maintain contact: Alban's mother clearly savors her son's revelations, vicariously enjoying the erotic thrill of the unhealthy situation. But the abbots in particular maintain this noxious climate. They tolerate close friendships, but only to the extent that they do not interfere with their authority or encourage any emancipation the of young people. Like Alban's mother, they enjoy it all from the sidelines, and the palpitations of the boys reverberate in them and disturb them deeply. Adolescent homosexuality becomes a problem only when it reveals adult homosexuality: the abbot de Pradts is in love with Serge Souplier, and works hard to keep from admitting it. He convinces Alban that his love (for Serge) is impure, that he must keep the moral well-being of his little friend in mind. Soon, the situation is reversed: "Virtue came back into fashion." Lastly, when Alban and Souplier are found closeted together, the wheels start to roll: Pradts gets Alban expelled, but the superior, who knows what Pradts is up to, throws out Souplier, as well.

The dénouement is edifying, for it perfectly sums up the cult of homosexuality. The scandal at the institution is revealed, and the abbots are dismissed and replaced by new-comers. The new generation at Park will not be protected. Alban discovers girls, and his "situational" (or *"occasionel"*) homosexuality comes to a sudden end. Adolescence is a closed world to which it is impossible to return: "The abbot de Pradts replied to the superior, who told him to find Souplier one day: 'It will be too late,' and to Alban: 'The kids, it's over so quickly.' So it was all a question of age."[352]

Still, Montherlant does not leave the question of adolescent homosexuality as merely a rite of passage; he shows that, consciously and unconsciously, it affects one's future life: "De Pradts tore up the photographs of Serge. Alban went out of his way not to pass in front of his house. Linbourg preferred not to have to see kids around." Later, they all send their children to Park, just as all those English fathers send their children to the same public school that they knew.

Homosexual relations in the religious schools are a fairly traditional topic. Daniel Guérin, at Bossuet, relates that he "also discovered, as a result of an indis-

---

351. *Ibid.*, p.294-295. Montherlant gave estimates that don't appear to conflict with the English examples: a little more than a third of the whole were part of the "protection," and in some years it was close to half.

352. *Ibid.*, p.469, and 484.

cretion, that certain abbots and their favorite pupils exchanged rather thorough embraces, in a dark little room close to the vault."[353] In *Le Cahier gris* (1922), Roger Martin du Gard makes veiled allusions to a romantic friendship between Jacques Thibault and Daniel Fontanin; there is no sign of the licentious atmosphere of the boarding schools, here. The young boys, candid, sincere and passionate, exchange fervent poems and oaths of eternal loyalty. They do not even suspect they are doing wrong. It is the abbot who, discovering the book, condemns the relationship as sinful: "The tone, the content of the letters, alas!, did not leave any doubt as to the nature of this friendship."[354]

Cheap popular novels exploit the theme of special friendships at religious schools, implying that they are a hotbed of perversion. This set of themes is part of a long anticlerical tradition; some examples would be *Adolescents: mœurs collégiennes*, by Jean Rodes (1904), *Antone Ramon* by Amédée Guiard (1914), *Les Adolescents passionnés* by Albert Nortal and Charles-Étienne (1927), and *L'Enfant de chœur* by René Étiemble (1937). Rodes states in his foreword that he does not intend to criticize only church schools but the entire school system and the very foundation of our moral system. His novel takes place at a college in Gascogne; it is run by Jesuits who follow "the British style." Special friendships develop as a result of "such an abnormal education" and "the de-virilizing scholastic program." The characters are caricatures and the tone is melodramatic. The romantic machinations are observed by a chaste pupil, who severely condemns the system and quits the school, complaining of "the strange doctrines that rule at Saint-Vincent, according to which kissing a woman is an unpardonable shame, an offense infinitely worse than same-sex licentiousness."[355]

L'Enfant de chœur (The Choirboy) develops the same theme. The hero, André Steindel, makes friends with another new boy, Maurice. The older boys jump in, immediately: "Ah hah! That's a good one! Already taking rabbits. You are way ahead of yourselves. That's not allowed.... Only big kids are entitled to rabbits."[356] The system very quickly pulls them apart. André becomes "the rabbit" of a bigger boy and, "by Christmas, Maurice had slit open his left pocket."[357] André becomes a choirboy with Maurice; they make love in the sac-

---

353. Daniel Guérin, *Autobiographie de jeunesse*, Paris, Belfond, 1972, 248 pages, p.71.

354. Roger Martin du Gard, *Le Cahier gris*, in *Œuvres complètes*, Paris, Gallimard, coll. "Bibl. de la Pléiade," 1981, t.I, 1 403 pages.

355. Jean Rodes, *Adolescents: mœurs collégiennes*, Paris, Société du Mercure de France, 1904, 219 pages, p.211-212.

356. René Étiemble, *L'Enfant de chœur*, Paris, Gallimard, 1937, 251 pages, p.25.

risty. In 1924, the climate changes: new students are no longer violated, and there is less rampant vice. The author indicates that the homosexual fad was related to the relaxation of morals and the loss of parental authority after the war. The situation would return toward normal within a few years.

In *Antone Ramon*, the institution is given as St. Francis de Sales of Bourg; the 13-year-old hero, Antone Ramon, falls in love with an older boy who takes him under his wing. Due to a series of misunderstandings and some malicious maneuvering on the part of some of their comrades, plus the opposition of George's parents, he loses his friend. He then sinks into more and more degrading conduct. The book ends with his accidental death, which comes as the just desserts for the sins he has committed.

Nortal and Charles-Étienne's book was a frontal attack on religious schools. The foreword sets the tone: "The calm of a friendly interview would be far preferable to the confessional booth where the ecclesiastic, by the pall of his very breath, by his perfidious questions, can create an incendiary vice, can ignite a full-blown debauchery."[358] The three heroes, pupils at St. Allaix college, run by the Fathers, are described as near caricatures — fair, slender, delicate. They are rivals for the attentions of Jean-Louis Massias, a feral, feline-like dissolute, with destructive inclinations. In the study hall, "thoughts of debauchery permeate the air, flitting through everyone's minds, brutal, fast, fleeting, and shameful." The book obligingly renders the details of the complex relations between the boys. One, who is ugly, contents himself with looking at photographs of beautiful young men. Another, called "pet," "rabbit," or "Jesus," is under Massias's thumb. Their relationship starts with a love letter, whereas, generally, "this kind of union begins with a pummeling or a stinging cuff on the ears."[359] The competition was relentless: "Bégot kissed me on the neck and Bahier went after me in the urinal."[360] The atmosphere is noxious; Page and Massias sleep together, but after the holidays Page is replaced by Ferrari. Massias is also secretly in love with his male cousin. Fernand sinks into sex and promiscuity; his health and his grades suffer. There are rapes and other attacks; the boys are expelled; some fail their baccalaureates. When Massias tells his cousin he loves him, the other condemns him, saying: "I was born normal,... not every schoolboy is full of vice." He

---

357. *Ibid.*, p.45.

358. Charles-Étienne and Albert Nortal, *Les Adolescents passionnés*, Paris, Curio, 1928, 253 pages, p.13.

359. *Ibid.*, p.37.

360. *Ibid.*, p.45.

has read medical books in his father's library and understands what's "wrong" with Massias. He offers to take him to the doctor, but Massias defends his own point of view, citing Oscar Wilde, Jean Lorrain, Pierre Louÿs, Rachilde, Proust, Gide and Havelock Ellis! During a night of drinking, Massias sleeps with his cousin. The book ends, after some further adventures, with Massias committing suicide. Once more, adolescent homosexuality is shown as the result of the corrupting influence of a misguided teaching establishment that fosters an unhealthy environment. The pupils have only two possible choices: to give themselves up to vice and sink into prostitution, or to die.

Thus, in France and Germany, the school years left a sense of disillusionment. Adolescent loves left an aftertaste of betrayal, vice and guilt. Those who were confirmed homosexuals hardly wished to revive such memories; and those who turned to women, in adulthood, preferred to forget such wayward behavior. In England, by contrast, the literature celebrates the adolescent years and definitively associates the cult of homosexuality with that of the public school. The teen years are depicted as pure and free, an ideal of friendship that can never be found again. After the passionate attachments that formed at school, adult loves will always appear to lack the spontaneity and enthusiasm of youth.

The cult of the public school was also widespread as regards girls. Starting in 1902, alumnae of Roedan would come back to the school on weekends; they'd wear their old uniforms, and act as if nothing had changed. Other public schools would hold events where the school anthem was sung and girls would talk over the good old days. A literature developed on this theme, as well, albeit to a lesser extent. Enid Blyton published a dozen works on the subject.[361] Angela Brazil had a successful series celebrating the days spent at public school.[362] Her tales of friendship between schoolgirls, and sometimes teachers, include kissing scenes and naïve jealousies. It is hard to say whether any readers identified with char-

---

361. One wonders why the novels of Enid Blyton were in such disrepute in France, in contradiction to her phenomenal success in the bookstore. This literature is centered around just one theme: life in autarky of children or teenagers (*The Club of the five, The Clan of the seven*, etc.). Police schemes serve as a pretext for a survey of adolescent mores, in a closed world, made up of secrets and codes. Even more striking are the scenes directly dedicated to life in boarding school (the *Mallory School* cycle, *The Two Twins*). In each book, exclusive relationships are formed that provoke jealousies typical of love; relations between the girls are sensual, passionate. The subversive character of this literature is obvious: it develops feelings in the reader which cannot be manifested in the French school system, which doesn't encourage the formation of a team spirit and the development of a homoerotic climate founded on admiration.

acters called Lesbia Ferrars or Lesbia Carrington, "The Lady Lavender," or were attracted by titles like *A Terrible Tomboy*.[363] Gillian Freeman suggest that although Angela Brazil's writing was based on her own memories of youth and personal experience, she was not conscious of the sexual implications of her novels. But, for the reader, the atmosphere of the schools seems heavily charged with eroticism and sentimentality. That thousands of readers saw themselves in such descriptions does indicate that, however much real sexual activity was going on, such passionate attachments between girls were far from uncommon.

The subversive aspect of these works cannot be ignored; these novels were very unpopular with school directors. In 1936, a novella about St. Paul's in London was severely denounced by the principal, Ethel Strudwick, who then announced at morning prayers that she would collect all the Angela Brazil books and burn them.[364]

Public school and the homosexuality that was implicitly linked to it took on mythic connotations in the English culture, gaining legitimacy and glorification. Christopher Isherwood accurately traces the process of idealization that occurs in adulthood, noting that gradually, in absolute secrecy, he started to develop a cult of the public school. Not that his own progress through school had been marked by anything particularly romantic, heroic, dangerous, or epic. Rather, he concocted a fantasy in which he was an austere young professor called in unexpectedly to head up "a bad house," surrounded by scornful detractors and declared enemies, and that he set himself to combat the delinquency and moral decay, severely repressing his own romantic feelings for a

362. Gillian Freeman, *The Schoolgirl Ethic. The Life and Work of Angela Brazil*, London, Allen Lane, 1976, 159 pages; Rosemary Auchmuty, "You're a Dyke, Angela! Elsie J. Oxenham and the Rise and Fall of the Schoolgirl Story," *in* Lesbian History Group, *Not a Passing Phase. Reclaiming Lesbians in History, 1840-1985*, London, The Women's Press, 1989, 264 pages.

363. In 1936, Lord Berners amused his friends in London by publishing a satire entitled *Les Filles de Radclyffe Hall, by* Adela Quebec. The book is a double parody: on the one hand, it describes relations between girls at a college, caricaturing the schemings of Angela Brazil, but in a spicier style; and the name of the boarding school is, obviously, that of one of the best known British lesbians: "John" Radclyffe Hall; and then, it proves to be a rigorously exact transposition of events and relations in love concerning well-known homosexuals, notably Cecil Beaton and Peter Watson. Cecil Beaton actually succeeded in having nearly all the existing copies destroyed. See Hugo Vickers, *Cecil Beaton, op. cit.*, and Adela Quebec, *The Girls of Radclyffe Hall*, "printed for the author for private circulation only," London, 1935, 100 pages.

364. Reprted by Gillian Freeman, *The Schoolgirl Ethic, op. cit.*, p.19.

younger boy and, finally, triumphing over all the obstacles, having passed the test, and emerged — a man.[365]

The myth and the idealization reach their climax in the imagination of Isherwood and his friend Edward Upward, then in his relations with W.H. Auden. With this last, he imagines heroic sagas, whose heroes would be the alumni of their school. For Auden and Isherwood, adolescent sexuality is the referent, the ideal, and at the same time the symbol of an immaturity which they sought to preserve as long as possible:

> — Their friendship was deep-rooted in the memories of schoolboys and the nature of their sexuality was adolescent. They had slept together, without romanticism but with much pleasure, during the ten last years, every time the occasion presented itself, as they now did. They could not see themselves in quite the same terms as before, however, sex had brought an additional dimension to their friendship. They were aware of that and it bothered them, a little — in fact, sophisticated adults were embarrassed by their sexual partners from school.[366]

Cyril Connolly also recalls how his experiences at school prefigured the rest of his love life. At the age of 30, he looks back on his youth at St. Cyprian: — The boy that I loved during my last three years at [school] ... was small, brunette, vigorous, good at sports... His type kept turning up throughout my life, giving me trouble... At the age of 12, the four types to which I was sensitive had already appeared.... the Faun, the Redhead, the Extreme Blond, and the Brunette Friend.[367]

When the boys separated, at the age of 18, they exchanged addresses and promised not to forget each other. They should not have worried on that score; they never forgot. Several years later Connolly went to the theater with a friend, and suddenly noticed a man with a ruddy face and a white moustache, and looked at him long and hard. In the taxi going home, he suddenly burst into tears, saying: "At... school... he smelled... of tangerines."[368] A symbol of lost youth, fleeting love, and vanished dreams, homosexuality thus became the ideal of a generation. The public schools contributed substantially to the creation of the myth.

---

365. Christopher Isherwood, *Lions and Shadows, op. cit.*, p.47-48.

366. Christopher Isherwood, cited by Humphrey Carpenter, *W.H. Auden, a Biography*, London, Allen & Unwin, 1981, 495 pages, p.63.

367. Cited by H.Carpenter, *The Brideshead Generation, op. cit.*, p.22.

368. Cited by John Gathorne-Hardy, *The Public-School Phenomenon, op. cit.*, p.180.

TWO GENERATIONS OF HOMOSEXUAL INTELLECTUALS

In England, the cult of homosexuality was propagated by many intellectuals who, for the most part, had experienced public school life personally. When they went on to university, the high point of British homosexuality, it only reinforced their tendencies. Their many personal accounts, in the form of novels or autobiographies, disseminated the mythical view of the 1920s as years of homosexual liberation, unique and never to be repeated.

The First Homosexual Generation: Precursors

The first homosexual generation grew up at Cambridge, and then went on to form the Bloomsbury Club. This was a meeting ground for intellectuals who valued human relations and combated the Victorian spirit; they made themselves known by their militant pacifism during the First World War and their political, economic and moral liberalism. This generation of intellectuals, born in the 1880s, played a central role in changing how homosexuality was looked upon in England. By 1919, they were the role models for the next generation.

Cambridge and the "Apostles"

For this first generation, Cambridge was the symbol of the cult of homosexuality. The majority of the professors encouraged male relationships, which they practiced themselves more or less openly. A.E. Housman was a famous poet praising pedophile loves. His poem, "A Shropshire Lad" (1896), was a kind of touchstone for homosexuals during the inter-war period. The philosopher C.G. Broad expressed a clear penchant for Scandinavians. D.A. Winstanley, a professor of Victorian history; Gaillard Lapsley, a medievalist; H.O. Evennett; F.A. Simpson; Andrew Grew; and the economist A. C. Pigou (who took his prettier students along with him for hikes in the Alps); A.F. Scholfield, the librarian; professor of ancient history F.E. Adcock; and, finally, the vice-chancellor himself, J.T. Sheppard, were also known. The most famous figure was Oscar Browning, professor of history, tutor to E.M. Forster, and a former director of Eton, but who was fired in the wake of an enormous homosexual scandal.[369]

---

369. Cited by Noel Annan, *Our Age, op. cit.*, p.102.

The tendency was appreciably the same among the students. It is fair to say that, from 1895 to approximately 1910, Cambridge was as idyllic a setting for homosexuals as Oxford was in the inter-war period. One observer noted that:

> — in Cambridge there is, considering the nature of the business, an unusual number people of such a [homosexual] temperament, although they are not always conscious of it; and I do not doubt that besides the relations between the young people themselves, relations of a personal nature with obliging professors may be the best thing that Cambridge has to offer.[370]

However, whereas Oxford looked to the triumph of aestheticism and proclaimed the glory of homosexuality, Cambridge was characterized by its discreet tolerance, good taste, and restraint. The students, if they were homosexual, regarded this preference as an almost intellectual choice and very often kept their sexuality within a framework of asceticism and chastity. The adoration of boys was asserted as a philosophical ideal derived from the Greeks; it was idealized to the point of removing any sensuality and any concrete sexual implication. These ideas had a lasting influence on the first generation which — on the basis of such premises — could defend homosexuality as a noble activity, an ideal of purity and abnegation as opposed to heterosexual debauchery and the shameless quest for pleasure. At the same time, this attitude did nothing to facilitate a liberation of morals; the ideas were tolerated but the acts were not.

The first reflections on homosexuality were developed by those who went on to become the founding members of the Bloomsbury Club and who were, at the time, members of the Apostles, a secret society founded in 1820. Many of its members are now famous: Bertrand Russell, Desmond MacCarthy, Leonard Woolf, Lytton Strachey, E.M. Forster, H.O. Meredith, Clive Bell, Thoby Stephen and J.M. Keynes. In addition to intellectual concerns, most of the Apostles also shared a taste for boys. After Keynes was elected to join the Apostles, students came to be recruited more for their beauty and charm (Arthur Lee Hobhouse) than for their intelligence (although Rupert Brooke combined both). Bertrand Russell noted that homosexual relations became common, whereas they hitherto had been unknown.[371]

---

370. Cited by John Gathorne-Hardy, *The Public-School Phenomenon, op. cit.*, p.146.
371. See Robert Skidelsky, *J.M. Keynes, Hopes Betrayed, 1883-1920*, London, Macmillan, 1983, 447 pages.

A theoretical basis for homosexual love was developed in tandem with this new trend, and that was decisive in the expansion of the cult of homosexuality. Love of boys was defined as the highest form of love (higher sodomy) that one could experience, women being inferior in body and spirit. E.M. Forster wrote, in *Maurice*, "I feel the same thing for you as Pipa for her fiancé, only far nobler, deeper, more absolute; neither sensuality nor medievalism disincarnate, but a particular harmony of the body and soul of which I think women can have no idea."[372] Here, we find Platonic themes renewed, an apologia for masculine relations that defines homosexuality as the final stage in intellectual and aesthetic development, the only choice for a man of taste. The Apostles' theories were tinged with misogyny, which exasperated Virginia Woolf. While their influence was liberal, in the sense that they removed the shame from homosexuality, their actions were consistent with a conservative masculine and patriarchal framework.

The Apostles tended to see a link between intelligence and homosexuality. The perception of homosexuals changed, little by little; and after the war, the new generation internalized this model and had no further qualms about asserting its homosexuality as a positive thing.

Deprived of female company and generally living in a closed world, students at Cambridge organized their life around male friendships. This helped them preserve some sense of their childhood and isolated them from a world which they perceived as hostile. Swithinbank said that, at college, — emotions and desires were directed almost exclusively toward the male sex. [He] did not know anyone, in other words, who ever gave any thought to women. That does not mean that there was much "sex"; that was looked down on with a disapproval that was not entirely free of envy on the part of those who repressed their desires out of timidity or virtue.[373]

Sentimental friendships were the prevailing trend; homosexuality was more a myth that an act and the first generation certainly could not be accused of indulging in unfettered sexuality. The school years remained highly evocative in the homosexual imagination; the final chapter of *Maurice* recreates that eternal nostalgia: "To the end of his life, Clive was never sure of the exact moment when [Maurice] departed and, over the years, he came to doubt that he had ever left.

---

372. E.M. Forster, *Maurice* [written in 1914], Paris, Christian Bourgois éditeur, 1987, 279 pages, p.97-98.
373. Bernard Swithinbank, cited by R. Skidelsky, *J.M. Keynes, op. cit.*, p.104.

The blue room radiated gently, the ferns undulated and, with Cambridge in the distant background, he seemed to see his friend making signs to him sign, haloed by the sun, among the confused rumor and the perfumes of the May trimester."[374]

Bloomsbury

March 1905 is the accepted date for the foundation of the Bloomsbury Club, since it was then that Vanessa, Thoby, Adrian and Virginia Stephen launched their Thursday soirées at 46 Gordon Square, in London. It is more difficult to pin down when the Club dissolved, but we can date it to roughly 1931 (when Lytton Strachey died) to 1934 (when Roger Fry died). It would be hard to draw up a complete list of the group's members, for some maintained fairly loose ties throughout the entire period, and some took an active part for a limited time. Still, we can name the most essential active members: Leonard and Virginia (Stephen) Woolf, Vanessa (Stephen) Bell (her sister) and Clive Bell (Vanessa's husband); Adrian Stephen (their brother), Lytton Strachey, James and Marjorie Strachey, E.M. Forster, David Garnett, Desmond and Molly MacCarthy, Roger Fry, Duncan Grant, Saxon Sydney-Turner, J.M. Keynes and Francis Birrell.[375]

The meetings were informal, friendly get-togethers to discuss painting, literature and life in general. The very idea of men and women discussing such things together freely was already avant-garde. But Bloomsbury also went on to develop a theory of sexuality and human relations which questioned the moral foundations of the Victorian Era. They were influenced by the Neo-Pagans, whose followers had been students with them in the same colleges. Virginia Woolf had caught everyone's attention by skinny-dipping in a pond with Rupert Brooke at Cambridge and going camping with him without a chaperone. The influence of Edward Carpenter can also be felt. E.M. Forster had met Carpenter and Merrill at Millthorpe. According to Forster, Carpenter exerted "a magnetic influence" on him and Merrill, by touching his lower back, gave him a new erotic sensation that left a lasting impression.[376]

---

374. E.M. Forster, *Maurice*, *op. cit.*, p.279.

375. According to the list given by Quentin Bell in *Bloomsbury* [1968], London, Weidenfeld & Nicolson, 1990, 127 pages, p.15.

376. This encounter inspired him to write *Maurice*. Francis King, *E.M. Forster*, London, Thames & Hudson, 1978, 128 pages.

They were up on all the latest sexual theories: Lytton Strachey, Virginia Woolf, Vanessa and Clive Bell had read and discussed Havelock Ellis; and all of them had felt the influence of G.E. Moore, whose book *Principia Ethica* would be used as the basis of their ideas. For Moore, state of mind was more important than action or achievements. Since love is generally considered a very positive state of mind, it becomes almost synonymous with a successful life (the good life). The innovative aspect of Moore's philosophy lay in the difference he delineated between what is "good" from the human perspective and what is "good" from the moral perspective. This distinction was re-examined by Bloomsbury, which always put the human considerations first. Consequently, the Club repudiated both politics and accepted sexual conventions as symbols of hypocrisy; it replaced religion with skepticism; it rejected material success in favor of glorifying art; and it rejected the ineluctability of the First World War by defending the pacifist cause.

Most of the men in Bloomsbury were homosexual and at least one woman, Virginia Woolf, had lesbian tendencies.[377] Homosexuality could not have failed to be a frequent topic of discussion. Bloomsbury promoted very free speech when it came to sexuality, regardless of gender differences or any question of decency. Vanessa Bell noted that one could speak about intercourse, sodomy, fellatio or a cat, without raising any eyebrows.[378] And Virginia Woolf seconded her, saying that sexuality penetrated the conversation regularly, with the word "pederast" coming up all the time; copulation was discussed with the same fervor and freedom as the question of "what is good."[379]

Virginia Woolf frequently complained about the superficial nature of certain meetings, where the men amused themselves describing their conquests in terms of visits to a urinal. Still, this freedom of language was revolutionary and, by taking away the shock value, by looking at homosexuality as a personal and not a social matter, Bloomsbury denied the dangers of perversion and the need to isolate homosexuals.

The following generation took this teaching to heart. As Virginia Woolf saw it, — There was nothing one could not say, nothing one could not do at 46

377.Ottoline Morrell's daughter remembers that epoque in these terms: "I do not recall ever meeting a man who was sexually normal at my mother's."

378. Cited by Robert Skidelsky, *J.M. Keynes, op. cit.*, p.248.

379. Virginia Woolf, *Instants de vie* [1976], Paris, Stock, 1986, 273 pages, p.240-241. Virginia Woolf's remarks, in her *Journals*, cited by Philip Hoare, *Serious Pleasures: The Life of Stephen Tennant*, London, Penguin, 1992, 463 pages, p.152.

Gordon Square. It was a great progress in civilization. Pederast loves may not be a subject of paramount importance (if one is not a member of that brotherhood); but the fact that one can mention them openly leads to the fact that there is nothing wrong with them if they are kept private. Also, many customs and convictions were revised. Indeed, the Bloomsbury that was to come would prove that one can play many variations on the topic of sexuality and with such happy results that my father himself would have hesitated before thundering the single word he considered the only one appropriate for a pederast or an adulterer; which was: Scoundrel![380]

But the tolerance was not only verbal in Bloomsbury. While the Club did not exactly consist of sexual anarchists, it was still very much the creator of an extremely relaxed way of life. Homosexuality or bisexuality was standard, accompanied by a frequent change of lovers or partner-swapping. Honesty of feelings took precedence over jealousy. Most members of Bloomsbury had extremely active and agitated sex lives, which they discussed among themselves in detail. Keynes, for example, had had several affairs at school (in particular with Dilwyn Knox, Bernard Swithinbank and A.L. Hobhouse), then he conceived a passion for Duncan Grant. Grant initially had been the lover of Lytton Strachey (who had, himself, coveted Hobhouse). Grant subsequently left Keynes for Hobhouse, then for David Garnett. The same David Garnett had had a fling with Keynes, who then kept up a parallel liaison with Francis St. George Nelson (seventeen years) and Francis Birrell. Dora Carrington, who was in love with Lytton Strachey, married Ralph Partridge, with whom Strachey was enamored, and they lived together in an eternal triangle.

It is useless and basically impossible to draw an exhaustive diagram of the various connections which linked the members of the group; but it is quite obvious that such nonconformity influenced young people like Christopher Isherwood who came to visit. Even those who had less turbulent love lives all the same followed their inclinations freely. E.M. Forster, who had been in love with H.O. Meredith in school, had his first sexual experience in India with Mohammed el-Adt, a tram driver; then, he had several flings, in Alexandria especially; in London, he lived with a police officer, Bob Buckingham, for several years.

Forster's example illustrates another aspect of the Bloomsbury message. Homosexual liberation must not to be limited to unbridled sexuality; the purity

---

380. Virginia Woolf, *Instants de vie, op. cit.,* p.241.

of homosexual feelings must be confirmed. In *Maurice*, Forster expresses what thousands of boys had hitherto felt, without daring to acknowledge it: — He vaguely visualized a face, he vaguely heard a voice saying to him: "Here is your friend," and he awoke bedazzled and bewildered by tenderness. He would have been willing to die for such a friend, he would have accepted that such a friend should die for him; they would have made any sacrifice for each other, not caring about either the world or death; nothing could have separated them, neither distances nor obstacles."[381]

For this reason, *Maurice* can be regarded as the manifesto of a generation. Written in 1914, it was published only after Forster's death 1970. But the book circulated among homosexuals and was recognized as the expression of their desire to be free to fully exercise their love. For the first time, male homosexuality was described without shame nor remorse and without either punishment or separation at the end of the road. "Two together can defy the world," that was the general idea.[382] A new feeling had been born: pride.

At the end of the novel, Maurice and Alec give up their bourgeois life, their careers and their social aspirations, to live their love completely. This happy end, full of hope, nonetheless leaves the reader unsure. *Maurice* does not guarantee that their love will succeed; it merely heralds a new age where such a love will be possible. Also, the message which Bloomsbury bequeaths to homosexuals is balanced, but rich in hope. It stresses the importance of the individual and the sacred character of human relations. "Only connect," wrote Forster: we must recreate the bond between the body and the soul, which Victorian morals had so efficiently severed. By celebrating the wisdom of the body and the regenerative power of love, Bloomsbury opened the way to more radical combat. Homosexuality became the symbol of a generation.

The Second Homosexual Generation: The Apogee

To summarize the entire generation of the 1920s and 1930s in just three names may seem bold, but given the works of W.H. Auden, Christopher Isherwood and Stephen Spender, it may be justified. They embodied the common attitude of the intellectuals of their epoch,[383] and that of most of the middle- and upper-class homosexuals as well.[384] They described their experiences and their

---

381. E.M. Forster, *Maurice, op. cit.*, p.22.
382. *Ibid.*, p.149.
383. Noel Annan, *Our Age, op. cit.*, p.98-135.

opinions in their novels (Isherwood), their poems (Auden), and their autobiographies (all three). The amount of dissimulation or alteration (even involuntary) of which their testimony might be accused is, in itself, indicative of the era, its desires and its fears. In that, their accounts are irreplaceable. Christopher Isherwood was born in 1904, W.H. Auden in 1907 and Stephen Spender in 1909. The years 1919-1939 are those of their youth, their first sexual intercourse and, at least until 1933, of their exploration of Germany, which was to mark them deeply. For Bloomsbury, sexual nonconformity was closely tied to rejection of Victorian society. The succeeding generation did not have this reference mark, and therefore it would build its design of homosexuality on new values.

The Succeeding Generation

The succeeding generation wanted above all to claim the legacy of Bloomsbury and in particular that of E.M. Forster, whom Isherwood met in 1932. "My England is that of Edward Morgan,"[385] he would say. Isherwood read *Maurice*. Although he was bothered by the use of certain euphemisms (to share, rather than "to make love," for example), he was impressed and felt indebted to those who had fought these earlier battles for him. He credited Forster with the "miracle" of producing this novel in the age when it was written, the ability to get beyond the "jungle of prejudices" of the pre-war period and managing to express in words such "inadmissible opinions."[386] And when Forster humbly asked him what a member of the generation of the 1930s might think of *Maurice* and whether he found the novel dated, Isherwood answered him: "Why shouldn't it be dated?"[387] The book announced, indeed, that a happy ending is possible for homosexual loves; thenceforth, it was only a question of proving it.

The succeeding generation would take a more advanced position on homosexuality. It not only wanted to be frank about its homosexuality, it was proud of it. The sentiment was, — Who wants to be encumbered with women? They're no fun. They think only of themselves. Our best moments were those that we spent together, weren't they?[388]

---

384. For anonymous homosexual testimonies, see Kevin Porter and Jeffrey Weeks (ed.), *Between the Acts. Lives of Homosexual Men, 1885-1967*, London, Routledge, 1991, 153 pages.

385. Christopher Isherwood, *Down there on a Visit*, London, Methuen, 1962, 271 pages, p.134.

386. Id., *Christopher and his Kind* [1929-1939], London, Methuen, 1977, 252 pages, p.99.

387. *Ibid.*

The issue was not to be able to advertise everywhere a practice that was still criminal in England, but to stop making a mystery of it. Auden's and Isherwood's friends and parents knew their inclinations. When their first works were published, some part of the well-read public also found out.[389] Not content with admitting their homosexuality, the members of the rising generation aspired to change society. In *Down There on a Visit*, one of the characters describes, tongue in cheek, "the kingdom" which he hopes to found one day. There, he thought, it would be impossible to legalize heterosexuality right off the bat — "there would be too many protests." Maybe after twenty years or so, the resentment would die down. In the meantime, officials would close their eyes to heterosexual acts committed in private; and there might even be special bars in certain parts of town for people afflicted with such proclivities. Of course, care would have to be taken to protect innocent foreigners from straying in by mistake and getting upset by what they saw. And for anyone who did wander in, in error, "We will have a psychologist on hand to explain to him that such people exist, that it is not their fault, and that we must feel compassion for them and try to find a scientific means of reconditioning them."[390]

From now on, homosexuals had only one battle to fight: their own. Anyone who refused to help them was regarded as an enemy. Isherwood commented that — "Girls are what the State and the Church and the Law and the Press and the Medical Profession approve and command me to desire. My mother approves of girls, too. She silently, brutally asks me to marry and give her grandchildren. That is the will of Almost Everyone, and their will means my death. MY will is to live according to my nature, and to find a place where I can be what I am... But I must admit this — even if my nature made me like them, I would still fight them in one way or another. If boys did not exist, I would have to invent them."[391] From now on, homosexuals were a symbol of society's oppression of minorities. Homosexual liberation and the liberalization of morals became part of a larger game plan that questioned the domination of the middle-class. On the eve of the war, homosexuality became political.[392]

---

388. Christopher Isherwood to one of his friends, Waldemar, in *Down there on a Visit*, *op. cit.*, p.156.

389. On this topic, see Norman Pittenger, "Wystan and Morgan," in *Gay News*, n° 156.

390. Christopher Isherwood, *Down there on a Visit*, *op. cit.*, p.83.

391. Id., *Christopher and his Kind*, *op. cit.*, p.17.

392. See Chapter Six.

One of the first pillars of "middle-class" (i.e., patriarchal, conservative and authoritative) morality to be called into question was the family. Auden's and Isherwood's relations with their mothers were already strained. And then, they were constantly expressing their contempt for family, using one of their favorite weapons, derision, which they wielded against that respectability that is so dear to the bourgeoisie. One of the forms this would take was the factitious marriage, whose only purpose was political. Auden married Erika Mann (daughter of Thomas Mann) in order to obtain a passport for her to leave Germany; David Gascoygne did the same with a German girl named Ingrid, and John Hampson married Erika Mann's friend, the actress Therese Giese.

But it was their unbridled sexuality that was the most severe attack on family values. While sentiment may not have been entirely absent, the search for partners specifically for sexual ends became more prevalent, and more open. Auden's behavior in this sense is typical: at Oxford, he would spend entire evenings downtown seeking partners and, upon his return, he would treat his stunned but secretly envious friends to clinical accounts of the experience. He would report on the fellatio (his preferred form of sex) in detail, in order to liberate his audience, to show to them that the sense of guilt can be overcome. Following his example, the new generation rehabilitated sexual pleasure — the greatest taboo still attached to homosexuality. However, it is difficult to free oneself from secular prejudices; while they were free in their attitudes, the new generation still had to fight doubt. Auden's position vis-à-vis his homosexuality was not always clear. In 1922, he fell in love with one with his comrades, Robert Medley, when he was 15 years old. In his public school, Gresham, the "code of honor" was very strict on this point; and one may assume that at that time he was not completely sure of his feelings. From then on, his detachment, even his cynicism, alternated with phases of remorse and doubt. In 1927, he wrote that he still felt that there was something indecent in sharing homosexual relations. And even in 1933, he noted: "Homosexuality is to a certain extent a bad habit, like sucking one's thumb."[393] In spite of these periods of depression, his concerns remained quite circumscribed and his friends saw him as the apostle of their liberation. — Auden didn't feel at all ashamed or guilty about his sexual preferences. He felt guilty only on those occasions where, according to him, he had shown himself to be heartless, cruel or negligent.[394]

---

393. Cited by Humphrey Carpenter, *W.H. Auden*, *op. cit.*, p.105.
394. Norman Pittenger, "Wystan and Morgan," *loc. cit.*

In the 1970s, Christopher Isherwood would become a very active member of the homosexual liberation movement in the United States; he seems to have been acting out of a guilty feeling that he should have done more during the inter-war period. Isherwood deeply regretted that he had not been more explicit in his first autobiographies and novels, had not publicly announced his homosexuality. Installed in Santa Monica, having lived to see the blossoming of the homosexual community in San Francisco, he set to work to correct the errors of his youth and to analyze the homosexual experiences of the earlier days. Other members of his generation never really did come to terms with their condition and went as far as to repudiate it. Stephen Spender would complain of "choking in this world of pederasts," and he ended up marrying, in 1939, when the homosexual cult was over.

Oxford

"Everyone in Oxford was homosexual at that time."[395] Such a generalization is undoubtedly exaggerated, but Oxford (much more than Cambridge) certainly went through a great period of homophilia between the wars. Since Oscar Wilde, the university had always seen waves of effeminate young men, dressed in the fashions of the preceding century, posing in their rooms filled with blue porcelain. In the 19th century, Oxford's theatrical companies had made a specialty of farces featuring young men disguised as women. However, after the war, Noël Annan noted that "homosexuality has become normal." Evelyn Waugh is one of the more striking examples of the homosexual trend in Oxford in those days. Isaiah Berlin remembers having seen him on a settee of the Club of Hypocrites kissing a friend, and Christopher Hollis knew him to have had at least two major homosexual relationships, one with Richard Pares, the other with Alastair Graham.[396] However, Waugh married upon graduating from the university and claimed, afterwards, to hate homosexuals. Nevertheless the implications of this university homosexual activity are undeniable.[397] While homosexuality continued to be illegal under English law, it suddenly became the ideal for cultivated youth. The heterosexual poet Louis MacNeice comments

---

395. John Betjeman, cited by Noel Annan, *Our Age, op. cit.*, p.113.

396. Christopher Hollis, *Oxford in the Twenties, Recollection of Five Friends*, London, Heinemann, 1976, 136 pages; and Françoise du Sorbier (dir.), *Oxford 1919-1939*, Paris, Éditions Autrement, série "Mémoires," n° 8, 1991, 287 pages. The character of Sebastian Flyte in *Brideshead Revisited* would be modeled on Alastair Graham (Evelyn Waugh, *Return to Brideshead*, Paris, Christian Bourgois éditeur, 1991, 429 pages).

that he discovered that, at Oxford, "homosexuality and intelligence, heterosexuality and musculature went hand in hand." He remained an outsider, and turned to drinking.

As in the public schools, homosexuality was encouraged by the relative restriction of the students, who spent most of their time at the university. But in the inter-war period, homosexuality was fashionable, too; it was a choice. Students could go into town, and some were known to pick up waitresses; moreover, there are female colleges affiliated to Oxford, which could have facilitated heterosexual relations. That such relationships did not materialize can be attributed to the fact that heterosexuality carried negative connotations, it was scorned as vulgar and degrading. One writer observed that, — to run after the easy petticoat catalogued you irremediably. Romantic love affairs, even prudent physical experiments — disastrous, preferably — outside of the university and during the holidays were tolerated, and might even earn you a certain respectful consideration. But the mere mention of the female colleges that were already popping up in the university could render you ridiculous.[398]

In fact, the cult of homosexuality in Oxford is clearly linked to an omnipresent misogyny, a contempt for woman, born mainly of ignorance and fear. This education given by men to men, without contact with any aspect of the female world, guaranteed the cohesion of the elite, bonded by shared experiences and goals. From the day they entered public school, the pupils were encouraged to get rid of the only notable female influence that could block the educational process: that of the mother. The public school substituted maternal protection by the protection of a bigger boy, with or without sexual conditions, thus institutionalizing homosexuality to some extent. Upon their arrival at university, these boys had little desire to confront the female universe that was so deeply foreign to their rites and their childish myths. This public school past often had a strong influence on the sexual orientation of the students at Oxford; and to that a discreet but ongoing incentive was added. Graham Greene arrived at Oxford

---

397. Waugh himself admitted in an interview addressed to a specific public: "Have you had homosexual experiences? — Yes, first at school, and even later. — You mean that you fell in love with another boy. But surely that happens frequently, when one is young. — Yes, but the school years mark you for the rest of your life. I have always lived at the edge of homosexuality, and I have always been influenced by it," (in *Gay News*, 14-27 June 1973).

398. J.M. Stewart, in *Oxford 1919-1939*, *op. cit.*, p.23. Les femmes ont été admises à Oxford in 1920; elles ne le seront à Cambridge qu'in 1947.

after going through Berkansted, a day school, and thus he had not imbued the homosexual culture of his comrades; he kept himself at a distance from these milieux, but he was conscious of the strangeness of his situation. — Perhaps, he wrote, this was really just my naivety.... That never appealed to me or interested me.... Evelyn Waugh used to tease me.... He claimed that I had missed a lot by not going through a homosexual phase.[399] As in the public schools, homosexuality was encouraged by certain professors; at Oxford, professors F.F. Urquhart and Maurice Bowra were known for their talents as go-betweens. Bowra, for example, having learned of Cyril Connolly's interest in Bobbie Longden, expressed his approval to him and let him know that his friend spent time in certain dubious places; he advised him to invite him along to an isolated spot on the Oxford campus. Anthony Powell found that the university authorities were "indifferent to homosexuality but disapproved of heterosexual interest."[400]

The younger generation's attraction to homosexuality can be also understood as a reaction to their parent's generation, which had condemned Wilde and then kept silent on this type of subject. John Betjeman was corresponding with Lord Alfred Douglas; his father found out and subjected him to a sermon along these lines: — He said: "You have received letters from Lord Alfred Douglas." I could not deny it. "Do you know what kind of man he is?... He is a fag. Do you know what fags are? Fags are two men who put themselves in such a state of mutual admiration that one of the two sticks his prick up the other's bottom. What do you think of that?"[401]

Above all, homosexuality, as well as literature and art, would be used to distinguish a certain faction of the avant-garde, young people in the know, up on all the latest trends of modernity. Alan Pryce-Jones summarized the situation, saying: "It was chic to be a fag, the way it was chic to know a little something about dodecaphony or the *Nude Descending A Staircase* by Duchamp."[402]

At Oxford, indeed, homosexuality was not only a practice, it was also a way of separating the college into two mutually detesting clans: the heterosexual athletes (the hearties) and the homosexual aesthetes. Stephen Spender sums it up — To them, my interest in poetry, painting and music, my lack of interest for sports, the eccentricity of my clothing and my personal appearance were signs of decadence.[403]

---

399. Cited by Humphrey Carpenter, *The Brideshead Generation, op. cit.*, p.111.
400. *Ibid.*, p.113.
401. *Ibid.*, p.81.
402. *Ibid.*

In fact, the aesthetes were pleased to accentuate the originality of their costume and practiced affecting poses in response to what they regarded as the brutishness and the coarseness of the athletes. In this play-acting, one can distinguish the origins of a homosexual identity and a disguised rejection of the conformist bourgeois society. And Spender adds that he became affected, wore a red tie, cultivated friendships outside of the college, "became a bad patriot," declared himself a pacifist and a socialist, a genius. He hung reproductions of Gauguin, Van Gogh and Paul Klee paintings on the walls. And when the weather was fine, he made a habit of sitting on a cushion in the courtyard, reading poetry.[404] The athletes, for their part, painted an ironic and afflicted picture of those whom they regarded as degenerates. One of them recounts that when he met one of them and asked him his name, the pretty young man answered: "François Capelle." In fact, his name was Frank Curtis. He wore a pink jacket, a tuxedo waistcoat and purple trousers, which was hardly common, even in those days. And when he asked him which college he was going to, he said: "My dear, I don't even remember, really."[405]

The center of aesthetic and homosexual activity was the Club of Hypocrites, where young men danced together — in spite of prohibitions. Evelyn Waugh explains that its members were known — not only for their drunkenness, but also for the flamboyance of their costumes and their manners, which were in certain cases obviously homosexual.[406] The George Restaurant was also a meeting place for Oxford homosexuals during the inter-war period. The most flamboyant homosexuality at Oxford was embodied by two aesthetes, Harold Acton and Brian Howard, who had already been together in Eton from 1918 to 1922. Their homosexuality was aggressive, pretentious, and based primarily on style, posing, effect. Similarly, their "aestheticism" was intended to be a philosophy of life, a literary and artistic viewpoint, and not solely a sartorial caprice. Acton and Howard were at the avant-garde of an Oxonian aestheticism which strove to be in touch with the modern world and not locked up in a dusty fin-de-siècle cult. In distinction to their comrades, who concentrated on cultivating their uniqueness while never venturing beyond their own rooms and by associating only with certain carefully selected people, they met enormous numbers of

---

403. Stephen Spender, *World within World* [1951], London, Faber & Faber, 1991, 344 pages, p.33.
404. *Ibid.*
405. Sir Isaiah Berlin, in *Oxford 1919-1939, op. cit.*
406. Cited by Humphrey Carpenter, *The Brideshead Generation, op. cit.*, p.79.

people and made a name for themselves through their social talent and their journalistic or poetic writings, and they organized a propaganda campaign for their "movement." Martin Green describes them as "children of the sun" (Sonnenkinder) who refused to grow up after the war and who embodied all the adolescent arrogance at the heart of the Oxonian homosexual myth.[407] Evelyn Waugh saw Brian Howard as an "incorrigible homosexual," and his total lack of shame frightened him. The aesthetes made no mystery of their homosexuality, but it was not so much that as their affectations and the sense of their artistic superiority which earned them the hatred of the athletes. And if the hostility between the two camps frequently led to the ransacking of the aesthetes' rooms by tipsy athletes, it was more a means of defense against a lifestyle and sexual orientation that was beginning to submerge them than a witch hunt organized against the untouchables. Homosexuality may still have been under attack, but it was already recognized.

However, the climate of license and permissiveness often placed the university in a difficult position. The scandals and the expulsion of certain pupils for offending decency caused waves of hostility in the national press, which called Oxford a "den of debauchery and effeminates" and implied that the majority of students were actually "little women with made-up faces and precious gestures."[408]

Between approximately 1930 and 1933, there was a sudden proliferation of writings devoted to Oxford; some paint a severe portrait of a life characterized by laziness, drunkenness and vice, whereas others set out to defend, often apologetically, their dear Alma Mater calumniated by philistines. In the first category, one may cite *Oxford in the Melting-Pot*, by P.H. Crawfurth Smith, and *Letter to Oxford*, by T.E. Harrisson. The former does not refer directly to the students' supposed homosexuality, but emphasizes the decadent atmosphere of the university and the lack of virility in everything they do: "Let me repeat that the entire atmosphere of Oxford is foreign to labour and to study. It is unhealthy, it is superficial, it is saturated with sex."[409] Harrisson, for his part, establishes a clear distinction between Oxford, the place (which he venerates), and the students,

---

407. See Martin Green, *Children of the Sun: A Narrative of "Decadence" in England after 1918*, London, Constable, 552 pages; and Harold Acton, *Memoirs of an Aesthete* [1948], reedited., London, Hamish Hamilton, 1984, 416 pages.

408. *Isis*, 14 and 21 October 1925.

409. P.H. Crawfurth Smith, *Oxford in the Melting-Pot*, London, The White Owl Press, 1932, 24 pages, p.22.

who enjoy dishonoring this sanctuary of culture. In his chapter "Oxsex," he focuses particularly on homosexuality and paints an appalling picture of the students' sex life, rife with masturbation and perversion.[410] He links this phenomenon to the public schools (as he must):

> — When one says Harrow, one says perversion. It is one of the principal by-products of general public schools; and certain people are so seriously bitten that they never recover from a sexual hydrophobia [?]. Oxford is full of perverts — at least 20%, in my opinion. That is not counting the masturbators, who are the British standard. Some of the more outstanding perverts learned their tricks at Oxford.[411] [One may note that his inveighing against homosexuality is tinged with a vague argument against modernity and the cultivated elite:] Evenings for perverts are a characteristic of the university. The details are not printable, but I hope to publish them soon. Homosexuals and lesbians... flourish, particularly within the super-intelligentsia.[412]

Oxford alumni tried to clear their university of these attacks. Some, like Edward Thomas, in *Oxford*, stayed away from potential litigious subjects and contented themselves with ardent panegyrics, saying things like: — What an incredible thing it is to be a student at the university of Oxford! Other than being a great poet or a financier, there is nothing so absolutely fine available to a man!"[413] Others employed all their talent to defend the practice of homosexuality at Oxford. Terence Greenidge, in *Degenerate Oxford?*, in 1930, justified the basically homosexual life and feelings as a unique and enriching experience in a young man's life. He denounced the popular press for promoting scandals, asserting that it has already been mentioned that the popular press preferred the athletes, "and those are the students who are favorite heroes for the writers of magazine articles, as well."[414] By contrast, the aesthetes were qualified as "decadent" and "degenerate."

Greenidge may have preferred the homosexuals, but he endeavored to play down the extent of homosexual practices at Oxford, bearing in mind the fact that relations between men (other than platonic) were illegal. He claimed that,

---

410. T.E. Harrisson, *Letter to Oxford*, Reynold Bray, The Hate Press, 1933, 98 pages, p.24.
411. *Ibid.*, p.27.
412. *Ibid.*, p.28.
413. Edward Thomas, *Oxford*, London, Black A. & C., 1932, 265 pages, p.103.
414. Terence Greenidge, *Degenerate Oxford?*, London, Chapman & Hall, 1930, 245 pages, p.40.

in any event, romances at Oxford were often not pursued in any way that could generate conflicts with the penal code, for the simple reason that the students were immature enough to see value in platonic affections. Strange things may occasionally occur, he acknowledged, "among those who come from too emancipated a public school." And "perhaps some among us have read Havelock Ellis" and learned to see sex calmly and clearly.[415] He even declined to speak about homosexuality, preferring the term "Romantism." "The attraction of a man for a man, I will call it Romantism. One word is always preferable to two — the expression 'romantic friendship' is too heavy, and I do not approve of 'homosexuality,' for it seems too sinister and suggests more than is at question."[416]

Greenidge finds three justifications for the Romantism at Oxford: the boys are beautiful, Oxford is so original a city that "conventional frivolities with conventional girls simply would not do,"[417] and, finally, the authorities keep the two sexes separate: "To invite coeds to take tea at the college is in any event too difficult... There are always the complicated rules of chaperonage, and consequently one must invite a whole troop of girls or none at all."[418] As for the girls in town, — it is far too dangerous to pursue a relationship with one of them to any degree whatsoever. The critics seem to keep an exact list of all the ladies of Oxford who could be suspected of entertaining romantic dispositions. If you are seen speaking with one of these ladies, your university career is in danger."[419]

Greenidge also describes the more or less apparent homosexual culture which reigned at Oxford. He mentions that the college magazines often published love poems addressed to students. Like everyone, he recalls the athletes' aggression of the aesthetes, the shouts — "You, dirty aesthetes, you love men,"[420] but he is right to bring out the ambiguity of these relationships. Very often, indeed, an aesthete was in love with an athlete and the athlete admired the aesthete. Such complementary friendships could be beneficial. Homosexuality then served as a cement between different individuals, different ways of thinking. It helped preserve the unity of the college, and in a certain way it is the very spirit of the school: "Students who are not entirely lacking in personal charm — and few are — see no harm in lunching with one admirer, taking a long

---

415. *Ibid.*, p.90.
416. *Ibid.*
417. *Ibid.*, p.95.
418. *Ibid.*, p.96.
419. *Ibid.*, p.97.
420. *Ibid.*, p.92.

walk in the countryside with another, dining in some comfortable club at the university with a third and, perhaps, finishing the day with a whisky bottle in the company of a fourth."[421]

Greenidge, in fact, hardly knows which side to take. He wants to defend Oxford against the charges of perversion, but he cannot deny the facts. Moreover, he is endeavoring to get the public to see the positive aspects of this peculiar feature in Oxonian life, but without shocking sensibilities. That leads him to make some contradictions and compromises. Thus, he says that he is in favor of coeducation, as the only way to end Romantism; which he thus ends up exposing.

In the last lines of his book his fragmented outlooks appears most clearly, in sentences that recall the end of *Maurice* and that once again illustrate the permanent imprint left on a generation by these university years tinged with homosexuality:

> — When I contemplate the arid years which I spent since I left Oxford, alone in this old and tedious Bloomsbury and trying without much success to become an important actor, I can only go on eternally playing the role of Cyrano de Bergerac, I can only go on eternally regretting "my dead friend and my lost happiness."[422]

And so, Oxford in the 1920s became a myth, the symbol of the triumph of homosexuality in England. Alumni-turned-writers sought to describe the happiness of their youth; examples include Christopher Isherwood's *Lions and Shadows*, Stephen Spender's *World within World* and, especially, Evelyn Waugh with *Brideshead Revisited* — the book that most successfully disseminated the mythical image of Oxford as a homosexual paradise. Waugh captures the very essence of Oxford, the romantic passions (between Charles Ryder and Sebastian Flyte), the unrestrained aestheticism and flamboyant homosexuality (Anthony Blanche) and the nostalgia for adolescence (embodied by Aloysius, the teddy bear that Sebastian refuses to leave). Beyond the idyllic picture of a place that a whole generation would struggle to regain, he offers us a life-like description of homosexual life in those years. Love comes first and foremost,[423] and the rivalry

---

421. *Ibid.*, p.105.

422. *Ibid.*, p.245.

423. "For me, life at Oxford began with my first meeting with Sebastian," (Charles Ryder's confession in *Return to Brideshead, op. cit.*, p.35).

between the athletes and aesthetes is reported with humor,[424] but homosexual pride in particular is displayed for all to see with panache, irony and lubricity.

The character of Anthony Blanche,[425] facetious and extravagant, allows Evelyn Waugh to describe with a great flourish the cult of homosexuality that suffused the Roaring Twenties:

> At the age of fifteen, to win a bet, [Anthony Blanche] allowed himself to be dressed as a girl and taken to the big gaming table at the Jockey-Club in Buenos Aires; he had occasion to dine with Proust and Gide, and knew Cocteau and Diaghilev well. Firbank sent him his novels, embellished with enthusiastic dedications; he caused three inextinguishable vendettas in Capri, practiced magic at Céphalonie; got into drugs and underwent detoxication in California, and was cured of an Œdipal complex in Vienna.[426]

This passage touches all the literary and society landmarks of the homosexual world in the inter-war period. Homosexuality, for the elite, was more than a sexual proclivity; it was a style, a way of life.

In a scene where he is confronted by the athletes, Anthony Blanche shows his total lack of inhibition, his lack of complexes, and his natural affirmation of his homosexuality — and ends up defeating his adversaries:

> — He was approached by a horde of some 20 young people of the worst kind, and what do you think they were chanting? "Anthony, we want Anthony Blanche," in a kind of litany. Have you ever seen anyone declare himself so, in public?..."My very dear fellows," I said to them, "you resemble a band of very undisciplined lackeys." Then one of them, a rather pretty bit, honestly, accused me of sins against nature. "My dear," I said to him, "it may be that I am an invert, but I am not insatiable, even so. Come back and see me some day when you are alone."[427]

The character of Anthony Blanche[428] embodies the cult of homosexuality; confronted by a hostile or disconcerted society, the "invert" no longer hides his true nature. Once more, the contrast with the neighboring countries is great. In France, for example, there was no establishment that could entertain the myth

---

424. Stephen Spender describes similar episodes, in *World within World, op. cit.*, p.34; as does Christopher Isherwood, *Down there on a Visit, op. cit.*, p.93.

425. He might be compared to the character of Ambrose Silk, in *Down there on a Visit*.

426. Evelyn Waugh, *Return to Brideshead, op. cit.*, p.61.

427. *Ibid.*, p.64-66.

428. Evelyn Waugh based this character on Brian Howard.

that homosexuality was intellectually superior, the way Oxford and Cambridge did.[429] Of course, there are some personal accounts reporting on homosexual experiences in the universities, but they are individual cases which one cannot equate with a widespread social phenomenon. Daniel Guérin describes drinking with a good-looking neighbor who was a fellow student at the Saint-Cyr Military Academy and the rough-housing, pillow fights and wrestling that verged on more, and the arousal that resulted.[430]

The teacher training colleges were strongly associated with homosexual conduct, and sometimes they were presented as hotbeds of lesbianism. Thus, in *Claudine in Paris* (1902), Anaïs continues her exploits and describes how it is done: "Nothing special, she is 'with' a third year student…As you know, the dormitories are composed of two lines of open cubicles, separated by an alley for monitoring…. Anaïs found a way to go and find Charrelier almost every night, and they were never caught."[431]

The Advanced Teacher Training School of Sèvres was also supposed to be a breeding ground of homosexual friendships. Several old novels mention it, including *Les Sévriennes* (1900), by Gabrielle Reval, and *Jeunes filles en serre chaude* (1934) by Jeanne Galzy. *L'Initiatrice aux mains vides* (1929), by the same author, presents the emotional vacuum that overcomes a young educator, once her school career is finished. The years spent at Sèvres come to seem like an enchanted time, where hopes could still flourish.

Antoine Prost points out that these girls were in a very uncomfortable situation, in any case: the young high school graduates disembarked in a provincial town where there was nobody to welcome them. Their dubious status kept them apart from the townspeople, who viewed them with suspicion because of their independence and their culture. Only strong personalities could survive there, without sinking into depression. Simone de Beauvoir, having been appointed to a school in Rouen, was the object of attention for a number of her

---

429. In 1921, a pacifist bulletin, *La Jeune Europe*, published by some students including Pierre Brossolette, was banned after the third edition because of an article on homosexuality in boarding schools. In fact, the kind of relations with girls that was acceptable in the school from 1924 onward recall those of the Oxford students with regard to women's colleges: coldness and mistrust. See Jean-François Sirinelli, *Génération intellectuelle*, Paris, PUF, 1994, 720 pages, p.212.

430. Daniel Guérin, *Autobiographie de jeunesse, op. cit.*, p.155.

431. Colette, *Œuvres complètes*, Paris, Gallimard, coll. "Bibl. de la Pléiade," 1984, t.I, 1686 pages, p.323.

pupils, in particular one Olga Kosakiewicz, a 17-year-old White Russian who would go on to become Sartre's lover.

In 1936, in Paris, Simone de Beauvoir and Olga went to bars for women and posed as lesbians, even while denying there was any erotic component to their relationship.[432] However, they are a special case, and not very appropriate for generalization; their example is not enough to show that the university years could claim to be a decisive moment in the process of forming one's identity nor to have much to do with spreading a cult of homosexuality in youth. Conversely, for many English students, Oxford offered a real environment of homosexual freedom; Evelyn Waugh says that during those years he experienced "an extreme homosexual phase which, for the short period that it lasted, was without constraint, emotionally and physically."[433] Former students retained traces of their youthful experiences. Cyril Connolly has described the mentality of this new English elite as adolescent, with a spirit of school [camaraderie], affected, cowardly, sentimental "and, in the final analysis, homosexual."[434]

However, "real" homosexuals understood very quickly upon their departure from the university that they did not have any place yet in England. In their quest for new pleasures and freedom, they sought a place that would welcome them. Hints and echoes reported by friends returning from holidays, or something read in the scandal sheets, gave them reason to think that happiness lay in Germany. From this point until 1933, the history of English homosexuality would follow the German model.

Escape to Germany

For Christopher, Berlin meant boys.[435]

Germany is the only place for sex. England isn't worth a thing.[436]

In homosexual mythology, foreign lands have always held a great fascination. They seem to offer men who are often considered pariahs in their native land the possibility of escape or rebirth. It is simply easier to enjoy a satisfactory

---

432. See Deidre Bair, *Simone de Beauvoir*, Paris, Fayard, 1991, 854 pages.
433. Cited by Humphrey Carpenter, *The Brideshead Generation, op. cit.*, p.124-125.
434. *Ibid.*, p.443.
435. Christopher Isherwood, *Christopher and his Kind, op. cit.*, p.10.
436. Stephen Spender, *Le Temple* [1929], Paris, Christian Bourgois éditeur, 1989, 310 pages, p.24.

sexual experience abroad, where the weight of social strictures seems more distant. For this reason, the colonies became very fashionable at the end of the 19th century. This probably originated with the military: France's Africa Army was famous for its homosexual practices, symbolized at the highest level by Marshal Lyautey. By the same token, many of the imperial proconsuls of the English colonial army married extremely late (like Milner, Layard, and Baden-Powell), or not at all (like Rhodos, Gordon, and Kitchener). Most of them were surrounded by a circle of favorites. Similarly, explorers like Stanley and Edward Eyre always chose young men to be their companions on each expedition.

This phenomenon was not limited to the army. The lure of the exotic, and the rumors (strongly colored with colonialist attitudes) of willing natives, contributed to making the colonies seem like safe and discreet homosexual paradises. A French book, *L'Amour aux colonies (Love in the Colonies)* (1932), by Anne de Colney, describes how easy homosexual relations were in certain regions. First, the Asian countries: "Pederasty, an exceptional act in Europe, is accepted in Chinese morés as well as prostitution and opium, and that at all levels of the social caste." This characteristic is explained by resort to racist theories. Thus, the Annamite "is a civilized old man, who has all the flaws inherent in a refined mind." This kind of justification fended off any reproach with regard to Europeans practicing sexual tourism and taking advantage of their dominant position.

Asia did not have a monopoly on homosexuality. "The Arab is a born pederast."[437] This type of talk found an echo with certain homosexuals, who developed the myth of foreign lands that were open to homosexuality. Often, a stay in the colonies seems to have been a revelation. J.R. Ackerley, who was posted to Bombay in 1923, noted that the court of the Maharajah was the scene of "homosexual orgies." These discoveries led him to berate his own country for its sexual hypocrisy, noting that he liked to see men and boys holding hands when they walk, or standing with their arms around each other's shoulders, [as he had also seen in Egypt and in other Mediterranean countries]. — But the English would find that unmasculine in the extreme (or worse); and, he hinted, the Scots were still more hopeless.[438]

---

437. Anne de Colney, *L'Amour aux colonies*, Paris, Librairie "Astra," 1932, 214 pages, p.14, 45 and 92.

438. Cited by Peter Parker, *A Life of J.R. Ackerley*, London, Constable, 1989, 465 pages, p.74.

Those who were caught up in a scandal in their country of origin tended to retreat to the colonies. Robert Eyton, vice-chancellor of St. Margaret's, Westminster, exiled himself to Queensland in 1900 after a major scandal.[439] In the 1930s, two-thirds of the men posted to Malaysia were homosexual. Many were indicted after a Chinese male prostitute spilled the beans; deportations and two suicides followed.[440] Tangier also attracted many visitors in the 1930s — Bohemian intellectuals and homosexuals. Stephen Tennant explains this fascination for the city that symbolizes exoticism and expatriation. It is curious, he says, but here — so close to Spain — just thirty miles away — the sea is warmer, and the sun is burning. The spirit of Africa, which one breathes, which radiates in the streets — which is exhaled by the ground and the sidewalks, is strangely pleasing to me.[441]

Homosexual tourism was born in the colonies. For the foreigner, everything was easier: the fear of being recognized disappeared, and legislation could not reach him. The exoticism of the place added to the eroticism of the situation. Gide eulogized these easy relations. There were boys all over, blossoming in the sun, with gilded skin, marvelously complaisant, always available, free of prejudices and inhibitions.[442] Boys were passed from hand to hand. In the company of Wilde and Lord Alfred Douglas, Gide discovered that the trade in boys was organized for the purpose of satisfying demand from foreign visitors; one wonders whether he really was unaware that this was prostitution in disguise, that he believed in the spontaneity of the boys who were offered to him.[443] In *If It Die* and *AMYNTAS: North African Journals*, money is never mentioned. However, tipping or "baksheesh" was commonplace and pederasty is directly associated with those who have money. The colonizer, in his financial superiority, is sure to obtain satisfaction one way or another; consequently, he goes out of his way to show that money plays no part in his relations. The reader himself loses his faculty of judgment and Gide is an accomplice in that, for he makes a show of his

---

439. Ronald Hyam, *Empire and Sexuality: The British Experience*, Manchester, Manchester University Press, 1990, 234 pages.

440. *Ibid.*, p.109.

441. Cited by Philip Hoare, *Serious Pleasures, op. cit.*, p.295.

442. André Gide, *Si le grain ne meurt* [1926], reedited., Paris, Gallimard, coll. "Folio," 1986, 372 pages.

443. See on this subject Hédi Khelil, Sens, jouissance, tourisme, érotisme, argent dans deux fictions coloniales d'André Gide, Tunis, Éditions de la Nef, 1988, 172 pages.

weaknesses, his shortcomings, his hesitations. But, while he may question his sexuality, he never doubts his choice of partners.

Like *Gide*, Montherlant evokes life in Algiers as a continuous source of sexual adventure. He tours the Jardin d'Essai, and Bab-el-Oued, and goes to the cinema looking for yaouleds, Arab adolescents, whom he renames with his liking: The "Thorny Rose of Blida," "Jasmine of Belcourt," "Genêt of Médéa," "He who opens the doors of the sky." According to Montherlant, the North African colonials came to fulfill their fantasies in Algiers for all sorts of reasons: there was "the French dream": to conquer, control, exploit; the "artistic dream": dancers, jasmine, young men; and the "human dream": assimilation, justice, fraternity.[444]

Beyond the colonial experience, the Mediterranean countries were attractive in general. There again, the place is idealized, made legendary. Italy was particularly celebrated, by E.M. Forster and others; his novels, like *A Room with a View*, contrast an Italy bathed in sunlight, open to love, to an England that is Puritanical, sad, and dark. But the context remains strictly heterosexual. It was in his novellas, many of which were published only posthumously, that Forster expands on the idea of Italy as a homosexual paradise.[445]

Like the colonies, Italy was often selected as an adoptive homeland after various scandals drove one out of his country of origin. Douglas Norman, a friend of J.R. Ackerley, had been convicted of committing a moral offense on a sixteen-year-old minor; he exiled himself to Florence, where he could satisfy all his inclinations freely. J.R. Ackerley, who had barely disembarked from England, was flabbergasted to hear Norman's description of the young waiter standing before them, with the invitation, "When can you join us?"[446]

Ackerley visited Florence, accompanied by an Italian guide who was a friend of Douglas Norman, Giuseppe "Pino" Orioli, J.R. Orioli claimed that the Florentines wore gabardine trousers with the aim of displaying their attributes, and one of his favorite games was to stare at a young man, raising his gaze from the trousers to the face, with the aim of obtaining an erection. However, while the lads were often obliging, they did not wish to embark on a serious rela-

---

444. Cited by Pierre Sipriot, *Montherlant sans masque*, t.II, *Écris avec ton sang, 1932-1972*, Paris, Robert Laffont, 1990, 505 pages, p.30.

445. See for example *Un instant d'éternité et autres nouvelles*, Paris, Christian Bourgois éditeur, 1988, 305 pages.

446. Peter Parker, A Life of J.R. Ackerley, *op. cit.*, p.55.

tionship: after a night with his lover (who swore eternal fidelity), Orioli followed him and discovered that he went into a brothel.

Colonial and Mediterranean loves relate more directly to the first homosexual generation, that of Wilde, Gide, and Forster.[447] They preserve strong elements of Victorianism, especially with regard to their sexual choices: the object of desire is a young adolescent, even a child. Moreover, the relations are always venal, and the social and economic superiority of the visitors is constantly asserted. In Germany, the second homosexual generation began to go with their own peers, with males of the same age, without the contrast of exoticism or any other clear differentiation. The young lover was no longer "inferior," even if money continued to play a part — since the lovers were often male prostitutes or working boys who tacitly agreed to be being "kept." Even more important, young Germans represented the former enemy. Therefore, sexual liberation was mingled with social provocation. In this sense, escaping to Germany played a major role in the process of homosexual assertion.

So Germany, too, seemed like paradise to the English homosexual. Artistic innovations could be enjoyed along with the pleasures of the sun, flirtation, and sex. At least until 1933, Berlin was hot and became a very fashionable place. Charlotte Wolff, a doctor and lesbian, noted: "Berlin, with its reputation as the 'most permissive' city in Europe, had become a paradise for homosexuals. They came from all over the world, but particularly from England, to enjoy a freedom which their own country denied them."[448] By the end of the 1920s, a number of homosexual intellectuals, writers and artists were staying there, *inter alia* Christopher Isherwood, Brian Howard, W.H. Auden, Stephen Spender, Michael and Humphrey Spender, T.C. Worsley, Francis Bacon, Wyndham Lewis and John Lehmann. Isherwood lived there uninterruptedly from 1929 to 1933. Stephen Spender spent six months a year in Germany between 1930 and 1933.

Hamburg and Munich were also homosexual meeting grounds. Germany is surrounded by a mythical aura that quickly extended beyond specific locations. The publicity for Isherwood's second book, *The Memorial* (1932), plays up this sinful reputation: "In the deliciously prohibited world of Berlin of 1928, a World War aviation ace finds love in the muscular arms of his German lover."[449]

---

447. *Si le grain ne meurt*, written in 1919, partially published in 1921 and in its entirety in 1926, relates events that happened as early as 1893.

448. Charlotte Wolff, *Hindsight*, London, Quartet Books, 1980, 312 pages, p.72.

449. Cited by Paul Fussell, *Abroad, British Literary Travellers between the Wars*, Oxford, Oxford University Press, 1980, 246 pages.

Germany was an eye-opener for English homosexuals. Isherwood says that his first visit to Berlin was short, a week, ten days — but sufficient; it was one of the decisive events of [his] life.[450] They discovered that they were not alone, but belonged to a world community that was standing up for its rights. A visit to the Hirschfeld Institute was a revelation for Isherwood. For the first time, he saw his "tribe." Hitherto, he had acted as if homosexuality were an intimate way of life that he and his friends had discovered for the first time. Coming from a privileged background and having lived until then in a restricted circle, he discovered how Hirschfeld was fighting for the abolishment of §175, the help he was providing for men who could not express their sexuality, and the hostility to which many were subjected by the Nazi Party. Once he overcame his initial reserve, Isherwood, like many others, took up the cause and joined the nascent homosexual movement.[451]

But Germany was not only the battlefield where this conflict was being played out, it was a playing field in general. Post-war England still found it difficult to throw off its Victorian prejudices, but in Germany the body was coming into vogue. Stephen Spender discovered sun worshipping there: the naked body, healthy, shamelessly exposed. According to him, the sun was one of the primary social forces in Germany. "Nudity is the democracy of the New Germany, the Weimar Republic."[452] The heroes of the time were the naked, bronzed boys basking in the sun around the public swimming pools, or along the lakes and rivers. The sun had healed the war wounds, and that made them even more conscious of the beauty and the frailness of the body. The idea of sin seems to have been dissipated by memories of the great inflation of 1923; the only goal now was to live from day to day and to take advantage of what is free: sun, water, friendship and bodies. But it was not easy for these Englishmen to meld into this universe free from prejudices. Spender, for example, remarked that at first he was so nervous, so inhibited and complexed by his physique that it kept the young Germans from behaving with him as they did among themselves. However, he soon blended in, and found that "all one had to do was undress."[453]

In Germany, English homosexuals found both repose and exhilaration. In a country where homosexuality was seen as natural, they no longer had to hide or,

---

450. Christopher Isherwood, *Christopher and his Kind, op. cit.,* p.10.

451. According to anecdote, Isherwood visited the Hirschfeld Institute with Gide, who seems not to have apreciated the display of clinical cases.

452. Stephen Spender, *Le Temple, op. cit.,* p.65.

453. Id., *World within World, op. cit.,* p.109.

conversely, to show off; in the many entertainment spots that were offered, they learned of the existence of a whole homosexual lifestyle, conceived solely for male pleasure. They discovered easy sex and love expressed in broad daylight. There was a compete confusion of values and nothing was really important. The boys looked feminine, the girls took on a masculine allure and the sex of one's partners didn't matter: — I was grabbed by the waist, by the neck, I was kissed, embraced, tickled, with my clothes half off, I danced with girls, boys, two or three people at the same time."[454]

Lasting passions were born, between Isherwood and Heinz, Spender and Joachim, Auden and Pieps, Brian Howard and Toni. The Englishmen were fascinated by the beauty, the strength, the gleaming health of these boys, and also by their ease. In their novels and their autobiographies, they would try to express the admiration and desire that they inspired in them.[455] The German boys appeared to be something right out of a homosexual fantasy: 16 or 17 years old, tanned, with longish blond hair. They seemed like hooligans with disarming smiles, and beneath their innocent airs they hid considerable experience. They were very proud of their bodies, which they built up by various exercises and which they liked to show off in rough-housing. The English male submerged himself in this physical force, from which he drew an energy that he was lacking. In the confrontation of these bodies, two nations met and understood each other — briefly. The Germans had strength; the English had will. "Otto is only a body, Peter is only a head. Otto moves with fluidity, without effort. His gestures have the wild, unconscious, grace of an elegant and cruel animal. Peter... [has only a] will ...."[456]

But Germany was more than sun and water, and Berlin was reputed to offer visitors sensations far less innocent than these vacation pleasures: "Berlin is a dream for pederasts. There are 170 male brothels under police supervision.... [My friend is] a cross between a rugby player and Josephine Baker. D.H. Lawrence would pass for a choir boy. I am covered with bruises."[457] The young Englishmen sometimes had trouble recognizing that they were dealing with male prostitutes, they created such a friendly and convivial relationship: "Either

---

454. Christopher Isherwood, *Mr Norris Changes Train* [1935], London, Chatto & Windus, 1984, 190 pages, p.48.

455. *Ibid.*

456. Id., *Adieu à Berlin* [1939], Paris, Hachette, 1980, 246 pages, p.99.

457. W.H. Auden, cited by Humphrey Carpenter, *W.H. Auden, op. cit.,* p.90. On the nature of prostitution in Berlin, see Chapter One.

Heinz did his job very well, or he sincerely liked me. We spent ten days happy together making a tour of the city and going out on excursions — oh, German excursions! — to the surrounding lakes."[458] The relationship was in fact very simple: "I like sex and Pieps likes money; it is a good exchange," W.H. Auden would soberly observe.

There was also an element of danger, and that rendered this form of sexual pleasure more exciting: John Layard is quoted as describing his friend Wystan as liking "to be mistreated a little": — It happened once in my room. It started with a pillow fight, but ended up with fists; then they made love. Wystan did not much like to be seen this way.[459]

For T.C. Worsley, and for other homosexual English who never or almost never had sexual intercourse in their home country, the German male prostitutes were a godsend — and a revelation. He says that:

> — one could judge [his] lack of experience by the surprise, the skepticism that he showed, when one of [his] colleagues .... [told him] that there were places in Germany — Munich for example — where boys offered their services for a modest sum. Guys who gave out! Did such a thing really exist? [He] arranged to leave for Germany for the upcoming holidays.[460]

Distance, combined with the liberal attitude and the skill of the German boys, got them over their own taboos. The English intellectuals initiated sexual nomadism. W.H. Auden, for one, started to draw up suggestive lists in his journal.[461]

When Hitler put an end to the liberal and carefree Germany of the Weimar Republic in 1933, English homosexuals cherished the memory of practices and sexual experiences which they decided to continue in their own country: "After Berlin, everything was different."[462] At the same time, they were unable to be reconciled with their home country and become perpetual travellers and refugees. Isherwood, Howard, Spender, John Lehmann, Auden were eternally

---

458. T.C. Worsley, *Flannelled Fool, op. cit.*, p.130.

459. John Layard, cited by Humphrey Carpenter, *W.H. Auden, op. cit.*, p.90.

460. T.C. Worsley, *Flannelled Fool, op. cit.*, p.124.

461. "The boys I had in Germany: 1928-1929: Pieps/ Cully/ Gerhard/ Herbert/ an unknown transient/ a stranger from [the name of the bar is illegible]/ a stranger in Cologne/ stranger from [the name of the bar is illegible]/ Otto/I regret [name illegible]. He wasn't nice and was very dirty. The others were great" (cited by Humphrey Carpenter, *W.H. Auden, op. cit.*, p.97).

462. Christopher Isherwood interviewed in *Gay News*, n° 126.

uprooted, drifting from one country to another to preserve a sexual freedom that was, in fact, nonexistent even in their new adoptive homes. When Heinz, Isherwood's lover, was arrested in 1933 by the Nazis and convicted of perverse sexual practices, he was accused of having committed reprehensible acts with his friend in fourteen different countries, in addition to Germany.

The future of the English homosexual struggle was forged in the German crucible, through the experiences of an adventurous youth whose hours of happiness were all the more precious since they were halted by repression and the war. Germany thus has its place in the cult of homosexuality which defines the years 1919-1933. To the mythic dimension, it added the joy of liberation fully experienced, which proved that homosexuality was not universally condemned to secret nor to frustration.

The role Germany played in the homosexual consciousness is understood more intuitively through the homage paid by W.H. Auden in six of his poems. Despite his poor command of the language, he wrote most of them in German; they evoke the Berlin cafés, the one-night stands, and the holidays in the sun with eroticism and tenderness, and humor:

> Es regnet auf mir in den Schottische Lände
> Wo ich mit Dir nie gewesen bin
> Man redet hier von Kunst am Wochenende
> Bin jetz zu Hause, nicht mehr in Berlin
>
> So kommt es inner vor in diesen Sachen
> Wir sehen uns nie wieder, hab' dein Ruh:
> Du hast kein Schuld und es ist nichts zu machen
> Sieh' immer besser aus, und nur wenn Du
>
> Am Bahnhof mit Bekannten triffst, O dann
> Als Sonntagsbummelzüge fertig stehen
> Und Du einstigen willst, kuk einmal an
> Den Eisenbahn die dazwischen gehen.
>
> Sonst, wenn ein olle Herr hat Dich gekusst
> Geh mit; ich habe nichts bezahlt; Du must.[463]

* * *

201

Ronald you know, is like most Englishmen,
By instinct he's a sodomist
but he's frightened to know it
So he takes it out on women.[464]

The cult of homosexuality was an original and complex phenomenon that concerned primarily the British male elite. Women had little part in it and one cannot truly speak of a cult of homosexuality in France and Germany, even though traces of quasi-institutionalized homosexual activities may exist.

It is very difficult to analyze this phenomenon. First of all, it testifies to the sexual liberalism that began to be seen after the First World War. The death of thousands of young men on the battlefields traumatized the cadets, who set about celebrating the beauty of their school-fellows and reveling fully in the hallowed years of their adolescence.

The works of the Bloomsbury intellectuals and the second generation, that of Auden, allowed more open discussion of sexual questions; homosexuality was no longer taboo and, in certain sectors of society, it was no longer accompanied by shame and remorse. The cult of homosexuality made it possible for many homosexuals to express their sexuality more freely, without fear of being stigmatized and rejected. A whole generation became familiar with this sexual practice; it would be more tolerant and more understanding. The compelling experiences of youth would render unacceptable to the adult those prejudices based on ignorance and fear.

Nevertheless, limits to the tolerance were clearly perceptible: outside of a restricted and protected milieu, the British homosexual, even if he came from the elite, was at the mercy of the dictates of society, and that explains why they fled to Germany. We must not exaggerate the changes taking place in British society. While the cult of homosexuality had to do with a greater sexual freedom, it was also a symptom of an identity crisis among the English youth, which sought to

---

463. Septembre 1930. Literal translation: "It rains on me in the Scottish lands/ Where we were never together / One speaks of art here at the weekend, / I am at home. I am not anymore in Berlin. / / It always happens like that in these matters / We will never meet again, be calm: / You've done nothing wrong and there is nothing to do/ Become more and more handsome, and only / / If you meet some friends at the train station, oh then / When the Sunday buses are ready to leave / And you want to get on, watch / The big trains that go between them. / / Otherwise, when an old gentleman kisses you / Leave with him; I didn't have to pay. Go ahead."

464. D.H. Lawrence, *Pansies.*

disavow the Victorian generation that generated the war and to establish a new values system. The boys lived in a closed environment, all male, and that was their only frame of reference. Woman was an unknown being, almost an enemy imposed by society's morals. Homosexuality was touted as a sexuality of subversion, a sexuality that could be substituted for the patriarchal model; it was a fraternal sexuality that protected its members and created unbreakable bonds. It was also a rebellious adolescent sexuality that disputed and destroyed. Outside the mainstream and proudly so, it could not really contribute to any lasting transformation of British morals, but it did secretly wear away at their foundations. In its sexual dimension, the cult of homosexuality must be considered as the proud assertion of a difference finally assumed; but it must also be understood as the symbol of a total rejection of society, a deeply political act. The inversion of moral values and bourgeois traditions presaged more radical upheavals, like the turn to communism on the part of certain homosexual intellectuals.[465]

The years of homosexual liberation can be summarized in the impressions of an American writer who lived in France, Julien Green. He experienced both the Anglo-Saxon and Latin trends. In an American university he saw the equivalent of a cult of homosexuality, or in any case the diffusion of a liberal homosexual model. His literary activity brought him into contact with the French homosexual elite, while his travels in Germany brought him experiences similar to those of the British homosexuals. His mixed cultural background kept him from identifying with any particular milieu; and he constantly tried to reinterpret his experiences in the light of Catholicism. All the homosexual hopes and illusions of the inter-war period show in him. Klaus Mann summarized this complex personality in his journal: "...it is astonishing how he keeps any hint of his private life from creeping into his books; he maintains a strict compartmentalization: 'There is another Me who writes my works.'" To recover, he writes homo texts every day. [He is] incredibly passionate and at the same time [has a] cold relationship with all that is sexual.... — He shows me pornographic works by Tchelitchev: heroic pyramid of vice."[466]

---

465. See Chapter Six.
466. Klaus Mann, *Journal. Les années brunes, 1931-1936*, Paris, Grasset, 1996, 452 pages, 27 March 1933, p.132.

PART TWO

Unacknowledged Fears and Desires:
Ambiguous Speech and Stereotyped Images
Homosexuals become commonplace during the inter-war period

Private faces in public places
Are wiser and nicer
Than public faces in private places.

— W.H. Auden, *Collected Shorter Poems, 1927-1957*

CHAPTER FOUR
AWAKENING: WORKING TO CONSTRUCT A HOMOSEXUAL
IDENTITY

In the 1920s and 1930s, references to homosexuality were everywhere. Scholarly, artistic, anecdotal, or moralistic, they all add up to show that the collective imagination of the time was fascinated with homosexuality. The often-caricatured images that were current were balanced by representations developed by homosexuals themselves. The process of forging an identity was underway. The homosexuals and lesbians were on their way to asserting their singularity.

The homosexual identity, unlike the homosexual act, is a historical phenomenon. It is not universal, but temporal; it is not induced, but constructed. Therefore, it supposes the creation of a specific environment and an awareness that enabled homosexuals to define themselves as a group.[467]

The origin of the homosexual identity is difficult to pin down. At what moment can one say that a person recognizes himself as a homosexual? Is it simply that time when he accepts his sexual preferences, when he calls himself "homosexual," or is it only when he asserts his membership in a homosexual community, as a political statement? Just as it is hard to say when one person

---

467. The question of the homosexual identity is at the heart of homosexual historiography and raises many questions. Here and in the following notes I list some of the works that shed light on the topic: Salvatore J. Licata and Robert P. Petersen (dir.), *The Gay Past: A Collection of Historical Essays*, New York, Harrington Park Press, 1985, 224 pages; David F. Greenberg, *The Construction of Homosexuality*, Chicago, The University of Chicago Press, 1988, 635 pages.

takes on the identity of a homosexual, it is hard to say when the homosexual identity was created at all. Indeed, the date varies, depending on the country, the region (the notion of a homosexual identity emerges earlier in major cities than in rural areas) and the social class. (An intellectual can more readily define himself as homosexual simply because he will have access to the debates on the question of homosexuality, to medical writings, and so forth.)

Depending on how you look at it, the theorists of homosexuality have assigned a wide range of dates to the birth of the homosexual identity.[468] For some, the presence of homosexual "signals" in clothing and language, and the existence of meeting places, are enough to mark the existence of a homosexual identity.[469] If we take that view, the homosexual identity must have existed from time immemorial, since one can find homosexual codes, camouflaged to a greater or lesser extent, in every society and every era.[470] Others say that the homosexual identity could only have been constituted very recently, with the beginnings of gay militancy in the 1970s.[471]

Most historians of homosexuality, however, agree to date the emergence of a homosexual identity to the end of the 19th century, when the term "homosexual" came into wider use, doctors defined homosexuality precisely, and condemnations of homosexual acts were definitively inscribed in the laws of the European countries.[472]

This is a sound view; however, various nuances must be taken into account. The first homosexual generation was deeply marked by the medical theories and the scandals of the turn of the century. Bonded by their shared status as social outcasts, they remained very much affected by public opinion

---

468. For a discussion on this topic, see Kenneth Plummer, "Homosexual Categories: Some Research Problems in the Labelling Perspective of Homosexuality," *in* Kenneth Plummer (dir.), *The Making of the Modern Homosexual*, London, Hutchinson, 1981, 380 pages, p.53-76.

469.Mary McIntosh proposes that the 17th century was seminal period in creating the homosexual identity in ENgland. See "The Homosexual Role," *ibid.*, p.30-44.

470. See for example, in *Amour et sexualité en Occident*, Paris, Éditions du Seuil, coll. "Points histoire," 1991, 335 pages: Maurice Sartre, "L'homosexualité dans la Grèce antique"; Paul Veyne, "L'homosexualité à Rome"; Michel Rey, "Naissance d'une minorité."

471. John Marshall, "Pansies, Perverts and Macho Men: Changing Conceptions of Male Homosexuality," in Kenneth Plummer (dir.), *The Making of the Modern Homosexual*, *op. cit.*, p.133-155.

472. See Jeffrey Weeks, *Coming Out. Homosexual Politics in Britain from the 19th Century to the Present*, London, Quartet Books, 1979, 278 pages, and Sex, Politics and Society, London, Longman, 1989, 325 pages.

and had difficulty in asserting any positive image of themselves. In fact, only a male elite was truly capable of asserting a homosexual identity. By comparison, it was easier for homosexuals of the second generation to identify themselves as such. They integrated more easily into the nascent homosexual scene, and they were less at the effect of moral judgments. A lesbian identity appeared, based on a certain number of female models in particular. Consequently, a homosexual community was formed, unified by a shared a culture and frame of reference — but that did not necessarily induce a feeling of solidarity.

THE MEDICAL MODEL: AN IDENTITY IMPOSED FROM OUTSIDE

The homosexual identity was built around different definitions of homosexuality, arising from the abundant turn-of-the-century medical literature, among other sources. Since the theories varied, it is certainly hard to say what was their effect. However, the arrival of the doctor on a scene that had been reserved for the judge was certainly significant.

By inventing the "new" field of "perversions,"[473] psychiatry created "types," and the homosexual was one of them. A new creation as far as other people were concerned, the label was news to homosexuals themselves, too — they were now reduced to a single sexual characteristic, generally represented as a "disease," if not proof of "degeneracy." Other preexisting identifying characteristics became blurred, like the social bonds that were formed by socializing at the same places, the knowledge of certain codes, the wearing of certain signs. If they survived the "medical" shock, they became "accessories" to the development of a new round of definitions that pretended to be globally applicable. However, the extraordinary variety of the definitions that were proposed, and the contradictions that they revealed, not to mention the extreme confusion of the vocabulary, all contributed to muddying the waters — and that left homosexuals the opportunity to build their own identity, personally and to a large extent independently.

---

473. The term "perversion" was used for the first time in 1885 par Victor Magnan, in a communication on fetishism.

The Doctors Intrude

Until the end of the 19th century, the field of sexual perversion had remained the prerogative of the courts of justice. The law punished acts like sodomy, but did not recognize a particular criminal status. But then, the psychiatrists began to take an interest in sexual perversions. Now, the criminal was defined by his perversion: he was a homosexual, pedophile, sadist, or fetishist.

But he was also a victim (of heredity, his genes, his education), which meant he was not responsible. He no longer belonged in the dock, but at the doctor's.

Until the mid-19th century, reports on trials and collections of jurisprudence had provided the bulk of the scientific "knowledge" on homosexuality.[474] However, the law did not define specific categories of perversions nor of perverts; it used fuzzy but defamatory terms, which were intended to encourage the reader to recognize the horror of the act without being able to describe it precisely.

The medical study of homosexuality arises from this incapacity of the law to define homosexuals and thus to work out a specific repressive strategy. The most famous work of the time, *Psychopathia Sexualis* (1885) by Krafft-Ebing, is subtitled: "A medico-legal study for the use of doctors and lawyers." Krafft-Ebing was a professor of psychiatry at the University of Vienna and a medical examiner for the courts. Similarly, Tardieu's pioneering work in France, *Pederasty* (1857), testified to a new interest in homosexuality and paved the way for other books which sought to define the homosexual criminal — books like *La Prostitution antiphysique* (1887) by François Carlier. Tardieu based his conclusions on the study of 205 individuals whom he had examined with a maniacal care, looking for "signs of pederasty."[475] His research was conducted in the guise of forensic medicine and was intended to enable a more effective monitoring of homosexual locales that had been linked to robbery, prostitution and blackmail.

Following Tardieu, many doctors took an interest in homosexuality. While it may have been studied first as a demonstration of hysteria, it soon spilled over into the realm of mental illness and came to form its own distinct category, with its own characteristics, internal classifications and symptoms.

---

474. See Jean Danet, *Discours juridique et perversions sexuelles (XIXe-XXe siècle)*, Nantes, université de Nantes, 1977, 105 pages.

475. For example, the "infundibuliform deformation of the anus" is a "sign" of "active pederasty."

The new researchers relied on the preceding works, and they often based their speculations on existing depictions of homosexuals, if they were not content merely to roughly summarize earlier analyses. Havelock Ellis notes, for example, that he knew many doctors who had never encountered a case of sexual inversion. Thus, research on homosexuality, even though it made spectacular strides in the late 19th century, rested on a very narrow base. The picture remained very blurry, despite the outpouring of books and articles.

The theorists of "degeneracy" were the first decisive influence. At least they denied the "criminal" basis of homosexuality, while insisting on its "innate" character; but they did not offer any but a very negative model, centered on the concepts of "perversion" and "degeneracy," which so deeply marked the first generation. Thus, Carl Westphal, a young Berlin neurologist and the first psychiatrist to study inversion on a scientific basis, asserted (just like Johann Ludwig Casper) that homosexuality was a congenital disease and not a vice. According to Arthur Schopenhauer, male homosexuality was provided by nature as a means of regulating the birth rate. Albert Moll, a neurologist, was more circumspect: in his principal work, *Die konträre Sexualempfindung* (1891), he clearly distinguished innate homosexuality and acquired homosexuality; however, he regarded the latter as exceptional.[476] The baron von Schrenck-Notzing gained a name for himself in 1892 by claiming to have cured homosexuality by hypnosis.

The uncontested expert in homosexuality was Richard von Krafft-Ebing. In *Psychopathia Sexualis*, he distinguishes four stages in the constitution of a homosexual personality, from the simple perversion of the sexual instinct to the belief in sex changes. He also distinguishes four stages of homosexuality: the psychosexual hermaphrodite, who preserves some traces of the heterosexual instinct; the homosexual; the effeminate; and the androgyne.

Only Karl Heinrich Ulrichs, himself a homosexual and the inventor of the concept of uranism ("the heart of a woman in the body of a man")," stood out. He agitated for the decriminalization of homosexuality, initially under the name of *Numa Numantius*, then under his own, and asserted that homosexuality was not a disease but a simple sexual variation which was of no more consequence than the color of one's hair.[477] His definition of homosexuals as "a third sex," which he

---

476. Albert Moll did an about-face in 1936 in his autobiography, *Ein Leben als Arzt der Seele*. There, he claimed that homosexuality is as a rule the result of unhealthy sexual experiences and that only a small fraction of homosexual cases are innate. This reversal enabled him to welcome the repressive measures of the Nazi regime.

tried to define through a complex classification system, met with an extraordinary success and was picked up by Hirschfeld.

In France, Brouardel, Lacassagne, Chevalier and Raffalovitch studied homosexuality. Raffalovitch published a major work in 1896, *Uranism and Unisexuality*. Nevertheless Jean Martin Charcot (1825-1893) and Victor Magnan (1835-1916) were the first Frenchmen to abandon the criminal model of homosexuality in favor of a medical and pathological model. They authored the first publication on the subject, "Inversion du sens génital et autres perversions sexuelles," initially published in numbers 7 and 12 of the *Archives de neurologie* in 1882. Their theories were still being discussed in the inter-war period.[478]

French psychiatrists looked at sexual inversion primarily as it related to hysteria, and homosexuality was studied only in relation to neurosis; this bias skewed their conclusions in an inevitably perverse and pathological direction. Homosexuality was only an isolated symptom of a general disorder, "degeneracy." However, the discourse was more innovative than one might expect; Charcot based his work on the study of a case which he describes in close detail; the patient, a man of 31 years, had been attracted to boys since his childhood, he practiced Onanism up to the age of 21, and would have liked to dress as a woman. Charcot notes that he was not in any way effeminate, that he was "large, quite well-built," and "cultivated a certain military style." He was consulting the physician not because he suffered from his homosexuality,[479] but because he had been prone to hysterical attacks since the age of 15. For Charcot, he was "quite a unique sexual anomaly," but that was only "the most salient sign of a much more serious psychopathological state." He prescribes what is a fairly classic treatment for that era (putting him in touch with a woman, physical and moral hygiene, cold showers, bromide), but only the hysteria was regarded as dis-

---

477. "And they tried him just because of the color of his hair" (A.E. Housman, about the trial of Oscar Wilde).

478. Freud was inspired by Charcot's studies on neuroses, which he carried further. In his book *Le Centenaire de Magnan* (1935), Claude Vurpas recalled his studies of sexual inversion. Similarly, various works at the popular level made much of it — such as *Invertis et homosexuels* by Dr Georges Saint-Paul (preface by Émile Zola), published in 1896 and reprinted many times (Paris, Éditions Vigon, 152 pages) and *De l'inversion sexuelle à la détermination des sexes* by Dr Henri Allaix (Le Chesnais, Imprimerie moderne de Versailles, 1930, 10 pages).

479. He never actually acted upon it, which is a recurrent phenomenon in the choice of examples offered by doctors — as though it were more tolerable to present imaginings rather than actual experiences.

abling. Since homosexuality was considered to be innate, the subject was not responsible. As a mental patient, he could not be regarded as a criminal.

Female homosexuality does not seem to have stirred the interest of more than a very finite number of doctors. In fact, the number of medical models offered to lesbians proved particularly restricted, which perhaps helps to explain the delay in creating an identity. Moreover, the poverty of the analyses is striking — a consequence of a lack of interest on the part of both doctors and the public (lesbianism was not condemned by law), and also of the low number of cases observed. Krafft-Ebing, the first to take a closer look, had distinguished four types of female "deviants" in his *Psychopathia Sexualis*: women who do not betray their abnormality by their external appearance or by their mental characteristics, but who nevertheless are responsive to approaches by masculine-looking women; women who prefer to wear masculine clothing; women who pretend to be men; and, finally, "the last stage of degenerate homosexuality. The only female attribute remaining to the woman of this type is her genitals: her thinking, feelings, action, and external appearance are those of a man."[480] According to this analysis, "true" lesbians are those who most resemble men, and any masculine aspiration in clothing or behavior is a symptom of lesbianism.

Such assertions were still a mainstay after the War, promulgated by such writers as Mathilde de Kemnitz, in *Erotische Wiedergeburt* (1919); Dr. Caufeynon, in *La Perversion sexuelle* (1932); and André Binet, who claims, in *La Vie sexuelle des femmes* (1932), that "complete inversion is rare in women; more often, one observes bisexuality."[481] Similarly, Albert Chapotin, after having described lesbians as having, "accentuated facial features, breasts of the virile type but with nipples very elongated and erectile, thighs of the male type, contralto voices," affirms: "What one euphemistically calls 'light inversion' is very frequent among women, marked and well-developed inversion is rarer."[482] Erich Stern, Julie Bender and James Broch still considered it worth publishing articles in *Zeitschrift für Sexualwissenschaft* (in 1920, 1921 and 1929, respectively) tending to prove that lesbianism did exist.[483]

---

480. Krafft-Ebing, cited by Esther Newton, "The Mythic Mannish Lesbian: Radclyffe Hall and the New Woman," in Martin Duberman, Martha Vicinus and George Chauncey Jr. (dir.), *Hidden from History*, London, Penguin Books, 1991, 579 pages, p.287.

481. André Binet, *La Vie sexuelle de la femme*, Paris, L'Expansion scientifique française, 1932, 240 pages, p.183-184.

482. Albert Chapotin, *Les Défaitistes de l'amour*, Paris, Le Livre pour tous, 1927, 510 pages, p.18 and 183.

Countering the theory of innate homosexuality was the view of a "congenital anomaly" susceptible to being "treated." This was very much the minority view, but interest in it was renewed in the 1930s and was exploited and encouraged by the Nazi power. Steinach was the leading proponent of this view; from his experiments on rats, he deduced that it was possible to cure homosexuality by a surgical operation on the testicles. His research was periodically seconded by German doctors, for instance Dr. Josef Kirchhoff, in *Die sexuellen Anomalien* (1921); and Heinz Schmeidler, in *Sittengeschichte von heute, die Krisis der Sexualität* (1932). In *Zum Problem der Homosexualität* (1921), Dr. Otto Emsmann weighed the various medical theories on homosexuality and emphasized Steinach and Schrenck-Notzing's research: homosexuality could be cured either by implanting healthy sexual glands, by the transplantation of healthy testicles, or by hypnosis. Nevertheless, in the most serious cases such treatment would not suffice; in those cases, the will of the patient is the determining factor in the success of the treatment.

At the first congress of the World League for Sexual Reform, the fight between the psychiatric and the organic approach was at the heart of the discussions. Dr. Rogge and Haag gave a presentation on the "significance of Steinach's research for the question of pseudo-homosexuality." Here, the explanation lay in the sexual glands of both sexes being present in one individual. Dr. Weil, speaking on "Proportions of the body and intersexuality of forms as expressed by internal secretions" (!), asserted that homosexuality is primarily constitutional, as did Dr. Schwarz, who maintained that homosexuality could be modified by injecting hormones.

Medicine at the "Service" of Homosexuals

As a counterpoint to the new psychiatric theories, certain doctors were gaining renown (in public opinion as well as in homosexual circles) for the originality of their analyses and the progressive stance they took. The most famous was obviously Magnus Hirschfeld. We will not recapitulate his hypotheses here, as they are covered in Chapter Two; but it should be stressed that his theory of the "third sex" was an essential part of the foundation of the homosexual identity, since, in a way, the latter was built upon it and as a reaction to it.

---

483. Erich Stern, "Zur Kenntnis der weiblichen Inversion" (1920), Julie Bender, "Zur Frage der Homosexualität der Frau" (1921), James Broch, "Über Tribadie: eine Jungfrau als Konsulatssekretär" (1929), in *Zeitschrift für Sexualwissenschaft*, vol.6, 7 and 15.

Indeed, the theory could apply only to a fraction of the homosexual population, those who felt "feminine," "the heart of a woman in the body of a man."

Goldsworthy Lowes Dickinson, in a letter to his friend Frederick Schiller, devotes a good ten pages to an analysis of his homosexuality according to the theory of the third sex, saying that

> — It is a curious thing to have a feminine soul captive in a man's body, but it seems that that is my case. This physical impulse, however, has never been the key to my relations with men, because on the spiritual plane I have a still more urgent need to preserve my independence and my self-respect, and I have had in fact as much to give as to receive.[484]

Still, the theory of the "third sex" posited the bases of a powerful homo-sexual identity, autonomous and assertive, since as a group apart from society in general homosexuals would have to unite to claim their rights and to make the world recognize their difference. However, as we have seen, this view was severely criticized by the proponents of pederasty, who situated homosexuality in the Greek tradition and vigorously denied any "femininity." Misogynists, they looked on homosexuality from the historical and cultural, but also the political, point of view. This view was defended in Germany by Adolf Brand and Hans Blüher, and in France by André Gide.

Hirschfeld's theories were promoted in his books, which became best-sellers. They were translated into French and English, sometimes in digest form in order to be more accessible to the general public; and they had considerable impact. Another figure, however, was also important, for the construction of the homosexual identity as well as for the evolution of public opinion, in particular in England.

Havelock Ellis (1859-1939) was the most influential sexologist of the inter-war period. He was close to the radical socialist faction which emerged in the 1880s, and associated with leading figures of the new left like H.M. Hyndman, Eleanor Marx, Edward Aveling and the first Fabians. He was familiar with the works of Hirschfeld and Freud, with whom he disagreed, rejecting in particular the notion that sex is at the basis of all human behaviors. — There are certain psychoanalysts, he said, who, when they recognize signs of homosexuality, accept them, as most people do, as signs of homosexuality. But when they see the

---

484. Dennis Proctor (ed.), *The Autobiography of G. Lowes Dickinson*, London, Duckworth, 1973, 287 pages, p.10.

opposite, even a strong antipathy, they also take that as a sign of homosexuality, the reaction of a repressed desire. "Heads, I win; tails, you lose," they seem to say.[485] For his part, he preferred a personal approach of medicine and worked starting from accounts which were spontaneously brought to him by his correspondents and visitors. Unlike other doctors, Ellis was very familiar with homosexuality. He had strong friendships with recognized homosexuals like J.A. Symonds and Edward Carpenter (who brought him several homosexual autobiographies, including his own). His wife Edith Lees was a lesbian, and left him to live with women. His biographer, Vincent Brominates, raises the question of whether Ellis himself was not a repressed homosexual; he did not have any sexual intercourse with men, but all the women in his life complained about a lack of virility, about his scant sexual desire. His main work, *Sexual Inversion* (1897), was inspired by Symonds.

Sexual Inversion was definitely a landmark for homosexuals in the 1920s; it presented homosexuality under a more positive rubric than its contemporaries, affirming that is was an inborn characteristic and refusing to regard it as a "disease." Right in his introduction, Ellis justified his view: "I realized that in England, more than in any other country, the law and the public opinion combined to place a heavy criminal burden and a severe social stigmatization on the expression of an instinct which, for the people who have it, frequently seems natural and normal."[486] In its form, the work is not very original, citing preceding works and listing animals, countries, and civilizations that were known to exhibit homosexuality; but then Ellis presented many cases of homosexuals who — and this is what was new — were not "neurotic." Its limitations were many, however: sexual practices are scarcely documented, and sodomy, although some examples are presented, is largely avoided — no doubt because it was a crime according to English law and because in his quest to rehabilitate homosexuals in public opinion, Ellis wanted to marginalize certain types (sodomites, cross-dressers, queens), who in any case had difficulty find a place in the incipient homosexual community. Also, the analysis of lesbianism appears less relevant, perhaps because of personal reservations having to do with his wife and also because few female cases were studied. Ellis charts Sapphism along a scale which starts with passionate friendship and ends in "active inversion." He states

485. Cited by Vincent Brome, *Havelock Ellis, Philosopher of Sex*, London, Routledge & Kegan, 1979, 271 pages, p.220.
486. Havelock Ellis and J.A. Symonds, *Sexual Inversion* [1897], New York, Arno Press, 1975, 299 pages, p. XI.

that, "the principal characteristic of the female invert is a certain degree of masculinity." Ellis builds the lesbian couple on the heterosexual model. The "pseudo-
lesbians" are in fact really heterosexuals who have been "seduced" by true homosexuals, suggesting that,

> — These women are different from the average normal woman in that
> they are not disgusted and do not repel advances from members of their
> own sex. Their faces may be unattractive or even ugly, but they often have a
> good figure, which is more important for the inverted woman than the
> beauty of the face. They are affectionate by nature... and they are feminine.
> One might say that they are among the elite of the women whom the aver-
> age man would reject. This must be one of the reasons why they are open to
> homosexual advances, but I do not think that it is the only one...They seem
> to have a natural preference, although not precisely sexual, for women
> rather than men.[487]

That is a pretty negative description. However, it formed the basis for separating "true" and "pseudo" lesbians, two models which turned out to stay with
us for a long time and they influenced the identifying process profoundly.

Sexual Inversion was published in Germany in 1896, but the English edition
ran into trouble. In the maelstrom of the Oscar Wilde trial, the 1897 edition had
to be revised and Symonds' name was removed. The second edition was immediately withdrawn and the book was banned. The lawsuit proceeded without any
scandal, but the book was classified as obscene. It was then published in the
United States. The publicity generated by the lawsuit had positive consequences: hundreds of homosexuals wrote to Ellis to share their experiences with
him. He then used this documentation as the basis for further research.

Moreover, the book became the main reference work on homosexuality
prior to the Second World War, and Hirschfeld noted that "*Sexual Inversion* was
very important for the homosexual question in Germany. The spirit of the book
was so noble and scholarly that we preferred it to *Konträre Sexualempfindung de
Moll*. From this point, the name of Havelock Ellis became very popular in
Germany."[488] In England, Ellis had more influence than Freud; moreover, his
attentive and sympathetic treatment of homosexuality enabled him to influence
people who would have remained insensitive to a purely medical approach.[489]

---

487. *Ibid*, p.87.
488. Cited by Vincent Brome, Havelock Ellis, *Philosopher of Sex, op. cit.*, p.95.

Psychoanalytical Shock

Psychoanalysis brought about a major shift in the concepts, the approach, and the way of thinking about homosexuality; it created a shock by its method as well as by its conclusions and played a part in shaping the identifying process.[490] Freud did not start from scratch, however; in *Three Essays on the Theory of Sexuality* (1905), he pays homage to the research of his predecessors Krafft-Ebing, Moll, von Schrenck-Notzing, Löwenfeld, Eulenburg, Bloch and Hirschfeld, and he uses their inventory of examples as well.[491] However, he draws very different conclusions: where they say "innate," he says "acquired"; and he counters their biological explanations with the hypothesis of "seduction" in childhood: the homosexual is neither a criminal nor a congenital mental patient, he is a neurotic: the predisposition to homosexuality arises in a man from the discovery that the woman does not have a penis. If he cannot give up the penis as the essential sexual object, he will inevitably be turned off by a woman. She may even represent a threat, if the absence of the penis is perceived as the result of mutilation (castration anxiety).

Freud goes much further in his analyses: he establishes a parallel between neurosis and perversion. "[N]eurosis is so to speak the flip side of perversion."[492] According to him, symptoms of inversion can be found in the unconscious life of all neurotics (especially the hysteric).[493] In fact, neurosis is the product of the repression of perverse tendencies. This theory unfortunately opened the door to many erroneous conclusions, for Freud's readers were quick to equate neurosis and perversion.

---

489. A surprising number of books have been devoted to him and they show a profound sense of admiration: in 1926, *Havelock Ellis. A Biographical and Critical Survey*, by Isaac Goldberg; in 1928, *Havelock Ellis, Philosopher of Love*, Houston Peterson; in 1929, *Havelock Ellis in Appreciation*, under the direction of Joseph Ishill, who compiled a panegyric based on celebrities opinions on Ellis from the likes of H.L. Mencken, Edward Carpenter, Henri Barbusse and Thomas Hardy.

490. Clearly, Freudians have made immense contributions in many domains and, equally clearly, we do not intend to present here a complete history of psychoanalysis or psychoanalytic theory between the wars.

491. Furthermore, Freud went to Salpêtrière to learn from Jean Martin Charcot.

492. Sigmund Freud, *Trois essais sur la théorie de la sexualité* [1905], Paris, Gallimard, 1987, 211 pages, p.81.

493. On this topic, see the chapter "Les fantasmes hystériques et leur relation à la bisexualité," in *Névrose, psychose et perversion* (1894-1924; Paris, PUF, coll. "Bibl. de psychanalyse," 1992, 303 pages). By the same token, Freud maintains that the paranoïac is struggling with homosexual tendencies.

As regards female homosexuality, Freud initially paid it relatively little attention; later, he filled in with several psychoanalytical cases.[494] The genesis of female homosexuality is symmetrical to the male; castration anxiety still plays an essential role, for, if the girl does not accept her lack of a penis, she will struggle to assert her masculinity.[495] Freud insists that it is almost impossible to "cure" homosexuals; he does not even seem to think it desirable. He notes that most of the people who come to consult him do so primarily for social reasons. The women are generally brought in by their families, who absolutely want to marry them off or who fear a scandal. According to him: "Psychoanalysis is not going to solve the problem of homosexuality. It must be satisfied to reveal the psychic mechanisms which lead to the decisions governing the choice of the object and to trace how these mechanisms relate to instinctual drives."[496]

What did Freud contribute to the study of homosexuality? First of all is the importance of method: all conclusions are drawn from interviews with patients; this process was already used by other doctors, but Freud systematized it and transformed it by the practice of analysis. Then, Freud refuted the old concept of degeneracy, the idea of innate homosexuality and, finally, the myth of a psychic hermaphrodism. He made the point that "the most complete psychic virility is compatible with inversion."[497] According to him, inverts go through an intense phase of fixation on their mothers during childhood, and then, identifying with her, they take themselves as sexual objects (in the narcissistic way of young boys, they seek someone similar to themselves whom they will love as their mother loved them). Freud insists that all men are capable of making a homosexual choice, as that is formulated in the unconscious. The heterosexual choice also depends on a complex process and thus is no more natural than the other one. There exists, according to him, a considerable proportion of latent homosexuality in heterosexuals. He goes on to distinguish the absolute invert, whose sexual object can only be homosexual; the "amphigene," that is, in fact, the bisexual; and the part-time or occasional homosexual, who may have homo-

---

494. See the chapter "Sur la psychogenèse d'un cas d'homosexualité féminine," in Névrose, psychose et perversion.

495. Helen Deutsch worked out a different psychoanalytical theory of feminine homosexuality: for her, giving birth and motherhood were at the heart of the feminine homosexual relationship and originated in a pre-œdipal attachment to the mother — a hypothesis that is in stark contradiction to the Freudian orthodoxy.

496. Sigmund Freud, *Névrose, psychose et perversion, op. cit.*, p.270.

497. Id., *Trois essais sur la théorie de la sexualité, op. cit.*, p.47.

sexual relations only because of circumstances. In fact, Freud tended to think that mankind was originally bisexual;[498] and in so doing he raised questions about the foundations of patriarchal society and opened the gate to all kinds of minority movements. Indeed, if sexual attraction comes in all gradations, if anyone is likely to be attracted by a member of his or her own sex, it becomes difficult to condemn homosexuals unilaterally.

The Freudian theory was picked up by many disciples, who always did not follow his conclusions to the letter. Whatever the validity of the Freudian analysis as to the causes of homosexuality, it had the merit of not stigmatizing "inverts" and of questioning the idea that "heterosexuality = normality." Those who popularized his work often forgot this detail, including Sacha Nacht, who claimed that "the invert is impotent vis-à-vis women, before he is homosexual."[499] The Austrian psychiatrist and psychoanalyst Alfred Adler, in *Das Problem der Homosexualität* (1930), blames the feminist movements for spreading the "plague" and affirms that "homosexuality is a temporary and unnatural expedient that is not well understood" on behalf of men who have difficulty accepting female independence.[500]

Freud's successors developed divergent theories on the homosexual question. For Wilhelm Reich, homosexuality is "a purely social phenomenon, a question of education and sexual development;"[501] "it only develops when normal relations between men and women are impossible or difficult."[502] The best means of avoiding it, therefore, is coeducation and the practice of sexual relations whenever desired. Reich called for the decriminalization of homosexuality, a disease which he said caused great suffering to the individual. He did, however, believe it possible to cure some of them by following a suitable psychic treatment. Reich is the only psychoanalyst to consider the homosexual question in its social dimension, while giving it a political significance:

---

498. Freud sems to have borrowed this theory from a doctor in Berlin, Wilhelm Fliess. For the renewed interest in the theory of androgyny, as it was initially proposed by Plato, see Chapters Five and Six.

499. Sacha Nacht, *Pathologie de la vie amoureuse: essai psychanalytique*, Paris, Denoël, 1937, 198 pages, p.155.

500. Alfred Adler, *Das Problem der Homosexualität*, Berlin, Verlag von S. Hirzel, 1930, 110 pages, p.65.

501. Wilhelm Reich, *La Lutte sexuelle des jeunes* [1932], Paris, Maspero, 1972, 148 pages, p.90.

502. *Ibid.*, p.89.

Many young proletarians, because of their poverty, are also led to give themselves to homosexuals from wealthier backgrounds. Thus, in politically reactionary circles, such as among nationalist students or among officers, homosexuality plays a role which is not insignificant and which is very closely related to the strong imprint of moral and sexual inhibition in these milieux.[503]

Carl Gustav Jung was not much interested in homosexuality, either. Like Freud, when he explained that homosexuality corresponded to an infantile phase of sexual life, Jung claimed that it was a resurgence of a primitive phase of humanity. He called it psychological immaturity, and thus a behavioral disturbance. Psychoanalysis would enable the homosexual to mature psychologically, to pass from a state of individualism to social integration.

Freud met stiff opposition in France.[504] The usual hostility ignited by his theory of "initial seduction" was intensified by a fundamental hostility to any idea of German and Jewish origin.[505] Moreover, the French, proud of their own psychiatric discoveries, were not much inclined to recognize any other authority. The pioneers of French psychoanalysis thus set out to diminish the role of the initial seduction and to emphasize instead that of the imagination.

Angelo Hesnard, a member of the French Society of Psychoanalysis,[506] was particularly interested in homosexuality.[507] He borrowed heavily from Freud,[508] but he worked from a broad variety of sources, as much medical (Havelock Ellis,

---

503. *Ibid.,* p.90.

504. Freud began to be tranlated into France in 1922; the Société française de psychanalyse and the *Revue franÇaise de psychanalyse* were launched in 1926.

505. Poincaré's Minister of Education is quoted as saying, in 1928: "I am told that German youth have been poisoned by Freud. Freudism is nordic phenomenon. It cannot take hold in France" (cited by Marcelin Pleynet, "La Société psychanalytique de Paris," in Olivier Barrot and Pascal Ory [dir.], *Entre-deux-guerres,* Paris, François Bourin, 1990, 631 pages).

506. There were nine founding members: Princess Georges of Greece (née Marie Bonaparte), Evgénia Sokolnicka, Angelo Hesnard, René Allendy, Adrien Borel, René Laforgue, Rodolphe Loewenstein, Georges Parcheminey and Édouard Pichon. This group was formed rather tardily, as psychoanalytical societies had existed in Vienna, Zurich, Budapest, Berlin, London, and the United States since 1914.

507. This subject features prominently in *L'Individu et le Sexe. Psychologie du narcissisme* (Paris, Stock, 1927, 227 pages), *Psychologie homosexuelle* (Paris, Stock, 1929, 208 pages) and *Traité de sexologie normale et pathologique* (Paris, Payot, 1933, 718 pages).

508. According to Marcelin Pleynet, Hesnard practiced a "moderate anti-Freudism; he saw Freud as no more than one scholar among many; see Marcelin Pleynet, "La Société psychanalytique de Paris," *loc. cit.*

Magnus Hirschfeld) as artistic (he cited Proust, Margueritte, Binet-Valmer, Miomandre, Carco, Gide, Porché). However, his approach remained conventional: he opposes the Freudian analytical rigor with the usual recitative tone, descriptive, more sociological than scientific and, following the example other works of the time (except those of Freud), he begins his discourse with a history of homosexuality through the ages. While in broad outline he follows the Freudian theory, he distinguishes certain telling points: he sees the homosexual as "disgusted by sexuality," a "chaste" sensibility offended by female sexuality. According to him, homosexuals have completely dissociated tenderness and sensuality: "The homosexual only seldom obtains complete satisfaction."[509] Such an assertion is based on his unilateral interpretation of sexuality according to heterosexual terms: "....the absence of complete satisfaction — which only normal intersexual relations can give, the only ones that conform to the physiology of the respective organs — develops the unsatisfied sexual appetite to the point of exasperation."[510] On lesbianism, he puts forward the novel idea of a female predisposition to homosexuality: "Woman is, in the psychogenetic sense, originally homosexual. The normal adult woman is a being who has had to triumph over her original homosexuality to arrive at the result, which is harder for her than for the man, of sexual development, heterosexual and in accordance with the rules."[511] In conclusion, he draws a facile parallel between lesbianism and frigidity; the lesbian is in fact only seeking simple body contact, not specifically genital in nature, and may have somewhat sadistic tendencies.[512]

In fact, the Freudian influence in the design of the homosexual identity is paradoxical. Freud was mostly known through those who popularized, and often distorted, his thought, particularly in France. Certain countries (like England) were little influenced by Freudian theory for, in fact, the biological theories dominated. In Germany, the psychoanalytical movement was divided since the mid-1930s.

---

509. Angelo Hesnard, *Psychologie homosexuelle, op. cit.*, p.109.
510. *Ibid.*, p.113.
511. *Ibid.*, p.198.
512. *Ibid.* the same kind of assertions show up in the work of other psychoanalysts, like René de Saussure in his book, *Les Fixations homosexuelles chez les femmes névrosées* (Paris, Imprimerie de la Cour d'appel, 1929, 44 pages). Saussure Saussure especially insists on the desire for a penis and the feeling of castration, and the notion that women see the vulva as a wound.

Moreover, psychoanalysis did not liberate homosexuals. On the contrary, it imposed on them an external explanation of their condition, an obligatory model which they could hardly contest, since all their protests could be dismissed by the notion that it was unconscious. Lastly, categorizing homosexuality as an arrested stage of development could hardly be considered as favorable.

However, there was a fascination with psychoanalysis during the interwar period, especially among French intellectuals, thanks to the influence of Evgénia Sokolnicka, a student of Freud, and the Nouvelle revue française group where she met Paul Le Bourget.[513]

André Gide notes in his journal how much the Freudian revelations matched his own concept of homosexuality: "

> Freud. Freudism... For ten years, fifteen years, I have been [homosexual] without knowing it.[514]
> [Analyzing his own case, he resorts to characteristic medical jargon:] "No, I do not believe by any means that my particular tastes could have been transmitted by heredity: [these are] acquired characteristics, non-transmissible. I am this way because I was thwarted in my instincts by my education, and the circumstances... what I imagine, you see, is that I must have inherited an inordinately demanding sexuality, which was thwarted, repressed voluntarily by several generations of ascetics, and of which, to some extent, I am now subjected to the built-up pressure.[515]

In 1921, he read the *Introduction to Psychoanalysis* and participated in six psychoanalysis sessions with Evgénia Sokolnicka; she had opened a salon in Paris in the autumn of 1921, and already was seeing a number of Parisian intellectuals, including Roger Martin du Gard, Jules Romain and Jules Schlumberger. Gide gives a hilarious report on these meetings in his journal.[516]

The best example of the influence of psychoanalysis in homosexual intellectual circles comes from England, at the very center of the Bloomsbury Club.

---

513. On this topic, see Jean-Paul Nordier, *Les Débuts de la psychanalyse en France, 1895-1926*, Paris, Maspero, 1981, 274 pages; and Marcel Scheidhauer, *Le Rêve freudien en France, 1900-1926*, Paris, Navarin, 1985, 227 pages. Bergson's influence was a determining factor in arousing the literary world's curiosity about psychoanalysis.

514. André Gide, *Journal, 1887-1925*, Paris, Gallimard, coll. "Bibl. de la Pléiade," 1996, 1840 pages, p.1170-1171. Gide seems to have learned about Freudism through his friend, Dorothy Bussy, the sister of James Strachey, who translated Freud into English.

515. Avril 1921, cited by Roger Martin du Gard, *Notes sur André Gide (1913-1951)*, in *Œuvres complètes*, Paris, Gallimard, coll. "Bibl. de la Pléiade," 1983, t.II, 1 432 pages, p.1374.

516. André Gide, *Journal, 1887-1925*, op. cit., 17 March 1922, p.1173.

James and Alix Strachey were indeed the official translators of Freud's works into English and they contributed largely to its recognition in Great Britain. Both had a history of homosexual activity. Alix, born Sargant-Florence, suffered from neurotic disorders; she was a friend of Rupert Brooke, and had done her studies at Bedales, then at Cambridge. She had had romantic friendships with several women, without actually engaging in the act, itself. A nervous breakdown brought her to Vienna, for analysis by Freud, then to Berlin, and Karl Abraham. James Strachey was the brother of Lytton; he was in love with Brooke, like so many others, while he was studying at Cambridge, and he became a member of the Apostles and sacrificed to the homosexual fashion of the moment. Thereafter, he dismissed the sexual experimentation of his youth, joking that they divided their time between sodomizing one another and listening to the "Appassionata" being massacred by Donald Tovey.[517] He was in love with Alix, and explained his choice as follows: "Women are hateful, except for one delicious young lady at Bedales who resembles a boy."[518] James Strachey is the perfect example of the young man from a good family but who associated with Bohemians, who rejected his homosexuality but still could not face women. He thus chose a woman who was, herself, androgynous, and who was likewise unable to clearly define her sexual identity. It is interesting to note that it was precisely these two pure products of their time and their background who were charged with promoting Freud's work in England. Their writings, universally recognized, are regarded as the best interpretation of Freudian thought. As a result of their social origin and their social ties, they brought psychoanalysis into the most brilliant intellectual circles of England, thus contributing to its adoption in a country that had been quite closed to these new techniques.

Medical theories also played an essential part in the process of crafting an identity. Traces of these theories crop up throughout the homosexual literature of the time. Radclyffe Hall based the book *The Well of Loneliness* on Krafft-Ebing's and Havelock Ellis's theories. Proust's *œuvre* is an admirable digest of the latest medical theories; Proust read the principal authors and managed to weave in, almost imperceptibly to the unsuspecting reader, a whole series of specific signals suggesting homosexuality. In *In Search of Lost Time*, he expands on the hypothesis of "the third sex" so dear to Karl Heinrich Ulrichs and Magnus Hir-

---

517. Perry Meisel and Walter Kendrick, *Bloomsbury/Freud. James et Alix Strachey, Correspondance 1924-1925*, Paris, PUF, 1985, 395 pages, p.31.
518. *Ibid.*, p.37.

schfeld; he also evokes psychiatric and Freudian interpretations, Carpenter's theories, Walt Whitman's homosexuality and the Greek tradition. Having boned up on the medical literature, many homosexuals sought to explain their own cases in light of the most recent discoveries. Medicine had granted them the right to speak about homosexuality, and by discussing the theories, homosexuals took back some of the right to define their own identity.

From now on, the struggle to define their identity started with scientific comprehension. To be homosexual involved a host of questions which could only be answered by reading specialized works: "Medical books were the only thing that existed in great number. We got Hirschfeld's books, but ended up limiting our readings to clinical cases; to get them, these books, I called myself a doctor, and I hid them under my bed."[519] The idea of a hypothetical treatment for homosexuality was in the air and homosexuals discussed this possibility among themselves. Virginia Woolf reported that when she discussed it with E.M. Forster, he said that Dr. Head could convert sodomites. "Would you like to be converted?" asked Leonard Woolf. "No, certainly not," Forster answered.[520]

Moreover, the meeting between patient and doctor was very often disappointing. The homosexual who had expected to find help from his doctor ran into distrust and incomprehension: "[The doctor] had not read scientific works on the question. There weren't any, back when he was attending hospitals, and those that had appeared more recently were in German, and therefore suspect. Temperamentally opposed to these morals, he endorsed society's verdict, i.e. his condemnation was of a religious nature. One would have to be completely depraved, he felt, to turn toward Sodom, and when an individual who was morally and physically fit confessed this penchant to him, he spontaneously cried, 'Nonsense!'"[521]

Michel Foucault showed that medicine and psychiatry were the disciplines best positioned to authoritatively explore the territory of sexuality.[522] Psychiatry claimed to hold the key to sexual knowledge: it could diagnose and

---

519. Testimony of André du Dognon, recorded by Gilles Barbedette and Michel Carassou, in *Paris gay 1925*, Paris, Presses de la Renaissance, 1981, 312 pages, p.60.

520. Cited by Philip Hoare, *Serious Pleasures: The Life of Stephen Tennant*, London, Penguin, 1992, 463 pages, p.161.

521. E.M. Forster, *Maurice* [written in 1914], Paris, Christian Bourgois éditeur, 1987, 279 pages, p.178.

522. Michel Foucault, *Histoire de la sexualité*, t.I, *La Volonté de savoir*, Paris, Gallimard, 1976, 211 pages.

even cure. While the judge could only consider delinquents, the doctor could meet all sorts of deviants. As Jean Danet said, "According to all the evidence, then, the law and psychiatry are obviously competing to impose their own form of control over the perverts."[523]

The medical discourse was tending toward an emancipation movement in favor of homosexuals, but it was destructive at the same time. Instead of perceiving the doctor as an external agent in the service of the dominant power, homosexuals thought they could rely on him as an ally, an accomplice, even a savior. Instead of calling for the abolition of anti-homosexual laws in the name of justice and equal rights, homosexuals pleaded irresponsibility. Without necessarily realizing it, they sided with the medical men on this and contributed to their victory.

BEING HOMOSEXUAL: PROCLAIMING AN IDENTITY

The homosexual identity is more than a set of medical clichés. In the slow process of forming one's identity, other factors come into play: the social environment, contact with the homosexual scene, individual experience. To be homosexual means, first of all, to define oneself as such, to recognize one's uniqueness and to try to accept it. Depending on the case, this identity may by accepted very early on, or maybe only as a result of a long and painful process. There must be as many identifying constructs as there are individuals, but the study of first-hand accounts indicates that there are certain constants and certain standard patterns, beyond the whims of individual fate.

Homosexual confessions proliferated.[524] They are often presented as justifications: whether they were memoirs intended for publication, collections of personal correspondence, or private diaries, the author sought to explain what made him different. If the same individual had been heterosexual, he would not likely have considered it useful to explain to the reader what he thought was the key to his sexual orientation. As a homosexual, however, he feared that his proclivities would be misunderstood. By relating how he came to realize that he was

---

523. Jean Danet, *Discours juridique et perversions sexuelles, op. cit.,* p.46.

524. The written testimonies essentially come from the middle and upper classes. Among the oral histories, some concern the working class, but they are rare. We have no reports relating to the peasantry. One must hope that new archives will be discovered that will enable us to balance this presentation.

a homosexual, he has a chance to emphasize the innate nature of his sexual preference and to wipe out any suspicion of perversion. More rare were the militant
homosexuals who testified in order to advance their cause and who did not hesitate to be provocative.

Reading these personal accounts, one can evaluate the degree to which
each individual accepted his situation; of course, that varied enormously
according to the personality and his education. Age, too, played a big part.
Homosexuals of the first generation (born in the years 1870-1890) rarely felt
serene about their inclinations, but that was less and less true for the following
generation (born between 1900 and 1910). Even if we adjust for the *a posteriori*
revisions that one might expect to have crept in (even in good faith), the
accounts are instructive as to the image that the writer wished to project.

An Early Revelation

For many, the revelation of homosexuality came quite early, generally
during childhood. Maurice Sachs says,

> I passionately wished to be a girl, and I was so unaware of how grand it
> was to be a man that I went so far as to piss sitting down. Even better! I
> refused to go to sleep before Suze [his nanny] had sworn to me that I would
> wake up to find my sex had been changed.....As this occurred when I was
> about four years old, one would have to believe that since my earliest child-
> hood I had inclinations which very especially predisposed me toward
> homosexuality.[525]

Sometimes, homosexuality was revealed during an initial sexual experience, which might be precocious. Generally, the younger boy is initiated by an
older boy. Marcel Jouhandeau had his first experience at the age of eight, with a
19-year-old employee who showed him his sex; at the age of ten he had his first
pleasure with a boy of the same age, who masturbated him. Thereafter, he had
many revelations at school.[526]

Most of the authors obligingly relate all the details of their youthful adventures. This will to peg their homosexuality to a remote, almost indefinable past,
has to do with the individual's need to attach his sexuality to his most profound

---

525. Maurice Sachs, *Le Sabbat* [written in 1939, published in 1946], Paris, Gallimard,
1960, 298 pages, p.21-22.
526. See Chapter Three.

sense of self; it also corresponds to the influence of medicine, and in particular of psychoanalysis, as deciding factors in the construction of the sense of identity. When inversion is defined as innate, or as the consequence of an Œdipal complex that was handled poorly, the homosexual seeks at all costs to fit his personal experience into a general outline. This initial stage, recognition by his peers, is fundamental.

Homosexual Discomfort

This first awakening is, however, seldom positive. Most of the writers admit their discomfort. Recognized homosexuals whom one might have thought would have no complexes acknowledge fighting every minute against their inclinations. The photographer Cecil Beaton acknowledged as much, even while admitting that his friendships with men were more marvelous than with women. He "was never in love with a woman and [he did] not think that [he] ever would be in the same way as with a man. [He was] really a terrible, terrible homosexualist and [he tried] so much not to be."[527]

Hans Henny Jahnn met Gottlieb Harms, his great love, at the age of fourteen at the Sankt Pauli school in 1908. He fought his sexuality until 1913. After their "wedding," in July of that year, they still could not reconcile their physical desires with their spiritual aspirations: "We talked it over. He told me that having lain together with me made him insane .... He perceived me, my man, as if I were a prostitute sick with desire. He felt disgust for my body and my soul.... Now, I am dirty and sinful, and he is, too. And we cannot purify ourselves."[528]

Somerset Maugham was haunted all his life by the thought that his homosexuality might be publicly revealed. He always discouraged biographers and requested that his letters be burned after his death. After going through Cambridge, he met John Brooks and discovered Capri in 1895, the year of the Oscar Wilde trial. The scandal upset him and he understood that it would be impossible to go on as a homosexual and maintain a professional career as well: "I tried to persuade myself that I was three-quarters normal and only one-quarter homosexual — whereas in fact the opposite was true."[529] Until the end of the First

527. Cited by Hugo Vickers, *Cecil Beaton*, London, Weidenfeld & Nicolson, 1985, 656 pages, p.40.
528. Cited by Friedhelm Krey, *Hans Henny Jahnn und die mannmännliche Liebe*, Berlin, Peter Lang, 1987, 458 pages, p.423.

World War, he tried to pursue heterosexual relations, but his male friendships always won out. Thus, although he married Syrie Bernardo in 1917, he lived with his secretary, Frederick Gerald Haxton, whom he had met in Flanders in 1915. The marriage was a failure and Maugham held Syrie responsible. From 1920 on, Maugham was exclusively homosexual and he had relationships with various young writers and journalists who visited him, like Godfrey Winn, Beverley Nichols and Alan Frank Searle. However, within the Moorish villa where he received his friends, the homosexuality remained hidden.

For some, recognizing their homosexuality or, at least, bisexuality was absolutely impossible. D.H. Lawrence wavered between a violent aversion for the homosexual act, which he expressed particularly in his contempt for Bloomsbury, and an irresistible attraction for the myth of virile friendship, which appears many times over in his writings, in particular in *Women in Love*. Astute people were not deceived; Violet Trefusis noted that it was not difficult to guess, judging from the relations between "Birkin" and "Gerald," what kind of man is Mr. Lawrence. "He betrays himself at every turn."[530] In fact, it seems that it was the war that awoke D.H. Lawrence to the fear of being homosexual. He was haunted by images of the war, by the thought of rape. He acknowledged a violent hatred of sodomy and complained of nightmares on this subject; however, he did not find sodomy with a woman revolting. Talking with Bertrand Russell, he told him that he could not bear the odor of Cambridge, which he associated with decay and depravity. He explained to David Garnett that [he] simply could not bear it [love between men]. It is so bad... as if it came from some internal slime — a kind of sewer![531] However, he seems to have managed to consummate his love for a farmer, William Henry Hocking: one finds an echo of this relationship in *Kangaroo*.[532] Lawrence has a very ambiguous vision of homosexuality: for him, as for Bloomsbury, it is the "highest" form of love, which goes beyond simple sexuality and must lead to a total, mystical fusion of the two partners, but at the same time sexual intercourse between two men appears impure to him, perverse,

---

529. Confided to his nephew, Robin Maugham, cited by Robert Calder, *Willie. The Life of W. Somerset Maugham*, London, Heinemann, 1989, 429 pages, p.68.

530. Letter dated 19 July 1921 à Vita Sackville-West, *in* Violet Trefusis, *Lettres à Vita, 1910-1921*, Paris, Stock, 1991, 509 pages, p.493.

531. Cited in Brenda Maddox, *The Married man: A Life of D.H. Lawrence*, London, Sinclair-Stevenson, 1994, 652 pages, p.203-204.

532. Similarly, in *Le Paon blanc*, the bathing scene is an evocation of his friend Alan Chambers, and *Femmes amoureuses* recalls his friendship with amitié avec Middleton Murry.

against nature, the female body being "naturally" more beautiful than the male body. These two themes are constantly opposed in his life as in his work, and prevent any complete satisfaction.

T.E. Lawrence ("Lawrence of Arabia") is also an excellent example of maladjustment to sexual reality. He was attracted by men but never went beyond platonic enthusiasm and he restrained desires which he judged unhealthy. Confronted by homosexual advances at Oxford, he affected not to understand. His friend, Vyvyan Richards, evokes this episode with bitterness:

— There was in him neither flesh nor sensuality of any kind: he quite simply did not understand. He accepted my affection, my sacrifice, in fact, finally, my entire subordination as if they were his due. He never showed in the least way that he understood my reasons or guessed my desires.[533]

The most painful episode of his life, his capture and rape by the bey,[534] accentuated his feeling of shame and guilt. His repulsion with respect to sexuality was lifelong, and never found a solution. In a letter to a friend in 1937, he described himself as "a chaste bachelor"; he does not deny the restrictive nature of his situation, but says he prefers it to friendships which "can be easily transformed into sexual perversions." Barracks life is odious for him because of the libidinous climate that reigns there and he expresses indignation at the vulgar carnal instincts. However, at other times, he savagely denies the existence of homosexual relations within the army: the men are too dirty, there, and physically too close for any one to be attracted to the others; and they wish to stay in good shape. His attraction to young RAF aviators does not seem to have been fulfilled in any specific physical action.

The difficulty of accepting oneself as homosexual shows up differently, depending on the individual. Some manage to overcome their fears and their anguish, sometimes with outside help. Such was the case of the composer Benjamin Britten: until the age of 26, he did not have any sexual intercourse and expressed the greatest reserve with regard to any physical relations. His friends W.H. Auden and Christopher Isherwood, very liberated, badgered him with advice, without much success. In one of his poems, "Underneath an Abject Willow," written in March 1936, Auden evokes Britten's physical loathing and urges him to get into a loving relationship. The death of his mother in 1937 seems

---

533. Cited in Jeremy Wilson, *Lawrence d'Arabie*, Paris, Denoël, 1994, 1 288 pages, p.84.
534. See T.E. Lawrence, *Les Sept Piliers de la sagesse* [1926], Paris, Payot, 1989, 820 pages.

to have been truly liberating for Britten; released from maternal judgment, now he could live for himself. In 1937, he met the tenor Peter Pears, who was three years older than him. Pears had had several adventures in Lancing, his public school, and then at Oxford, and he had no trouble accepting his homosexuality. However, the two men's friendship took a long time to mature; Pears finally seduced Britten during a trip to America, to Grand Rapids, in June 1939. After that, they stayed together. Their relationship was patterned after the adolescent model of the public school: Pears was the dominating lover, uninhibited and physical, whereas Britten was more dependent, anxious and romantic.

In a different way, J.R. Ackerley's inability to find satisfaction shows in his unending quest for the "ideal friend." Despite his years of wanton sexual activity, totaling 200-300 conquests, Ackerley was still driven by a romantic faith in absolute love which he summed up by saying, "Incapable, it seems, of finding sexual satisfaction in love, I started a long quest for love through sex."[535] Like many other homosexuals of his time, he thought that other homosexuals were not real men and that they consequently were not desirable. A heterosexual, on the other hand, would constitute a valuable conquest. Ackerley tended to believe that the men who agreed to sleep with him must inevitably love him, whereas most of the time it was a casual fling, for them, an adventure with no future, easier to manage than a mistress. Forster and Daley constantly tried to draw his attention to this contradiction, without success:

> — When one wants to give a normal young man long kisses on the mouth (ugh!) and to entertain him with endless romantic speeches on eternal love (you and I under the arbor, oh my love, etc.), one must recognize that there is little chance a soldier who offers himself in a pub for 10 shillings a go will fit the bill.[536]

Ackerley's very explicit autobiography seems to have been undertaken partly in order to confront these problems.[537]

The rejection of homosexuality could be even more violent. Marcel Jouhandeau could not reconcile his spiritual aspirations and his sexual life. His book *De l'abjection* is a terrible testimony of self-rejection: "Rot! I am nothing but

---

535. Cited by Peter Parker, *A Life of J.R. Ackerley*, London, Constable, 1989, 465 pages, p.117.

536. *Ibid.*, p.119.

537. Ackerley also suffered from premature ejaculation.

flesh. Is this all that so many, so noble, promises have amounted to?"[538] The recognition of a broken life and career is added to this feeling of dirtiness and failure. Homosexuality becomes the major sin which determines all one's existence.

Asserting Oneself

Homosexuality is not inevitably experienced as a burden. Harold Nicolson seems to have expressed his homosexuality without any major difficulty. He managed to maintain a traditional family life, a diplomatic career and homosexual relationships, in parallel, with perfect serenity. Unlike many of his friends, he never expressed the least attraction for men of the working class and preferred the company of young intellectuals of the same social background as his. For him, homosexuality was only one aspect of his personality, a part of his life that was amusing, distracting, that it was best not to take too seriously and which there was no need to brag about.[539]

Rare, however, are the homosexuals who can completely accept their sexuality and their lifestyle, and who dare to assert it. Daniel Guérin, in his *Autobiographie de jeunesse* (1972), lists many flings that entailed no heart palpitations nor romantic illusions:

> The contact of naked bodies, which the Church and my education had made seem dramatic, was nothing more for me than a hygienic formality, like drinking and eating...what's more, the skins which I dared to rub belonged to the proscribed sex. Taboo was routed. Freedom triumphed. I tasted pleasure in its pure state, without mixing in either sensitivity, nor

---

538. Marcel Jouhandeau, *De l'abjection*, Paris, Gallimard, 1939, 156 pages, p.130. Jouhandeau went hrough phases of self-acceptance and disgust. Thus, in *Chronique d'une passion*, published in a private edition in 1938, then re-released in 1949, he rejects the judgment of society, and notably of the Church: "After the Father's departure, I retract into myself, I correct my confessions, I regret them: that is this disorder that he spoke of? What was so serious about it? What was so bad, after all, about disturbing an "order" that is, itself, so artificial, so miserable as the "conjugal order?" All night long I cursed myself for having calumniated homosexuality in my last book; it doesn't necessarily lead to abjectness, when sentiment plays a part," (*Chronique d'une passion*, Paris, Gallimard, 1964, 223 pages, p.135-136).

539. See James Lees-Milne, *Harold Nicolson, a Biography (1886-1929)*, London, Chatto & Windus, 1980, t.I, 429 pages.

intelligence, nor self-respect. I was not embarrassed anymore by what had become for me mere accessories (the fumbling and small talk of sublimation), and I sought the essential. The essential: a young naked body in fresh bedclothes.[540]

Quentin Crisp is the best representative of the flamboyant homosexual and his course throughout England in the 1920s and 1930s is rather unique. He recalls his youth in his autobiography, *The Naked Civil-Servant* (1968), which is as impertinent and funny as he was himself. While he is quite critical of the homosexuals of his era, he also has trouble seeing himself in a positive light: "I looked on all heterosexuals, even the lowliest, as superior to every homosexual, even the noblest."[541] However, Crisp's assessment of homosexuality was not unilateral. Thus, while he could not prevent himself from feeling a sense of inferiority personally, he did not intend that others, especially heterosexuals, should think the same way. When he heard that one of his friends had been engaging in thievery, he noted: "I did not object to these crimes because they were against the law. My very existence was illegal. I was embarrassed by their pettiness and angry because, if I were apprehended in relation to one of them, the snow-white image of the homosexual, which I had been working on intermittently, would have been sullied."[542]

Indeed, Crisp took it upon himself to educate the public about homosexuality. Rather than try to fit into one of the prevailing models, he decided to reinforce his singularity by exposing it publicly:

> — I became not only a confirmed homosexual, but a blatant homosexual. That is, I submitted my case not only to the people who knew me but to those who were completely foreign, as well. It was not hard to do. I wore make-up at a time when, even on women, eye shadow was a sin.[543]

This will to assert himself before all the world led him to display his difference under every circumstance and to face up to all affronts. He said that what he was looking for, in a regular job,

---

540. Daniel Guérin, *Autobiographie de jeunesse*, Paris, Belfond, 1972, 248 pages, p.168.
541. Quentin Crisp, *The Naked Civil Servant* [1968], London, Fontana, 1986, 217 pages, p.68.
542. *Ibid.*, p.44.
543. *Ibid.*

— was the opportunity to interact with the heterosexual world in order to be accepted as a homosexual. This evangelical zeal was the sole motive for all that [he] did.[544]

For the same reason, Quentin Crisp also liked to make a spectacle. One can only picture him, in the 1920s, on this suicide mission to make the man in the street accept the flagrant homosexual: — With a weary voice, [the police officer] beseeched [the crowd] to circulate. I was excited, exhausted, and annoyed by the crowd, but, as it had not yet torn me to pieces, I was not frightened. Because I believed that I could educate them, I was happy.[545]

Homosexuals did not build their identity on single experiences. One can, however, find recurring arguments in their speeches, which Quentin Crisp summarizes roughly as follows:

> — Soon I learned by heart almost all the arguments which could be raised in the climate of the time against the persecution of homosexuals. We were not harming anyone; we could not help it; and, although it was not necessarily irrefutable from a juridical point of view, we had enough to deal with, already. Certain speakers went so far as not only excusing our sin but glorifying it, by designating it a source of national culture. The great names of history since Shakespeare were recited one after another like the beads of a rosary.[546]

It was through these exercises in self-justification that homosexuals built a common identity in the inter-war period. It required a fundamental reversal of perspectives. Crisp remarked that: "By this process I managed to transform homosexuality from a burden to a cause."[547] The homosexual identity was built with, and against, the others.

There was, however, a considerable difference in perspective between the first generation of inverts, who often had lived their homosexual lives in secrecy, even in shame, and often without achieving sexual fulfillment, and those who were twenty years old in the 1920s or 1930s, who benefited from medical advances, better social visibility, greater sexual opportunities and the example of other activists engaged in the cause.

---

544. *Ibid.,* p.73.
545. *Ibid.,* p.50.
546. *Ibid.,* p.30.
547. *Ibid.,* p.33.

A Generational Example: Thomas and Klaus Mann

The example of Thomas and Klaus Mann enables us to study a member of the first and second generation in parallel. Both were homosexuals, but they experienced their sexuality in very different ways and one may read their stormy relationship as a metaphor of the construction of the homosexual identity in first half of the 20th century.

Thomas Mann had a very difficult relationship with his sexuality; he always tried to restrain his instincts, either through continence, or through marriage.[548] At the age of 25, he fell in love with Paul Ehrenberg, a young painter who reminded him of one of his first schoolboy infatuations (Armin Martens, who became Hans Hansen in *Tonio Kröger*). Ehrenberg was a ladies' man and he did not respond to Mann's overtures. Indeed, Thomas was always attracted by men who could not satisfy him, men who were his exact opposite: fair, with blue eyes, heterosexual, lacking in artistic sense. He desired them because he aspired to be like them, to join the "normal" world. Four years later, in 1905, he married Katia Pringsheim, who fascinated him. However, his journals from 1918 to 1921 reveal that he had great difficulty in overcoming his homosexual desires. For instance, in May and June 1911, he stayed in Venice with his wife and her brother Heinrich; and it was there that he met the Polish family and the beautiful adolescent who would be used as models for *Death in Venice*. The young boy cast a spell on Thomas Mann, who made no secret of his enthusiasm: "My husband was very much struck by him. He immediately had a weakness for this adolescent, whom he liked extraordinarily, and he did not stop watching him on the beach, him and his comrades. He did not follow him all over Venice, no, but the boy had fascinated him and he often thought of him."[549] When Mann published his novella, he indirectly acknowledged his homosexuality. His character Tadzio also represented an evolution on the sexual level: he is not a grown man, but an adolescent. From now on, Thomas Mann recognized his true sexuality by his taste for young beardless lads, whom he seduced and dominated.

Thomas Mann's journal allows us to follow his psychological evolution fairly closely; all his failures, misgivings, and desires are there. He wanted to make his marriage succeed, but was only too conscious of his handicap: "Approached K[atia]. Am not very clear on my state on this subject. Certainly it

---

548. For this analysis, see Marianne Krüll, *Les Magiciens. Une autre histoire de la famille Mann*, Paris, Éditions du Seuil, 1995, 398 pages.

549. Katia Mann, cited by Marianne Krüll, *ibid.*, p.174.

can hardly be a question of true impotence, but rather confusion and the usual unpredictability of my 'sex life.' No doubt, there is a weakness that might be exacerbated, as a consequence of desires that go in the other direction. What would happen if I had a boy 'under my hand'? In any case, it would be unreasonable to allow myself to feel depressed by a failure whose reasons are not new to me. Not to be concerned, good humor, indifference, and self-confidence are the appropriate behaviors, if only because they are the best 'remedy.'"[550]

The disorder increased as his son Klaus reached puberty; his androgynous beauty made him desirable. In his journal, Thomas makes many allusions to the ambiguous charms of his child: "In love with Klaus these days. Elements for new 'Father and Son' (July 5, 1920). "Charmed by Eissi [Klaus], pretty enough to be frightening, in the bath... Eissi was reading in bed, and his tanned chest was bare, which disturbed me" (July 25, 1920). "Read a story of Eissi's yesterday, imprinted with a heart-rending melancholy, and criticized it at his bedside while lavishing caresses on him which pleased him, I believe" (July 27, 1920). "I heard some noise in the boys' room and surprised Eissi, completely naked, in front of Golo's bed doing silly things. Strong impression of his startling and already almost virile body, what a shock" (October 17, 1920). The father's feelings for the son are very ambiguous and the family's biographers, Gerhard Härle and Marianne Krüll, judge that his desire had a destructive effect on the son.[551]

Klaus Mann was aware of his father's attraction to him, and that he kept it hidden; he himself already felt homosexual inclinations, but saw in his father's attitude only dissembling and confusion. This false situation influenced his own course toward identification; he took the opposite tack, provocative, assertive. In 1926, he married Pamela Wedekind, who was probably his sister Erika's lover; at the same time, Erika married Gustaf Gründgens, a homosexual actor. They would divorce in 1929. These fictitious marriages, willfully grotesque, may be seen as a denunciation of the paternal example, of his falsely proper life, his concessions to normality. Marriage did not make any sense, it did not represent the truth, so one might as well make it completely ridiculous. Thus, all that his father kept under wraps, Klaus exposed in an outrageous and grandiloquent way, and as a consequence attracted the paternal disfavor. Thomas Mann dis-

---

550. July 1920, *ibid.*, p.190.

551. 5 May 1932: "I dreamed about the Magician's secret life as a homo (his liaison with Kruse [Werner Kruse, a musician])" (Klaus Mann, *Journal. Les années brunes, 1931-1936*, Paris, Grasset, 1996, 452 pages, p.208).

covered his double, lubricious and wanton, the side of his personality that he had always refused to recognize in the name of moderation and propriety.

Klaus Mann was aware of his homosexuality from an early age; in 1921, he fell in love with various schoolmates. He was 16 years old when he met Uto Gartman: "I did not dare to understand the warnings and the signs of my destiny."[552] Then he read Wilde, Whitman, Rimbaud, Verlaine, and Stefan George. He did not make any secret of his homosexuality, and he did not hesitate to tackle the question in his writings. He mingled with all the homosexual intelligentsia of the time, Cocteau, Sachs, Green, Gide, Crevel, Auden, Spender, Isherwood, and Forster, but he preferred not to discuss the subject in public and did not mention it in his correspondence with close relatives. Nevertheless, his sexuality very quickly became known to the general public, since he and his sister Erika were involved in many scandals. Together they plunged into the shady swirl of Berlin and Klaus quickly found himself torn by two strong impetuses: the desire for freedom associated with homosexual pleasure, and guilt stemming from his bourgeois education. The loose morals of Berlin in the 1920s led to instability more than to fulfillment. What can one fight, what can one stand up for, when everything is possible, when everything is allowed? "We could not deviate from a moral standard: there was no standard."[553]

This lack of purpose explains why he did not engage in German homosexual movements: "Pr. Magnus Hirschfeld invited me, with the greatest civility, to make a speech in his 'Institute' on the role of eroticism in modern literature. Der Eigene paid me homage in the most compromising way."[554] His privileged situation seems to have dimmed his judgment, for a time; he did not realize that other homosexuals were not enjoying this kind of freedom; thus the letter which he sent to Stefan Zweig after the publication of *La Confusion des sentiments*: "*Thank heaven* that a destiny as horrible as that of the professor is no longer possible today — or is at least no longer inevitable."[555] His friend, the editor Fritz Landshoff, felt that this attitude was explained by too great a certainty of the acceptance of homosexuals, not by an egoistic lack of awareness: "The equal rights of homosexuals were so obvious to him that he did not believe that it had to be included as an 'agenda item' for the homosexual combat."[556] This attitude would

---

552. Klaus Mann, *Le Tournant* [1949], Paris, Solin, 1984, 690 pages, p.164.

553. *Ibid.*, p.161.

554. Letter to Erika Mann, 1926, cited by Stefan Zynda, *Sexualität bei Klaus Mann*, Bonn, Bouvier Verlag, 1986, 156 pages.

555. Letter to Stefan Zweig, September 1927, *ibid.*, p.58. Underlined in the original.

change radically in 1933, when Klaus realized that homosexuals were among the first targets of Nazism.

The crumbling of values went hand in hand with the banalization of the act of love and of sexual choice. Mann was fully aware of the charge of decadence associated with the Berlin liberation. His romantic aspirations found no outlet in casually waltzing from partner to partner:

> — They are all well matched, it doesn't matter. This girl is just as well suited to this young man as to any other, and if the young lady has pretensions (perhaps she has a special relationship with her horse or her chef), the two young men — hup! hup! — can manage very nicely and have plenty of fun without the girl at all ..."[557]

His novel *Pious Dance* (1925), very representative of the social environment in those days, was the first openly homosexual novel in German literature. It draws an oppressive picture of German youth, drifting, trying to find meaning in sex, drugs or art; most of the characters are homosexual, like Miss Barbara, "strong and virile," flaunting her relationship with a pallid dancer who "often spends the night with her," or Petit-Paul, hopelessly in love with the hero, Andréas, who is himself enamored (in vain) of Niels, a gigolo. Disappointments in love end in suicide or in a slow decline, as evoked in the song that Andréas languidly sings in a basement cabaret:

> And now we're walking the street
> A red scarf at our neck,
> Walking, walking the street,
> And really, who gives a fuck!
>
> Soon, we'll collapse,
> No one lasts long this way,
> It's straight down hill, to rack and ruin
>
> And then comes Judgment Day! [558]

---

556. Cited by Stefan Zynda, *ibid.*, p.87.
557. *Ibid.*, p.167.
558. Klaus Mann, *La Danse pieuse* [1925], Paris, Grasset, 1993, 272 pages, p.107.

After he finished his number, he is mobbed by bourgeois gentlemen filled with desire for his "dubious beauty."

Thomas Mann took his son's public confession very badly; however, at the same time, he was giving himself up in complete abandon to a 17-year-old boy, Klaus Heuser, and revealed his feelings to Klaus and Erika. Curiously, he warned Klaus-Eissi not interfere in his concerns: he most particularly did not want his affair to be known; on the other hand, he seems to have been boasting that he, too, was able to give in to passion, as Klaus's example had convinced him to throw himself into the swirl of life. One gets the impression that father and son influenced one another, without ever arriving at an accord: "Eissi is invited to keep out of my affairs....[and not to rock the boat]. I am already old and famous; why would you be the only ones to *sin* because of that?... *the secret and almost silent adventures of existence are the greatest.*"[559] Thomas Mann's love for Klaus Heuser was apparently one of most significant in his life. It was the ultimate fulfillment, the experience he had wished for all his life, the unique abandonment to his deepest instincts: "*[This experience] was the unhoped-for realization of something I had longed for all my life, 'happiness' as it is recorded in the book of humanity — even if not in that of practice — and because its memory means 'me too.'*"

Writing, finally, was the only means of fully realizing his homosexuality, for Klaus Mann as for his father. Several of his works depict young women in homosexual relations. In *Flucht in der Norden* (Escape to the North), the heroine, Johanna, "a girl who resembles a boy," stands in for Klaus Mann. The tale evokes his trip to Finland in 1932, when he fell in love with a young landowner, Hans Aminoff. In *Pathetic Symphony*, he pays homage to Tchaikovsky; significantly, he modifies the ending so that Tchaikovsky does not die of cholera but commits suicide. In fact, in most of his novels, homosexuality is presented as a very dismal thing: death or suicide seems to lie in wait for the hero. Thus, in *The Volcano*, Martin Korella (another disguised portrait of Klaus Mann) has relations with Kikjou, but cannot save him from destruction. All around him, his homosexual friends were committing suicide, most notably Ricki Hallgarten and René Crevel.[560]

---

559. Cited by Marianne Krüll, *Les Magiciens, op. cit.*, p.239, as well as the following citation. Italics in the original.

560. In *La Mort difficile*, René Crevel had already depicted the fatality of love based on sex. His hero Pierre, a homosexual cocaine addict, falls in love with a sensual young man, Arthur Buggle (who is attracted as much by men as by women), and commits suicide when he abandons him.

Thomas Mann did not help his son to accept his sexuality, and the latter absorbed to a degree many homophobic prejudices. In his journal, he recalls an extremely revealing dream: "I was followed by the police at a seaside resort, for various reasons: Eukodal, my homosexuality... But they were hoping, thanks to my homo relations, to obtain some information on the position of the Austrian army."[561] However, Klaus was not really conscious of his doubts and mixed feelings, and he held dear the myth of complete liberation and fully asserted sexuality. He was obsessed with his relationship to his father and, in his journal, he compares the homosexual identity of each generation.

> Tonight, reading "Wagner," noted that the theme of "seduction" is very characteristic for the Magician [Thomas Mann] — contrary to me. The motif of seduction: romanticism — music — Wagner — Venice — death — "sympathy with the abyss" — pederasty. The repression of pederasty as causes of this motif (going beyond the "seduction" of Nietzsche; see Wagner). — Different for me. Primary influence: Wedekind — George. Concept of "sin" — didn't have it. The cause: lived fully. Pederasty. Intoxication (including that of death), always accepted with recognition as exaltation of life; never as "seduction."[562]

Thus, according to his own interpretation, for the first generation homosexuality was "a seduction," an external influence, which one could resist, one could fight against. It is associated with negative images — death, downfall. Therefore it was necessary to stifle one's feelings and, at least, to hide them from the world. For the second generation, on the other hand, homosexuality was not a sin, nor an external seduction, but a constitutive principle of being, to which one must give oneself up, which one must assert. However, the idea of death remained present, associated with drugs or suicide. Haunted by paternal rejection, by his failures in love, the disastrous demise of his friends, Klaus Mann gradually went down. The Nazi repression that came crashing down on homosexuals and the Berlin life of his youth reinforced his fears and bitterness. He traveled, he fought, he wrote, but failure dogged him.

After several suicide attempts, he finally died on May 21, 1949. The long road to recognition came to a dead end: the suicide of Klaus Mann, symbol of Berlin's golden age, testified to the failure of a dream: that of homosexuality rec-

---

561. Klaus Mann, *Journal, op. cit.*, 24 March 1932, p.64.
562. *Ibid.*, 4 April 1933, p.134.

ognized, militant, affirmative; and to the retreat of homosexuals back to the private sphere, where his father had lived.

DEFINING ONESELF AS A LESBIAN — AN IDENTITY UNDER CONSTRUCTION

There is a problem in defining the lesbian identity: is it simply a variation on the homosexual identity, or is it something distinct? Some might even ask whether it exists at all. Before the 1920s, lesbians never formed a coherent group. While the 19th century did include some lesbian lifestyles,[563] they were either evanescent (no sexual intercourse, strong sentiment without recognition of the nature of the desires), or they were extremely peripheral: the aristocratic or financial periphery — like Natalie Barney's circle, the social periphery — the Sapphic loves among prostitutes, or peripheral experiences, like the Ladies of Llangollen, a lesbian couple who served as an example for following generations and who gave credence to the idea that lesbianism could be admitted and accepted.

Since the 1920s, thanks to the creation of the Berlin scene, to the propagation of lesbian models disseminated by public figures, and to changes in women's roles in society, a lesbian identity began to take shape. Homosexual women, like homosexual men, could live out their sexuality in a very different way. And similarly, the lesbians of the second generation had more opportunities to express themselves than those born at the turn of the century. However, the reality of the lesbian experience did not match that of homosexual men, and most of the time they had nothing to do with each other. Admittedly, lesbians were very much in the minority; but they had the benefit of legal tolerance, even though a particularly wild set of anti-lesbian themes was promoted during the inter-war period. Moreover, they could pass as normal in social settings, for they were often thought of as "old maids." This relative lack of danger means that they were under no pressure to form an interdependent and militant lesbian community, so that in the inter-war period the lesbian identity was in an earlier stage of formation than the homosexual identity.

---

563. See Lilian Faderman, *Surpassing the Love of Men*, New York, Morran & Cie, 1981, 496 pages.

The Dominant Model and Alternatives

At the end of World War I, Sapphism was marginalized and reduced in its definition to a particular type of women: the "masculine lesbian" (butch, *mannisch*). Whereas the model of the effeminate invert had been rejected and denied by homosexuals, the model of the masculine lesbian would be retained as a symbol not only by the public, but by lesbians themselves, and for many long years this meant that they were associated with medical cases one could only look upon with pity. This restrictive representation of the lesbian is a direct consequence of the medical discourse, and of the influence of certain famous lesbians, in particular Radclyffe Hall. However, this image was not accepted everywhere and certain women succeeded in developing a different model, in terms of both appearance and conduct.

Radclyffe Hall

Marguerite Radclyffe Hall must have been the most famous lesbian of the inter-war period; she was known as "John" (1880-1943).[564] Just like Stephen Gordon, the poetess and novelist Radclyffe Hall embodied the heroine of her book, *The Well of Loneliness* (1928) — the image of the lesbian in the eyes of the public. Her life and manners may have shocked proper English society, but one cannot say that John led a scandalous existence. Beginning in her adolescence, she developed romantic friendships with two of her cousins, but it was her meeting with Mabel Batten "Ladye," a woman of great beauty, mature, and married, that was the turning point. John was then a very lovely young woman who dressed rather severely (but still as a female, until about 1920), and wore her ash-blonde hair long. Ladye introduced her to the existence of a lesbian world, and in particular to the salon of Winaretta Singer, Princesse de Polignac. In 1915, John also met Una Troubridge, likewise married, with whom she would spend the rest of her life. She was more feminine than John; Una never wore men's clothes. Thus, the two women typically embodied the lesbian couple such as it was defined in those days by Havelock Ellis and the majority of sexologists: a "true" lesbian, Radclyffe Hall, who was identified with the man, and a "seduced" lesbian, playing the traditional role of the woman, Una Troubridge. This life match was satisfactory and Radclyffe Hall (unlike, for example, Vita Sackville-

---

564. See Michael Baker, *Our Three Selves: A Life of Radclyffe Hall*, London, Hamish Hamilton, 1985, 386 pages.

West), did not go on chalking up conquests. Only Evgenia Souline, in the late 1930s, disturbed the arrangement between John and Una.

The name of Radclyffe Hall remains associated with the image of the lesbian in this period largely because she embodied the "New Woman" to the extreme, and because her principal book, *The Well of Loneliness*, drew the attention of British society to Sapphism and opened the eyes of many people who had been completely unaware of the very existence of lesbians. Radclyffe Hall took to wearing men's clothing more and more, after 1920: very strict tailoring, ties, men's hose with garters, heavy shoes with flat heels, and gaiters, with a pipe or cigarette without filter. In 1930, she tried wearing trousers. Finally, she had her hair cut extremely short. She socialized with the smart lesbian set: Natalie Barney, Romaine Brooks, Renata Borgatti, Mimi Franchetti, Marchesa Casati, and also Edy Craig's more circumspect circle in Rye.

Radclyffe Hall's first poems and novels touch on the topic of lesbianism only indirectly. They show a strong autobiographical influence; *After Many Days* refers implicitly to her relations with Ladye and Una. The novella *Miss Ogilvy Finds Herself* and the novel *The Unlit Lamp* are particularly revealing. However, *The Well of Loneliness* remains paramount: in it, John endeavors to recount the painful destiny, from childhood to maturity, of a young invert who has always felt that she is different from the other girls. Judging from its repercussions among lesbians as well as the broader public, this novel may be taken as the best representation of the "New Woman." Stephen Gordon is a model; thanks to her — or because of her —lesbians of the inter-war period wanted to be masculine. The book seems to have been inspired by a reading of Havelock Ellis's *Sexual Inversion*: John recognizes himself in that description of the congenital invert. The portrait which she traces of the heroine, Stephen Gordon, was very much influenced by the medical model, but is also based on personal experience. It has been said that such a book could be written only by an invert, as only they would be qualified enough through personal knowledge and experience to speak "in the name of a misunderstood and misjudged minority."[565]

Hall also read many authors who dealt with homosexuality, like Clemence Dane, Rosamund Lehmann, Natalie Barney, Colette, Liane de Pougy, Willy, Proust. She did not model her books on them, however, for she wished to display her own vision of the lesbian. She thus eschewed adolescent loves, which society finds easier to excuse, and focused on adult homosexuality. Armed with good

---

565. Una Troubridge, cited in *Gay News*, n° 148.

intentions, Hall wanted to awaken the public to the painful fate of the "invert." To achieve that objective, she did not hesitate to exaggerate and draw an apocalyptic picture of a life of suffering, frustration and sacrifice.

Hall summarizes the heroine's childhood through a series of medical banalities. Her parents wished for a boy, and they baptize her with a boy's name; as a child, Stephen likes neither dresses nor long hair, and falls in love with the maid. Her mother does not love her, and her father, who suspects the truth, spends his time reading medical works, such as Ulrichs and Krafft-Ebing. Upon reaching adulthood, she is more or less shunned in the local community; she repulses one suitor, then falls in love with a married woman (who initially responds to her advances, then, frightened by the girl's passion, reveals everything to her husband). A scandal erupts; Stephen is driven out of the house and leaves for France. There, she achieves literary success and discovers the Parisian lesbian community, at the side of Valerie Seymour (a pseudonym for Natalie Barney). When the war breaks out, she signs on with the ambulance corps and distinguishes herself brilliantly. She meets a girl, Mary, and falls in love. They settle together in Paris and live in harmony for a few years; but Mary finally falls for a man and Stephen sacrifices herself for her happiness.

Beyond the melodrama, certain points are worth mentioning. First, the congenital invert looks masculine. One passage basically says,

> — That night, she stood looking in the mirror; and even at that moment she detested her body with its muscular shoulders, small, compact breasts, and the slim hips of an athlete. All her life she would have to drag along this body like a monstrous weight imposed on her spirit.[566]

The difference is physical, it is visible, it is immediately apparent to a casual observer: "It is my face; there is something wrong with my face,"[567] she notes. Stephen does not think there is any hope of fitting in; she is shut out by her body, and then by her sexuality.

The only solution is exile; there, life is easier, but it is also depressing and humiliating. Going out with women, lesbian bars, everything is only makeshift

---

566. Radclyffe Hall, *The Well of Loneliness* [1928], London, Virago Press, 1982, 447 pages, p.187.

567. *Ibid.*, p.71. It is interesting to note that, to bolster her theory of physical predestination to homosexuality, Radclyffe Hall had the oortraits of her as a child touched up. On one of them, where she was shown with her face framed by long blond curls, she had the bottom repainted to show her hair very short, like a little boy's.

since public life is prohibited. Love itself is fleeting; Stephen suffers for not being able to marry Mary, not being able to offer her either security or public recognition. If she sacrifices herself, it is because she knows that only a man is able to guarantee her honor in the eyes of society.

In that, Radclyffe Hall ratifies the separation between the masculine lesbian, the true lesbian, whose destiny is inevitably dismal, and the pseudo-lesbian, feminine, romantic, who can always revert to the traditional role. The two women who shared her life were both married. One may suppose that she felt she was in direct competition with the men and that to supplant them in the heart of her friends would be a fitting revenge and proof of her true virility. The masculine lesbian is the one who must take on the challenges and face the external world. This very traditional understanding of the couple, copied on the heterosexual model, shows clearly that Radclyffe Hall took in the prejudices of the external world and perpetuated the concept of male domination.

Her lesbianism is not feminism. In fact, John regarded himself as a man captive in a woman's body; she regretted that she did not receive the regard that is due to one of her true nature. Therefore, her attire and her conduct were intended to reveal her true identity to the world. Moreover, like Una Troubridge, she openly acknowledged her lesbianism in society and professed only scorn for lesbians who were ashamed to show themselves. This distinctive attitude does not mean, however, that Radclyffe Hall accepted her sexuality easily. The fatalism which underlies her novel is the consequence of a very profound sense of guilt and inferiority, reinforced by her adherence to the Catholic religion. For John, inversion was certainly not a natural thing; it was a disease, a mark of destiny, which made her a being apart.

In describing Stephen Gordon this way, in showing her difficulty in adapting to society, Radclyffe Hall voluntarily places lesbians in a marginal position. By taking up the cause of masculine lesbians, Radclyffe Hall not only ratified the classifications of the sexologists, but she posed a cruel choice to the pseudo-homosexuals: from now on, they had to come out in public in order to get themselves accepted as lesbians (and thus risk derision and exclusion), or savor the sweetness of their romantic friendships without ever knowing what view of womanhood to identify with.[568] Hall's vision of lesbianism is at the foundation of a very powerful sense of identity, for it rests on the acceptance of difference and exclusion. By making lesbians unique, she reinforced the bonds between them and called for solidarity based on their shared fate. Even long after her death, Radclyffe Hall enabled thousands of young women to recognize themselves as lesbians, to forge a system of references. However, while *The Well of Loneliness* may be held to be the symbol of one generation of lesbians, there were other models which refuted the assumption of masculinity.

Natalie Barney and Colette

The Parisian lesbians were first to reject the vision of the "New Woman." They exemplified the Sapphism of the aristocratic and intellectual milieux, mixing Greek references into the French erotic tradition. Natalie Barney is the best representative of this trend.[569] With Renée Vivien, she tried to found a school of poetry to the glory of Sappho at Mytilene, then founded a lesbian salon at 22 rue Jacob, dubbed the "Temple of friendship." In fact, the rediscovery of Sappho played an important part in the crafting of the lesbian identity; she appeared to be the requisite model in antiquity, at a time when homosexuals were making constant references to the Greek example to justify their existence. Natalie Barney and Virginia Woolf even undertook to learn Greek in order to better understand the poetess.

Natalie Barney's refuge, a cult hang-out during the Belle Epoque, continued to illuminate the lesbian world of the inter-war period. Rich, good-looking and famous lesbians mingled there, enjoying a precious and cosmopolitan atmosphere: — Young women, transported by literature and champagne, danced like mad in each other's arms, remembers Matthew Josephson.[570] Janet Flanner, who was a regular there, summarizes these get-togethers as introductions, conversations, tea, "excellent cucumber sandwiches and divine little cakes baked by Berthe," but the result was a new place of rendezvous for women who were enamored of each other or who simply wished to see each other again.[571]

---

568. This question is at the heart of modern feminist historiography. *The Well of Loneliness* is reexamined from the perspective of its influence on the lesbian identity; the faulty assimilation between lesbianism and masculinity is criticized briskly. For a discussion on this topic, see Lilian Faderman and Ann Williams, "Radclyffe Hall and the Lesbian Image," in *Conditions*, n° 1, April 1977; Lilian Faderman, *Surpassing the Love of Men, op. cit.*, p.322-323; Anne Koedt (dir.), *Radical Feminism*, New York, Quadrangle Books, 1973, 424 pages, p.240-245.

569. Much has been written about Natalie Barney; particularly interesting are George Wickes, *The Amazon of Letters, Natalie Barney*, London, W.H. Allen, 1977, 286 pages; and the remarkable work by Shari Benstock, *Women of the Left Bank, Paris 1900-1940*, Austin, University of Texas Press, 1986, 518 pages.

570. Cited by Lilian Faderman, *Surpassing the Love of Men, op. cit.*, p.369.

571. *Ibid.*, p.370.

Barney's salon thus created a specific, although restricted, lesbian culture and identity. The visitors' love lives were the main topic of conversation; sexual freedom was extensive and homosexuality, at last, was not interdicted. When someone asked Natalie Barney about one of her new conquests, she replied: "Do I love her? God in heaven, no, we made love, that's all."[572]

Natalie Barney's declaration was regarded as the basis of future lesbian combat: "I do not feel any shame; one does not reproach the albino for having pink eyes and white hair, why should anyone hold me accountable for being lesbian? It is a question of nature; my homosexuality is not a vice, it is not deliberate and does not do any harm to anybody."[573]

To Barney's great credit, she rejected any definition of lesbianism imposed by society, and in particular by the medical world. She was hostile to the theories of the third sex and to the idea of a woman that is half man, and she rejected compassion and the status of victim. At the same time, she remained on the periphery of lesbianism according to Radclyffe Hall, because she rejected provocation and the strategy of exclusion. For her, acceptance meant integration into the rest of society and not the formation of separatist groups. Nevertheless, the elitist atmosphere of her salon, her dilettantism, her tendency to consider homosexuality as a game of love and a good excuse for intrigues, make her more of a hold-over from the 1900s rather than a representative of modernity. Barney was 43 years old in 1919, and hardly resembled the Amazon. However, her influence remained strong throughout the inter-war period.

Her *New thoughts of the Amazon* wonderfully illustrates her concept of female loves and her taste for a lascivious woman, fully given over to passion, completely detached from man (materially as well as physically): "They came to us with burning hands,"[574] she confided. Barney contrasts the idea of the Butch with the extreme sophistication of an aristocratic femininity: "I travel as badly as a basket of raspberries."[575] She looked down on women who took on a more masculine style. She herself posed as a nymph, sporting long hair floating freely and tunics modeled after antiquity. She cautioned against confusing radical thought with radical appearances, the latter being only a pale substitute of the first. According to her, masculine women were only a passing fashion, having

---

572. *Ibid.*
573. *Ibid.*
574. Natalie Barney, *Nouvelles pensées de l'Amazone*, Paris, Mercure de France, 1939, 215 pages, p.198.
575. *Ibid.*, p.122.

more to do with society's aspiration to androgyny than any real lesbian movement; they even contribute paradoxically to the standardization of the genders and the victory of masculine values. Thus, her lesbian theory is also a feminist reflection.

Natalie Barney was one of the first to affirm lesbian sexuality as a form of liberation for women. As lesbians, they retained control of their own bodies, and no longer needed to fear the violence of the heterosexual act and childbirth. This counter-model, while it has the advantage of not reducing the lesbian to a medical anomaly, offers little grounds for claiming rights or asserting differences. It is an individualistic, even independent, model and would be preferred by women who were already free socially and financially. On the other hand, it seems to have had no impact on the main population of lesbians, who were indifferent to Greek tradition and who were in no position to impose on those near and dear to them a scandalous and sumptuary mode of life.

Colette, who frequented Barney's salon, however, managed to detach herself from Sapphic mythology and build a modern image of woman. She thus embodied a model of lesbianism that the general public could grasp, in her widely disseminated novels as well as in her private life (which was full of scandal). Colette separated from Willy in 1905 to be with a woman, "Missy," i.e. Mathilde de Morny. The lesbian scandal was exacerbated by the women's appearance: Missy was a masculine lesbian, 42 years old. Colette was 32. With Missy, she discovered lesbian nightclubs in Paris like Palmyre, on place Blanche. She made a spectacle at Natalie Barney's, dancing naked as "Mata Hari." At the Moulin Rouge, January 3, 1907, she danced a mime with Missy, "Dreams of Egypt": Colette was naked, Missy embraced her, and the scandal was enormous. In 1929 and 1930, like so many others, she was in Berlin, sizing up the distance between Parisian lesbianism and German militancy. In 1932, she wrote the subtitles of *Girls in Uniform* for the film's previews in France.

Colette felt the need to clarify her position on lesbianism after *The Well of Loneliness* was published. Like many others, reading the book dismayed her; she also wrote to Una Troubridge to explain her position: "One who is abnormal must never feel abnormal; quite to the contrary."[576] It was in response to Radclyffe Hall that she published *The Pure and the Impure*. It caused her great pain to write that book: "It makes me vomit, of course," she declared to Lucie Delarue-

---

576. Cited by Herbert Lottman, *Colette*, Paris, Gallimard, coll. "Folio," 1990, 496 pages, p.295.

Mardrus.[577] Sapphism, which had been presented in a ludic form in her novels, is displayed here under a cruel light. She denounces the Don Juans, the "goules," the lesbians out for conquest and pleasure, restless and incapable of true feelings: "There can never be enough blame put on the casual Sapphos, those of the restaurant, the dance hall, the Blue Train (*Le Train bleu* was a posh rail link to the Riviera) and the sidewalk, those who are merely provocative, who laugh instead of sighing."[578] Such a woman leaves only disaster in her wake; thus, "her credits consist of despairing young girls, young women committing suicide under her window, broken households, and sometimes bloody rivalries."[579]

This condemnation of the lesbian way of life must be placed in its context, however: that of very liberal Paris during the inter-war period and relating only to a narrow segment of society that could shrug off criticism. Colette is an eyewitness of her milieu. Her reproaches are not limited to flirtation and sexual nomadism. The principal danger which threatens lesbians, according to her, is that of masculinization; on this point, she agreed with Natalie Barney: "You understand, a woman who remains a woman is a complete being. She does not lack anything, even with regard to her 'friend.' But if she gets it into her head to want to be a man, it is grotesque. What could be more ridiculous, and sadder, than a ... fake man?"[580]

In spite of this denigration, Colette admired unusual personalities. She draws up an intriguing portrait of the "Chevaliere," a determined and influential butch who is perfectly comfortable with her masculine side and who makes no concessions to fashion. She leads a solitary life, outside of time and without any lover, for her aspirations are too far apart from those of the new wave. This lack of solidarity between the generations testifies to the fragility of the lesbian community. Colette contemptuously notes that these women who are so sure of themselves, so open, suddenly become discreet and conformist as soon as their social position is at stake. Love affairs are only acknowledged privately: "Only one dared to say, 'ma légitime' ("my wife"),"[581] and they have no stomach for scandal when it cuts too close to them: "'It is not that I am hiding it,' the viscountess of X briefly explained, '... it is just that I do not like to make a show of it'."[582]

---

577. *Ibid.*, p.296.
578. Colette, *Le Pur et l'Impur* [1932], Paris, Hachette, 1971, 189 pages, p.123.
579. *Ibid.*, p.109.
580. *Ibid.*, p.112.
581. *Ibid.*, p.78.

The Pure and the Impure, a book that was celebrated for its tolerance and its sincerity, is undoubtedly a deeply lesbian book, a book about the love of women. But it is also a critique, sometimes indulgent, often severe, of the circumscribed Parisian world, the meanness and superficiality of those lesbians who had made it and who did nothing, despite their position, to advance the lot of other women.

Vita Sackville-West and Virginia Woolf

Perhaps the most modern counter-model and most relevant to contrast to Radclyffe Hall is that of Virginia Woolf and Vita Sackville-West. The two women greeted *The Well of Loneliness* with considerable reservation. They considered it not only poor in form, but also dangerous in its premises. In fact, Virginia Woolf's and Vita Sackville-West's lives and loves are evidence that a lesbian model could exist that was different from the one asserted by sexologists and the militant lesbians, and that it was valid. However, it was largely obscured by feminist historiography, because it was incompatible with the very strict definition of the lesbian identity as it had been formulated: starting with self-sufficiency with respect to men, a self-sufficiency which often meant the complete rejection of men. Virginia Woolf, Vita Sackville-West, and Violet Trefusis were married. Their meetings, their exchanges of often passionate letters, and their sexual intercourse — conducted with discretion and reserve — were closer to the model adopted or dreamed of by the anonymous lesbians than to the hard-hitting arrogance of Radclyffe Hall.

Vita Sackville-West certainly did not conform to the prototype of Stephen Gordon. True, she too had dreamed since her earliest childhood of being a boy, but that came out mainly in an extraordinary vitality, an exuberance mixed with authoritarianism. If she preferred men's clothes (they were more practical), she leaned toward riding breeches and gaiters, not Radclyffe Hall's tuxedo. And if she regretted that she was not a man, it was above all because she could not inherit the family palace. By no means did Vita consider her masculine traits as symptoms of a "congenital inversion." In her love affairs, she showed all the enthusiasm of a seductress, a magnetism intended to bend her conquests to her whims.

Vita was aware of her deep nature very early on; she seduced her childhood friend Violet Keppel. In a journal that she was keeping at the time,[583] she

---

582. *Ibid.*

describes her conquest in detail, with a striking freedom and absence of guilt. On November 11, 1918, the two women left on a journey to Paris; there, Vita (who was going by the name of Julian), dressed as a boy. During the day they went visiting, and they ended the night in a hotel, on their way to Monaco. According to Vita, "It was marvelously amusing, especially as one was always likely to be discovered." For her, there was no difference between homosexual love and heterosexual love, and there were certainly no moral implications. She was perfectly frank about her sexual passions and her needs. "I took her along [to my room], I treated her savagely. I made love to her, I possessed her, I made fun of her, I simply wanted to hurt Denys [Violet was engaged at the time to Denys Trefusis], even if he would never know it."[584] Not until March 15, 1919 did Vita agree to join her husband, Harold Nicolson, for a "peace conference." On June 16, 1919, Violet married Trefusis; that very night, Vita created an incident at the hotel and took Violet. The following days were terrible; Denys and Violet stayed in separate rooms during their honeymoon in France. Returning to England, Violet took up again with Vita and planned a new escapade to Monaco, in October-November. After a new scene with Denys in February, Violet was separated from Vita by her family, who banded together to put an end to the scandal. By then, Vita began to lose interest, having learned that Violet had slept with her husband.

Both women presented their versions of this adventure in novels. Vita Sackville-West started to write *Challenge* ("*Ceux des îles*") (1924) during their escapade in Paris and Monaco. It was at the same time a self-justification, the vision of what her love for Violet could have been, and an account of suffering. Likewise, Violet Trefusis tried to justify her behavior in *Broderie anglaise* (1935); the book, written in French, was not translated into English. Rather than rewrite the history of a love affair, Violet sought to examine the reasons for its failure and the personalities concerned.

Virginia Woolf had a different fate. Her childhood was painful: she lost her mother, Julia Stephen, then her sister Stella was 13 years old. After a first period of insanity, she was sexually accosted by her half-brother, George Duckworth.[585] She fell in love with two women, Madge Waugham and Violet Dick-

---

583. This journal was published by her son Nigel Nicolson in 1973 in *Portrait of a Marriage* (*Portrait d'un mariage*, Paris, Stock, 1992, 319 pages).

584. Vita Sackville-West, cited by Lilian Faderman, *Surpassing the Love of Men, op. cit.*

585. For detail on this period in Virginia Woolf's life, see *Instants de vie* [1976], Paris, Stock, 1986, 273 pages.

inson; but Vita Sackville-West was her great flame. She was already over forty, and had been married to Leonard Woolf since 1913 when she met Vita for the first time. Virginia Woolf had always been very reticent with respect to sexuality, and her love of women was closely related to the softness that it offered in contrast to male brute force. Woolf herself said that the vague and unreal world, without love, heart, or passion, without sex, that is the world that [suited her] and that [she was] interested in.[586] Even her husband, for whom she felt a deep tenderness, did not inspire any physical desire in her.

However, she was aware of her lesbian inclinations and when she met Vita, in 1922, she was dazzled by the elegance and self-assurance of the young woman. "I love her and I love to be with her, in her splendour."[587] To Virginia, Vita represented woman, and to Vita, Virginia represented the writer; their relationship was built on these images. In her letters to her husband, Harold Nicolson, Vita Sackville-West reveals "the feeling of tenderness mixed with protection" which she felt with regard to Virginia. Nevertheless, she struggled to avoid getting into a physical relationship, which she feared might have consequences for Virginia's mental health. Woolf did have some physical experiences with Vita Sackville-West, but that was not the basis of their relationship. Sackville-West soon began to seduce other women again, but she continued to see and to love Woolf.

Woolf wrote *Orlando* (1928) for Vita — a kind of dreamed autobiography of Vita and a lesbian anthem. Orlando is a young aristocrat who, after many adventures, finds himself transformed one day into a woman. From then on, time is abolished, and he/she traverses the centuries, in love alternately with men and women. Orlando casts a very different image than *The Well of Loneliness*. In lieu of fate and the separation of the sexes, Woolf displays the glory of the androgyne, the confusion of the genders, the negation of categories: — As Orlando had never loved anyone but women and since it is human nature to hesitate before adapting to new conventions, though a woman in her turn, it was a woman whom she loved; and if the awareness of belonging to the same sex had any effect on her, it was to revive and deepen her formerly male feelings.[588] The book is a satire of the precise constructs of sexologists and a celebration of beauty and of sex which resist being used throughout the centuries. Whereas powers dis-

---

586. Letter from Virginia Woolf to Madge Waugham, June 1906.

587. Louise de Salvo and Mitchell A. Leaska (ed.), *The Letters of Vita Sackville-West to Virginia Woolf*, London, Hutchinson, 1984, 473 pages.

588. Virginia Woolf, *Orlando*, Paris, Stock, 1974, 351 pages, p.178.

sipate, dynasties die and countries are devastated, Orlando lived on, always beautiful and always loved. Woolf thus affirmed the historical vocation of the lesbian (who is not an invention of the 1920s but is one of the many faces of woman), her scorn for oppressive powers and her ambition to live serenely within society, despite being different. For Woolf, and as Sackville-West had shown so well, Sapphism was good luck, not bad; an additional reason to live and love: "It is certain that she collected a double harvest, the pleasures of life were increased for her.... She exchanged for the rigor of trousers the seduction of the petticoat, and so knew the joy of being loved by both sexes."[589]

Virginia Woolf and Vita Sackville-West had wanted to prove that what was valid for homosexuals was also valid for lesbians. They lived out their "inversion" freely, with discretion but without fear. They proved that Sapphism could fit into society, because lesbians were women like others. But lesbians of the inter-war period did not rally around the model of Orlando, although the book resonated here and there.[590] In choosing Radclyffe Hall as their emblem, most lesbians set themselves in reaction against society. They gained an identity, but lost any chance of integration.

Individual Answers

Reading the accounts of lesbians who lived in the inter-war period, one is struck by the ignorance that prevailed. The scarcity of meeting places does not explain it fully. Lesbians, like other women, suffered from a want of information on sexuality. Many accounts confirm the existence of indubitable lesbian tendencies, and sometimes they were acted upon, in parallel with a total ignorance of the significance of such practices and with the pursuit of normal marital activity.

Ignorance

Like a good many others, Rachel Pinney discovered that she was a lesbian by reading *The Well of Loneliness* in the 1930s. She had had a fling with a woman at

---

589. *Ibid.*, p.239.

590. — A woman has written to tell me that she has to stop and kiss the page when she reads O[rlando]: – I imagine she is of the same race. The percentage of lesbian is on the rise in the United States, all because of you — (Virginia Woolf to Vita Sackville-West, February 1929, in Vita Sackville-West/Virginia Woolf, *Correspondence*, Paris, Stock, 529 pages, p.379).

the age of eighteen at Bristol University, without being particularly affected by it. She had married out of conformity and only came to understand that she was lesbian during the first days of the war. Similarly, Charlotte Wolff, a German Jew who became a doctor specializing in female sexuality, acknowledged her long sexual ignorance; she considered that her good fortune. Unconscious of being different, she lived freely: "Neither Ida [her friend] nor I had ever heard the term 'homosexual' and we did not know anything either about love between two people of the same sex. We enjoyed our relationship without any fears or labels, and we did not have any model for making love."[591]

Homosexuality was often an abstract concept that young women did not think of as having anything to do with their day-to-day experience.

> When did I recognize myself as a lesbian? It is a concept which came to me only very late. I lived as I was without saying, "I am a lesbian." That kind of problem did not affect me. I had [girl] friends, I was attracted to women and I had been, I believe, from my early youth... I had what now seems like a great amount of experience, without any difficulty, because I basically did not realize, I did not ask questions, I lived like that because I wanted to, that's all.[592]

In the same way, B insists she was completely unaware:

> I always had fancies for others apprentices in the couture houses down the street... It was my mother who figured out what that meant.[593]

Pat James remembers that at the age of thirteen she understood her inclinations, and was not troubled about it:

> — I did not even wonder what was going on, I did not feel different, I did not even think about it. I just wasn't much interested in boys that way.[594]

---

591. Charlotte Wolff, *Hindsight*, London, Quartet Books, 1980, 312 pages, p.26.

592. Testimony of A., recorded by Claudie Lesselier, in *Aspects de l'expérience lesbienne en France, 1930-1968*, mémoire de DEA de sociologie, Paris-VIII, under the direction of R. Castel, November 1987, 148 pages, p.57.

593. Testimony of B., *ibid.*, p.56.

594. Pat James was born in 1921; since the age of 8, she worked at the market. Memoir recorded in Suzanne Neild and Rosalind Parson, *Women like us*, London, The Women's Press, 1992, 171 pages, p.57.

This ignorance of sexuality particularly affected the lesbians of the first generation, born in the mid-19th century. And it was not only the uneducated women who missed defining themselves as lesbians. The English writer Vernon Lee (Violet Paget, 1856-1935) had female relationships all her life, without drawing any conclusion; the limits of a good Victorian education and the negation of the body kept her from the realization:

> — Vernon was homosexual, but she never could face sexual realities. She was perfectly pure. I think that it would have been better if she had admitted it. She went through a whole series of passions for women, but they were all perfectly correct. She avoided physical contact. She was completely frustrated.[595]

Charlotte Mew, an English poetess born in 1869, had a series of disastrous loves: she was passionately attracted by a young woman, sought to give her her support, to show her love to her, but did not know how to go about it; finally she was rejected by the young lady, who refused to consider going further. This pattern was repeated without any solution.[596] The relationship between Vera Brittain and Winifred Holtby was more complex, but also revealing. They met in Somerville College, one of the female colleges at Oxford, in 1919. After completing their studies, they shared an apartment; and when Vera Brittain married George Catlin, Winifred continued to live with the couple. Their friendship ceased only when Winifred died. However, neither of the two women saw the relationship as lesbian. On the contrary, Vera Brittain, a notorious feminist, took care in her memoirs to deny it. She also took the trouble of editing out of her letters any tendentious allusion.

Winifred Holtby was less reserved in her writings. She contested Radclyffe Hall's definition of lesbianism, which she refused to regard as pathological; and she refuted the presumed linkage between celibacy and frustration. Vera Brittain, on the contrary, adopted a traditional vision of sexual relations: marriage is essential, and celibacy is a source of neuroses for women. Brittain's position is also symptomatic of a conflict between feminists and lesbians, with feminist concerns always coming first.

---

595. Irene Cooper Willis, heir and friend of Vernon Lee, cited by Burdett Gardner, *The Lesbian Imagination (Victorian Style): A Psychological and Critical Study of Vernon Lee*, New York, Garland, 1987, 592 pages, p.85.

596. For further details, see Penelope Fitzgerald, *Charlotte Mew and her Friends*, London, Collins, 1984, 240 pages.

The case of Edith Sitwell is even more unusual; her strange physique was not attractive to men and she never had any sexual adventures. In addition, she was surrounded by homosexuals, notably her brother Osbert, and she fell in love with the Russian painter Pavel Tchelitchev, also homosexual. Observers of the time took her for a lesbian, although she never had relations with women. She found Wyndham Lewis's caricature of her in *The Apes of God* (1930) and her portrait as a lesbian by Noël Coward revolting. It is difficult to determine, here, whether this was a case of homosexuality that was never accepted or simply an inability to face sexuality in general, a result of a difficult childhood and significant physical complexes.

Assuming an identity

Still, it would be a mistake to believe that most lesbians kept their loves platonic, without daring to give physical expression to their sexuality. Natalie Barney racked up many conquests and she is considered to have had more than forty lovers, not counting casual flings. Many lesbians gave full expression to their attraction for the female body and their pleasure in making love. The tell-all book by Djuna Barnes, *L'Almanach des dames (The Almanac of ladies)* (1928), hails the female pleasures in a devilish satire of the Parisian lesbian microcosm. Djuna Barnes arrived in Paris in 1919 with her friend, the American sculptor Thelma Wood. She did not regard herself as lesbian: "I am not lesbian. I only love Thelma," she replied to an insinuation by Ottoline Morrell.[597] Marguerite Yourcenar also lived out her homosexuality very freely. In the 1930s, she led a dissipated life including many love affairs, until she met the American academic Grace Frick, in 1937, with whom she shared the rest of her life. She was a regular on the Paris lesbian scene, at the Thé Colombin, rue du Mont-Thabor, and Wagram, 208 rue de Rivoli, and she was a mainstay of the local night life.

The most remarkable example is definitely Vita Sackville-West, whose extraordinary vitality we noted above. Her life was marked by a series of scandalous episodes, like her flight with Violet Trefusis, and she was considered responsible for breaking up several marriages, including that of Dorothy Wellesley. Other affairs were pursued with the tacit agreement of her husband, including with Mary Campbell and Virginia Woolf. A veritable Dona Juana, Sackville-West took one lover after another, without the least scruples. The list

---

597. Cited by Shari Benstock, *Women of the Left Bank, op. cit.*, p.245.

includes Rosamund Grosvenor, Margaret Voigt, Hilda Matheson, Evelyn Irons, Christopher St John, and Gwen St Aubin, *inter alia*.

Her marriage with Harold Nicolson was a perfect incongruity in English high society of the inter-war period. Both were homosexual, and both pursued their affairs in parallel, without any concerns and without denting their deep attachment to each other. Sackville-West was also sympathetic to the news that her elder son, Ben, was homosexual. She wrote him a long letter, in which she managed to reconcile the defense of homosexuality with an apologia for marriage, the gist of which said,

> — But Daddy was wrong on one point: that doesn't bother me. What would bother me, is if you believed that that will inevitably keep you from what you call "all the happiness and joys of marriage." Remove that idea from your head immediately. Two of the happiest married couples that I know, whose names I must conceal out of discretion, are both homosexuals. For you undoubtedly know that homosexuality exists among women as well as men. And then, look at Duncan [Grant] and Vanessa [Bell]; they are not really married, but have lived together for years, which amounts to the same thing. They love each other as Daddy and I do, although Duncan is completely homosexual. Therefore, you can see that it is not necessarily an obstacle to our kind of happiness.[598]

Violet Trefusis's letters to Sackville-West reveal a bubbly temperament, a great emotional freedom and total abandon to sexual desire. There is no sign of the reserve which one might expect from a well-bred young lady. In her letters, Violet often calls Vita by a man's name, whether Julian, Dimitri or Mytia, and she boldly makes the most compromising statements. Furthermore, it is Vita who moderates their relationship and tries to keep it within manageable bounds, whereas Violet, in the exaltation of her love, clearly would have been willing to sacrifice her reputation. — Oh my God, Mytia, a demonic force has broken out in me, ... I would have you with me before you had time to do a thing, and you remain blind.... One of these days, the clouds will burst and you will be carried with all the rest.[599]. Trefusis's love is explicitly carnal; she loves Sackville-West with all her body and sends explicit invitations and erotic provocations, with no decency, no shame. Sex is natural, love is healthy: — My days are consumed in an

---

598. Cited by Victoria Glendinning, *Vita, la vie de Vita Sackville-West*, Paris, Albin Michel, 1987, 437 pages, p.290.
599. Undated letter [1918?], in Violet Trefusis, *Lettres à Vita, op. cit.*, p.169.

impotent desire for you, and my nights are haunted by unbearable dreams.... I am dying of hunger for you, if you really want to know.[600]

Katherine Mansfield's journal similarly reveals that a young lady from a good family, raised in an environment sheltered from sexual realities, could fully enter into and assume her sexuality, without scruples or remorse. One passage may be summarized thus

> I spent last night in her arms — and this evening I hate her — which, once you think about it, means that I adore her: that I cannot lie in my bed without feeling the magic of her body... I feel more deeply with her than with any man all those impulses known as sexual... And now she is coming — and pressed against her, holding her hands, her face against mine, I am a child, I am a woman, and more than half a man.[601]

There were other very original alternative lifestyles developed during the inter-war period which called into question the bases of patriarchal society. One of the best examples of an experiment in lesbian life fully engaged is the "community" founded in the 1930s by Edith Craig, daughter of the actress Ellen Terry. Edy lived with Christopher St John (a pseudonym of Christabel Marschall) until his death, in 1947. Christopher defined himself as a congenital lesbian, whereas Edy was bisexual. She established a triangle with Christopher and Clare Atwood (Tony) in Smallhythe, in the English countryside, and they made their house a special meeting place for lesbians. In July 1931, she invited her neighbors Radclyffe Hall and Una Troubridge (who lived in Rye) to attend a show at the Barn Theatre. Everyone dressed as a man for the occasion. In 1932, Vita Sackville-West was invited to read her poem, "The Land"; her husband Harold Nicolson, Virginia and Leonard Woolf, Stephen Spender, Raymond Mortimer and William Plomer were also invited — the flower of British homosexuality. In 1933, Virginia Woolf joined the group. The sexual intercourse was very free; Vita Sackville-West even spent a night with Christopher. The neighbors did not appear to have any problem with these goings-on; the threesome was considered an intriguing eccentricity and did not set off the hostility to which Radclyffe Hall and Una Troubridge, for example,[602] were accustomed.

---

600. *Ibid.*, 30 June 1919, p.154.

601. Katherine Mansfield's journal, 1 June 1907, about her relations withEdie Bendall, cited by Antony Alpers, *The Life of Katherine Mansfield*, New York, The Viking Press, 1980, 466 pages, p.49.

This type of experiment remained very rare, however. Most lesbians of the inter-war period, whether well-known or unknown, stuck to a traditional-looking family life which in the end differed very little from the heterosexual model. Such cases were more numerous, but there are few accounts on them since they did not attract attention.

Sylvia Beach and Adrienne Monnier fit that picture perfectly. The shy young American met Monnier in 1917 while visiting her bookshop. They were friends until 1937, when they broke up. With Monnier's assistance and advice, Beach founded the Shakespeare & Co. bookshop. They led an undramatic life; for entertainment, they would go to visit Natalie Barney and thus they were in touch with the Parisian lesbian community.[603] Neither one was very loquacious about their relationship, which appears to have been a model of equilibrium. They did not mimic heterosexual roles, but each assumed her own identity, without reference to male models, and they did not fall into conflict and destructive relations.

The journalist Janet Flanner (Broom), too, avoided any public show and preferred discretion to the flamboyance some of her friends. An American by origin, Flanner was part of the loose group of Left Bank lesbians, intellectuals and artists who gathered around Natalie Barney. Like many others, she left the United States in order to be able to live more freely, without being subjected to the constant pressure of public opinion. Her relationship with the writer Solita Solano was unremarkable; both felt that their way of life was normal and natural, so there was little scope for making them the subject of any scandal or scene.

Many anonymous lesbians who were interviewed also insist that their relationships were natural. "Me, I always considered myself very normal... But at the same time I was normal and I was glad to be different. Because, fundamentally, I was in rupture with the idea of family, whereas everyone had a family; I was in rupture with marriage, whereas all the women were marrying; I was essentially lesbian whereas most women loved men... I was rather glad to be different, that's all."[604]

---

602. For further details, see Joy Melville, *Ellen & Edy: A Biography of Ellen Terry and her Daughter Edith Craig, 1847-1947*, London, Pandora, 1987, 293 pages.

603. For further details, see Noel Riley Fitch, *Sylvia Beach and the Lost Generation*, New York-London, W.W. Norton & Co, 1983, 447 pages; and Shari Benstock, *Women of the Left Bank, op. cit.*

604. Testimony of N., recorded by Claudie Lesselier, *Aspects...*, *op. cit.*, p.60.

The relationship with one's parents was complex, however. Sylvia told me, "One did not speak about sex at that time, but from the age of eleven I started falling in love with girls. When it became more apparent, my mother started making fun of my feelings.[605]

However, not all lesbians inevitably suffered from peer pressure, and the assertion of one's homosexuality did not necessarily cause a break with the parents. An affair with another girl, if it remained discreet, was less likely to attract scandal than a too evident flirtation with a young man. Thus, B testifies: "My mother left me a great deal of freedom. The only thing she was terrified of was that I might become pregnant without being married. 'You can do what you want, but not that,' she said. To be an unmarried mother, to her, was an abomination. Seeing that I was not attracted to boys, she thought: at least, she won't have a baby that way! Then she left me more freedom than my sister..."[606] Another says: "They allowed my friend to visit at our house, and one day after she left, there was one of those scenes between my mother and me, my mother saying that this was unacceptable, that I was heading for trouble,... that she did not understand me, etc. I answered: 'Okay, mom, if that's the way it is, I'll leave.' My father, who usually did not get involved, basically a good and reasonable man, said to me: 'Okay; you can leave tomorrow, on the understanding, have no fear, that we will talk it over again here.' Actually, no one ever mentioned it again. It was settled then and there."[607]

A. lived with her friend for forty years, and the rest of her family considered her a full member. The couple was accepted in the neighborhood, and in the village they moved to thereafter: "We didn't have any problems... For decades, we lived in peace; we were two friends, we were 'the little household at Number 25,' if you will, and it should be said that we never had serious trouble, in our case. Me, I was pretty quiet, and I didn't get in anyone's way. Maybe they laughed behind our backs; I couldn't have cared less."[608]

Charlotte Wolff, who came from a middle-class Jewish family, also enjoyed a great tolerance: "The Jewish middle class in general was ignorant on subjects like unorthodox sex, but my parents and their family were not. I was agreeably surprised when my aunt Bertha once remarked: 'I believe you are in love with

---

605. Testimony of Sylvia in *Women like us, op. cit.*, p.63.

606. Testimony of B., recorded by Claudie Lesselier, *Aspects..., op. cit.*, p.56.

607. Testimony of A., born in 1907 in Paris, to a father who worked and a mother who stayed home, *ibid.*, p.74.

608. *Ibid.*

Mrs. X.' I answered: 'In love, but not very much attracted.' She smiled." Wolff noted: "I was accepted for myself in my private and professional circles, and I suppose that I naively assumed that the whole world would do the same."[609]

Relations with one's parents were not always so easy. For Valentine Ackland, adolescence was the major turning point. Paradoxically, it was her parents who revealed to her that she was different and led her to become radical. In 1922, at the age of sixteen, she fell in love with Laura, who was three years older. In all innocence, they embraced, exchanged gifts, and wrote passionate letters — which were soon discovered. Father and daughter clashed, in mutual incomprehension:

> I did not understand at all what he sought to discover. I said to him that we loved each other. I have a very sharp memory of the expression of disgust on his face... He became completely furious — more furious than I had ever seen him. He asked me whether I knew what an indecent thing I was doing. I said no, I had not done anything indecent; it may have been weird, but it wasn't evil. I thought that some of us must have been built wrongly. He asked me, in a rage, what I meant. I answered that Laura ought to have been a man. I thought that Laura must have been one in an earlier incarnation.[610]

After the scene with the father, who felt that his authority was being flouted, Valentine had to face maternal recriminations: "No man will ever want to marry you if he hears of this"; "It is a disgusting thing, unpardonable." If Valentine remained unimpressed, Laura was convinced: "Her mother said that unless she married, she would remain an old maid, dishonored, poor and rejected."[611]

The arguments of respectability were powerful in a society governed by others' opinions. When that was not enough, medical arguments would be used to terrorize them: Valentine was told that she would go blind and lose her mind if she continued her practices "against nature." Standing up to her parents, Valentine gradually discovered the realities that were being hidden, and she came to terms with her identity. After an unconsummated marriage, she decided to live independently. She had her hair cut in a bob and developed female friendships.

---

609. Charlotte Wolff, *Hindsight, op. cit.*, p.73.

610. Valentine Ackland, *For Sylvia: An Honest Account*, London, Chatto & Windus, 1985, 135 pages, p.67.

611. *Ibid.*, p.68-69.

In 1926, she met Sylvia Townsend Warner. They moved in together in 1930, composing poems together and settling in Dorset. They were very committed politically, fighting Fascism and serving in the volunteer ambulance corps in Spain. They lived independently for forty years and managed to assert their lesbian identity without any major problems.

Self rejection

Not all lesbians managed to accept their identity and to live their lives accordingly. Many women did not admit they were different, or rejected the most extreme aspects. A freedom of morals and provocative dressing might go hand-in-hand with a certain conformity and an uncomfortable question about one's identity. The painter Romaine Brooks exemplifies this schizophrenia. Like others, Brooks built her identity gradually, in reaction to her mother, who rejected her, and then as a result of contact with the cosmopolitan homosexual community which she became a part of in Capri and then in Paris. Brooks remained sexually innocent for a very long time, although she fell in love with several of her counterparts during her adolescence. She had difficulty accepting her sexuality and the fact of being different. Far from being a positive experience, for her lesbianism seemed to be a matter of bad luck and a flaw. This feeling was reinforced by many failures in love. Her meeting with John Brooks turned the corner. Like other British homosexuals, Brooks had left England following the Oscar Wilde trial and had settled in Capri, where he shared a house with E.F. Benson and Somerset Maugham. He met Romaine, whose mother had died and bequeathed an immense fortune to her, and he married her — at her request; neither one was in love. The marriage lasted only one year because Brooks, keen to retain his respectability, was unable to accept his wife's transformation: she cut her hair and started dressing like a man. Then she struck up friendships with the princesse de Polignac, Ida Rubinstein, Renata Borgatti, D'Annunzio, Montesquiou, Cocteau, and Whistler. She met Natalie Barney in 1912, and that was the great love of her life.[612] However, that hardly provided any satisfaction either: Barney went on with her conquests, without regard for Romaine's fidelity.

---

612. On Romaine Brooks, see Meryle Secrest, *Between Me and Life: A Biography of Romaine Brooks*, London, Macdonald & Jane's, 1976, 432 pages; Françoise Werner, *Romaine Brooks*, Paris, Plon, 1990, 334 pages; Shari Benstock, *Women of the Left Bank, op. cit.*

Romaine Brooks's attitude with regard to the lesbian community is ambiguous. She was a full member, a celebrity among the homosexuals of Paris, and was satirized in *Extraordinary Women* (1928)[613] by Compton Mackenzie, whom she depicted in a savage and cruel portrait in her own work. Her two favorite targets were Radclyffe Hall and Una Troubridge, whose affectations and victim mentality she despised. Still, she socialized with them constantly and she herself wore only men's clothing. Her portrait of Troubridge, one of her most famous tableaux, is a caricature of the "New Woman," and an indictment against lesbian stereotypes, in all:

> — A hard gaze, the left eye magnified by a monocle, the mouth pinched, the hair short and tight,.... And clothing that is hardly more flattering: the high collar of a white shirt interrupted by a tie which strangles the neck; a black jacket over a gray and black striped skirt — this is the kind of over-done costume, the type of get-up that encourages ridicule of lesbians.[614]

Brooks never managed to get beyond these contradictions. According to her biographer, Françoise Werner, she "adored traditional values; make no mistake: the great rebel, the nonconformist, enjoyed her female society that saved appearances."[615] Her inability to accept herself as a lesbian reflects on her social attitude: she didn't like women who resembled her too much. This love-hate relationship led her to take a political stance to the far right. [616]

Sometimes, the different road is too fraught with suffering, and too lonely to be followed to the end. Annemarie, Klaus and Erika Mann's friend, was born in 1908 into an ultraconservative Zurich family of wealthy industrialists who became Nazi sympathizers. Her mother, Renée Schwarzenbach, a very respectable woman of the upper middle class and the daughter of a general, was nonetheless lesbian. Her invasive personality stifled her daughter, whom she forbad to admit her homosexuality, all the while encouraging her masculine tendencies and her attraction for women. She herself had an affair with the professional singer Emmy Krüger, who lived in their house. In 1928, Annemarie left home for Paris, then Berlin. Everywhere she went, her attractive and desperate beauty inspired passions — including in Erika Mann, Carson McCullers, Ella

---

613. See Chapters Five and Seven.
614. Françoise Werner describing the picture, in *Romaine Brooks, op. cit.,* p.267.
615. *Ibid.,* p.262.
616.See Chapter Six.

Maillart, Barbara Hamilton and the baronne Margot von Opel. Her whole life was one long escape into drugs, travel, and writing. In *Nouvelle lyrique* (1933), she creates a male stand-in for herself, a depressed man in love with Sibyl, a cabaret singer. The impossibility of homosexual love is represented here in the opposition between the well-bred young man on his way to a diplomatic career, and the muse of Berlin night life. Looking for a pretense of stability, Schwarzenbach married the homosexual Claude Clarac, Second Secretary at the French embassy in Persia, in 1935. In spite of all, she sank into a morphine habit and died at the age of 34 in a fall from a bicycle, after having made several suicide attempts.

Thus, the first lesbian identities appeared in the 1920s, but they still remained very polemical. The majority of lesbians were defined according to the model of the masculine lesbian, patterned on Radclyffe Hall. "I believe I liked it better when we all martyrs!" declares Valerie Seymour, in *The Well of Loneliness*.[617] However, this model was not the only one and we should not forget that certain lesbians were able to propagate optimistic ideals and an identity based on acceptance of oneself and integration into society.

THE BIRTH OF A HOMOSEXUAL COMMUNITY?

Was there any homosexual community to speak of, in the 1920s? The term conjures up images of coherent homosexual groups, interdependent, sharing the same cultural reference, the same aspirations and, presumably, the same goals (militancy, educating the public, mutual support) and so forth. And can we speak of a homosexual community in the broad sense (homosexuals and lesbians) or must we keep them in mind as two separate groups? Based on what we have seen, there appears to be little basis for imagining a homosexual and lesbian community. The two groups lived completely autonomously; they had little or nothing to do with each other, and they did not have the same references and certainly not the same goals: lesbians were not under any legal pressure in any of the three countries concerned. The first point is more delicate. In fact, the most persuasive sign that there was a homosexual community — and at the European level — is that of shared references. English, French and German homosexuals all looked to a certain number of "famous ancestors," they read certain authors,

---

617. Radclyffe Hall, *The Well of Loneliness, op. cit.,* p.391.

they went to see certain plays and enjoyed certain painters. This reality exists and it unites the homosexual populations more effectively than the militant movements, which affected only a minority. On the other hand, the homosexual community was certainly still not very coherent: it may have functioned relatively well at the level of the elites, but it was far from integrating all the social classes and all the categories of homosexuals.

Sharing a Common Culture

Between the wars, the foundation for a homosexual community was laid in the establishment of common references. Literature was one of the most fertile fields for developing the essence of the homosexual culture. Certain names were quoted time and again, demonstrating that there was a sort of "homosexual literature." The classics, like Plato, played an important part for students, who might discover the mysteries of Greek love through hints and allusions — when the text was not expurgated: "Mr. Cornwallis stopped the student who was going over the text and indicated, in a neutral voice: 'You can skip that line, it is just an allusion to the unmentionable vice of the Greeks.'"[618] Certain texts developed a wicked reputation, including Shakespeare's Sonnets, Marlowe's plays and, more recent, the works of Walter Pater and Johann Joachim Winckelmann. The very name of Oscar Wilde was an evocation of vice, as was that of Renée Vivien in France — which became part of their attraction: "I have all the works of Renée Vivien in the original, my friend knew my passion for Renée Vivien very well and, every time she could, she took the opportunity to buy one of those little books from Lemerre, illustrated..."[619]

In England, "uranian" poetry enjoyed certain a vogue in homosexual milieux.[620] Many of the poets were related to the BSSP, besides. "A Shropshire Lad" (1896) by A.E. Housman became a cult poem enjoyed by a whole generation. Contemporary poets were the most read, and they were often quoted, for they were able to evoke the personal experiences of homosexuals who identified with the choices, the doubts, the suffering, and sometimes the struggle and the pride evoked. In the first generation, Edward Carpenter and J.A. Symonds were

---

618. E.M. Forster, *Maurice, op. cit.*, p.54.

619. Testimony of A., recorded by Claudie Lesselier, *Aspects..., op. cit.*, p.102.

620. For a complete study on this topic, see Timothy d'Arch Smith, *Love in Earnest, Some Notes on the Lives and Writings of English "Uranian" Poets from 1889 to 1930*, London, Routledge & Kegan, 1970, 280 pages.

very popular in England, as well as Ronald Firbank (whom Siegfried and Cecil Beaton enjoined Stephen Tennant to read). Among the best-known novelists and poets in England were D.H. Lawrence, Compton Mackenzie, Walt Whitman, E.M. Forster, Virginia Woolf, Rupert Brooke and, a little later, Christopher Isherwood.

Radclyffe Hall's book, for its part, clearly became the touchstone of the lesbians in the inter-war period. It is constantly cited by women when they are asked to name their major influences. Eleonor read it when she was sixteen: "We all wanted at all costs to get our hands on *The Well of Loneliness* and we passed it around, even when it was forbidden. It was completely dog-eared. We thought it was marvelous simply because we knew we were like that."[621] Its scope went far beyond England. Even Frenchwomen testify to its impact in their life:

> That was a big thing, it was a whole époque (which I did not live through, in its entirety, of course...) But finally, when we in France started to read this book which had been burned in England... Then, obviously, that created a certain fashion for lesbians to carry it around... I always the think of the ties from Sulka, the tie was a little bit an imitation of Radclyffe Hall ... In the end, it wasn't great literature, but it was dear to the hearts of lesbians.[622]

In Germany, Thomas Mann's writings were replete with homosexual insinuations, skillfully dissimulated. His son Klaus soon made himself a reputation as a homosexual writer, in particular with the publication of his very explicit book, *The Pious Dance*. The high priest of homoeroticism was Stefan George, whose poetry celebrating the beauty of a young boy was reserved for a very limited elite readership. Jelena Nagrodskaya's novel, *The Bronze Door* (1911), was a great success. It went through five printings in Germany and was translated into several languages. The 1000-page novel by A.E. Weirauch, *Der Skorpion*, became the major reference of the lesbian public. Hilde Radusch, a former municipal adviser of the KPD, noted: "For me, the book was a revelation, I recognized myself there."[623] In 1931, *Die Freundin* described it as "the most beautiful of all the women's novels." The work was fairly traditional, at that, in the "homo-

---

621. Eleonor, testimony reported in *Women like us, op. cit.*, p.34.

622. Testimony of A., recorded by Claudie Lesselier, *Aspects...*, *op. cit.*, p.101.

623. Cited by Claudia Schoppmann, *Der Skorpion, Frauenliebe in der Weimarer Republik*, Berlin, Frühlings Erwachen, 1984, 81 pages.

sexual coming of age" genre with all its obligatory stages. And it imitates Hall's novel, *The Unlit Lamp* (1924), in many points.

In France, of course everyone was reading Verlaine and Rimbaud, and the turn-of-the-century dandies like Robert de Montesquiou and Jean Lorrain, whose *Monsieur de Phocas* (1901) tells the story of a man obsessed by the death of one of his friends at the age of eleven. The Proustian influence is undeniable; even those who did not read his works knew how ambiguous they were. The homo-sexual elite read *Sodom and Gomorrah*, but they did not always like it. On the subject of male homosexuality, the dispute usually centered on Proust's dissimu-lation of his own homosexuality, and in particular his use of the subterfuge of Albertine: "That Proust, for example, made Albert into Albertine, makes me doubt the whole work....This cheating kills our confidence."[624]

When it came to the lesbians, they harshly disputed both his description of their morals and his general view, which they considered masculine, partisan and degrading:

> But was he confused, was he ignorant when he assembled such a Gomorrah of abysmally vicious girls, denounced an understanding, a com-munity ... having lost the comfort of the earth-shaking truth which guided us through Sodom — the fact is, with all due respect to Mr. Proust's imagi-nation or error, that there is no Gomorrah. Puberty? loneliness, prisons, aberration, snobbery... Those are thin seedbeds, not sufficient to account for the generation and feeding of a vice so widespread, so well-established, and the indispensable solidarity that goes with it. Intact, enormous, eter-nal, Sodom contemplates from above its pale shadow.[625]

Reading Proust also amounted to a provocation — the pleasure of finally seeing the subject broached and being able to wave the book around without actually knowing what to make of it. Vita Sackville-West wrote to Virginia Woolf, to that effect, in 1926: — The rest of the time, I read Proust. Since no one on board had ever heard of Proust, but had enough French to be able to translate the title, they rather looked at me askance....[626]

But it was Gide who became the ultimate reference on homosexuality in France in the inter-war period. Gide was read by the men, and by lesbians alike: "André Gide, that was when I was at the teachers' college, so I was nineteen

---

624. René Crevel, *Mon corps et moi*, Paris, Éditions du Sagittaire, 1926, 204 pages, p.62-63.
625. Colette, *Le Pur et l'Impur*, *op. cit.*
626. Vita Sackville-West/Virginia Woolf, *Correspondence*, *op. cit.*, p.129-130.

years old (1936). *If It Die* was about a man's homosexuality, but I understood that it was the same problem. *Corydon?* I read that one, too. He was a great guy, Gide."[627] For some homosexuals, Gide was a revelation; his influence is palpable: "At a certain moment, having read André Gide, 'families — I hate you,' *Nathanaël* — I threw it all in. I left the teachers' college, I left my family, I left everything. I came to Paris (1937).[628]

Homosexual culture was not limited to the private pleasures of literature. It was entirely possible to go into town to see homosexual shows. In addition to the traditional transvestite cabarets that could be found in many homosexual establishments and of which Germany had made a specialty, it became possible to see homosexual spectacles in perfectly traditional settings. In England, the literary and art critics were openly pro-homosexual. *New Stateman* and *Listener*, one due to T.C. Worsley, the other due to J.R. Ackerley, defended homosexual artists.[629]

In addition, Diaghilev and the Ballets Russes had made the treatment of homosexuality on stage a familiar item since before the war. Diaghilev's homosexuality was notorious, as was his affair with Nijinsky. The success of the Ballets Russes among the homosexual intelligentsia was extraordinary: Proust, Cocteau, Lytton Strachey became fanatics.

After 1919, the dancer Ivor Novello and the actor Noël Coward[630] perpetuated the homosexual myth in the world of entertainment. All his life, Coward distinguished himself by his relative discretion; he never made a public statement about his homosexuality and, while his immediate entourage was perfectly aware of his tastes, those watching his ambiguous plays often remained unaware of the subtext. Still, he helped to popularize the image of the chic, decadent homosexual on the British stage in the 1920s. In *The Young Idea* (1923), the

---

627. Testimony of N., born in 1904, living in the provinces with her grandmother, recorded by Claudie Lesselier, *Aspects...*, *op. cit.*, p.104.

628. *Ibid.* For her part, Vita Sackville-West read *Les Faux-monnayeurs* and *Si le grain ne meurt* in March 1927 and was not charmed in the least: "The African part bored me; I don't think that lust is interesting *as such*, and it did not inspire me in any way to know that Gide "had" a young Arabian boy five times in one night... But the part relating to Wilde is good, although revolting," (Vita Sackville-West/Virginia Woolf, *Correspondence*, *op. cit.*, p.238).

629. All references in Noel Annan, *Our Age: English Intellectuals between the Wars: A Group Portrait*, New York, Random House, 1991, 479 pages, p.114-115.

630. On Coward, see Philip Hoare, *Noel Coward: A Biography*, London, Sinclair-Stevenson, 1995, 605 pages.

two heroes, Sholto and Gerda, embody the two extremes of the androgynous fashion, the effeminate boy and the flapper. In *The Vortex* (1924), Nicki Lancaster takes drugs, which was interpreted by critics as a substitute for homosexuality. In 1929, he put together *Bitter Sweet*, a musical based on the homosexuality of the Oscar Wilde generation, in another skillful maneuver. One outstandingly transparent allusion is in the line, "We are the reason for the 'Nineties' being gay." And, finally, in *Design for Living* (1930), he broaches the topic of bisexuality.

The best-known English actors of the time, John Gielgud, Max Adrian, Gyles Isham, Henry Kendall, Charles Laughton, Ernest Milton, Esme Percy, Eric Portman, Ernst Thesiger and Frank Vosper, were homosexual or bisexual. In Germany, actors like Wilhelm Bendow, Max Hansen, Adolf Wohlbrück, Hubert von Meyerinck, and Hans Heinrich von Twardowsky made no secret of their homosexuality. In France, Jean Marais was the biggest celebrity. Among women, Marlene Dietrich, Zarah Leander, and Greta Garbo were bisexual. Many homosexuals were also found in the fashion and art world, in particular, in England, the interior decorator John Fowler, the set designer Oliver Messel, the great dressmaker Norman Hartnell and the photographer Cecil Beaton.

In Germany, there was an attempt to create a homosexual theater, the Theater of Eros, which was founded in Berlin-Steglitz on July 6, 1921, by Bruno Matussek. It was an itinerant theater which put on shows for private individuals or in hotels. It specialized in plays with homosexual themes like *Satire et tragédie de Caesareon*, which was about the life of an invert. The homosexual newspapers published the program in their advertisements. *Der Hellasbote*, in its May 26, 1923 issue, announced the June 4 presentation of a play by Reinhold Klugs entitled *Who is Guilty?* Not much is known about this experiment; it seems that, for all his goodwill, Matussek lacked dramatic talent.

Several plays with homosexual themes were played in a more traditional setting in the inter-war period. In Germany, Klaus Mann's play *Anja and Esther* was directly inspired by the adolescence of the Mann children. On stage, Erika and Klaus interpreted their own roles, Esther was played by Pamela Wedekind and Jakob by Gustaf Gründgens. This was already scandalous in itself, since Pamela was Erika's lover, and Klaus and Gustav were also homosexual. The play was put on simultaneously in Munich and Hamburg in October 1925, but was not received very favorably. In 1926, it went on the road, with a different cast, and it had a great success, especially in Berlin and Vienna. Another play with homosexual overtones, *Le Mal de la jeunesse* (1925) by Ferdinand Bruckner, also deals with young people adrift in a Berlin pension. The gender dictates the conduct: out of love for a boy, a girl goes into prostitution; another commits suicide out of love for her friend.[631] In England, J.R. Ackerley's *The Prisoners of War* (1925) was announced as "the new homosexual play," and it was the first to cover the subject in a contemporary way. The reviews were good and the homosexual intelligentsia was delighted: Stephen Spender, Christopher Isherwood, T.E. Lawrence, and Siegfried Sassoon raved about it. Ackerley was having an affair at that time with Ivor Novello, anyway. *The Green Bay Tree*, by Mordaunt Shairp, was produced in London for the first time on January 25, 1933, at the St Martin Theatre, with Laurence Olivier as a young man seduced by an aging homosexual. In France, Roger Martin du Gard's *Un taciturne* was shown in 1931 at the Louis-Jouvet Theatre. The play is very dark and dramatic.

The most famous play with homosexual themes of the inter-war period was unquestionably *The Captive (La Prisonnière)*, by Édouard Bourdet.[632] It was played in France for the first time on March 6, 1926 at the Femina Theatre and was also staged in England and Germany. It became a cultural mainstay for homosexuals in that period, and was constantly cited as an example of the recrudescence of lesbianism. The heroine, Irene, is under the influence of a married woman. Her father pressures her to marry a childhood friend, Jacques, who is warned by the husband of the older woman, that,

> They are not like us. Stay away from them! Under cover of friendship, a woman introduces herself into a household whenever she wants, at any hour of the day, and she poisons everything there; she ransacks everything before the man whose home is being destroyed sees what is happening. By the time he realizes it, it is too late, he is alone! Alone, facing the secret alliance of two beings who understand one another, who divine each other's wishes, because they are alike, because they are of the same sex, from a different planet than him, the foreigner, the enemy.[633]

The play is striking in its fundamental anti-lesbianism and the number of prejudices it reveals. Curiously, its success was attributed to its modernity, and its temerity(!); it was judged by many to be scandalous and symptomatic of the

---

631. Many plays taking Oscar Wilde or the Eulenburg affair as their themes were also presented.

632. Édouard Bourdet, *La Prisonnière*, a comedy in three acts, Paris, Les Œuvres libres, 1926, 116 pages.

633. *Ibid.*, p.70-71.

epoch. It became a symbol of the homosexual culture of the period, and sparked a fashion for strict tailoring, ties and a short haircut — "La Prisonnière."

That same year, another play which also gave the worst possible view of lesbians, *Les Détraquées (Ruined)*, was played at the Theatre of the Two Masks, featuring two criminal, homosexual teachers.[634]

Few movies that could be called homosexual were made in the inter-war period, but there were some interesting references.[635] Generally, the homosexual themes are disguised or barely hinted at. In a German comedy from 1927, *Der Fürst von Pappenheim (The Prince of Pappenheim)* by Richard Eichberg, Curt Bois plays an actor in a variety show who does a transvestite number. The film was later used by the Nazis to associate Jews and homosexuality. In *Geschlecht in Fesseln (Chains)*, by Wilhelm Dieterle, 1929, a man in prison discovers homosexuality. When he is released, his lover makes him sing; he ends up committing suicide.

These examples show that, as far as cinema, homosexuality was still treated in a very simplistic way. The homosexual is either a transvestite, the source of comic misunderstandings, or a figure of tragedy, guaranteed to end in dishonor and death. The only completely homosexual film, *Anders als Andern* (1919), had already dealt with the topic of homosexuality in a tragic mode. At least, it provided a message of hope.[636] In another pessimistic film, *Mikael*, by Carl Theodor Dreyer (1924), a painter falls in love with his model, Mikael, who is only interested in his money and leaves him for a woman. Dying, the painter makes Mikael his sole legatee.

In 1929, *Revolte im Erziehungshaus (Revolt at the reformatory)* and, in 1931, Karl Anton's *Der Fall des Generalstabs-Oberst Redl (Colonel Redl)* also featured homosexual characters. *Zéro de conduite (Zero for Comportment)*, by Jean Vigo, in 1933, broke the paradigm and used homosexuality as a sign of rebellion, of rejecting the established order. Now, it took on a political, anarchistic dimension. The film was called subversive and was banned until 1945.

Lesbianism was treated in a very limited way in movies; examples are *Claudine At School*, by S. de Poligny, 1937, and especially *Girls in Uniform* by Léontine Sagan (after Christa Winsloe), 1931 — the most famous lesbian film of the inter-war period. It marked a generation of lesbians as surely as Radclyffe Hall's book. "I must say that one film that changed me, when I was young, was

---

634. André Breton raved about this play in *Nadja*.

635. For further details, see Bertrand Philbert, *L'Homosexualité à l'écran*, Paris, Henri Veyrier, 1984, 181 pages.

636. See Chapter Two. Most copies of the film were burned during the 1930s.

'Girls in Uniform.' I even said so, to my grandmother: 'I have to go see this film.' And what a film! I was fourteen or fifteen years old when it came out. I had seen the posters, and that is what made me say to my grandmother: 'You know, you have to give me money to go to the movies.'"[637]

The film gets its power from the faithful evocation of the noxious atmosphere of a German boarding school. One of the most remarkable scenes takes place in the dormitory, where all the girls wait until their beloved teacher, Miss von Bernburg, gives them a good-night kiss. The girls are kneeling by their beds, heads lowered. The heroine, Manuela, gives herself fully to the kiss, in ecstasy. In the novel, the drama culminates in Manuela's suicide. In the movie, when she is about to jump out the window, she is held back by her comrades and carried forth in triumph, the whole college revolts against the authority of the director — all the pupils having, in fact, been in love with a fellow pupil or a professor, like Manuela. This triumphal and entirely improbable dénouement show that there was a desire to break the fatalistic paradigm of homosexuality, substituting certain death with an awakening and a revolt. In this sense, the film could be considered a call to rise up, to form a lesbian movement and assert one's rights and proudly affirm one's identity. At the time, it was especially interpreted as a criticism of Prussian authoritarianism, and homosexuality was seen as a sign of political dissidence.

The other major film touching on lesbianism was *Loulou* (1929), by Georg Wilhelm Pabst, with Louise Brooks in the principal role. Countess Geschwitz is in love with Spitz, who toys with her, without ever giving her satisfaction. The ambiguity of the relationship did not escape the censors. In several countries, England in particular, scenes with the countess were removed. The film did not suggest a lesbian identity as powerfully as *Girls in Uniform*, for homosexuality was only as minor topic; and the character of Spitz, an easy woman, a *femme fatale*, reproduced the inevitable stereotype of the lesbian as a depraved woman, eager to try any new sensation.

However, even if the cinema in the inter-war period was still marked by prejudices and conventional treatments, it was an eye-opener for many homosexuals. They could identify with a hero of their own sex, and certain figures became cult figures of camp, like Marlene Dietrich or Zarah Leander.

Popular songs also became homosexual references. French lesbians looked to Susy Solidor, a singer and manager of a lesbian nightclub, who put out a

---

637. Testimony of B., recorded by Claudie Lesselier, *Aspects...*, *op. cit.*, p.105.

record (for limited distribution) in 1932, *Lesbian Paris*. The singer Damia, a bisexual, was also much appreciated: "I always listened to Damia. I remember [the lyrics] that could apply to two women as well as to a man and a woman, so we took them for ourselves. Many things were not intended for lesbians, but they were transformed; instead of masculine, we cast them as feminine."[638]

Another emblematic figure of the time was Barbette, the transvestite trapeze artist who fascinated the crowd, and in particular Maurice Sachs, who was a spectator in 1926: "I may never have seen anything more graceful than this girl dressed in feathers who sprang so boldly from the trapeze, did a somersault and caught herself in full flight by a foot, and then, taking a bow, pulled a big curly wig off her head and revealed that she was a young man! This little American appears at the Variety under the name of Barbette; I went to see him at the Daunou Hotel where he is staying, and found him lying completely naked on his bed, his face covered with a thick layer of black pomade. Bisexual on the stage and bi-colored at home. He had just three books on his bedside table: *Ulysses, Le Grand Écart*, and Havelock Ellis's *Onanism Alone and for Two*."[639]

The homosexual community finally recognized itself in certain artists who took a homoerotic approach in their work.[640] At the end of the 19th century, male homosexuality was often only suggested. It appeared in certain works in the aesthetic (and decadent) movement, in Antiquity or a medieval context, in the form of languid, androgynous young men — for example, in the tableaux of the pre-Raphaélite painter Burne-Jones. Kitsch paintings by the autodidact Elisar von Kupffer, a member of Gemeinschaft der Eigenen, evoke the androgynous figure of disguised adolescents, transported to a homosexual paradise. More suggestive were the photographs of Baron von Gloeden, Guglielmo Plüschow and Baron Corvo, featuring nude young Sicilians; there was little attempt to mask their homosexual motivation. The erotic drawings of Aubrey Bearsdley, full of beautiful young men and satyrs with oversized phalluses, were equally unequivocal, as were those of the German Maurice Besnaux (Marcus Behmer), a member of the WhK, who also illustrated Oscar Wilde's *Salomé* and whose drawings appeared in *Simplicissimus* and *Die Insel*.

---

638. *Ibid.*, p.106.

639. Maurice Sachs, *Au temps du "Bœuf sur le toit"* [1939], Paris, Grasset, 1987, 235 pages, p.194.

640. See Emmanuel Cooper, *The Sexual Perspective: Homosexuality and Art in the Last 100 Years in the West*, London, Routledge & Keagan, 1986, 324 pages; *also 100 Jahre Schwulenbewegung*, Berlin, Schwules Museum, 1997, 384 pages.

Homosexual and lesbian themes were shown far more directly in the 1920s. Particularly in Germany, many painters and illustrators contributed to re-examining homosexuality or had links to the homosexual movements. Many homosexual books included illustrations. Several houses published such works, in particular Editions Heinrich Böhme, Zweemann, and Paul Steegemann. The art merchants and publishers Fritz Gurlitt and Alfred Flechtheim were the principal intermediaries in Berlin for this kind of production. The artists were no longer presenting idealized figures of androgynous young men, transported to an imaginary Antiquity, but the modern Berlin scene, its bars, its balls, its openly sexual atmosphere.[641] Homosexual leaders were also used as models: Magnus Hirschfeld was caricatured in *Simplicissimus* by Eduard Thönys in April 1921; Erich Godal made two portraits of him. Rudolf Schlichter represented him in the company of his friends, while Peter Martin Lampel painted Richard Linsert, the Secretary of the WhK, in 1928. Arnold Siegfried did a portrait of Adolf Brand in 1924. Otto Schoff (1884-1938) produced many homosexual drawings and he illustrated books by Pierre Louÿs and August von Platen. He also made many drawings of the Berlin homosexual subculture, including people like Christian Schad, Guy de Laurence (Erich Godal), Renée Sintenis, Georg Ehrlich, Martel Schwichtenberg, Margit Gaal, Paul Kamm and Karl Arnold.

Most of the drawings showed only very young people; it was still taboo to depict adults. The painter and educator Peter Martin Lampel, who had ties to the WhK and Gemeinschaft der Eigenen, specialized in portraits of young boys on their own in the big German cities. He started out as a member of the Irregular Forces, then joined socialism and militated for youth education. He tried to help the unemployed youth and the male prostitutes who were victims of the economic crisis. He made a portrait of these young people in his book *Jungen in Not* (1928), then mounted a play, *Revolte im Erziehungshaus*, which soon led to the film mentioned above. Most of his paintings and drawings have disappeared.

Homoerotic art was also finding a place in France and England, but it was less clearly integrated into the homosexual subculture. In the 1930s, Cocteau's drawings, for example, emphasized the plastic forms of virile soldiers and sailors, pure products of the homosexual phantasmagoria of the time. Stephen Tennant's illustrations for *Lascar* testify to the same inspiration. Duncan Grant, a member

---

641. On this topic, see Andreas Sternweiler, "Das Lusthaus der Knaben, Homosexualität und Kunst," in *100 Jahre Schwulenbewegung, op. cit.*

of the Bloomsbury Club, produced paintings that sometimes showed his bisexuality — in particular "Bathing," (1911) where a naked man with a muscular body, dives, swims, then climbs up into a boat. The photography of Cecil Beaton, like that of Horst P. Horst and Herbert List in Germany, also had a powerful homoerotic connotation.

In England, one of the specialists in homosexual art was H.S. Tuke (1858-1929).[642] His canvases of nude young boys enjoying nautical activities were very much in vogue in homosexual circles. One of the professors who taught at the same public school as T.C. Worsley hung a large Tuke painting, "Dreams of Summer," on the wall of his room, showing a nude adolescent lying in the grass.

Lesbian art made particularly great strides in the 1920s, developing its own references and at the same time coming out from under the shadow of male homosexual works and the traditional Sapphic representation. Among the most famous lesbians artists were Gluck (Hannah Gluckstein), Dora Carrington, and Romaine Brooks, whose severe precision emphasizes the tortured personalities of her portraits. Her nudes present the ideal of an asexual female body, pale, very thin, with a child's breasts, and no pubic hair. "The Crossing" (1911), which represents Ida Rubinstein as basically a white line on a black background, is the best example. Thelma Wood, the American who was the partner of Djuna Barnes, evoked the female genitalia through floral compositions, and the Argentinean émigré Leonor Fini (who moved to Paris, the heart of surrealism), produced women-goddesses with mysterious powers, with long hair framing a face of transparent palor.[643]

Jeanne Mammen, a German, may be the most famous: her caricatures of the Berlin lesbian scene, published in *Simplicissimus*, fixed in the mind's eye the sharp-edged features of flappers, with elongated eyes, plaited hair and cigarettes, dancing corps-a-corps in men's suits, in tuxedos, in smoke-filled clubs. Mammen also worked for fashion magazines; she illustrated many homosexual reviews and did a number of book covers. Most of her work was destroyed during the war and most of the magazines were burned by the Nazis.

The homosexual culture was particularly rich in the inter-war period; the public was not over-reacting when it protested that the mainstream was being

---

642. See Emmanuel Cooper, *The Life and Works of H.S. Tuke, 1858-1929*, London, Gay Men Press, 1987, 72 pages.

643. Portraits of Tamara de Lempicka, a Polish woman who emigrated to the US, shows a woman brimming with sexual energy, nicely shaped,

jouissant de la vie et s'offrant indifféremment aux hommes et aux femmes.

overrun with scandalous images. This new visibility reinforced the homosexual identity by creating literary and visual types, and by providing a stock of references common to all.

Solidarity and Exclusion

The image of a homosexual coterie forming a universe apart, ruled by codes and secret signs of recognition, is one of the dominant topics of homophobic thought. It is as though homosexuals had founded a mafia of vice, with its affiliates infiltrating everywhere, recognizing each other without ever being seen, understanding without speaking and, in particular, taking care to introduce any new arrival to his fellow-members, who will welcome him with open arms or who, by paying for his favors, will give him the means to earn a living if he has no resources — a form of mutual aid.[644]

This fantasy vision contains a shadow of truth: like any persecuted minority, homosexuals tended to live in hiding and to develop codes accessible only to initiates. Quentin Crisp notes that the atmosphere of perpetual danger in which they lived bonded them together.[645] Homosexuals were frequently shown in the inter-war period to make up a parallel group within the society, linked by sexual ties and banding together in some occult way. Michel de Coglay thus speaks of an "international pederastic freemasonry."[646] François Porché, in the same vein, imagines a broadly ramified secret society: "Consequently, homosexuality will be, firstly, a collection of individuals who share certain morals; but in the second place, it will be a view of the world, which includes a philosophy, an ethics, an aesthetics, even a politics, with freemasonry, cards, newspapers and reviews, affiliated salons, expositions, press campaigns, intrigues, secret agreements, and various forms of fraternity and mutual support."[647]

However, homosexuals are different from other minority groups in that they have no distinctive sign. Thus, whereas the Jewish community has held together over the centuries due to a family and social solidarity, the homosexual remains an isolated individual. His homosexuality generally becomes clear to

---

644. François Carlier, *La Prostitution antiphysique* [1887], Paris, Le Sycomore, 1981, 247 pages, p.94.

645. Quentin Crisp, *The Naked Civil Servant, op. cit.*, p.29.

646. Michel du Coglay, *Chez les mauvais garçons. Choses vues*, Paris, R. Saillard, 1938, 221 pages.

647. François Porché, *L'Amour qui n'ose pas dire son nom*, Paris, Grasset, 1927, 242 pages, p.134.

him only at adolescence and thus the discovery that he is different comes late. Young homosexuals can turn neither to their family nor their usual associates. Homosexual solidarity, like homosexual militancy, always has to start over: nothing is passed down through the family or society. Young homosexuals born during a period of social tolerance do not work to protect their interests in case of a backlash. Very often, homosexual solidarity is purely fictitious and homosexuals do not feel linked by their sexuality. Thus we may question the extent to which the nascent homosexual community could have been a coherent and interdependent structure, protecting the interests of its members and sticking together in adversity.

The most original phenomenon of the era was the "Homintern." Indeed, the cult of homosexuality among English intellectuals led them to form a distinct group within society, linked only by a sexual factor. The constitution of a homosexual community within the elite only intensified the public's mistrust and jealousy with regard to intellectuals, who were reproached for being a cult, a polarizing force, an anomaly within English society. This growing antagonism was summed up in the nickname Cyril Connolly (a homosexual, himself) gave to the homosexual intellectuals: The Homintern.[648] The word play is significant. From the inception of the Comintern, these homosexuals had been seen as a symbol of a foreign force that had penetrated the country and was trying to "convert" followers.[649]

W.H. Auden and Christopher Isherwood, who had been lovers since college, personified this sexual and intellectual fraternity. The poet and the novelist were one of the pivots of the Homintern — due to their open homosexuality as well as their leftist sympathies. In fact, the Homintern did function as a secret society whose members, unperceived by the public, recognized each other and defended their common interests. The group was bound by the knowledge of intimate details of its members' lives and by the use of personal signs in alluding to homosexuality. In Foster's *Goldsworthy Lowes Dickinson*, the writer's homosexuality is camouflaged, but this biography became a cult item for Auden, Sassoon and Isherwood, who, knowing the history, could read between the lines and recognize references to Edward Carpenter, Gerald Heard, Joe Ackerley and Dickinson himself. The system of dedications also reveals the interactions within the

---

648. Arthur Waley called Forster, Ackerley and Plomer's group a homosexual "gang."

649. In 1951, when two English diplomats, Guy Burgess and Donald Maclean, "went East," it only confirmed the suspicion that there were ties between the two organizations. See Chapter Six.

group. W.H. Auden, Christopher Isherwood, and Stephen Spender dedicated their works to each other; Spender dedicated several of his works to T.A.R. Hyndman, his secretary and lover. Forster dedicated *Abinger Harvest* to William Plomer, Joe Ackerley, Bob Buckingham and Christopher Isherwood, all four homosexuals.

In the same manner, an auxiliary group came together around Lionel Charlton, who had served as a general during the First World War, then as a brigadier general in the Middle East. He retired with an old RAF pal, Tom Wichelo. He wrote his autobiography, dedicating it to Wichelo, Forster and J.R. Ackerley, and then wrote adventure novels for adolescents, featuring athletic boys who loved aviation. Personalities like Raymond Mortimer, Duncan Grant, and actors like John Gielgud revolved around him. They met in London at Gennaro's, in New Compton Street, which was famous for the beautiful waiters selected by the owner during visits to Italy.

These groups of homosexual intellectuals were generally open to people from the outside, mainly good-looking young men. They might be students at Oxford, but boys from more modest backgrounds were also recruited, primarily for their looks. That is how Forster met Bob Buckingham, a police officer who became his companion, during an evening organized by J.R. Ackerley in 1930. Buckingham was there as a friend of Harry Daley, Ackerley's lover.

What bothered people about the "Homintern" was that it succeeded in setting up a loose network of influence intended to help homosexual young people improve their social position. Jackie Hewit describes the homosexual world of the 1930s, saying that

> — the gay world of those days had a style that it no longer has today. There was a kind of intellectual freemasonry that you do not know about at all. It was like the five concentric circles [sic] of the Olympic emblem. A person in one circle knew those in another, and thus people met. And some people, like me, went from one to another. I was not a whore. Amoral perhaps, but not a whore.[650].

John Pudney, Auden's former lover, was working for the BBC and secured positions for Auden and his friend, the composer Benjamin Britten, collaborating on a program on Hadrian's Wall. Stephen Spender found a part-time job for his

---

650. Cited in Donald Mitchell and Philip Reed (ed.), *Letters from a Life, Selected Letters and Diaries of Benjamin Britten*, vol.1, *1923-1939*, London, Faber & Faber, 1991, 619 pages, p.606.

lover Hyndman with the *Left Review*, then asked Isherwood to participate in it, as well. John Lehmann, a homosexual publisher, also published his friends, including William Plomer, Forster, Isherwood, Spender and John Hampson. According to E.M. Forster, Joe Ackerley always helped his friends; as a literary and artistic director of *Listener*, he supported the careers of his many young lovers. Reviews of Ackerley's own works were written by Isherwood or Forster. Ackerley got into the BBC in 1928 thanks to one of his homosexual friends, Lionel Fielden. Subsequently, he used his influence to find work for a number of his acquaintances: E.M. Forster became a regular on BBC, G. Lowes Dickinson had a show on Plato, Lionel Charlton gave a talk on pacifism. Lytton Strachey was invited, but his voice was not good enough. Virginia Woolf, Desmond Mac-Carthy and Harold Nicolson followed one after the other. In March, 1929, he invited one of his lovers, Harry Daley, to talk about the daily life of a police officer on the radio. And Hilda Matheson invited Vita Sackville-West and Hugh Walpole to discuss "the modern woman" on the BBC. Wyndham Lewis called these practices "the intense *esprit de corps des hors-la-loi*," the solidarity of those who are above the law.

This was not anything really specific to homosexuals: these intellectuals helped each other first of all because they had done their studies together, they came from the same social background, they visited the same families, they had the same friends. But what is striking to an outside observer is the sexual specificity and the sometimes tendentious nature of the recruitment, which was not always necessarily conducted according to professional criteria. That is apparently what was most shocking to contemporaries. One Mrs. Leavis actually published a vengeful article saying, in substance,

— Here is how these elegant members of the unemployed infiltrate the highest places of journalism and even the university world, and how reputations are made: all you have to do is go find the good people, whom you already know or to whom you have just been introduced, and have one write the best things about you in the best places. The odious spoiled children of Mr. Connolly and the childhood friends of so many other writers ... arrive en masse in the universities to become stupid, pretentious young people, and then they go on to invest the literary milieu, where they replace a batch of the same species. Mr. Connolly and his group hope to succeed Rupert Brooke and are watching out right now to make sure that the literary world remains a private hunting preserve for them. Those who have been wondering how critics who are obviously so unqualified could gain such prominent positions in our literary magazines no longer need torment themselves. They were "the finest young men at school," or had a feline charm, a sensual mouth and long lashes.[651]

The arrogance of the intellectuals, added to their elitism based on sex, must have been a contributing factor in the conservative wave that swept through an England that was apprehensive to see a pole of subversion developing in the very heart of the leading classes. However, when Stephen Spender talks about those days, he probably comes closer to the true essence of what was baptized "Homintern" than most of its detractors: — I never lost that need for friendship, that desire to share my intellectual adventures with a man whose quest was similar to my own.[652]

However, homosexual solidarity, apart from these few examples, seems to have been very limited. Admittedly, the German homosexual militants were working toward a common goal, but they also fought each other. The elites had a sense of solidarity, but it was often based on factors other than homosexuality, which on the contrary could be a source of discord and rivalry. It was quite difficult to belong to Gide's circle and Cocteau's at the same time. In fact, homosexuals did not display a united front and personal quarrels often took precedence over the common fight.

Klaus Mann evokes a typical instance of this absence of homosexual solidarity: "In the *Nouvelle revue*, a disgusting and repugnant article by André Germain: 'Klaus Mann, the Narcissus of the mud pit' — the worst spite that could come from an 'aunt.' — I would take great pleasure in crushing that spider."[653] More serious were certain typical scenes of denunciation between homosexuals, which would seem to be a form of self-punishment. The homosexual, who dislikes himself, transfers his guilt feeling onto one of his peers and treats him particularly severely, in line with his own self-deprecation. When the political situation was deteriorating in Germany, Christopher Isherwood asked his friend Heinz to come to join him in England. Heinz was stopped at the border by the immigration department, which asked the purpose of his journey. The immigration officer refused to believe that Heinz could be Isherwood's

---

651. Cited by Valentine Cunningham, *British Writers of the Thirties*, Oxford, Oxford University Press, 1988, 530 pages, p.149.

652. Stephen Spender, *World within World* [1951], London, Faber & Faber, 1991, 344 pages, p.185.

653. Klaus Mann, *Journal*, op. cit., 8 March 1932, p.60.

domestic servant and sent him back to Germany. When Isherwood expressed his astonishment, Auden explained: — As soon as I saw his bright little rat's eyes, I knew that we were done for. He sized it all up at first glance, because he was the same as us.[654]

The desire to be integrated into society fueled the most profound injustices. As a stigmatized group, the homosexual community reproduced the same exclusion of which it was the victim. Even as the homosexual community was affirming its legitimacy, even as it was managing to obtain a certain amount of recognition (for example, by opening homosexual clubs), it was developing more conservative standards and imposing a consensual view of what the homosexual should be: blending in, discreet, a good sort. The militancy of Quentin Crisp, his insistence on playing the "queen," thus made him a particular victim of homosexual ostracism. As he says, himself,

> — In my most optimistic days, I went into two or three of these homosexual clubs and I observed that every year they became more respectable or, at least, more sober. Even in the beginning, when they were slightly sordid, I did not feel at home there. The management feared that my arrival and my departure might draw the inopportune attention of the authorities. That, I could understand, but it was with a pained fright that I came to see that, even among the clientele, my arrival caused a thunderous moment of silent resentment. I started to meet a greater number and a larger variety of homosexuals and I had to face the fact that, almost without exception, they did not like me.[655]

This phenomenon of exclusion even at the heart of the homosexual community was a disturbing experience for those who were its victims. Crisp notes: "To discover that homosexuals did not like me was more difficult to bear than the hostility of normal people."

In the same way, the Parisian lesbian and homosexual circles prized discretion. The princesse de Polignac's salon was made up almost exclusively of homosexuals of both sexes. When a new potential member was introduced to her, she simply asked: "You are homosexual, aren't you? Of course. Then, it's perfect."[656] Moreover, there was stiff competition between the various Parisian

654. Christopher Isherwood, *Christopher and his Kind* [1929-1939], London, Methuen, 1977, 252 pages, p.125.
655. Quentin Crisp, *The Naked Civil Servant, op. cit.*, p.84.
656. Michael de Cossart, *Une Américaine à Paris. La princesse de Polignac et son salon, 1865-1943*, Paris, Plon, 1979, 245 pages, p.173.

homosexual salons; the princess did not host the same people as Natalie Barney or Gertrude Stein, and the competition was savage. Maryse Choisy, a friend of Rachilde, was reproached for her infidelity:

> ... I went twice to cocktails at Natalie Barney's. Rachilde made such violent scenes when I went to rue Jacob that I gave it up. "Natalie and Colette both have bad reputations, I do not want you to see Colette."[657]

Similarly, Ruth Röllig, who published *The Lesbians of Berlin* in 1928, saw the lack of female solidarity as the explanation for the weakness of the lesbian movements: "But, as we know, all women, without exception, have no team spirit, and even lesbians do not derogate from this rule. For this reason, there can be no question of forming a united front."[658]

The lack of common goals is another explanation for the lack of solidarity between homosexual and lesbians. Lesbians always kept away from the homosexual movements, because they themselves were not targets of police repression. On the other hand, the homosexual community held a very chauvinistic attitude toward women that often went beyond heterosexual prejudices. Many homosexuals based their identity on the cult of the penis, the celebration of virile friendships, the rejection of women. Misogyny is very apparent in certain novels. In *Maurice*, the women are incapable of real feelings and are described as little idiots; in *A Handful of Dust* (1937), by Evelyn Waugh, the woman is behind the destruction of the hero. Women are almost entirely absent from Isherwood's novels, if one excludes the character of Sally Bowles.

By the same token, certain lesbians entertained a deep revulsion with regard to homosexuals. In a letter which she sent to Hemingway, Gertrude Stein listed the prejudices, basically asserting that:

> — The act between homosexual males is ugly and repugnant and then they are disgusted with themselves. They drink and take drugs to compensate, but they are disgusted by this act and they change partners constantly and cannot really be happy.... Women do not do anything of which they can be disgusted and nothing which is repugnant, and then they are happy and they can lead a happy life together![659]

---

657. Maryse Choisy and Marcel Vertès, *Dames seules*, Paris, Cahiers Gai-Kitsch-Camp, n° 23, 1993, 53 pages, p.33.

658. Ruth Röllig, *Les Lesbiennes de Berlin* [1928], Paris, Cahiers Gai-Kitsch-Camp, n° 16, 1992, 140 pages, p.41.

Thus, the question of homosexual solidarity remains doubtful. While obvious examples of solidarity existed, they did not prevent the formation of clans according to criteria that went far beyond sexuality alone: social origin, profession, financial means, personal affinities, and partisan orientation. Therefore, we can only speak of the homosexual community in the 1920s in a very measured way. It was a new phenomenon, still in gestation, and certainly cannot claim to have encompassed the whole of the homosexual population of the countries concerned.

* * *

The homosexual identity was built on two axes: self-discovery, one's view of oneself; and other people's views. Homosexuals took advantage of the relative permissiveness of the 1920s to establish a personal definition. The slow course toward self-affirmation had begun, before the war, with the popularization of medical theories and the beginnings of German militancy. But these efforts, at first, had only a peripheral effect. In the 1920s, the homosexual identity became a reality, for it was disseminated by more powerful media (primarily cultural), and by the homosexual scene, which offered anonymous meeting places. The lesbian identity was less well-anchored and more conflicted, because it was more recent and it did not benefit from such an organized structure. Moreover, the lesbians did not have any well-defined combat to carry out.

In sum, during the early part of the 20th century, homosexuality enjoyed something of a vogue; it was no longer unmentionable, although it was certainly still fraught with negative perceptions — among the general population and among homosexuals, themselves.

Advances on a personal scale were not matched by advances at the "community" level. The lack of solidarity is partly due to dissatisfaction with the initial definitions. While they tried to assert themselves personally, they did not really succeed in detaching themselves from externally imposed concepts. Many did not want to be associated with proponents of the third sex or with congenital inverts, and they did not do much to support theses which they did not believe in and which they suspected of serving contrary interests.

---

659. Cited by Emmanuel Cooper, *The Sexual Perspective, op. cit.*, p.112.

In Volume Two, we will examine the position of the Church, then watch the changing tide as the Roaring Twenties gives way to an era that was far less broad-minded.

The memory and mythology of both "the good old days" and the backlash that followed are still with us today, coloring perceptions and projecting models to emulate or avoid.

INDEX

A

Abraham, Karl, 87, 224
Ackerley, Joe Randolph, 29, 62, 64–67, 149, 194, 196, 231, 268, 270, 277–279
Ackland, Valentine, 155, 261
Acosta, Mercedes d', 21
Acton, Harold, 45, 186–187
Adams, George, 120
Adcock, Sir Frank Ezro, 173
Adelsward-Fersen, baron Jacques d', 25, 140
Adler, Alfred, 220
Adrian, Max, 176, 269
Agostinelli, Alfred, 128
Alcibiade, 135
Alençon, Émilienne d', 20
Allan, Maud, 27
Allard, Roger, 125
Allégret, Marc, 133, 143
Allendy, René, 221
Aminoff, Hans, 239
Annan, Noel, 145, 174, 179, 183, 268
Anton, Karl, 271
Armand, Eugène, 28, 142, 146
Armengaud, André, 35
Arnold, Karl, 274
Arnold, Thomas, 156
Atkin, Gabriel, 30
Atwood, Clare, 258
Auden, Wystan Hugh, 34, 41, 52, 67, 157, 172, 179, 181–182, 197, 199–202, 205, 230, 237, 277, 279, 281
Audoin-Rouzeau, Stéphane, 28
Aveling, Edward, 215
Axieros, 141

B

Bab, Edwin, 96, 196
Bacon, Francis, 197
Baden-Powell, Robert, 194

Bahn, Walter, 105
Baker, Joséphine, 74, 199, 242
Bankhead, Tallulah, 45
Barbedette, Gilles, 10, 68, 73, 142, 225
Barbette, 273
Barbusse, Henri, 137, 218
Barnes, Djuna, 256, 275
Barney, Natalie, 20–21, 241, 243–244, 246–249, 256, 259, 262, 282
Bauer, Gérard, 137
Beach, Sylvia, 21, 259
Beaton, Sir Cecil, 44–46, 148, 157, 171, 228, 266, 269, 275
Beauvoir, Simone de, 192–193
Bebel, August, 84
Bell, Clive, 174, 176–177
Bell, Graham, 67
Bell, Quentin, 176
Bell, Vanessa, 177
Bellen, Paul de, 125
Bellenbaum, Ernst, 101
Bender, Julie, 213–214
Bendow, Wilhelm, 269
Benson, Edward Frederic, 262
Berlin, Sir Isaiah, 186, 189
Bernard, Raymond, 65, 67, 175, 178
Bernardo, Syrie, 229
Berners, Lord Gerald, 171
Bernstein, Eduard, 83
Besnaux, Maurice (Marcus Behmer, called), 274
Bessunger, August, 86
Betjeman, Sir John, 149, 183, 185
Beyria, Gustave, 140
Bibesco, Antoine, 128
Billing, Noel Pemberton, 27
Billy, André, 137
Binet, André, 124–125, 166, 213, 222
Binet-Valmer, Gustave, 124–125, 222
Birrell, Francis, 176, 178
Bismarck, Otto von, 23

Printed in the United States
24106LVS00001B/288

9 780875 862521